CRYSTAL TABLE GLASSWARE
SAMPLE ROOM 623 SMITHFIELD ST. BET. 6TH & 7TH AVES.
NO ALLOWANCE FOR BREAKAGE.
PAY NO MONEY TO AGENTS ON OUR ACCOUNT.
Toy Set
BRYCE, HIGBEE & CO. PITTSBURGH, PA.
Over
MUSTARD'S OR HORSERADISHE'S
BRYCE, HIGBEE & CO. PITTSBURGH, PA.
FULL SIZE
FULL SIZE
Bear Mustard or Horse Radish
FULL SIZE
Over

Homestead Glass Works

BRYCE, HIGBEE & COMPANY

1879–1907

PAUL KIRK JR.

Schiffer Publishing Ltd

4880 Lower Valley Road • Atglen, PA 19310

Library of Congress Control Number: 2016932617

Designed by Danielle D. Farmer
Cover concept by Paul Kirk, Jr.
Cover design by Molly Shields
Type set in Algerian/Seagull Lt BT/Adobe Caslon Pro/PhyllisD

ISBN: 978-0-7643-5035-1
Printed in China

Published by Schiffer Publishing, Ltd.
4880 Lower Valley Road
Atglen, PA 19310
Phone: (610) 593–1777; Fax: (610) 593-2002
E-mail: Info@schifferbooks.com
Web: www.schifferbooks.com

To Messrs.

Bryce and Higbee and all those who had a part in the creation of the glassware made by Bryce, Higbee & Company. Your memories will forever remain alive in the glassware handed down to us and future generations.

Epigraph

It is not our right to alter what history has so graciously bequeathed; rather, it is our duty to preserve the past and record it as accurately as possible.

Contents

Foreword

As editor of the Museum of American Glass in West Virginia's quarterly publication, *All About Glass*, there are a number of things that I look for in judging the contributions of the many glass historians and researchers with whom I have been fortunate enough to be associated. There are many diligent historians whose ability to write is adequate at best—and many fine writers who do a good job of synthesizing the findings of others, but bring little or nothing new to the discussion in hand. Far less often do I encounter someone who does both—writes clearly and covers a subject in a comprehensive manner—and then goes a step further by conducting primary research and adding to, validating, or effectively contradicting the "facts" presented by previous researchers. As anyone who has read Paul Kirk's articles knows, he does all three and does them well.

This book bears this out. Yes, the topic has been addressed before and well enough, considering the level of knowledge available at the time. But research is an ongoing process and Mr. Kirk has gone to great lengths to find previously unknown or under-used resources, presenting his findings with careful consideration of the facts, logical interpretation, when necessary, and clarity. I commend Mr. Kirk to you, the reader, with full confidence that you will not only find this volume educational, but highly enjoyable as well.

—Tom Felt, West Virginia, 2015

Introduction

There were scores of factories that produced pressed glass during the last half of the nineteenth century and into the first few decades of the twentieth century. Many of the smaller factories did not succeed in such a highly competitive market as it was, and much of their history and production has been lost in the dusty annals of time. For the most part the larger, more prolific companies have been well documented, some more recently than others, by dedicated researchers. Though previous authors have written about Bryce, Higbee & Company, there still are many gaps and much misinformation regarding the company's output.

Minnie Watson Kamm was perhaps the first to research and document this factory's products over sixty years ago. Author and researcher Bill Heacock continued by attributing patterns to Bryce, Higbee based on Butler Brothers assortments. This added considerably to what was known of the company's output, but errors persisted and there still remained a paucity of specific information and a lack of clarity between the products of Bryce, Higbee and J. B. Higbee. To this day certain patterns are attributed to the wrong company, even in many of the major reference books widely used by collectors. The glassware made by the companies is all too often arbitrarily labeled "Higbee glass," a designation that does not do full justice or give credit to the men who operated these factories. Despite what many may think, they were not the same company. A child shares traits common to the parent, of course, but at the same time is also a unique individual. Each deserves to be acknowledged as a distinct entity. Lola and Wayne Higby's book *Bryce, Higbee and J. B. Higbee Glass* was the first in-depth study of these companies, and a noble attempt it was; but, unfortunately, the book is laden with misinformation and errors. Errors are inevitable when compiling such an extensive study, and the authors are not faulted by any means for penning the book. They are commended for taking on this ambitious task. Their book has assisted in making the products of these companies more widely known and better appreciated, but collectors deserve more accurate and updated information.

Over fifteen years have passed since the Higbys' book was published, and perhaps there are resources available now that were not available to the authors. Sometimes less obvious paths must be sought and trodden to yield information and results. As much as other authors are respected, what they present should not be thoughtlessly repeated by the next. This is not merely a measure of doubt; it is becoming actively involved in the research process, born from the desire to understand one's subject to the fullest extent. It is through questioning that we become truly motivated to seek more information for ourselves. This active involvement often yields previously undiscovered material, a very compelling and satisfying reward which benefits all.

A huge stumbling block for the researcher is the lack of original Bryce, Higbee & Company material. The only company catalog pages known are the ones shown in Minnie Watson Kamm's *An Eighth Pattern Glass Book,* first published in 1954. The comprehensive Rakow Research Library at the Corning Museum of Glass has none and does not know the whereabouts of any. The author's numerous queries to major libraries around the country, as well as smaller libraries and historical societies in the United States and even Canada, proved fruitless.

In the absence of original catalogs needed for documentation, the researcher must seek other contemporary sources to attribute patterns, assign their correct OMN (Original Manufacturer's Name), and date them. Trade journals reported on the new products of the glass companies, and in some cases this is the only record we have of certain patterns manufactured by Bryce, Higbee & Company. These firsthand accounts are the best and most reliable source available to document when patterns were introduced. Unfortunately, not every pattern made was mentioned, and there are many gaps where the company is not mentioned at all. There are also numerous patterns and items cited with very little or no description given. Some of these are patterns the collector knows by their made-up names, but until they can be identified through period sources, it is merely guesswork to assign the correct name given by their maker.

Over the years, speculation on the part of some authors has somehow magically turned into *documentation*. It is amazing how one author's statement "circa 1885" eventually becomes *made in 1885* because someone publishes it as such with no evidence whatsoever. These errors are then simply repeated by subsequent authors to the point where they are accepted as *fact*. Each passing year only serves to strengthen the misguided conviction that the information is accurate, for surely, if someone wrote it sixty years ago, it *must* be correct! The spread of misinformation is hastened at lightning-fast speed through the Internet, where anybody who possesses an ability to regurgitate information gleaned from dubious sources is considered an "expert." The validity is hardly questioned or challenged, for it is on the Internet and, therefore, *must* be correct! These people confuse research with looking something up. Research involves much more than just opening a book or a web page and gleaning the information found there. It includes methodical studying, finding facts for oneself from firsthand sources, evaluating that information, and weighing those findings against data compiled by yourself and/or others. This regularly involves spending days on end in research libraries poring over various materials until one is completely vertiginous and cannot even see to see. Sometimes all of this effort yields little or nothing and there are times when one must completely go back to the drawing board and start anew on a different path. Facts are not always available, of course, and this is where speculation comes in. Speculation is the result of the inability to find hard documentation. It is based on careful research and validated by experience and a thorough understanding of one's subject.

It is nearly impossible to ignore speculation, especially when writing about Bryce, Higbee & Company. There simply is not enough original company material to document all that they made. Information that cannot be documented can be left out, but that would include the majority of their production and there would be very little to present. Oftentimes good speculation can lead to documentation. When speculation is included in this book it is identified as such and is based on much research and study.

Never one to mince words, Ruth Webb Lee, pioneer author about EAPG (Early American Pattern Glass), once said "it is a perverse habit misinformation has of spreading more widely than the truth and of persisting more obstinately." This statement was made over eighty years ago and still holds true today, probably even more so since the advent of the Internet. It is the author's hope that this book, which contains the most current research available, will clear up misinformation that has persisted for so long and prove a useful resource for many years to come.

Research is definitely a labor of love, and a most enjoyable one at that. I am proud to share my findings and observations and invite the reader, whether a researcher, serious student, or casual collector of Early American Pattern Glass, to learn about and appreciate the beauty of the glassware made by Bryce, Higbee & Company.

—Paul Kirk Jr., 2015

Note:

The company was originally called Homestead Glass Works and Bryce, Higbee & Company. In this book, the company is referred to as Bryce, Higbee & Company; Bryce, Higbee & Co.; and simply Bryce, Higbee, for this is how they are best known now and how they were mainly referred to while they operated.

All factory-given names are referred to throughout the book as OMN (Original Manufacturer's Name) in regular type. Names that collectors and researchers have coined for patterns are referred to as AKA (Also Known As). These names are presented in *italics.*

Some Words Regarding the Use of OMNs Versus AKAs

Keeping track of all the different names for one pattern can prove to be very confusing and frustrating, especially to newer collectors. Most EAPG patterns have multiple names. This is due to different authors publishing the same patterns under different names over the course of many years. In some cases writers were satisfying collectors by using the names in common usage; however, in many cases they made the names up themselves. A few authors even gave the same pattern more than one name. Made-up names are often descriptive, and really should be to fulfill their intended purpose of simply identifying a pattern when the OMN is unknown, but many are not descriptive and have nothing to do with the patterns whatsoever. A few authors used OMNs when known. Ruth Webb Lee and Minnie Watson Kamm documented many OMNs, but did not always endorse them.

We raise our hats to the early authors and researchers of early American pattern glass, for they laid the groundwork for future collectors, authors, and researchers. We must remember, however, that the focus of collecting was very different in past decades than it is now. When many of the early references were written, most collectors were more concerned with how the glassware fit into their decorating schemes than with its historical significance. Keep in mind much EAPG that was popularly collected was only forty to sixty years old—or less—at the time. Author Alice Hullet Metz actually frowned upon those she considered "so-called collectors," who felt they needed to know exact details of where and when their glassware was made. To her, those people were merely gatherers of useless information; she stressed that it was completely adequate to estimate the age of glass by its quality, color, and pattern characteristics. In the 1930s, Lee stated, "Better [to have] a recognizable alias than a meaningless birth certificate!" regarding pattern names given by the factories that were long forgotten. Standardized accepted names were needed for collectors to identify patterns among themselves and to dealers. Buying glassware sight unseen through the mail was fast becoming popular and intensified this need.

Each generation looks at things differently and has different perspectives and goals than the previous generation. This is how progress occurs. It applies to collecting as well. Through my active involvement as a trustee and pattern identifier for the Early American Pattern Glass Society, as well as in my capacity as historian and lecturer for many other groups, I see that the vast majority of collectors seek education and want information and history about what they own. Some may disagree with the author on this matter, but a teacher does not cease to instruct because there exist students who do not care to absorb the material presented. A teacher sows seeds of knowledge. Consider that only a small percentage of the thousands of seeds a single maple tree strews each and every season will subsist. The tree continues to spread its seeds regardless of the number that may possibly take root because it is designed by nature to do so. Just as the tree is programmed to propagate, the teacher is determined to educate. We all appreciate different things in our collecting, but if collecting and research is to continue to grow we cannot cling to trends of sixty, seventy, and more years ago. A single pattern does not need multiple names, in some cases four or more! This is infinitely more confusing than remembering a single OMN.

Collectors who shun OMNs claim those titles are confusing and difficult to remember because there is no apparent connection with the designs. They prefer names that are descriptive, but not all AKAs include the pattern elements in their name. A good example is Bryce, Higbee's *Beautiful Lady*, a name given by Kamm over six decades ago in lieu of the OMN. A beautiful lady has nothing at all to do with the pattern, yet no other name based on its design has ever been given it; therefore, non-descriptive pattern names are obviously acceptable and can be easily remembered if given the chance.

Of course, when OMNs are not known, descriptive names are substituted until the OMN is found. To be useful and fulfill their temporary purpose, however, they should not duplicate AKAs already assigned to other patterns, for this would imply they are the same line of glassware by the same manufacturer. All too often the very same terms are used for an infinite number of AKAs. Words such as loop, bead/beaded, medallion, and jewel are sorely overused and are part of the AKAs for literally dozens of patterns. Many AKAs are confusingly similar, and if a single part of the name is wrong or out of order, one is dealing with a completely different pattern. It is true that different companies often used the same pattern names at the time of manufacture, and it is not up to us to alter what history has so graciously bequeathed, nor is it our prerogative to attempt to change or "improve" an artist's intent merely because we do not like or cannot remember the name of his/her work. Some concession can be made for patterns given only numbers originally. Lee truly considered pattern numbers a "meaningless birth certificate," and, though her words may seem a bit harsh, there is truth in her statement. There is little, if any, artistic merit in a mere number, and the use of them for pattern names reeks of cold, sterile capitalism in a mechanical world. Names are more easily remembered than numbers by most. Thankfully, Bryce, Higbee did not use numbers for their tableware patterns, only names. One will find references that list the OMNs of some as numbers, but the origin of these numbers is questionable and they did not originate with Bryce, Higbee & Company.

Some people apparently believe non-descriptive names coined by authors are far superior to the original names given by the manufacturers. Many collectors insist on using certain names because of resistance to change or out of respect for the pioneer authors. Why should we not have the same reverence for the manufacturers who gave us reason to collect in the first place? By using OMNs, we not only simplify and standardize by using only one name for a pattern, but we also show our respect for the men, women, and children who labored so well over the glassware we love and treasure. The names bestowed by the makers certainly are a product of their time and are very colorful and interesting. Bryce, Higbee & Company carefully chose the names of their patterns, many of them having a marked significance with obvious thought and creativity behind the titles. Knowing and using the OMNs places the glassware in the context of the era in which it was created, ultimately leading to a greater understanding and appreciation. It may be considered a great irony that we must look back in order to move forward, but this is the method history uses to instruct. The next generation of collectors deserves to be fully and correctly informed.

Values

The values given in this book are approximations of what one might expect to pay for items on the open market and should be used as a guide, not as gospel. Prices for the same item can vary according to the marketplace in which the piece is offered. Small rural auctions and flea markets generally will not yield the same prices as antiques stores or well-advertised glass shows. Clear EAPG, especially in patterns unidentified by or unknown to sellers, is often not highly regarded. It is in this area that the collector has particularly great potential to find bargains. Values given are for the same item pictured, in the same color and in excellent condition with no damage. Damaged items are worth less than the values quoted. It is ultimately up to the collector to decide what price is fair to pay for an item. The author's intent is not to set prices, but to report what items might realistically sell for. Neither the author nor publisher is liable for any losses incurred through consulting the values presented in this book.

1 Company Histories

HOMESTEAD GLASS WORKS: Bryce, Higbee & Company, 1879–1907

The John B. Higbee Glass Company, 1907–1918

CLOCKWISE FROM TOP

The Bryce, Higbee & Company factory in its early years.

Portrait of John B. Higbee.

Portrait of John Bryce.

Homestead Glass Works: 1879–1907 Bryce, Higbee & Company

From the very start, Bryce, Higbee & Company seemed destined for success. Highly competent men who were raised in the glass business and understood the trade well, John Bryce, his son Charles K. Bryce, and John B. Higbee (all formerly of Bryce, Walker & Co.), combined their expertise to create one of the most respected American glasshouses of its day. Joseph Doyle, formerly of Doyle & Co., was mentioned as a founder in early quotes in the trade journal *American Pottery and Glassware Reporter*, but he is not mentioned in any later accounts, even those written in retrospect while the company was still operating.

The firm was also known as the Homestead Glass Works. The factory was located at the foot of West Street in Homestead, Pennsylvania, six miles from Pittsburgh, on the south side of the Monongahela River. Its showroom and offices were located on Smithfield Street, a bustling thoroughfare in nearby downtown Pittsburgh. Construction of the factory began on May 26, 1879, and Bryce, Higbee & Company commenced operations on September 29, 1879. Early accounts make notable mention of how well-planned and efficient the factory was. Within the first few months, sixty workers were employed with a projected 150 needed when operating at full capacity. A cooper shop was completed by the end of the year to manufacture packages to ship the glassware, and the cutting and engraving shop was in full operation by late November 1880. Though much mention was made early on of the extensive line of engraved goods the company produced, very little is known about these wares today.

According to contemporary reports, Bryce, Higbee & Company maintained steady business during its twenty-seven years of operation by reliably offering good, honest, conservative patterns as well as a reasonably priced, quality product. They were noted at the time as being the first glasshouse in the country to use natural gas. The company had its own mould shop and mention was made of John Bryce's capability of designing patterns of "new and of novel ornamentation, not a single old mold being used." John Bryce designed and patented many patterns while associated with Bryce, Walker and Company during the 1870s, one being the well-known thistle design using the emblem from the land of his Scottish ancestry, but no design patents for the patterns he created for Bryce, Higbee are known to exist. Trade journals mysteriously report that several of the company's designs were copyrighted. This may have been merely talk to deter pirating of their designs because no such documents seem to exist; furthermore, designs are protected by patents rather than copyrights.

By the end of 1879, Bryce, Higbee had two salesmen, E. C. Long and Henry Clay Ranney. Mr. Long disappears from trade journal reports, but Ranney is noted in 1888 as being Bryce, Higbee's eastern agent who spent much time in New York City showing the company's wares at the Astor House. He is mentioned in early 1895 conducting business from Room 53 at the Metropolitan Building. In March 1904, he is listed at 32 Park Place. A brief death notice for a man named V. C. Gelwick appeared in *Crockery and Glass Journal* on January 6, 1916, and notes he was an "old-time glass salesman," who "for eighteen or twenty years was with the Bryce-Higbee Co." This span nearly encompasses the life of the company, yet no mention of Gelwick is found in trade journals while the firm was in business. It is not known when Gelwick worked for Bryce, Higbee. The author was not successful in locating other documents mentioning Gelwick, except for a simple listing in an 1866 Cincinnati, Ohio, city directory that records his occupation as a clerk.

The first full decade of operation saw much growth. Trade journals consistently mention how busy the factory was, and this must have been true, for in June 1886 the company's office and sample room on Smithfield

Street underwent a "complete transformation, with the aid of paper, paint, and carpeting." They also added more tables to display their growing assortment of wares. Some changes at the helm occurred as well. John Bryce died August 3, 1888 and it was reported in *Pottery and Glassware Reporter* that "the surviving partners, Messrs. J. B. Higbee and C. K. Bryce, will carry the business on as before under the old firm name and in the same way as heretofore." By this time Joseph Doyle is not mentioned at all. During the 1880s, Robert G. West became a salesman for the company, traveling about the country promoting and selling their wares. Henry Hand is mentioned as an engraver for Bryce, Higbee in May 1885.

It appears that Bryce, Higbee manufactured blown glass as well as pressed glass. Seeger & Guernsey's *Cyclopædia of the Manufacturers and Products of the United States* for the year 1891 lists the company in three categories: pressed flint glassware (in this time period flint referred simply to clear glassware), glassware novelties, and blown glassware. Bryce, Higbee has never before been associated with blown glassware, so this comes as a bit of a surprise. The company is listed in the same categories in the 1900 issue of the publication, so this obviously is not an error. Just what items of blown glassware Bryce, Higbee was manufacturing is a mystery. Unfortunately, no trade journal reports have been found that mention any such wares.

The big news in fall 1891 was Bryce, Higbee's conversion to a new type of furnace patented by M. L. Murphy of Coraopolis, Pennsylvania. The Murphy Improved Gas Producing Furnace was able to run on coal, oil, or natural gas. This was very noteworthy because alternate fuels could be used. Many areas were experiencing a dwindling supply of natural gas, which eventually closed down numerous glass factories. The cost to operate the Murphy furnace was about one-third of the usual furnace fueled by natural gas. Despite substantial savings such as this, the glass factories were not doing too well in the late 1880s and early 1890s, Bryce, Higbee included. Ironically, many of the practices that brought success to the glass companies were the very same ones that contributed to their downfall. New patterns were presented every January for the spring trade. Most companies brought out at least two new lines each year. An additional pattern was occasionally introduced in the fall. After some time, supply outweighed demand and the glasshouses found themselves with a surplus of product. Indeed, the *Pittsburgh Dispatch* newspaper reported on December 4, 1889:

> **Overstocked With Glass**
> The glass factories of Bryce, Higbee & Co., at Homestead, have suspended operations for a time. Trade is reported unusually dull and the factories have been accumulating stock.

The result was many idle hands at the factories. Prices began to drop and many factories were not able to handle the financial hardship. As early as the mid–1880s, serious discussions began about the benefits of forming a combine to build strength through the pooling of assets. The goal was to regulate production and return the industry to profitability. This was a highly competitive business, and the Pittsburgh area alone was home to numerous glass factories. Considering the abundance of glassware available and the depressed glass market at the time, it is quite amazing that Bryce, Higbee & Company was able to maintain and succeed on its own, unlike many others who succumbed to joining the large conglomerates of the United States Glass Company (formed in 1891) and the ill-fated National Glass Company (formed in 1899).

By the mid–1890s, there was improvement in the state of the market and sales were up, much of it likely due to the consolidation of factories that became part of the United States Glass Company. In July 1893 *China, Glass & Lamps* reported:

> Bryce, Higbee & Co. are offering some very dainty new patterns and crystal tableware and are doing pretty well as the season goes. They are not pushed with orders but are getting their share.

Bryce, Higbee weathered the storm and continued to grow and prosper. *History and Commerce of Pittsburgh and Environs: Consisting of Allegheny, McKeesport, Braddock and Homestead, 1893–4* reports a workforce of 250 to 300 employees. The book devotes a paragraph of high praise to Bryce, Higbee & Company reporting their success and notably mentioning their expansive market outside the borders of the United States. In part, it states:

> They are manufacturers of crystal table glassware, and turn out a distinctly superior class of goods. Their productions command extensive sale throughout the United States and Mexico, and are exported largely also to South America. The pressed glassware...is noted for beauty, variety and originality of designs and elegant workmanship, and are not surpassed for general excellence by anything of the kind on the market.

The company continued its success into the new century. *China, Glass & Lamps* consistently reports strong sales with much mention of Robert G. West traveling about the country promoting the company's wares. The showroom was greatly expanded and again tastefully renovated at the end of 1900. Fully stocked with beautiful displays of staples and new patterns, it was unveiled in January 1901. A 1905 newspaper relates that Bryce, Higbee was the largest independent producer of crystal (clear) glass tableware in the country; however, for some reason they and their products were mentioned in the trade journals less than previous years. No reference to specific patterns has been found after 1903, and the full scope of their production after 1900 is vague to say the least. Bryce Higbee's demise was apparently not due to lack of success, but rather to a series of events that were beyond their control. A scandal plagued their later years, causing a rift between the Higbee and Bryce families. In early February 1905, *China, Glass & Lamps* reported, with no reason given, that C. K. Bryce resigned and was leaving for Denver, Colorado. The December 16, 1905, issue of a Maryland newspaper, *The News*, clearly explains why he fled:

> Charles K. Bryce...was arrested at his home on information made by J. B. Higbee, president of the firm, who charges Bryce with the embezzlement of $5,000 and upward...it is said it may reach $75,000...other suits of a more serious character will be entered shortly. It is alleged Bryce secured the cash through falsifying the pay rolls, principally by placing names upon them of persons who had never been employed by the company.

This quote is rather thought-provoking, for one cannot help to wonder what charges (which had not yet been entered at the time of the report) could be considered more serious than embezzlement of up to $75,000. This was an exorbitant amount in 1905. Charles K. Bryce was well known in the community and had been highly esteemed, not only in his capacity at Bryce, Higbee & Company, but also for being the first chief of Homestead's fire department. One can only imagine the negative impact the scandal had on the factory and its workers. It must have been quite devastating to the whole community.

About a year later, Bryce, Higbee & Company prevailed. In December 1906 *Crockery and Glass Journal* reported:

> In the equity proceedings of Charles [K.] Bryce against Bryce, Higbee & Co. to compel an accounting of partnership funds, a decree has been handed down which finds in favor of Bryce, Higbee & Co. for $22,850.33.

It must be kept in mind that the settlement of nearly $23,000 was an extremely large sum in 1906, equivalent to approximately $500,000 today.

John B. Higbee died on December 9, 1906. Along with his photo, *China, Glass & Lamps* printed a write-up, which also appeared in the *Mt. Washington News*:

> John B. Higbee, aged 64 years, one of the best known glass manufacturers of Pittsburg, died suddenly Sunday morning, the 9th inst., at 5 o'clock, at his late residence, Grandview avenue, Mt. Washington. The deceased was a native of St. Clair township, Allegheny county, Pa. At the age of 17 years he left home and went to St. Louis to engage in the pottery business with a relative. At the age of 21 years he became a glass salesman for three leading glass firms of Pittsburg, Hamilton, Doyle and Atterbury. In 1879 he [founded the company] known as Bryce, Higbee & Co. Since the death of his partners, the Bryce brothers, he became the active

Photo postcard of the 1907 flood showing the Pittsburgh business district where Bryce, Higbee & Company's showroom was located. Note the canoe in the center of the street.

> member of the company, and so remained until his death, as above noted...In his business trips as salesman, he generally took his wife with him, so that at the hotel where he stopped he would have it much like home.
>
> His business relations were always of a pleasant character, and he enjoyed the esteem and respect of his employees, about 75 whom attended his funeral in a body and contribute [*sic*] a beautiful floral tribute to his memory, built in form of a glass house. Besides his wife, a son, O. J. W. Higbee, survives.

From this tribute something can be gathered about Mr. Higbee's character, and it seems that the real driving force behind the factory was now gone. With John's death came more legal battles between the Bryce and Higbee families. According to an account in *China, Glass & Lamps* on December 22, 1906:

> It is announced that Bryce, Higbee & Co., Homestead, Pa., have shut down their tableware plant and that they will not operate pending the settlement of matters due to the death of John B. Higbee, one of the members of the firm.

The final blow occurred the following spring with the infamous flood of March 1907. A photo postcard relates that it was the "greatest flood ever recorded in Allegheny county, Mononaghela [*sic*] river guaging [*sic*] 36.2 ft. of water, and Allegheny river 36.6 ft." Prior to this, the "Pumpkin Flood" of 1832 was the worst, followed by a flood in 1884 which was 3.3 feet less than the 1907 flood. Old photographs show men navigating the downtown business district in canoes.

Crockery & Glass Journal mysteriously reported on March 28, 1907, that it was first thought the factory was damaged very little from the flood, but the damage was actually so great that the factory would "have to be rebuilt if it is ever operated again." In early April, it was reported that the factory would be repaired and managed by C. K. Bryce, whereas the Higbee interests were to open a factory at Bridgeville, Pennsylvania. Then, in mid-June, the journal related:

> A charter has been granted the Bryce-Higbee Co., of Pittsburgh, with a capital stock of $10,000, the object of the company being to take over and operate the old Bryce-Higbee factory at Homestead. The directors of the new company are J. W. Hanley, Elliott Frederick, both of Allegheny, and C. L. Kerr, of Pittsburgh.

It is not completely clear why this did not come to fruition, but there were obviously legal battles and ill feelings between the Bryce and Higbee families, which may have put a halt to reopening the old factory. The next report, at the end of December 1907, details the "equity proceedings against Bryce, Higbee & Co." stating a grand total of $54,737.62. Of this, $1,212.22 was enumerated for "manufactured goods" and $2,665 for "machinery and equipment." It is not known how much inventory of glassware was lost or how many moulds were at the factory, as there is only mention that "every pot in the plant was broken." The figures reported give some sort of idea of how many moulds may have remained as well as the tremendous quantity of glassware. See chapter 8, Production of Bryce, Higbee's Patterns by Other Manufacturers, for detailed discussion.

In May 1908, *National Glass Budget* mentions glassware and machinery going to public sale. This journal also reported that the late John's son, Orlando, bought the "movable parts" to be used at his new factory. The name he gave it was an homage to his father, and the John B. Higbee Glass Company was born.

A postcard of the J. B. Higbee factory. *Photo courtesy of Bob Sanford.*

The Alpha pattern, introduced in 1908, marked the auspicious beginning of the J. B. Higbee Glass Company.

The John B. Higbee Glass Company 1907–1918

Because the main focus of this book is Bryce, Higbee & Company, the study of the J. B. Higbee Glass Company and its products will not be as in-depth. Some detailed information must be presented, though, to complete the story of Bryce, Higbee, to make the distinction between the two companies clear, and to understand the relationship between their products.

Orlando Joseph William Higbee, known as Ollie, was nearly thirty-three years old when he began the John B. Higbee Glass Company in Bridgeville, Pennsylvania. He had worked at his father's glass factory and understood well its techniques and products. Trade journals from early 1908 declare the first patterns of the new company to debut for the spring trade, Alpha (AKA *Rexford*) and Laurel, were being well received. Alpha is the first letter of the Greek alphabet and from this extends its meaning to "first" or "beginning." The name was of great significance and thoughtfully chosen because this was J. B. Higbee's first pattern, marking the beginning of the new company. Ollie applied for a patent for the Alpha design on October 14, 1907, and patent number 39,230 was granted to him on March 31, 1908. This in itself is notable, for not many of the busy imitation-cut patterns so prevalent during this era were patented. In Alpha one can clearly see motifs found in some of Bryce, Higbee's later patterns. Patents for other new patterns were also issued throughout the life of the J. B. Higbee Glass Company, including Gala (AKA *Hawaiian Lei*) in 1913 and Iris (AKA *Pineapple*) in 1916. Some collectors use the names in italics given by early authors and researchers, but the original (and in this author's opinion, far superior) names given by the factory were Gala and Iris. The company trademark, a small bee with the letters H I G placed over its wings and body, is a clever rebus on the owner's surname and has become synonymous with products of J. B. Higbee. This mark was not used by Bryce, Higbee, as some mistakenly believe. The firm led by Ollie Higbee achieved success and declared that only pot glass was made by them. Pot glass was a finer, more expensive product and was a more time-consuming process compared to the cheaper continuous tank glass some manufacturers were making.

Despite its apparent success, the J. B. Higbee Glass Company closed somewhat abruptly in 1918. The circumstances surrounding its demise are vague, but in November of that year the building, along with an unknown amount of equipment, was sold to the General Electric Company. Some moulds, and quite likely finished glassware, were bought by other companies, including the New Martinsville Glass Manufacturing Company and the Paden City Glass Company. Items in the Delta (AKA *Paneled Thistle*), Gala (AKA *Hawaiian Lei*), and Madora (AKA *Arrowhead in Ovals*) patterns are found in Catalog No. 21 of the Jefferson Glass Company, Limited, of Toronto, Canada. Late author and researcher Bill Heacock dates this catalog circa 1920–1925.

The factories run by John and Ollie Higbee, as well as the glassware they made, are often confused for one other. Though the quality of their glass and some of their products are similar, the companies were completely separate entities. Like most other glasshouses at the time, Bryce, Higbee & Company used no trademark on its glass. J. B. Higbee used the bee trademark mentioned earlier, but it is not known if that trademark was on each and every piece manufactured by them.

2 Trade Journals and the Presentation and Promotion of New Patterns

View of Smithfield Street at the intersection of Water Street, Pittsburgh, Pennsylvania. The famed Monongahela House is at left foreground, and down the street, within walking distance, is where Bryce, Higbee & Company's showroom and offices were located.

In the late nineteenth century it was standard practice for the glasshouses to introduce new patterns for the spring trade and display them at the annual glass and crockery show held every January at the famed Monongahela House. Located on the corner of Smithfield and West Street in Pittsburgh, Pennsylvania, this hotel was noted for its luxurious interiors as well as for the list of famous people who lodged there, including Abraham Lincoln. Some companies located nearby, like Bryce, Higbee, displayed wares in their own showrooms. The show lasted over a month and was highly anticipated, with much excitement generated by the trade journals. We are fortunate to have some firsthand accounts of the displays and descriptions of the products written by the trade journal reporters, often in flowery Victorian rhetoric. These reports are a bit of a time capsule and read as mini diary entries. In some cases they are the only records remaining of the products of the glass companies.

Most patterns were introduced for the spring trade. Toward the end of each year, the glass journals began reporting on the new lines of glassware for the coming season. Reporters viewed samples in the company offices and showrooms and were among the first to see them. From original accounts, it is apparent that, in some instances, reporters merely communicated with factory salesmen and owners about the new patterns without actually seeing them. It was important to create interest, yet not reveal too much that might give the competition an edge. Write-ups often included the names of patterns and mentioned how many items were planned for each set when complete. Patterns were loosely described and given high praise in general terms. A fair amount of the buzz was probably aimed at the other glasshouses to keep everybody on their toes, but most was meant to entice the buyers to examine the new wares in person. If buyers made the trek to Pittsburgh and had the goods beautifully and tastefully displayed in front of them, how could they possibly refrain from placing orders?

The December 28, 1899, issue of *China, Glass & Lamps* gives some interesting insight into the anticipation of the show and the importance of silence amongst the trade:

> None of the manufacturers has a word to say about the new patterns for 1900 and it seems there is an understanding to show nothing before January 1, when they will be sprung on the trade as a surprise. There are said to be many novel and unique features in some of the new lines and every house will have more or less of them. They have decided to keep on the quiet this year so that there can be no copying and each concern may stand on its own merits.

Despite the introductory sentence to this paragraph, this trade journal issue does include information about some of the new patterns for 1900, but, as usual, they were spoken of broadly and not described in any great detail.

Samples were brought to the annual January glass show in Pittsburgh by company representatives and were shown for the first time to the buyers, who came from all parts of the country as well as Canada. The glasshouses were able to see how popular (or unpopular) their patterns were and then had some idea of how much they needed to produce to keep up with the demand. The new lines were not presented to the public until the spring; therefore, when a journal reports on new patterns late in the year as they were apt to do, those patterns were not made available until after the first of the year. Collectors and students of glassware must realize this to use dates correctly. A pattern first mentioned in late 1899 was not made in 1899 or introduced in 1899; it was introduced for the 1900 market. The items spoken of before presentation to the buyers were samples. Some new patterns were brought out in the fall, but this was not as common.

After the grand unveiling, the reporters gave much more detailed descriptions of the patterns seen at the show. They commented on the displays over the course of several issues (most journals were published weekly) as a further means to attract more buyers. Interestingly, lists of buyers who attended the show, along with the firms they represented, were also detailed in the journals. In non-specific terms, the reports mentioned the great number of orders the salesmen were taking. They were sure to mention how elated and gratified the companies were with the response to their new patterns and how pleased the buyers were with them. Nothing negative was ever said about any of the wares displayed. Failures were completely non-existent in this venue. The reality is that they just were not mentioned, of course, and surely successes were exaggerated.

The companies then worked on fulfilling orders. Patterns that truly had a good reception kept the workers busy producing the goods, and in some cases new items were added to the set, facilitating the need for additional moulds. The wares the buyers did not respond favorably to may not have gone into production at all, or may have had a very limited production just to fulfill enough orders to recoup some expenses. Certain companies chose to retool moulds for patterns that were not popular. Bryce, Higbee did this for unpopular designs, but, in some cases, also for patterns that had a good run. This was a way to update a pattern that had been on the market for a while and an economic method of using existing moulds to create a new design when a particular pattern had successfully run its course.

The reporting of new products was a way of advertising, not to the general public, but to the buyers, many of whom were wholesalers, also known as jobbers. It is not known how much influence the glass companies might have had with the reporters. Some companies were mentioned more often than others, and the products of certain companies were described in greater detail for longer periods of time than others. The reports are not always consistent. Bryce, Higbee & Company was given a fair amount of coverage, especially in *China, Glass & Lamps* in the mid–1890s and just into the new century. After 1901 very little was written about their new patterns and only sporadic, brief mention was made about general matters pertaining to their business or sales. From 1902 to 1906 only three of Bryce, Higbee's new patterns are mentioned in two different trade journals, and those patterns are not described in detail.

Advertising space could be purchased in the glass journals. Small ads toward the end of the publication included only basic information that would normally be given on a business card. Some slightly larger ads included a cut of a small item from a new or recent line of

Trade Journals and the Presentation and Promotion of New Patterns

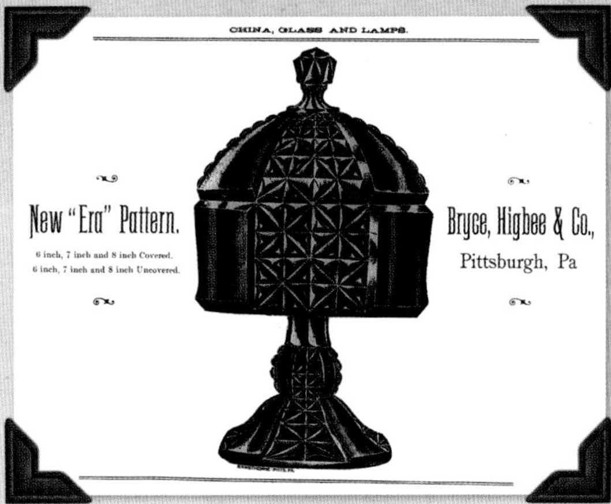

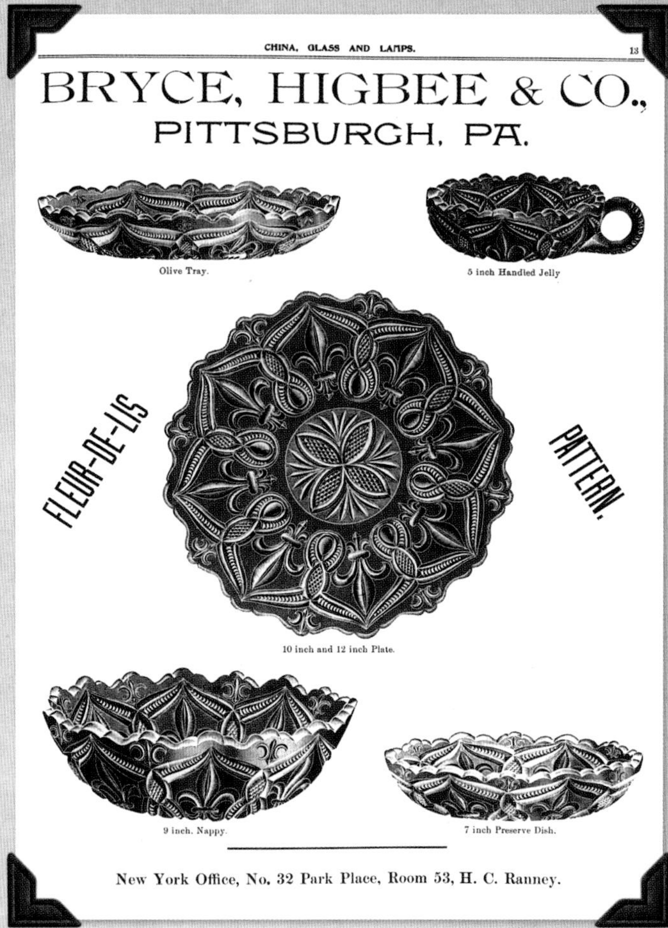

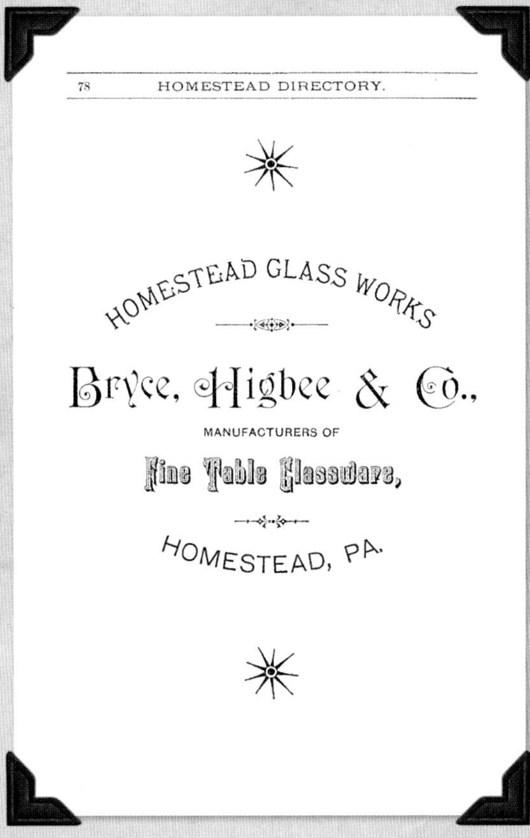

CLOCKWISE FROM TOP LEFT

Advertisement for Bryce, Higbee's Era pattern, which ran in the trade journal *China, Glass & Lamps* during spring 1891.

Advertisement for Bryce, Higbee's Fleur-de-lis pattern from *China, Glass & Lamps*, 1898.

This business card-size ad ran in each issue of *China, Glass & Lamps* for at least a decade. It remained nearly unchanged for all those years.

Bryce, Higbee advertisement from the *Homestead City Directory*, 1890.

glassware. Full-page ads appeared on the cover and near the front of the journal. During the 1890s, full-page ads from Fostoria, McKee & Brothers, United States Glass Company, and George Duncan's Sons regularly appeared in *China, Glass & Lamps.* Space was precious and was reserved for illustrations of what the companies considered their best and/or most novel goods. The most comprehensive advertisements appeared after the first of the year and in the weeks following the annual glass show in Pittsburgh. Some companies boldly illustrated new patterns in the last few weeks of the year, but clearly noted when and where samples would be available for viewing, usually at the Monongahela House in January. Being the first to illustrate a new line had its advantages and disadvantages. It gave the buyers who planned to attend the glass show impetus to seek that company's new line. Many jobbers, however, preferred to wait until wares from all the companies were on display to make their final choices, so the advertising dollars spent may not have made much of a difference. Though the premature unveiling of a pattern in a trade journal could potentially open the door for a certain amount of copying, the first firm to illustrate a new pattern was not suspect of plagiarizing; consequently, it would have been clearly understood within the trade who the culprit or culprits were.

The only known illustrated ads from Bryce, Higbee & Company show their Era and Fleur-de-lis patterns. *China, Glass & Lamps* ran ads for Era in three issues during March and April 1891. Each displays a different item or items. Fleur-de-lis ads appear in four issues of the same journal between January and February 1898. Each full-page ad is different and shows multiple items. Fleur-de-lis was given extensive coverage by the reporters, which may have been because the company purchased substantial ad space. The ads for Era are smaller, approximately one-third of a page, and the pattern received good coverage. Illustrations of a Fleur-de-lis table set and pitcher also appear in the March 1898 and April 1898 issues of *Illustrated Glass and Pottery World.* Beginning in the 1890s, a small Bryce, Higbee ad was included toward the back of *China, Glass & Lamps* regularly for at least a decade. The ad is very basic and remained nearly unchanged for all the years it ran. This was a much more economical method of advertising and implies the firm maintained sufficient business and had their share of regular customers who knew their product. Similar ads were put in the Homestead city directory.

No mention of specific patterns from Bryce, Higbee has been found in any trade journals from mid–1891, all of 1892 and 1893, and most of 1894. This is the time frame the author believes Worlds, *Bowline*, Gem, and *Teardrop Row* originated, and there were very likely other patterns and items that are unknown to us. General business matters were reported during those years with more detailed mention of Bryce, Higbee's furnaces and routine repairs than anything else. As with the other glass companies, business was generally reported as slow to average. *China, Glass & Lamps* began to consistently mention Bryce, Higbee every other week, and sometimes reported that the firm had a good share of orders. Most of the entries are mundane and read very much the same, however. New patterns are only mentioned in passing, but no names or specifics are given. It is not until September 1894 that we find one of their patterns, the Melrose, listed by name.

Trade journals that reported on Bryce, Higbee & Company include: *American Glassworker; American Pottery and Glassware Reporter; China, Glass & Lamps; Crockery and Glass Journal; Glass and Pottery World;* and *Pottery and Glassware Reporter* (formerly *American Pottery and Glassware Reporter*).

3 Jobber and Retail Catalogs

- Butler Brothers
- Pitkin & Brooks
- Other Jobbers
- Retail Catalogs

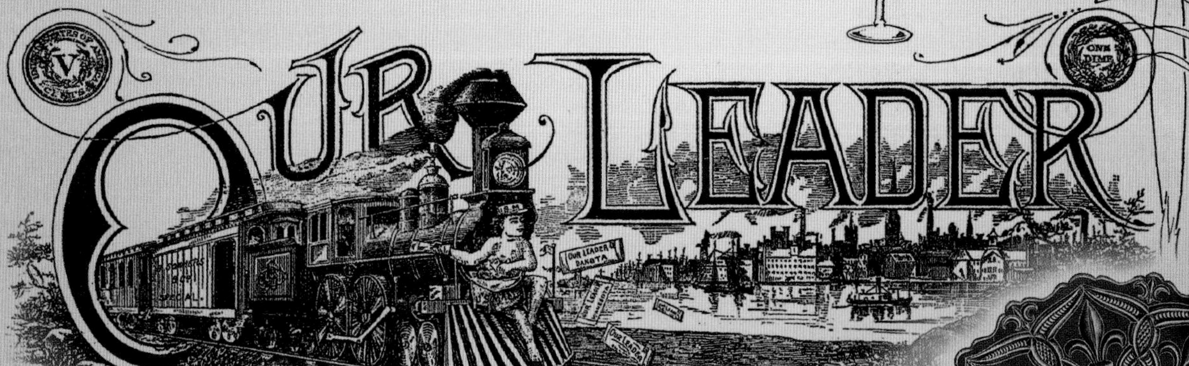

Wholesale distributors were referred to as jobbers in the nineteenth and early twentieth century. Many think that jobbers sold only old, outdated merchandise not marketable by any other means. While it may be true that some operated in this manner at times, there is overwhelming evidence to show not all did. An 1888 account informs the reader that Bryce, Higbee's goods "are sold to jobbers and are in widespread and growing demand in the trade." If jobbers only sold old product, a prolific company like Bryce, Higbee would not have used them as a primary method of selling their goods. It certainly is true that Butler Brothers carried an enormous amount of Bryce, Higbee's glassware. A bit of insight into the popularity of the items jobbers carried is given in an article published in 1905 in *Glass and Pottery World*:

> The jobber will go right on doing businesses at the old stand, handling the goods for which there is the greatest demand and which, therefore, pay him best. He will never disturb himself to create a demand for the goods himself. He simply supplies the ordinary, normal demand as it comes to him...The retailer continues to ask for goods which his customers demand...For a long time—in fact, up to within the last few years—the jobber, or his substitute, the commission man, carried the manufacturer in his vest pocket. He was in a position to say to him: "You manufacture this, that, or the other. Make it so and so. Sell it to me for so much." The manufacturer, having his orders set to work... and did just what the jobber told him to do. When the goods were all made, the jobber took them as he had promised to do, and paid just what he agreed to pay.

Not only does this show that jobbers demanded the most salable items for their customers, but it also clarifies the relationship between the jobbers and the glass manufacturers. According to this report, the jobbers called the shots. And why should they not have? They were the ones who were distributing large quantities of glassware to the retailers, who in turn sought to offer what the public wanted. The jobbers' profits depended on this. No doubt some good old-fashioned salesman schmoozing took place to sell their assortments from the glass companies, but that could only go so far for so long, for the buying public had to be pleased in order for anybody to remain in business.

Butler Brothers included this image on the cover of their catalogs with minor variations over the course of many decades. The *"Our Drummer"* title was registered as a trademark in 1886.

The salesmen who worked for the jobbers were called drummers and traveled from city to city seeking buyers from crockery and glassware shops, department stores, and other retail establishments. Butler Brothers was a bit unique in that they called their catalog "Our Drummer," implying that the goods sold themselves without the need of salesmen. This may be why their catalogs are so well and profusely illustrated.

Butler Brothers

Butler Brothers began in 1877 from a single twenty-foot by fifty-foot room on a back street in Boston and grew to become the largest wholesaler of general merchandise in America. By 1907, the company claimed to have over seventy acres of floor space between its four distributing houses and two large buildings devoted solely to the display of samples. A complete display of samples was viewable in six cities throughout the United States. All sorts of products for the middle class, including much pressed glass, were offered. Catalogs clearly inform the reader:

> We do not sell to anyone but merchants, neither do we sell to peddlers or agents. We send catalogs only to storekeepers who handle our lines. Any merchant, customer or not, who sees our catalog in the hands of anyone not entitled to same, will do us a favor by reporting the fact.

It is fortunate so many catalogs have survived because the assortments of pressed glass are quite valuable in researching the products of Bryce, Higbee & Company. At the beginning of the glassware section in their catalogs, Butler Brothers states:

> Our assortments are all made up and packed by professional packers at the factory before being shipped to us, and are not opened until they reach our customers' stores.

By this statement we know that all the items offered in a single Butler Brothers assortment have a common origin. Since there are so few original Bryce, Higbee catalog pages known, this can be a valuable means to date and attribute patterns when used judiciously in conjunction with other sources and methods. When studying Butler Brothers catalogs, the reader must keep a few things in mind:

1) Single items given their own number, though shown next to other items, are not assortments and can be (and often are) products of different companies.
2) Assortments of items decorated by outside firms can contain patterns of various manufacturers. Decorators bought glassware from different companies and sold it as their own product. In some cases,

TOP TO BOTTOM

Butler Brothers New York City building.

Butler Brothers Chicago buildings as they appeared in 1907.

1907 artist's rendition of Butler Brothers' St. Louis building, scheduled to open in 1908. Projected to contain 800,000 square feet of floor area, it was lauded to be "the largest structure in America occupied by any one wholesale concern."

the decoration merely consisted of gold trim.

3) There is a margin for human error at the time the catalogs were put together. Now and then an odd item known to have been made by another firm appears in an assortment. Assortments appear to have been constructed from cut-out illustrations of each individual item. Many times distinct outlines can be seen around objects. Indeed, a 1907 Butler Brothers catalog states: "We supply a duplicate of any cut in this catalog and keep on hand for quick shipment a stock of over 1000 cuts. Our "Catalog of Stock Cuts" explains everything. Send for a copy."

A rather large and varied assortment of Bryce, Higbee glassware from the spring 1906 Butler Brothers catalog showing patterns known to have been made by the firm, including Melrose, Banquet, Fleur-de-lis, Highland, Bonair, and *Ten-Pointed Star*.

Sometimes the wrong image was put into an assortment, either inadvertently or deliberately when a particular image was not available for the assortment in question. This has been encountered more than a few times, but also noted that later catalogs showing the same assortment are often corrected. It is not completely certain where the images used in jobber catalogs came from, but comparison shows that some images are identical to those found in other jobber and retail catalogs.

The author conducted a study of Bryce, Higbee assortments in Butler Brothers catalogs to judge their accuracy. In a total of 1,003 assortments of Bryce, Higbee glassware offered in over fifty Butler Brothers catalogs over the course of twenty-two years, only twenty-three of those assortments were found to contain errors or discrepancies. Of the twenty-three mentioned, there are only six different assortments that contain errors, but each was printed in subsequent issues, totaling twenty-three actual appearances. The errors occurred when the assortment was new or when the contents were slightly changed. It seems that much effort went into composing the assortments accurately, but with so many different items and images involved it is reasonable to expect errors. Of course, the errors are noted from catalogs observed, and it is possible that an issue showing the same error—or a different error—was not available for study. Still, the amount of error is approximately only two percent for the Bryce, Higbee assortments included in the study.

The images in Butler Brothers catalogs are rather accurately portrayed and contain enough detail that there is usually not much doubt of the identity of the object being represented. There

Our "BARGAIN DAY" 3c Assortment.

3c Possibilities, but comparable only with the 5-Cent Assortments Offered by Our Neighbors.

LC106—Although these *can* be sold for 3 cents, they are all large pieces which have never before retailed for less than 5c. All brilliant cut glass patterns, most of them full finished and fire polished.

Assortment Comprises 1 Doz. Each of the Following:

5½-Inch Footed Scalloped Edge Tray—Brilliant and attractive.
Large Handled Mug—Shapely and rich.
Medium Size Cut Pattern Salt and Pepper—Extra heavy with good tops.
4½-Inch Deep Footed Sauce Dish—Fancy scalloped edge.
Large Fancy Goblet—Brilliant and shapely.
5½-Inch Fancy Olive or Bonbon Dish—Footed, with turned-up sides.
Extra Heavy Rich Table Tumbler—Deep cut pattern.
4½-Inch Footed Comport—Extra deep, full finished.
Full Finished Wine Glass—Brilliant rich pattern.
4¼-Inch Beaded Edge Nappy or Sauce Dish—Extra deep, extra bright.
Rich and Heavy Toothpick Holder—A 5c gem.
¼-Inch Fancy Finished Plate—Always useful.
(Total 12 doz. in bbl. Bbl. 35c.) Per dozen, 24

Our "BARGAIN DAY" 3c Assortment.

3c Possibilities, but Comparable Only with the 5-Cent Assortments Offered by Our Neighbors.

C106—Although these *can* be sold for 3 cents, they are all large pieces which have never before retailed for less than 5c. All brilliant cut glass patterns, most of them full finished and fire polished.

Assortment Comprises 1 Doz. Each of the Following:

5½-Inch Footed Scalloped Edge Tray—Brilliant and attractive.
Large Handled Mug—Shapely and rich.
Medium Size Cut Pattern Salt and Pepper—Extra heavy with good tops.
4½-Inch Deep Footed Sauce Dish—Fancy scalloped edge.
Large Fancy Goblet—Brilliant and shapely.
5½-Inch Fancy Olive or Bonbon Dish—Footed, with turned-up sides.
Extra Heavy Rich Table Tumbler—Deep cut pattern.
4½-Inch Footed Comport—Extra deep, full finished.
Full Finished Wine Glass—Brilliant rich pattern.
4¼-Inch Beaded Edge Nappy or Sauce Dish—Extra deep, extra bright.
Rich and Heavy Toothpick Holder—A 5c gem.
6¼-Inch Fancy Finished Plate—Always useful.
(Total 12 doz. in bbl., Bbl. 35c.) Per dozen, 25c

Our "BARGAIN DAY" 3c Assortment.

3c Possibilities, but Comparable Only with the 5-Cent Assortments Offered by Our Neighbors.

C106—Although these *can* be sold for 3 cents, they are all large pieces which have never before retailed for less than 5c. All brilliant cut glass patterns, most of them full finished and fire polished.

Assortment Comprises 1 Doz. Each of the Following:

5½-Inch Footed Scalloped Edge Tray—Brilliant and attractive.
Large Handled Mug—Shapely and rich.
Medium Size Cut Pattern Salt and Pepper—Extra heavy with good tops.
4½-Inch Deep Footed Sauce Dish—Fancy scalloped edge.
Large Fancy Goblet—Brilliant and shapely.
5½-Inch Fancy Olive or Bonbon Dish—Footed, with turned-up sides.
Extra Heavy Rich Table Tumbler—Deep cut pattern.
4½-Inch Footed Comport—Extra deep, full finished.
Full Finished Wine Glass—Brilliant rich pattern.
4¼-Inch Beaded Edge Nappy or Sauce Dish—Extra deep, extra bright.
Rich and Heavy Toothpick Holder—A 5c gem.
6¼-Inch Fancy Finished Plate—Always useful.
(Total 12 doz. in bbl., Bbl. 35c.) Per dozen, **25c**

CLOCKWISE FROM TOP LEFT

"Our 'Bargain Day' 3c Assortment," Butler Brothers, July 1902. All items shown are Bryce, Higbee products except for the sweetmeat shown at lower right, which is McKee's Jubilee pattern.

The same assortment shown in the fall 1902 catalog. Note the image of the Jubilee sweetmeat is removed.

By spring 1903, the assortment was corrected to include a Highland salt shaker, as originally intended.

is no question that Butler Brothers distributed huge quantities of glassware, but many may not realize that the number of errors in their catalogs is quite low. Keep in mind there are even errors in original glass company catalogs. Not every single original document in any sort of research is infallible. Let us consider genealogy for a moment (which glass research is very much akin to). There are a great number of errors found on ship lists and, many times, even birth records or marriage applications, but this is not to say these documents should never be used to confirm a person's lineage. It is ideal, whenever possible, to compare assortments between catalogs and consult other catalogs as well. Many assortments remained the same over an extended period of time and contained the same core items with some items dropped to allow the addition of newer items or patterns. The same patterns were usually offered in different assortments from the same company, too.

A common misconception is that because Butler Brothers sold wholesale, they offered only old goods unsellable by the glass manufacturers themselves. Comparing the patterns the glass companies offered in each catalog with known dates of introduction does not substantiate this claim. It is true that not every single piece in an assortment was always brand new. It behooved the factories to include some older patterns that would not move as easily on their own. Every now and then a single odd item or two of a much older pattern is spotted in an assortment. These may have been old stock of discontinued patterns, but some may have been older staples that were still in demand. If they all were odds and ends of which the manufacturers were just trying to rid themselves, it does not seem likely that these same items would continually appear in assortments year after year, for all the old stock would have been purged by then. Assortments from United States Glass Company probably contain more old patterns than any other. This is because the company inherited warehouses full of previously made stock from all the member factories, which literally took years to sell. They also were producing some of the earlier patterns, introduced prior to their formation in 1891, which were in good demand, often in new colors such as Dewey blue and emerald green.

In their book *Pressed Glass in America,* the Welkers state that Butler Brothers "would buy lots at large discounts from a purchaser who had overpurchased at the annual glass shows, as well as directly from glass factory overstocks." There is proof that representatives from Butler Brothers and other jobbers were registered as buyers and came long distances to attend the January glass shows in Pittsburgh, where the focus was promoting new lines. Travel was not as easy then as it is now, by any means, especially in the winter. This trek to see new lines of glassware and place orders would not have been necessary if they purchased only old goods or overstock directly from the factory, and they certainly would not have attended the glass shows if they purchased lots from other buyers who had overbought at the very same shows. In short, it is not very likely that

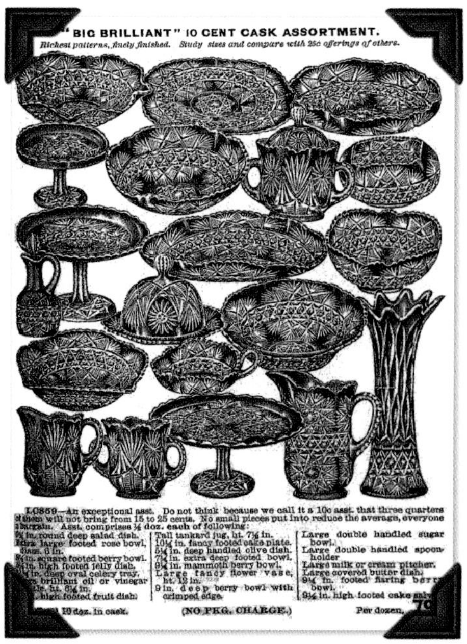

LEFT | The Butler Brothers spring 1902 catalog offered many assortments of Bryce, Higbee's Highland, proving that this wholesaler did carry new patterns. Highland was introduced for the spring trade that same year.

RIGHT | Butler Brothers offered a large assortment of Bryce, Higbee's new *Ten-Pointed Star* pattern in their spring 1906 catalog. The OMN has not been discovered yet.

representatives from Butler Brothers would have incurred extra expense and taken time to attend the shows if they had easier and cheaper methods of obtaining wares.

Compiling assortments and offering them to jobbers was a good method for the glass companies to reach a huge market, and it enabled them to move product quickly. In instances where the introduction years of specific patterns are known, it is worthy to note that the majority do appear in Butler Brothers rather soon after their introduction. This is particularly true of patterns from the mid- to late 1890s and early 1900s, when more and more items were being offered and, consequently, more comprehensive catalogs were issued with greater frequency. This observation does not support the Welkers' theory that lots were purchased at a large discount from those who overbought at the January show, for there would have to be quite a fair gap between the time the items were ordered, shipped, received, and displayed in their stores and when those merchants finally realized they bought too much because the goods were not moving. It would only be after this or a similar process that the excess would have been passed on to someone else. Considering that there would have been quite a bit of monetary loss incurred by those getting rid of the lots, it is reasonable to think that this would have been a last resort after ample time was allowed. Also, Butler Brothers offered tremendous quantities of glassware over the course of many decades, and it hardly seems likely that what they sold was obtained on a regular basis from incompetent buyers who did not know or understand their market. Products of the same companies were consistently offered and it would be a very strange coincidence for overstocks of only these manufacturers to make their way to this particular jobber. The possibility that some product was acquired through surplus cannot be completely discounted, but it does not appear that the majority was.

Some may feel Butler Brothers catalogs are not a valid research tool, but when closely studied they actually offer quite a bit of insight into the products of the glass companies and the marketing of those products. One drawback to Butler Brothers catalogs is the fact that patterns are rarely identified by their OMN. There are some instances where they are, but this is rather unusual. Butler Brothers assortments were given colorful and attention-getting names and included a list of the items with measurements, generally without naming the individual patterns in each grouping. It should be considered that if it were not for these catalogs, we would barely have any idea of what Bryce, Higbee produced and little, if any, approximation of when they produced it. Merely eighteen tableware patterns are documented to the company through the only known trade catalog pages shown in Kamm's *An Eighth Pattern Glass Book*. This is a paltry sum, indeed, considering the company produced glassware for over a quarter century. The sum of eighteen tableware patterns encompasses approximately one quarter of the firm's output and does not include novelties. In the majority of cases, jobber assortments are the sole method we have to link patterns to Bryce, Higbee and are the only visual record we have of the patterns when they were new.

PITKIN AND BROOKS

Pitkin and Brooks was a wholesaler in Chicago, Illinois, that began business in 1872. The company was established by Edwin Pitkin and J. W. Brooks and incorporated in 1891. They offered a large range of cut and pressed glass in addition to lamps and other decorative items.

During the late 1890s to early 1900s (and perhaps earlier), Pitkin and Brooks used very clear, detailed illustrations. Comparative study indicates many of these images were taken or directly copied from the company catalogs of the glass factories. They also offered some small assortments that link patterns to one manufacturer. The first dozen pages of their 1897, 1899, and circa 1900 catalogs feature the latest patterns offered by the glasshouses. Some older patterns within the catalogs may be staple items that remained popular with the public and found a ready market. Pitkin and Brooks

Pitkin & Brooks building, Chicago, Illinois, as it appeared in the late 1890s.

wholesale prices were higher than those of Butler Brothers for the same goods. For example, Bryce Higbee's Charm pitchers were offered in an 1897 Pitkin and Brooks catalog for $2.50 per dozen (about 21¢ each), but Butler Brothers sold the same pitcher for $1.63 per dozen (about 14¢ each) that same year. Neither price reflects the 35¢ barrel fee both charged. A dealer was required to order a minimum of two dozen pitchers for that price from Butler Brothers, but this still was cheaper than Pitkin & Brooks, even considering the 10% discount the latter firm gave for purchasing two dozen (which brought the price down to about 19¢ each). The difference in cost may seem rather insignificant to us today, but keep in mind the average weekly wage for a skilled white male laborer at the time was about $8.00, and a nickel had much more purchasing power than it does now. Pitkin & Brooks catalogs are not as comprehensive as those of Butler Brothers, but are quite valuable because the illustrations are outstanding and in the vast majority of cases they use the original names given by the glass companies.

OTHER JOBBERS

Baltimore Bargain House (Baltimore, Maryland), B. Sommers and G. Sommers (St. Paul, Minnesota), Spelman Brothers (New York, New York), and others offered assortments similar to Butler Brothers, but in lesser quantities. Not as many of these catalogs are found, and it may be that they were not issued as frequently or in such great numbers as Butler Brothers, which issued monthly catalogs beginning in 1907. The size of the company is an important factor. Smaller jobbers would obviously offer smaller quantities and turn over product less quickly, and, therefore, issue fewer catalogs. Illustrations vary in clarity depending on the jobber, and the age and assortment of the patterns offered varies as well.

The jobbers mentioned above (as well as some others not noted) used OMNs, some more frequently than others. Like Butler Brothers, all items in an assortment are supposed to be from the same maker; however, there is still a margin for human error that must be considered. Assortments were put together and packed by the glass companies. Sommers catalogs note:

> We sell glassware in full packages only, shipping the barrels in the same shape we receive them. This avoids repacking and saves much breakage. The goods are packed by experienced packers at the factories, and there is little breakage reported to us.

Spelman Brothers makes a similar notation:

> Original packages, just as they are packed at the factory, require the charge of 35¢ per barrel for

The B. Sommers *Our Leader* catalog cover for the 1884–1885 season is notably similar to the design Butler Brothers used on their *"Our Drummer"* catalogs.

Cover of *Spelman's Fancy Goods Graphic* for February 1882.

Bryce, Higbee's Our Toothpick presented as a match safe on a plush stand with a bottle of perfume. This was one of many novelties called "Bazaar Goods" and offered by Spelman Brothers circa 1888.

> packing. It is not our charge, but just what every purchaser pays in the glass regions. It is more honest to charge you just what we pay than to conceal the amount in the prices of the goods.

It was important for the objects shown in each assortment to be accurate representations of the actual items, as evidenced by this statement made by Baltimore Bargain House:

> We wish to call your particular attention to the fact that we illustrate in these glassware pages each and every item in an assortment, be the article large or small. In that way the merchant can see exactly what he will receive for his money.

This point is mentioned again on the same page, though with different wording, stressing the importance of the images.

Baltimore Bargain House rarely used OMNs and offered more stray items in their assortments than other jobbers, such as items from a table set in different patterns. Most of the patterns they offered were a year old or more at the time the catalogs were issued. The aesthetic looks of their assortments often have less continuity than other jobbers' and some images are very disproportionately portrayed.

B. Sommers changed their name to G. Sommers sometime between issuing their spring 1886 and fall 1887 catalogs. Many of the patterns they offered were new or recent. Spelman Brothers offered a large number of "Bazaar Goods" which they defined as "fascinating specialties that are remarkably elegant and wonderfully cheap." This included odd wine glasses, toothpick holders, and glass shoes, each containing a small bottle of perfume. When the perfume was gone the owner had a usable piece of glassware for the household. No doubt many odd items of EAPG were distributed in such a manner. Spelman

Brothers also offered small assortments of glassware.

Hollander, Bradshaw and Folsom (Boston, Massachusetts), H. Leonard's Sons & Company (Grand Rapids, Michigan), and Ogden, Merrill & Greer (St. Paul, Minnesota) are other jobbers that used clear images and OMNs as well. They sold mostly individual items, table sets, and water sets, but a few assortments were included. It is interesting to note that many images found in different jobber catalogs appear to have come from a common source and are either the same or appear to have been drawn or engraved from the same image. Of all the jobbers noted, Butler Brothers catalogs are unquestionably the most comprehensive and have survived in the greatest quantity. It is still valuable to seek other jobber catalogs to confirm the accuracy of items included in assortments as well as OMNs. Oftentimes different patterns and items were offered by different jobbers, the study of which gives more insight and a fuller understanding of the scope of Bryce, Higbee's production.

RETAIL CATALOGS

Sears, Roebuck & Company

There is hardly an American who is not familiar with the ubiquitous Sears catalog. Generally thought of as the king of mail order houses, the company was founded by Richard Sears. After moving to Chicago, Sears partnered with Alvah Roebuck. The first catalogs were issued in 1888 and retail stores were opened in 1925. Catalogs boldly state "Cheapest Supply House on Earth." By the references and language used throughout their catalogs, it is obvious the company aimed to make mail order as convenient and pleasant to the consumer as possible. Perhaps the greatest achievement of Sears was its ability to reach a strong customer base in rural areas, where residents had limited and usually more expensive selections based on what their closest general store carried. Their catalogs opened the window for average folk to own, or least aspire to own, goods previously viewed as unaffordable or unattainable. This may be what the company is most remembered for.

Sears sold a wide variety of merchandise including pressed glassware. Though some new patterns were offered, the majority were a year old or more. Their 1897 catalog is a bit of an exception in its offerings. In that catalog forty-four percent of the patterns shown were introduced that year, thirty-three percent were introduced in 1896, and twenty-three percent were introduced prior to 1896. Profit margins were much smaller back then. For example, in 1897, Pitkin & Brooks sold Bryce, Higbee's Crescent pitchers wholesale for $2.50 per dozen (a little over 20¢ each). Sears retailed the same pitcher to its customers for 28¢ each that year. Sears only provided order numbers for individual items and sets, unlike Montgomery Ward & Company, which very often used OMNs.

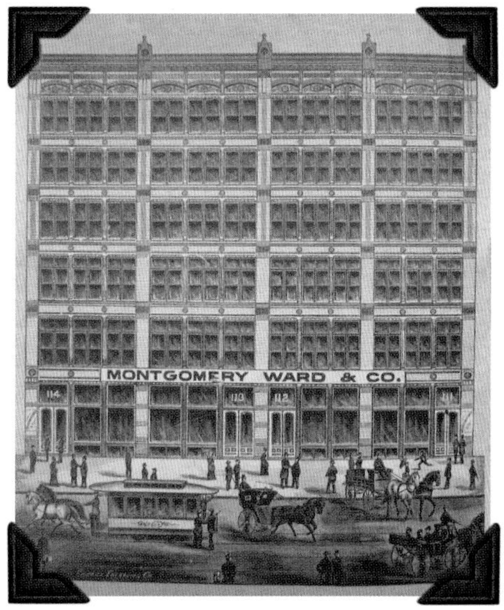

Montgomery Ward & Company, late 1880s.

Montgomery Ward & Company

Montgomery Ward & Company was founded in 1872 in Chicago, Illinois, by Aaron Montgomery Ward. The first catalogs were not illustrated, but beginning in 1876 woodcut images were used. The company quickly grew during the next decade. Like Sears, Roebuck & Company, Montgomery Ward offered all sorts of merchandise (including food) for the American home and farm. By the mid–1890s these two mail order houses were in fierce competition with each other. It was at this time that Montgomery Ward proudly declared themselves "Originators of

Montgomery Ward catalogs included beautiful cover art as these examples from the spring and summer 1893, World's Fair edition illustrate.

the mail order Business" on the covers of their catalogs.

Montgomery Ward began offering glassware in 1883, and their glassware sections are more comprehensive than those of Sears. From 1883 to 1885 assortments of glassware made by McKee & Brothers were sold. Beginning in 1886 the products of Atterbury & Company were added, and by 1890 an even wider range of manufacturers were represented. Montgomery Ward first offered Bryce, Higbee glassware in 1887. It is not completely certain how they acquired all the glassware they sold, but they may have had a direct relationship with some of the glass companies and/or jobbers. A February 1910 supplement presented a set of glassware for a special price. The leaflet states: "Six carloads for this sale. Order placed with the factory when business was dull—kept them busy—result, a low price." The pattern is McKee's Rock Crystal, neither a cheaply made nor old, outdated pattern in early 1910. With this bit of evidence, the thought that other glassware was obtained by Montgomery Ward in this manner cannot be disregarded.

Contrary to popular belief, Montgomery Ward did offer many new patterns. Their spring and summer catalogs show sets of brand new patterns the glass companies introduced the very same year for the spring trade. Many of the older patterns offered are individual pieces. No doubt some were popular items that had continual demand rather than closeouts of old stock, because they appear regularly over the course of many years. They are also found in catalogs of Pitkin and Brooks during the same time frame. More often than not patterns are given their OMNs in Montgomery Ward catalogs. Even when OMNs are not used, there are usually direct references to them or the manufacturer. For example, Fostoria Glass Company's Louise is called "Fostoria," United States Glass Company's Washington is called "White House," and National Glass Company's Reward is called "National." It is a mystery why some patterns were given different names, but it could have been a marketing decision made by the glass manufacturers themselves. There appears to have been some relationship between Montgomery Ward and Pitkin & Brooks, for not only did they offer many of the same patterns and items in the same year/season, but in some cases gave patterns the very same names that were not the ones used by the manufacturers.

4 Bryce, Higbee & Company Catalogs

BRYCE, HIGBEE & COMPANY CATALOG PAGES SHOWN IN MINNIE WATSON KAMM'S *An Eighth Pattern Glass Book*

Mention is made in trade journals of catalogs issued by Bryce, Higbee & Company. An issue of *American Pottery and Glassware Reporter* from December 1880 states the company has "just got out a new lithographic catalog." *China, Glass & Lamps* mentions another Bryce, Higbee catalog in January 1883: "Their new catalog is now ready, and it is neat and comprehensive. It is illustrated with engravings of the various articles they make." These catalogs would be particularly valuable to researchers because they must show their early tableware patterns, many of which are unidentified as to design and/or OMN. In early 1898, a reporter for *China, Glass & Lamps* wrote: "The firm [Bryce, Higbee & Co.] are getting out catalogs of the new ware, profusely illustrated, and will mail copies to dealers as soon as ready." None of these catalogs have ever been discovered. The only known Bryce, Higbee catalog pages are those reprinted in Kamm's *An Eighth Pattern Glass Book* (simply referred to as Kamm 8 by collectors), but none of those pages are from any of the catalogs noted here. Kamm alludes to other pages from the catalogs she chose not to reprint. She is not explicitly clear if she owned the catalogs illustrated, but her language indicates she did not. Mrs. Kamm does not give credit to any particular person or library for them, yet she consistently notes the owners of objects she sketched. The whereabouts of the catalogs Kamm reprinted is a mystery. If anyone has or knows of any Bryce, Higbee company catalogs, please contact the author at FiddlerPaul71@gmail.com.

BRYCE, HIGBEE & COMPANY CATALOG PAGES SHOWN IN MINNIE WATSON KAMM'S *AN EIGHTH PATTERN GLASS BOOK*

Kamm shows many Bryce, Higbee catalog pages in her eighth book on pattern glass published in 1954, the year of her death. Although a great deal of time has passed, many of the inaccuracies presented in her text still persist to this day and must be cleared up. Kamm's book is the only source for original Bryce, Higbee company catalog pages, and for that alone we are indebted to her for showing them. This is the only means to truly document the designs and their original names. Kamm mentions the catalogs are undated and places most of them to the mid–1880s. Due to this, subsequent authors assigned the date circa 1885 to many of these patterns, which has somehow magically (and in most cases, inaccurately) become *made in 1885*.

It is a bit perplexing that Mrs. Kamm erroneously states some of the pages are from the Greensburg Glass Company of Greensburg, Pennsylvania, when they are actually from Bryce, Higbee & Company. Because of this, it is fair to think the company name was not printed on the individual pages. On none of the pages shown in negative print (white images on black background) does the company's name appear, yet it does on the pages done in positive print (black images on white background). Kamm correctly documents all the latter-mentioned pages to Bryce, Higbee & Company. It is not known from how many different catalogs these pages were extracted. At least some of them may have been from separate catalogs or incomplete catalogs/loose sheets, for if they were bound as one volume, why would Kamm think some were from Greensburg and others from Bryce, Higbee? It is possible, though, that all the positive pages were from one catalog and all the negative images were from another and Kamm mixed things up after making prints for the book. The positive catalog pages are marked as the work of the Armor Lith. Company of Pittsburgh. The negative catalog pages are marked "CENTRAL LITH. CO. PITTSBURGH, PA." or "CENTRAL LITH. CO. PITTS. PA." and the known introduction years of the patterns shown on them are 1888, 1889, 1890, and 1891. If the negative printed pages are from the same catalog, it appears it would date from circa 1892/93. This is based on the inclusion of Worlds. As for the pages done in positive print, there are variations noted in the discussion of the plates that may link certain pages to each other; however, if this group of positive printed pages is from just one catalog, it must date between July 1888 and December 1888. This is based on the presence of the Royal goblet and the narrow window of time the Persian pattern was referred to as "Princeton" in trade journals.

It is a shame for the modern researcher that Kamm did not reprint the catalogs in their entirety, for, if she had, there might have been additional clues for dating them a bit more accurately. A more complete list of items, using their original company terms, would be possible, too, but trade journal quotes and other means can assist in this endeavor. One must understand Kamm's intent in reprinting the pages was merely to document patterns, manufacturers, and/or their OMNs. In this regard she truly was a pioneer, for at that time most EAPG authors did not concern themselves with such undertakings. I do not wish to convey a lack of respect for Kamm's work by scrutinizing it so closely; quite the contrary, I wish to update, correct, and add to the foundation she laid down for us.

Plates 16–17, Yale

Kamm states that these pages are from an undated trade catalog of around 1885; however, *Pottery & Glassware Reporter* verifies that Yale was introduced in January 1887, so these pages must date 1887 or after.

Plates 18–19, Homestead

Kamm dates Homestead to the mid–1880s. This author has found nothing to confirm or deny this, but the actual catalog pages shown, I feel, date to 1888 (see discussion of plates 31–33). Note the Anglo-Japanese and Neo-Grec corner ornaments.

Plates 20–21, New Grand

Kamm does not date these pages, but states elsewhere the pattern was found in a merchandise catalog for 1885 (but does not name it) and mentions the numerous stemmed compotes found in the pattern are typical of the mid–1880s. No evidence has been found to confirm an introduction date for Grand, but the earliest source this author has found for the pattern is a Bryce, Higbee invoice dated June 30, 1886. The names Grand and New Grand were not used intermittently; rather, New Grand referred to an updated version of the Grand pattern with different mould shapes. Though these pages show New Grand, the author feels the goblet shown actually originated with Grand. See Grand and New Grand discussions in chapter 9.

Plates 22–24, Persian

Again, this is arbitrarily stated by Kamm to be from the mid–1880s, but Persian is noted as a new pattern for the upcoming spring trade in the December 27, 1888, issue of *Pottery and Glassware Reporter.* It appears to have been first issued as "Princeton" in 1887, but by late 1888 the name was changed to Persian. See plate 38 and listing of Persian in chapter 9 for further discussion.

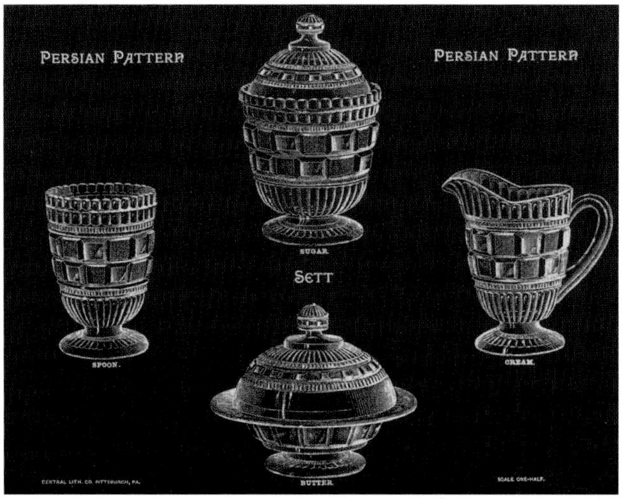

Plates 25–27, Era

Kamm says Era was made during the mid–1880s and reproduced or kept in stock until 1891, when the "New" was added to the name. This pattern was not called New Era by Bryce, Higbee. Her confusion comes from advertisements shown in *China, Glass & Lamps* in 1891 (plate 27 shows one). Note the quotation marks only encompass the word "Era." The word "New" is clearly outside these quotes, meaning that Era was a new pattern. In her fifth book, Kamm states, "In 1880, they [Bryce, Higbee & Co.] put out 'New Era,' probably the first pattern, the name significant in meaning." There is absolutely no evidence to indicate the pattern was their first pattern or even that it was produced prior to 1891, but there is plenty of evidence that it was first made for the 1891 market.

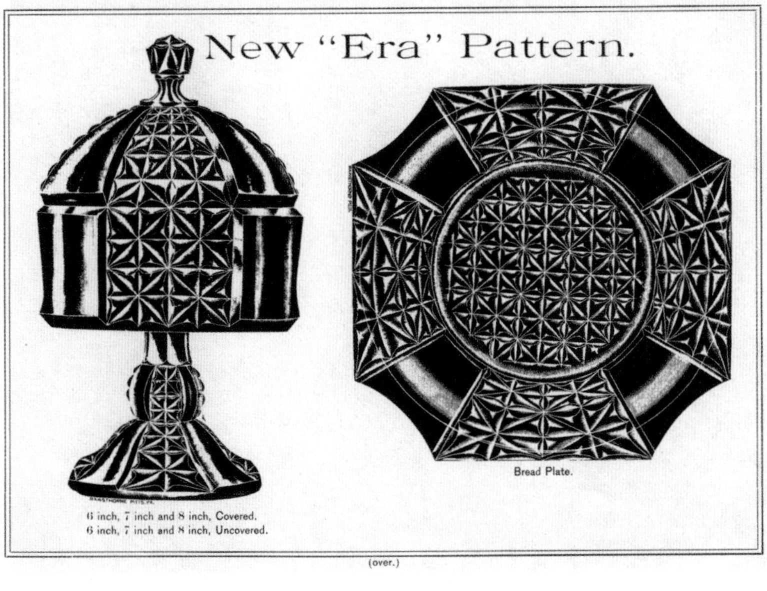

Plates 28–29, Royal

Dated to the mid–1880s by Kamm, but noted as a new pattern in the July 12, 1888, issue of *Pottery & Glassware Reporter*. Royal is not the same pattern as that commonly known as *Sprig*, despite what has been accepted for many decades. See Rival and Royal in chapter 9.

Plate 30, Miscellaneous Items

This catalog page is undated, but must be 1887 or after, for trade journal reports confirm the Busy Bee Hive Ink, Gatling Gun, and Tub Soap Dish were new novelties for 1887.

Plates 31–33, Menagerie Toy Set, Miscellaneous, Mustards or Horseradishes

There is little doubt these pages are connected, judging from the typeset and the Anglo-Japanese and Neo-Grec ornamental designs in the corners. They cannot be earlier than 1887 because each of the three pages includes an item listed as new in the January 13, 1887, issue of *Pottery & Glassware Reporter*. This author feels the pages date to 1888 (see discussion of plate 38). It is possible that plate 30 is from the same catalog. The border is different, but the typeset is the same. The typeset of plates 31–33 also appears identical to plates 18–19 showing the Homestead pattern; but, more importantly, each page contains the same distinctive designs found in the corners on plates 18–19. Plate 32 appears to be the reverse side of plate 38, as both say "over" and have the same ornamental corner designs. Plate 31 appears to be the opposite side of plate 33 for the same reasons.

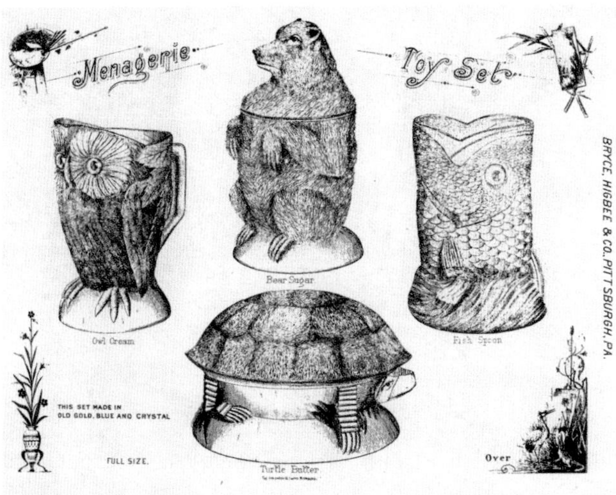

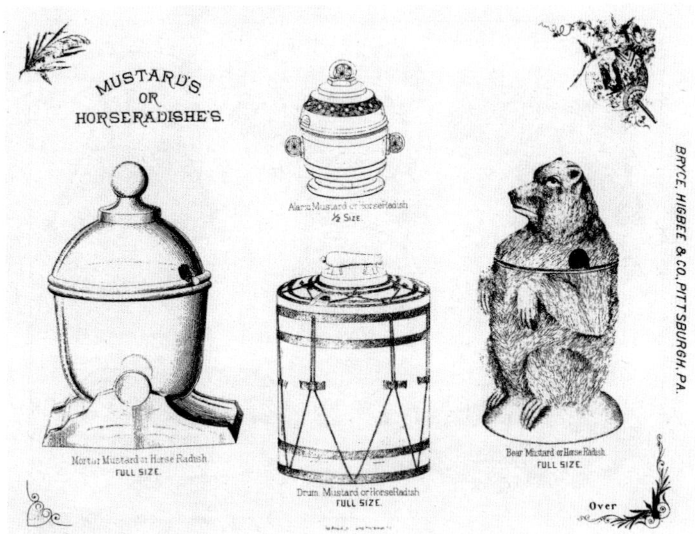

Plate 34, Novelties

Kamm gives the caption "Novelties by the same firm in 1887" to this page. Trade journals confirm that three of the four items shown on this page were introduced in 1887; the other, 1886. The typeset appears to be the same as plates 16–17 showing the Yale pattern, introduced in 1887. These three pages may have come from the same catalog.

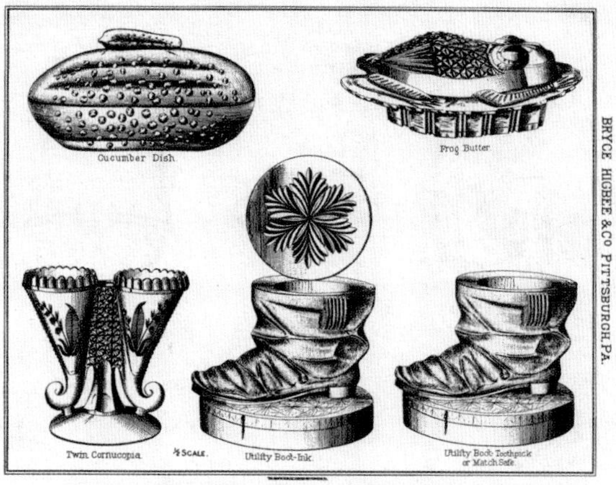

Plate 35, Kaiser Wilhelm Plate

If this item was made as a memorial, which it appears to be, it would date after Kaiser Wilhelm I's death in early March 1888. The typeset appears to be the same as plates 30–33, and very well could be from the same catalog. Note that author feels plates 30–33 date to 1888.

Plates 36–37, Grant Plate and Pope Leo XIII Bread Plate

The typeset of the headers on these two pages is the same and it appears they came from the same catalog. Trade journal quotes confirm the Grant Plate was new in 1885, and an 1888 jobber catalog offers the Pope Leo XIII plate. Note the recurring date of 1888 in the discussions of the positive-print catalog pages. See chapter 9 for detailed discussions of these commemorative bread plates.

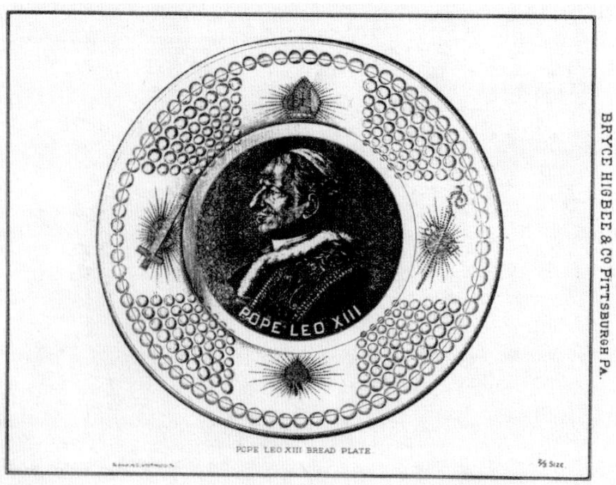

Plate 38, Stemware

Kamm dates this page circa 1885, but it is later because the Royal pattern introduced in 1888 is shown. Again, notice the typeset and the distinctive Neo-Grec designs in the corners which link it to plates 18–19 and plates 31–33. Plate 38 is probably the reverse side of plate 32. Interestingly, the Persian goblet is labeled "Princeton," which undoubtedly places this catalog page sometime between July 1888 when Royal is first mentioned in trade journals, and December 1888 when Princeton appears in trade journals as Persian. For further discussion see Persian on page 214.

Plates 42–44, Mirror

These are some of the catalog pages Kamm mislabeled as being from the Greensburg Glass Company. The date of "about 1880" she assigns to the pattern is also incorrect. Trade journal quotes confirm that Mirror was made by Bryce, Higbee for the 1890 market, and items are shown in Butler Brothers assortments with other known Bryce, Higbee patterns.

Plates 45–46, Gem

Though these catalog pages are undated, Kamm assigns Gem to the mid–1880s; however, it is more likely a pattern from the early 1890s. See discussion under Gem in chapter 9 on page 174.

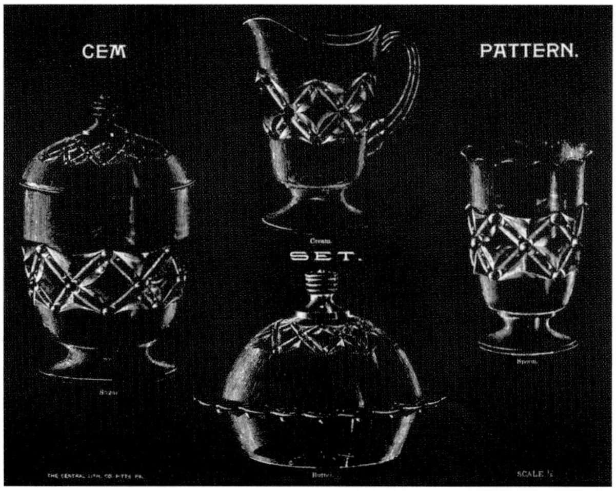

Plate 47, Worlds

Kamm states the pattern was put out in the mid–1880s, but the catalog page shown is undated. There is no proof Worlds was introduced in the 1880s, but there are indications it was introduced during the 1892/93 time frame. See Worlds discussion on page 246 in chapter 9.

Plates 48–49, Flora

Attributed by Kamm to Greensburg Glass Company during the mid–1880s, but Flora is first mentioned in July 1890 in trade journals as a product of Bryce, Higbee and also mentioned as a new pattern for the 1891 spring trade.

Plates 50–52, Tidal

Another pattern Kamm mistakenly attributes to Greensburg during the mid–1880s. *Pottery & Glassware Reporter* describes Tidal in July 1889 as a new pattern by Bryce, Higbee "got out for the fall trade."

Plates 53, Bijou

Although Kamm says Bijou was produced by Greensburg Glass Company in the mid–1880s, the July 12, 1888, issue of *Pottery & Glassware Reporter* tells us it was made by Bryce, Higbee & Company for the upcoming fall trade. Note the annotation "(C.)" after each item.

Plate 54, Bijou

This is also a page from a Bryce, Higbee catalog rather than Greensburg, as stated by Kamm. She identifies the bowls and pickle with the shell motif as Tidal, logically so, as they do resemble that pattern. Kamm notes the rectangular bowl at the top of the page labeled "sauce dish, 7 in." is yet another pattern. Though the items on this page are not the same design, Bryce, Higbee intended them all to be part of the Bijou line, hence the caption at the top of the page identifying them as such. There are initials in parenthesis denoting the three different patterns shown. The items with the fan and acanthus leaf design typically associated with Bijou are labeled "(C.)," items with the shell motif are labeled "(S.)," and the odd sauce dish is labeled "(F. D.)." It is not certain what the letters stand for, but "S." may denote "Shell," and "F. D." could be "Flat Diamond," "Fenced Diamond," or other similar designation. The July 12, 1888, issue of *Pottery and Glassware Reporter* gives a good, detailed report of the new Bijou pattern, specifically mentioning shell patterned items. The report states the line "*comprises several different varieties of shapes and patterns*" (author's emphasis). Without this quote we would not link these diverse items together. At first glance, the bowls and pickle dish with the shell motif appear to have more in common with Tidal, but close inspection reveals they actually are not the same. More importantly, the Tidal pattern did not exist until the following year, 1889. There are small bowls as well as 7" and 10" plates formed as shells not shown on this page which are also part of the Bijou line. See Bijou in chapter 9 on page 128 for further discussion.

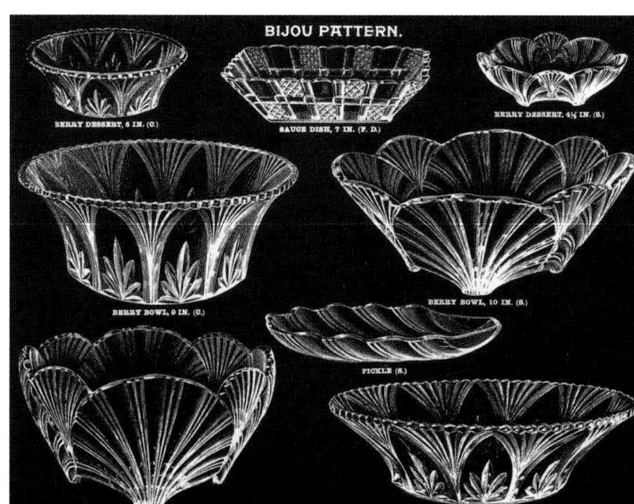

Plates 55–57, Ethol

Under plate 55, Kamm states Ethol is a Greensburg Glass Company pattern which was new in 1880. In the text of the book, she says it dates to the mid–1880s. Trade journals confirm that Ethol was made by Bryce, Higbee & Company and was new in 1890.

Looking through *An Eighth Pattern Glass Book,* one discovers how many patterns Kamm dates to the "mid-Eighties." For the time in which she wrote, it was completely acceptable to her audience to give a general and somewhat arbitrary range like this. Kamm was actually more of a researcher than most authors of her day and used original catalogs to document patterns and manufacturers when possible. Many company catalogs are not dated, however, so she guessed based on how she perceived the characteristics of the patterns. The companies never imagined future generations would collect the glass they made, let alone avidly seek information to document their products. Today's researchers, authors, and collectors strive to know as much as they possibly can about the history of Early American Pattern Glass. If more period documents were available to Kamm, she probably would have used them. We are fortunate to have access to so many of the important trade journals, which are the most accurate method of pinpointing when Bryce, Higbee introduced the patterns mentioned in them. It is the author's hope that the detailed information presented here, which is based on years of devoted research, will elucidate the facts and correct misinformation, which has persisted for so long.

5 Bryce, Higbee's Products

- TERMINOLOGY AND USE
- FORMS
- SETS
- INDIVIDUAL FORMS
- FAVORED FORMS

Terminology and Use

A question often posed by collectors is "what was this item used for?" Original terminology is an interesting subject unto itself. It often changed over the years within any given company, and some of it may have been influenced by the designer or the fashion of the time. Certain forms were called the same thing by nearly all the glass manufacturers, but many were given different and unique names. We look back well over a century later and wonder why they used the terms they did. Having studied literally thousands of original company, jobber, and retail catalogs from various factories and businesses, as well as trade journals and other documents, the author is able to form some conclusions.

Certain jobber and retail catalogs not only used OMNs, but they also used the same images and terms from the manufacturers' catalogs; however, even within the same company's catalog, different terms are sometimes encountered for the same form in different patterns. Many times, jobber catalogs used the terms given by the company; other times they did not. The same form is sometimes given a different designation in the same jobber catalog when it is shown elsewhere in the catalog. Terminology can also vary from season to season or year to year. There seems to be varying levels of consistency, and it appears that using different terms for the same form was primarily a marketing technique.

During the 1890s, Victorian excess reached its zenith. Companies boldly proclaimed how many pieces were produced in their huge lines of glassware. It was not unheard of for some to contain 100 to 150 or more different items. Moulds were very expensive and this was taking a huge risk in the sluggish market at the time, but the manufacturers needed to do something to stand above the rest. The glass market was highly competitive, so it was important to create distinct forms, as well as to coin interesting designations for them. The purpose was to convince the buyer to purchase their wares. This demand was fueled by the rising middle class's need to emulate the more prosperous upper class who used many specialty items for elaborate presentations at exclusive social events, oftentimes as a means of initiation into their society. In Victorian times, prosperity was judged by what and how much people owned and how tastefully they displayed it. An outward display of excess was a clear symbol of financial comfort and contentment, which implied a solid family unit. The virtue of a happy family was not only important to the individual members of the family, but to society as a whole. Nineteenth-century Americans prided themselves on being as advanced and civilized as possible. They believed contentment was an important element of a civilized society, and the root of this was at the family level. Raising a family amongst beautiful things in beautiful surroundings produced beautiful, well-bred individuals overflowing with gentility. Abundance could only lead to greater contentment, for it implied nobody was in want or need of anything. This certainly was not the actual reality for all, but an illusion was enough to satisfy and convince society that its own Utopia had been realized.

Illusion played an important role during the Victorian era. There was much that was implied and unspoken. If the family could not afford cut glass they could own something that looked like it for a fraction of the cost and nobody would know the difference. There is evidence of the concept of "keeping up with the Jones" in statements found in period catalogs, such as "Your neighbors will pronounce it genuine cut glass" in reference to pressed glass, and "Everybody wants it." In 1897, Sears, Roebuck & Co. offered a set of McKee & Brothers' Masonic pattern that Sears called an imitation of "the celebrated English 'Prism' cut glass." Special notice was given to the pitcher of the set: "The large pitcher, in particular, is a very handsome piece of glass, and, if it were genuine cut, would alone be worth $20.00...and very few could possibly tell the difference." The marketing strategy presented here is very indicative of the times. The appeal lies not in what the item actually is, but what it pretends to be. The Industrial Revolution caused Americans to value things in a different way. It was now highly desirable to be able to produce

something that closely resembled something much more expensive—concrete proof that America was advancing through modern technology unknown to our forebears. Along with this came the production of larger quantities of goods quite accessible to much of the fast-growing population. Was all of this glassware actually used as the companies and retailers labeled and intended it, or was it even used at all? Probably not. Some items may have been simply displayed on a shelf in front of the mirrored back of a sideboard, mantle, or curio and, just as today, people undoubtedly used the items to suit their own needs. A small footed plate could make itself just as useful in the bedroom holding trinkets as it could at the Sunday dinner table serving olives.

It is a common myth that Victorians spent hours gorging themselves on tremendous quantities of food served in many courses. While it is true that dinners commonly consisted of many different courses, only a small portion of each was generally taken and not each course was taken by all. Abundance was highly regarded and implied contentment; yet, paradoxically, moderation—and sometimes utter abstinence—was considered an esteemed virtue. Foods were grouped in a certain serving order and each grouping was considered a course, whether the offering was substantial or not. Punch, for example, was considered a separate course and was often served before game. Each course had its own set of serving pieces and dining implements, and food was savored and eaten slowly. In actuality, we probably eat larger portions of food than the Victorians did, but they likely had a greater variety of items at one dinner and took longer to serve and consume them. The great variety required something made of silver, china, porcelain, or glassware to properly present and display each item. The upper tier of society had the finest and greatest abundance of food and tableware, but the rising middle-class emulated their practices, or at least aspired to.

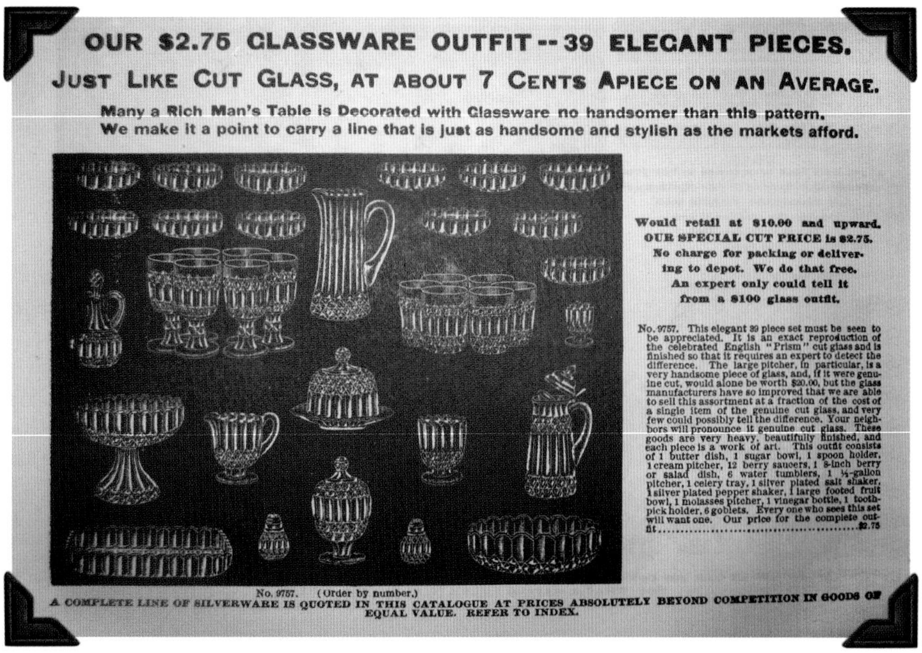

TOP LEFT | Many middle-class homes had parlor cabinets such as this to display glassware and bric-a-brac. This particular model was offered in the early 1900s by Tyrell Ward & Company as a premium in their catalog titled "How to Furnish Your Home and Clothe Yourself without Cost."

BOTTOM | Late nineteenth-century glassware ad using typical sales strategies of the time. Sears, Roebuck & Company, 1897.

FORMS

Being a manufacturer of glass tableware, Bryce, Higbee & Company made wares to compete in that market. A list of forms can be compiled, but keep in mind it will not be complete. It is likely that heretofore unknown forms in any given pattern will show up. Very few company catalog pages are known, but jobber and retail catalogs give us a good idea of what was made. In many cases they point to the name the company originally gave the form. Information which pertains to EAPG in general is also reported here. Though other companies may have used similar language, the specific terms presented apply to products of Bryce, Higbee & Company unless otherwise noted.

SETS

Table Set, originally called "set" or "sett"

- covered butter dish
- covered sugar bowl
- cream pitcher
- spoon holder

The four-piece table set was sometimes referred to as a "tea set" by retailers. The manufacturers simply called the four pieces a set or "sett." Note the latter is not a typographical error, but an archaic spelling of the word. Silver-plated butter dishes were made with either glass or metal drainers, yet, oddly, far fewer glass butter dishes were offered with drainers. EAPG sugar bowls are much larger than those of today. This is because sugar was less refined and more was needed to achieve the desired amount of sweetness. Today the terms creamer and spooner are more commonly used, obvious abbreviations of the complete terms noted above. Many believe these are more recent appellations coined by collectors, but the terms were used in the nineteenth century. The most notable, and possibly the earliest source for the word spooner is McKee's 1880 catalog. Pitkin and Brooks' 1897 catalog uses the terms cream, cream pitcher, and creamer as well as spoon, spoonholder, and spooner. The earliest source for the term creamer known to the author is an 1867 catalog of Meriden Britannia Company. Merriam-Webster cites the first known use to 1858, but it is unclear if the word referred to liquid cream or the cream pitcher. The majority of company catalogs use the words cream and spoon. Jobber catalogs often refer to the cream pitcher as a milk pitcher. Collectors use the term milk pitcher to denote a quart-sized jug.

As the name reveals, spoon holders are receptacles meant to hold spoons on the tea table or dining table. Sugar bowls missing their lids are often mistaken for spoon holders and are too often labeled as such. This may be due to honest confusion, but in some instances they are intentionally mislabeled to hide the fact that the item is not complete. Many spoon holders have scalloped edges with no inner rims. These are the easiest to properly identify. Some have plain edges (such as Earl and Ida), and some even have scalloped edges with an inner ledge (such as Beaunot and *Feathered Medallion*). In these instances, the collector will do well to remember that the spoon holder is just about the same size as the cream pitcher of the set. As a rule, when the sugar bowl of the set is handled, the spoon holder is handled as well. There are exceptions with the products of other companies, but this rule holds true for Bryce, Higbee and J. B. Higbee patterns. Sugar bases are larger and generally wider than spooners. Keep in mind that not all sugar bases have inner ledges. Sugar bowls are of two basic designs. The first type has a plain edge with no inner ledge, which takes a lid with an inner rim. The second type has an inner ledge and takes a lid with no inner rim. When possible, these details are included in the individual pattern listings in chapter 9 in instances where the sugar base could be confused for the spoon holder.

Berry Set (also see Bowls under Individual Forms)

- one large bowl, approximately 8" to 9" in diameter

CLOCKWISE FROM TOP LEFT

Feathered Medallion spooner and sugar, missing its lid. Note that both items have an inner ledge, but that the spooner is narrower. Spooner, 4.25" w., $25–$30; sugar, 4.75" w., $35–$40 (with lid).

Rival spooner and sugar base. Note that both items have smooth rims, but the sugar is larger than the spooner. Spooner, 3" w., $30–$35; sugar, 4.25" w., $45–$50 (with lid).

Comparison showing two styles of lids found on sugar bowls. Note the Rival sugar at right has an inner rim on the lid to hold it in place, whereas the lid of the Yale sugar rests on a ledge on the inside of the sugar base. $40–$50 each.

Assortments of *Ten-Pointed Star* bowls offered by Baltimore Bargain House in June 1906. Note the different styles achieved through hand tooling.

- six to twelve individual bowls, approximately 4" in diameter

Berries of all sorts were a seasonal favorite. Berry sets were extremely popular not only in glass, but also in china and porcelain. Large, elaborate silver spoons, often with gilded and embossed or engraved bowls, were made to serve the berries. Individual berry bowls are often quite small, which baffles collectors. Many now refer to them as honey dishes, but this term is not found in period sources in reference to this form. Portions were not as large in the nineteenth and early twentieth century as they are now. The berries were obviously savored, for silver companies made special tiny berry forks with fewer prongs than standard forks. Their size and fragility enabled the diner to eat just one berry at a time. Silver companies often fitted large berry bowls with elaborate silver-plated holders and sold them as their own product. Many have an arched handle. Collectors coined the term bride's basket for these fancy articles. They were quite popular as wedding gifts, but were simply called berry or fruit dishes when originally sold.

Water (or Lemonade) Set

- one pitcher, usually half-gallon
- tumblers or goblets

Some sets include a waste bowl and a matching glass tray. In that case, there were only two goblets or tumblers so everything would fit on the tray. Sets without a waste bowl included more goblets or tumblers.

INDIVIDUAL FORMS

Bowls

Bowls of many sizes, depths, and shapes were made for various purposes. Edges were often hand-tooled to flare, ruffle, cup, or square the edges. Bowls made by Bryce, Higbee often have a prominent collar base. The glass maker's term for a collar base is "marie." The peculiar designation casserole or berry casserole was used for what collectors might now call a collar-based berry bowl. The terms nappy, berry bowl, and berry dish seem to have been used interchangeably for bowls measuring anywhere from 4" and up. The word nappy is a diminutive of the Old English *nap*, meaning "cup or bowl." It is a term used quite frequently during the nineteenth century. Shallow bowls, flat or footed, measuring approximately 4" to 5" were often called desserts, fruit desserts, or berry desserts by the company. "Comportier" was often used for small and large collar based bowls as well as 3.5" low-foot bowls and is a term used frequently by Bryce, Higbee and later by J. B. Higbee. It is a corruption of the French *compotier*, a pedestaled serving dish. Some people refer to the 3.5" comportier form as a sherbet, sauce, or even a master salt dish, which it is not. Bryce, Higbee and J. B. Higbee used the term jelly dish or handled jelly for what modern collectors call a nappy or handled nappy, whereas the same dish tooled into a triangular shape was called an olive dish by the companies. Oval bowls were offered in graduated sizes and were simply termed ovals or oblongs. 7"-long rectangular bowls with sloped sides are found in some patterns and were called sauce dishes by Bryce, Higbee and J. B. Higbee. Very shallow oval bowls with upturned edges measuring about 10" long may have originally been called cake trays. A very popular form was a bowl with both sides hand-tooled upward. See Favored Forms on page 73.

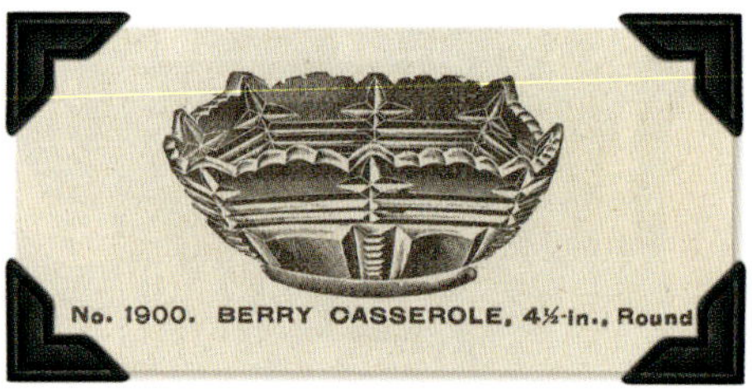

ABOVE | Paris 1900 berry casserole offered by Pitkin & Brooks circa 1900. Though square-shaped, note that the item is labeled "round." Even period catalogs sometimes contain errors. *Courtesy of the Rakow Research Library, Corning Museum of Glass.*

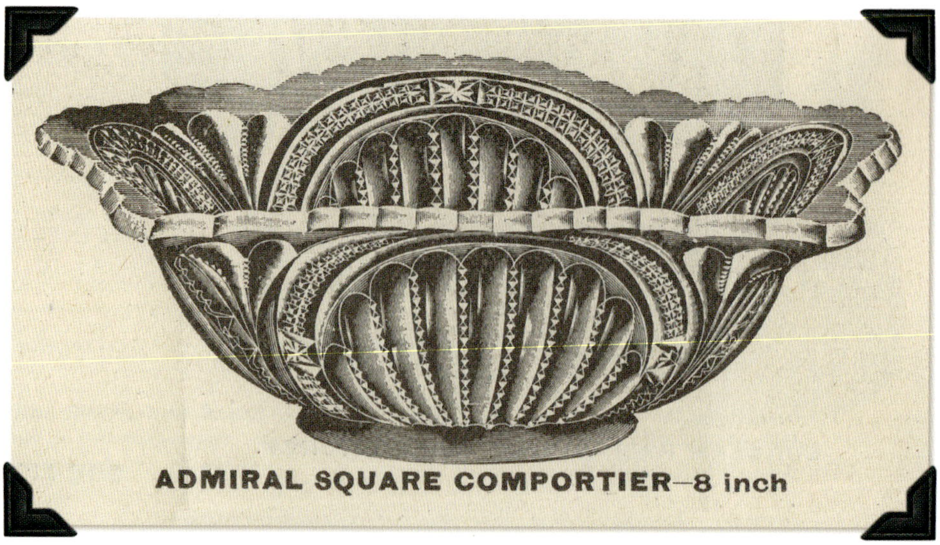

Admiral square comportier, Pitkin & Brooks, 1899. This Chicago firm used original company terminology. *Courtesy of the Rakow Research Library, Corning Museum of Glass.*

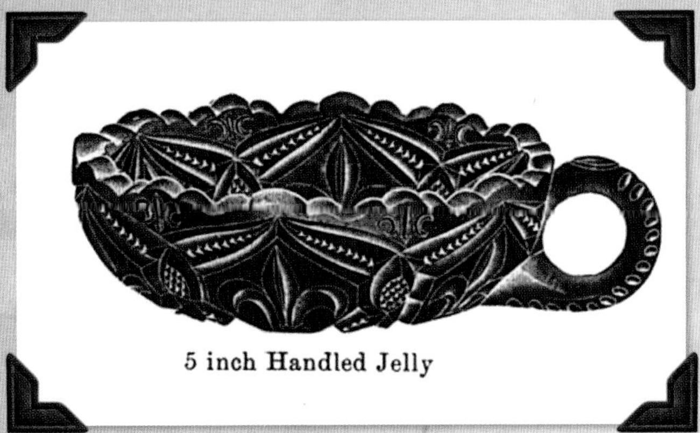

CLOCKWISE FROM TOP LEFT

Persian footed fruit dessert illustrated in a Bryce, Higbee company catalog. This form is what was later called a sherbet by most glass companies.

Madora 3.5" comportier, $10–$12. This form is found in nearly all of Bryce, Higbee's post–1904 patterns. J. B. Higbee used the same term and included comportiers in this same size and shape in their lines of glassware as well.

Bryce, Higbee catalog page, circa early 1890s, showing the form they called a sauce dish.

Fleur-de-lis handled jelly from an 1898 advertisement *in China, Glass & Lamps.*

Cake Stands

ABOVE | In Victorian times, good baking was a mark of domestic achievement. Montgomery Ward catalog illustration, 1899.

Fleur-de-lis salver from an 1899 Pitkin & Brooks catalog. Note the upturned edge. *Courtesy of the Rakow Research Library, Corning Museum of Glass.*

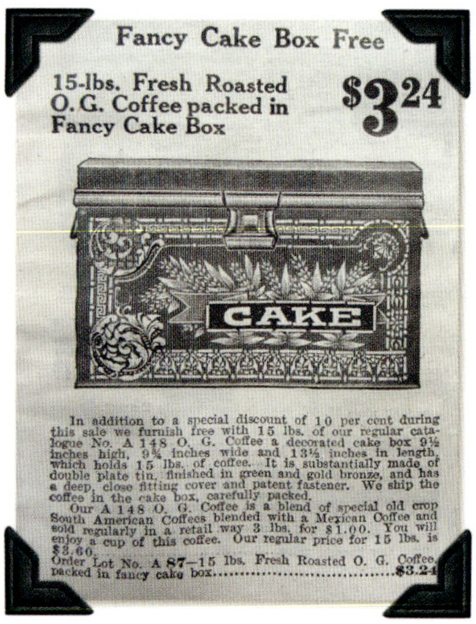

Montgomery Ward offered this elaborate tin cake box as a premium for buying coffee in February 1909. This was the type of receptacle used to keep cake fresh.

Originally called salvers, they were commonly offered in sizes ranging from approximately 6" to 10" and more, sometimes made in one-inch increments. The word salver is from the French *salve*, meaning "tray for presenting food to the king" and was first used in the mid-seventeenth century. Salvers made by Bryce, Higbee have upturned edges or gallery rims. Most were likely used for cakes and desserts, but the smaller ones would have been just as useful as calling card receptacles. It was a custom at the time to leave one's card when paying a visit. There was a whole ritual built around leaving cards, with strict rules that were carefully observed. A form similar to the salver, but with a flat rim, is found in nearly all (if not all) of Bryce Higbee's full lines beginning in 1900 and was most likely termed a wafer stand by the company as it was by J. B. Higbee. They are not always completely flat. Some have slightly sloped sides, but they do not have upturned rims like the salvers.

The very design of the salver, a plate elevated on a tall pedestal, indicates the contents served upon it were something special. Baking was quite difficult and time-consuming before the advent of gas and electric ranges with built in thermostats. Wood burning stoves were quite temperamental and required diligent attention to maintain an even temperature, essential for successful baking. Pure, fresh ingredients were a must and not always obtainable. A cookbook from 1871 instructs the baker:

> Use none but the best materials for making cake. If you cannot afford to get good flour, dry white sugar, and the best family butter, make up your mind to go without your cake, and eat plain bread with a clear conscience.

After many more paragraphs of firm instruction and terse, almost scolding commands, the author continues:

> If the cake be uneatable, throw it away upon the first beggar-boy who comes for broken meat, and say nothing about it. If streaky or burned, cut out the best parts… Then keep up a brave heart and try again. You *may* not satisfy yourself in a dozen trials. You certainly *will* not, if you never make another attempt.

These entries give an idea of what a daunting task baking was, as well as the importance of success in the kitchen. Good cakes and pastries were a mark of achievement for the home baker. Of course, these treats were obtainable in the larger cities from bakeries, but the prudent homemaker would have made them herself whenever possible, especially if she wanted to display her domestic skills to family and guests. Those in rural areas often had no other choice.

The so-called rum well or brandy well are recently concocted collector's terms to denote a concave area of varying diameter and depth found in the center of some salvers. The rather romantic theory is that some sort of spirit was added to this depression to keep a whole cake moist. This hardly seems plausible, as a cake would absorb any liquid immediately; besides, the moistened area would be confined to a small area on the bottom of the cake, resulting in a sticky mess. If the rum well was so intended, it seems that all salvers would have this feature, for why would anyone want to purchase a well-less salver which would not allow their cakes to remain moist? No mention of any such thing is found in period cookbooks, housekeeping guides, or advertisements from the glass companies; however, there are instructions given in Victorian era cookbooks to keep cakes moist by wrapping them in thick cloth before placing in tins with tightly fitting lids. To avoid dry cake the housekeeper was also instructed to cut no more than needed. The well found on some salvers is a result of the way the item was formed in the mould.

Comparison of celery vase, spooner, and flower vase. Patterns (l. to r.) are Anona, Admiral, and Paris 1900. Celery vase, \$30–\$35; spooner, \$35–\$40; vase, \$15–\$20.

Celery Vases and Celery Trays

Often confused for spoon holders, celery vases are also cylindrical, but generally measure no less than 6" tall and are usually about 4" wide at the top. A useful tip to remember when out shopping without a measuring tape or ruler is that a dollar bill (something most people have on them) is approximately 6" long. If a teaspoon completely fits inside the vessel, handle and all, it is a celery vase rather than a spooner. It is true that celery vases were very occasionally marketed as large spoon holders by some companies, but this was generally for soda fountain use and was not the norm. Unless one finds catalog evidence of a specific pattern offered this way, one cannot rightfully call their celery vase a spoon holder. Flower vases are sometimes confused for celery vases, too. If the vase is footed and tapers to nearly a point toward the base, it is for flowers. Remember, celery vases were designed to hold a bunch of celery and are large enough to comfortably hold more than just a few stalks.

Contrary to popular belief, celery was not a food exclusive to the wealthy during most of the period in which EAPG was produced. Beginning in the early 1870s, when the soda-lime glass formula was commonly used in America, glassware became cheaper to manufacture and was being made in larger sets and in larger quantities. The celery vase was included with nearly all, if not all, full lines of glassware from that point forward. If celery was only for the rich, why then would the celery vase be so commonplace and prolifically produced in such inexpensive pressed glass marketed to the middle class? The 1907 book *Celery Culture,* by W. R. Beattie, informs the reader that celery growing on a commercial basis practically began in 1884 with the introduction of self-blanching varieties that caused the industry to grow by "leaps and bounds" by the early 1900s. Beattie also clarifies an important misconception held to this day:

> Many persons have the impression that celery growing is an intricate process requiring special conditions, skill and equipment, but such is not the case. Celery is not more difficult to grow than the majority of garden crops, but it has a few peculiarities the understanding of which only adds interest to the work.

Nineteenth-century cookbooks also give some insight. *Common Sense in the Household* by Marion Harland (the pen name of Mary Virginia Hawes Terhune) includes instructions on how to prepare raw celery. It is apparent that the author wrote this book for the everyday housewife, and not with the rich or particularly affluent in mind. Her tone is very plain and unpretentious throughout; the recipes, advice, and remedies are very homey and basic. Her dedication, "To my fellow-housekeepers, north, east, south, and west" does not suggest the book was written with wealthy people in mind. Terhune's book went through many editions and millions of copies were sold—hardly the target audience of the rich. Fannie Merritt Farmer devotes space to celery as well in *The Boston Cooking-School Cook Book* (1896). She informs the reader that "Celery may be obtained from last of July until April. It is best and cheapest in December. Celery stalks are green while growing; but the white celery seen in market has been bleached." This does not imply an exclusive commodity, especially considering it was available eight full months of the year. Celery was highly decorative and enhanced the table setting, a very desirable quality to the Victorians. Incidentally, period cookbooks mention keeping the celery in cold water *until* ready to send to table. They do not instruct to put water in the celery vase as many today think it was served.

Celery trays are flat, oblong or oval dishes measuring approximately 10" to 12" long. Another misconception is that the celery tray completely replaced the celery vase when celery lost its distinction. Celery trays became prevalent during the 1890s and coexisted with the celery vase for decades to come. The glass companies continued to offer both forms in their full lines well into the teens and some even later. The celery tray may have been another way to display and serve plain, raw celery, but it is also likely that the celery tray was used to serve different dishes made from celery. It should come as no surprise that the popularity of the celery tray coincides with the inclusion of other, varied recipes for celery in cookbooks of the time.

Compotes (or Comports)

The word compote is from old French *composte* meaning "mixture." It was first used in the late seventeenth century and referred to stewed fruit in syrup. By association, the dish used to serve the dessert became known as a compote. Compotes were made open and covered, ranging from approximately 4" to about 10" in diameter, usually in one-inch increments. The largest covered compotes found made by Bryce, Higbee measure 9" wide. Original nineteenth-century terminology for an open compote was simply "bowl" or, if covered, "covered bowl." Bryce, Higbee tended to favor high-domed lids, which gave a solid, massive presence. It was also a practical design, for the lid could remain in place when greater amounts of fruit or other foods were piled in the vessel. One description of a large covered compote in an 1889 Butler Brothers catalog read, "The cover on this elegant bowl is so high and of such clear glass that fruit in the bowl may be 'heaped up' so as to present a wonderfully beautiful and tempting effect." Sometimes the height of a compote was indicated by adding "high foot" or "low foot" to the description since measurements were only given for the diameter of the bowl.

The smallest low-foot open compotes are generally called sauce dishes by collectors, but Bryce, Higbee seems to have called this form a footed fruit dessert. According to period sources, the larger open compotes were used for fruit bowls and for serving sauces, candy, crackers, etc. Covered compotes were likely used for just about anything that would keep fresh longer if stored in a covered vessel. Remember, this was decades before specific kitchenware was marketed, and obviously long before the advent of plastic wrap and disposable containers. Covered serving items were common in the south, but were just as welcome in other areas, especially during the summer months. Open, high-foot compotes measuring approximately 5" in diameter were called footed jellies, and those made by Bryce, Higbee are found with various edge treatments, usually round and square. The term comport was originally used for what we would simply consider a bowl with a slight foot or a low-foot compote these days. It is an alteration of the French *compotier*, which refers to a pedestaled serving dish. Collectors use the terms compote and comport interchangeably.

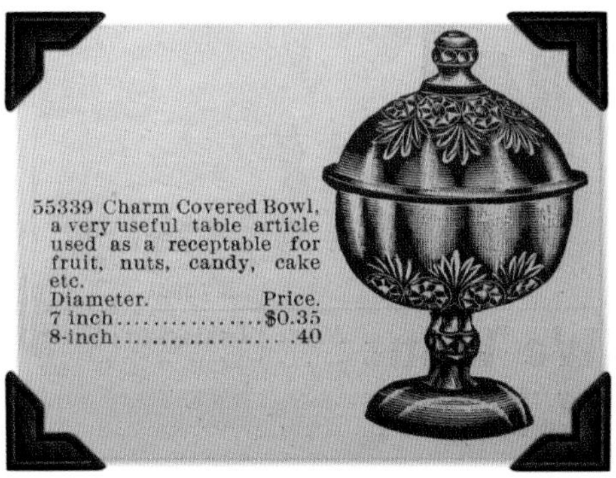

ABOVE | Early offering of Charm covered compotes by Montgomery Ward in their spring and summer 1895 catalog. Note the massive appearance due to the high-domed lid and the notation that it was a useful receptacle "for fruit, nuts, candy, cake etc."

Feathered Medallion 5.75" w. flared jelly with unusual plain edge, apparently tooled from a goblet. This form is usually found with small scallops on the edge. Value undetermined.

Cruets and Cruet Trays

Bryce, Higbee stopper #1.

Cruets were originally referred to as vinegar or oil bottles. It appears that the first cruet Bryce, Higbee made was in the Banquet pattern introduced in 1897. The author questions whether the cruet collected with the Ethol pattern (introduced 1890) was actually made by Bryce, Higbee. See discussion on page 161. There are four different stoppers that were used for a variety of cruets made by Bryce, Higbee & Company:

Stopper #1, designed for the Banquet cruet, is somewhat ovoid and is composed of nine sharply pointed diamonds arranged within four larger diamonds. This motif is in the Banquet pattern where the rings overlap in the design. This stopper is found with the Fleur-de-lis (introduced 1898) cruet, and is also shown in period catalogs with the Admiral (introduced 1899) cruet. Pitkin & Brooks, Montgomery Ward, and Butler Brothers all illustrate the large Paris 1900 (introduced 1900) cruet with a very similar stopper but it is more ball-shaped, much wider, and has sixteen pointed diamonds within each large diamond. Though catalogs of three different merchants show it the same way, an actual stopper matching the illustrations has not been observed.

Fleur-de-lis cruet with stopper #1, $45–$50.

Admiral cruets were sold with Bryce, Higbee's stopper #1. Note that the Paris 1900 cruet is illustrated with a similar but larger stopper. *Images from Pitkin & Brooks catalogs, courtesy of the Rakow Research Library, Corning Museum of Glass.*

Bryce, Higbee stopper #2.

Stopper #2 contains elements found in the Paris 1900 design and matches the butter and sugar lid finials of that pattern. It is shown in period catalogs with the small size Paris 1900 cruet as well as *Fine Cut and Fan* (introduced c. 1901). Not every stopper #2 will fit the latter cruet, so there was likely more than one size made.

Stopper #3 was made to match Bonair (introduced c. 1903) and is composed of three of the same vertical diamond and zipper panels found in the pattern (Bonair is the OMN for the pattern collectors have called *Palm Leaf Fan*). This stopper was used with cruets sold from 1903 onward including Bonair, *Beautiful Lady*, Anona, *Feathered Medallion*, *Ten-Pointed Star*, and Madora patterns. Butler Brothers illustrates the stopper in the *Fine Cut and Fan* cruet beginning in spring 1904. Stopper #3 has three vertical panels of diamonds.

Stopper #4 contains the same pattern as the previous stopper, but it is larger and has four vertical panels of the diamond and zipper pattern. This stopper has only been found in the large Paris 1900 cruet. Butler Brothers clearly illustrates the stopper beginning in spring 1904. Oddly, the stopper designed to match the Paris 1900 pattern has not been seen in the larger size, nor has a Bonair cruet been found that will fit this large

Bryce, Higbee stopper #3.

Bonair cruet with stopper #3. This stopper was designed for the pattern. $35–$40.

Bryce, Higbee stopper #4.

The large size Paris 1900 cruet was sold with stopper #4. $40–$45.

Bonair-patterned stopper. George Duncan's Sons' No. 42 AKA *Mardi Gras* (introduced 1899 and continued by Duncan and Miller) employs a stopper that is extremely similar to Bryce, Higbee's Stopper #4. There are several differences, but the most notable is that there is only one row of zipper design separating each panel of vertical diamonds. Bryce, Higbee's stopper has two rows of zipper between each panel of diamonds.

The combinations of cruets and stoppers noted are those the author has observed from period catalog illustrations. It is possible that other combinations were originally offered, such as a Fleur-de-lis cruet with Stopper #4, or Bonair cruet with Stopper #2. It was obviously more cost effective to use the same stopper for different cruets.

Bryce, Higbee stopper #4 (left) is very similar to the stopper used for George Duncan's Sons & Company's No. 42 AKA *Mardi Gras* cruet (right).

J. B. Higbee also had a "universal" stopper. It appears to have originated with Alpha and was sold in cruets of many different patterns as well. Madora cruets are often found with the J. B. Higbee stopper, but they were also sold with the Bonair stopper (Stopper #3). Madora cruets are illustrated with Stopper #3 in the circa 1910 J. B. Higbee Madora catalog as well as Butler Brothers catalogs until the "Crown Jewel" assortment was eliminated in the first part of 1911. Alpha cruets have been seen with Stopper #3, but it is quite impossible to know if they were originally sold this way because the base diameter is very close to the J. B. Higbee stopper and is a proper fit. An Anona cruet has been seen with the typical J. B. Higbee stopper. Though it adequately fits the cruet and contains a very similar star found within the Anona design, this does not confirm its authenticity. It looks quite disproportionate by comparison to the other combinations noted.

Stoppers often appear chipped at the base and many are found with an extra nib of glass at the end. This is due to the manufacturing process. To save time and resources, multiple stoppers were molded to a ring or plank of glass and broken off at the base. The stoppers were not ground by the factory, so the point at which they were broken off is clearly visible. This should not be considered damage.

Cruet trays have been found only in the Anona pattern, and it was also used with *Feathered Medallion* and *Ten-Pointed Star* cruet sets. It is uncertain whether a cruet tray was made with the *Ten-Pointed Star* motif.

This J. B. Higbee stopper was sold with several different cruets beginning in 1908.

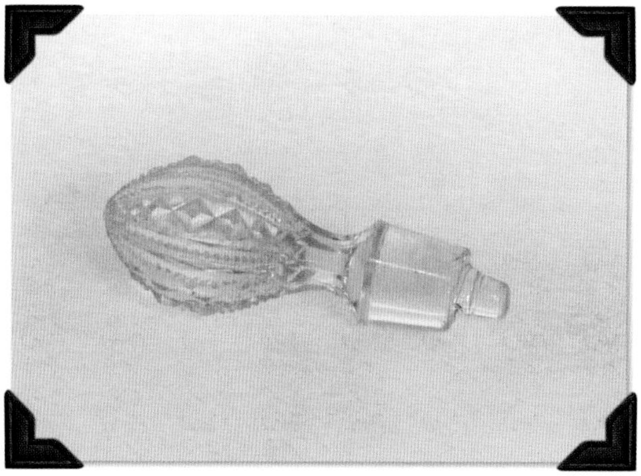

Many cruet stoppers made by Bryce, Higbee have rough bases or extra nibs of glass, like this #4 stopper. This should not be considered damage.

Mugs, Cups, and Stemware

Mugs were a popular form in china, earthenware, and glass during the nineteenth century. Bryce, Higbee made them in many patterns and sizes. At least one pattern, Acme, offered mugs in three different sizes. Some companies made mugs specifically as toys. This may also be the case with some of Bryce, Higbee's, notably the small Acme and Drum mugs, but no catalog proof exists.

Cups were used for custard, sherbet, cold desserts, and other refreshments rather than for hot beverages. The 1896 edition of *The Boston Cooking-School Cook Book,* by Fannie Merritt Farmer, includes over 100 recipes for cold desserts, including ices and ice creams, many with instruction to serve on a glass dish. No doubt many of these desserts were consumed from glass cups. Some collectors call them punch cups, but most companies referred to them as custard cups even if the line included a matching punch bowl. While other glass companies were producing punch sets in the

Teardrop Row custard cup (left), $18–$20; Bonair mug (center), $25–$30; Banquet mug (right), $20–$25.

1890s and early 1900s (some quite massive, in fact), Bryce, Higbee seems to have ignored this form completely, for no punch bowls are known in any of their patterns

Goblets of approximately eight-ounce capacity were intended for water. Wine glasses hold about two ounces, much smaller than those made now. Cordials, used for after dinner drinks and aperitifs, hold about one ounce. Claret and champagne glasses are less common and fall between goblets and wine glasses in size and capacity. Claret is a type of wine with a low alcohol content, which was deemed suitable for women to take. It was often recommended with game. Period cookbooks instruct to serve claret cool and champagne "very cold by allowing it to remain in salt and ice at least one-half hour before dinner time." Modern tastes prefer to use the water goblets for wine.

Visual comparison of (l. to r.) goblet, wine, and cordial. Patterns (l. to r.) are Melrose, Charm, and 5th Avenue. Goblet and wine, \$15–\$25 each; cordial, \$10–\$12.

Pickle Dishes and Pickle Jars

Pickling was widely done in the Victorian era, not just to make a tasty condiment, but also as a means to preserve food. When we think of pickles today, we envision a small cucumber, but in the nineteenth and early twentieth century many other things were pickled that seem unlikely to modern minds. Period cookbooks and housekeeping guides contain dozens of recipes ranging from green tomato and cantaloupe pickles to watermelon rind and walnut pickles. Chow-chow was a very popular type of pickle made from vegetables and spices that is less common today. With all of these options, it is no wonder so many pickle jars and trays were made. Many collectors call them relish dishes, but this does not seem to be a term that was widely used during the EAPG era. In a circa 1917 catalog, J. B. Higbee offered what they termed a "twin relish" in their Gala pattern (introduced in 1913). This is one of the few examples of the term the author has seen in period sources.

Capitola pickle jar in silver plated frame, $100–$125.

Pickle dishes are flat, oval bowls that are sometimes handled and measure approximately 8" long. These dishes were very popular and included in full lines of glassware. They were also made as novelties with no matching pieces.

In July 1880, a reporter for *Crockery and Glass Journal* relates, "They [Bryce, Higbee & Co.] have an assorted lot of pickle-dishes, some of them of an especially handsome design and which take well with the trade." Bryce, Higbee later called a similar form an olive tray. Pickle jars made by Bryce, Higbee & Company have matching glass lids. Some may be found in silver-plated holders with tongs and silver-plated lids. Metal companies commonly bought lidless glass pickle jars from the glass companies. They fitted them with metal lids and frames and sold them as their own product. While it may be true that some metal companies did special order specific inserts, many lidless jars are found in company catalogs of the glasshouses. Also, the glass inserts shown in catalogs of the silver manufacturers and retail establishments are often older patterns, some a decade old or more, whereas the silver holders are of the latest styles. This certainly indicates the metal companies bought older stock from the glass companies.

The terms jam jar and marmalade are often used for pickle jars. The first two terms have never been spotted in period catalogs for this particular form in EAPG. A Central Glass Works catalog, dated circa 1922 by Heacock, shows a thin-blown, cylindrical covered jar with a plate etched band of thistles. It is labeled "8 oz. Marmalade Jar," but it has a notched lid and is outside the EAPG era. Early collectors applied the names jam jar and marmalade to the similar pickle jar commonly found in EAPG. Pioneer author Ruth Webb Lee used the terms as early as the 1930s.

Admiral olive tray from an 1899 Pitkin & Brooks catalog. *Courtesy of the Rakow Research Library, Corning Museum of Glass.*

Plates and Oval Platters

Bryce, Higbee produced square plates measuring approximately 7.25" in many patterns (see Favored Forms on page 73). Round plates were made in numerous sizes, ranging from about 5.5" (usually called a tray or "tray plate" by Butler Brothers) to 12". The smallest plates are found in some post–1900 patterns with one edge turned straight upward. The original company term seems to have been "almond tray." Many collectors refer to the round plates (especially those measuring 9" to 10") as dinner plates, but they were intended as bread or cake plates. Consuming hot foods from glassware was a concept unknown to the Victorians and did not come about until the 1920s when complete sets of matched dinnerware became the norm.

Prior to this people ate their meals off china, porcelain, or earthenware. Glassware was commonly used to accessorize these sets.

Various Bryce, Higbee patterns have oval or oblong bread plates, including Alaric, Ida, Earl, Persian, *Bowline*, and Surprise. The Alaric bread plate mould was used for the Grand Army of the Republic commemorative, and novelty bread plates were made with portraits of famous individuals. Interestingly, Bryce, Higbee seems to have ignored the ubiquitous bread plate with the very popular "Give Us This Day Our Daily Bread" motto that so many other manufacturers included in their lines of glassware.

Fleur-de-lis plates were offered in 10" and 12" sizes in a Bryce, Higbee advertisement that appeared in *China, Glass & Lamps* in early 1898.

Salt Dishes and Salt & Pepper Shakers

Salt dishes are found in many Bryce, Higbee patterns. In some cases, table salts (now referred to as master salts) and individual salts, as well as salt and pepper shakers, were offered in the same pattern. Though open salts and shaker salts coexisted, the concept of dispensing salt from a shaker was an innovation that came about much later than serving it from a salt cellar. The salt shaker has become so commonplace that we now associate open salt dishes with old-world elegance. Celery was ordinarily dipped into individual salts rather than sprinkled with salt from a shaker. Unlike today, salt clumped and caked easily, preventing it from pouring freely from the shaker. Early salt shakers are sometimes found with their original metal agitators, intended to break up the salt as it was shaken. Judging from the amount of old patents dealing with mechanisms and innovations to effectively dispense salt from shakers, the agitators no doubt worked better in theory than practice.

Pair of Fancheon salt and pepper shakers with metal agitator, $50–$55.

Selection of Admiral 10.75", 7", 9.5", and 10.25" trumpet vases, $20–$30 each; rose bowl, $40–$45.

Vases and Rose Bowls

Trumpet-shaped flower vases were made in different sizes and first appear during the 1890s, continuing to be made in patterns introduced in 1900 and after. When the vessels were removed from the mould many were flared and cupped by hand. Swung vases are also found in some Bryce, Higbee patterns and were made by literally swinging the vase in arcs while the glass was still malleable. This technique stretched the glass and caused the pattern to become distorted. Height varies, depending on how much the vase was swung. The very tall vases are often called funeral vases by collectors. Swung vases appear to be an innovation of the early 1900s and were a common fixture in photography studios, often set on a table with some flowers next to the subject.

Rose bowls are globe- or egg-shaped receptacles used as decorative parlor ornaments, but could also hold potpourri or flowers. They are found on collar bases and stems. Flat rose bowls may have been called lily bowls or nut bowls. Stemmed rose bowls are called lily vases in J. B. Higbee company catalogs, and Bryce, Higbee most likely used the same terminology for this form.

Novelties and Miscellaneous Items

Novelties refer to items that have no matching pieces. Many were perennial favorites for the glasshouses, while others were commemorative and shorter-lived. Novelties include, but are not limited to, ABC plates, toothpick and match holders, inkwells, soap dishes, bread plates, and covered dishes. Each known novelty made by Bryce, Higbee & Company is listed and discussed individually in chapter 9.

For the purpose of this book, miscellaneous items denote those which do not appear regularly in lines of glassware made by Bryce, Higbee & Company. These include:

Baskets

There is indication that Bryce, Higbee used the term basket to refer to a collar-base bowl with both sides brought upward, though to avoid confusion, the term nick nack tray is used in this book. For our purposes, baskets refer to bowls with arched, applied glass handles. It is certain baskets were produced by Bryce, Higbee because they appear in their patterns in jobber catalogs before the demise of the company. Ribbed handles were applied to bowls tooled into an oblong shape. Two of the company's late patterns have been found that include baskets, *Ten-Pointed Star* and Madora, though others could exist. Baskets must be examined carefully on both sides where the handle attaches to the bowl. This is a vulnerable area where damage is easily overlooked.

Covered Honey Dishes

Two patterns are documented that include a covered honey dish, Ethol and Rival. The Ethol honey dish is square and comfortably fits a honeycomb. The Rival honey dish is diamond-shaped and quite unusual in its configuration. A honey dish likely exists in the Royal pattern, but it has not been documented. The Era butter dish could be confused for a honey dish since it is square, but square shapes are a feature of that particular pattern.

Cracker Jars

Cracker jars resemble very large sugar bowls and are sometimes called biscuit jars. The *Teardrop Row* covered sugar is quite large and often mistaken for

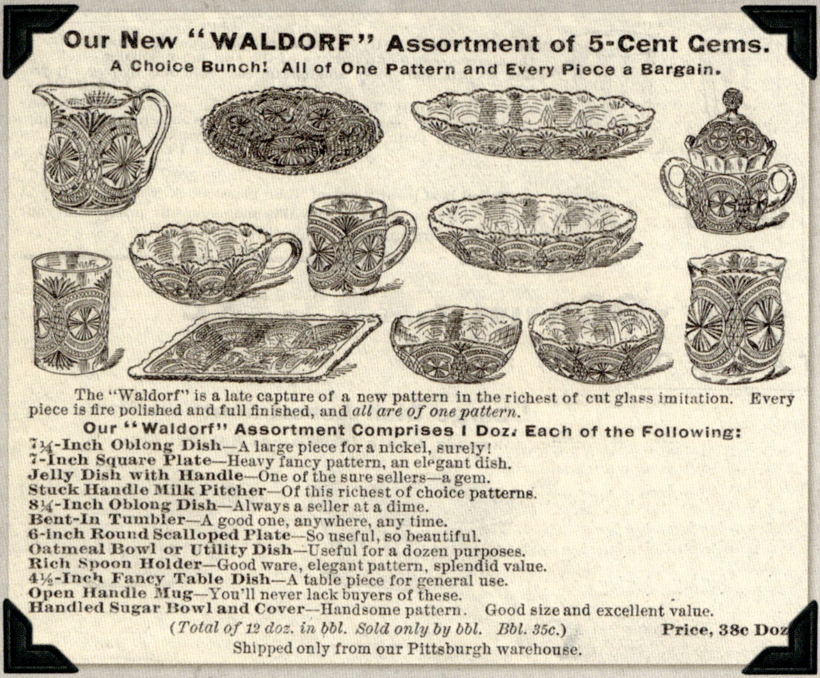

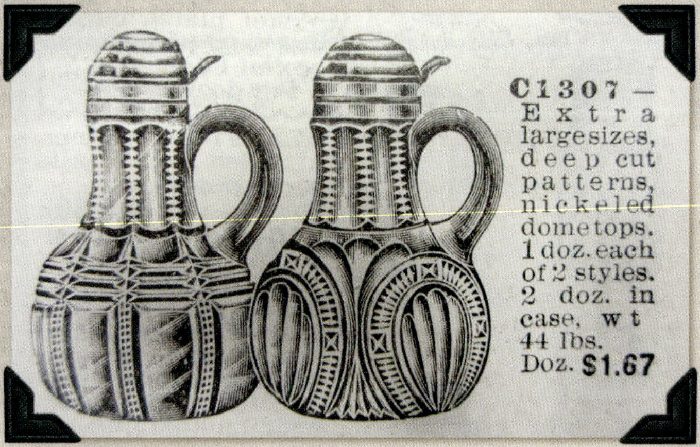

TOP | Assortment of Banquet. Butler Brothers, May 1898. Note the individual covered sugar bowl at far right.

CENTER LEFT TO RIGHT
Banquet mustard offered by Butler Brothers in fall 1902. The lid is quite difficult to find.

Bonair mustard or utility jar, Butler Brothers, 1904. Note wooden spoon inside jar.

BOTTOM LEFT TO RIGHT
Paris 1900 and Admiral syrups, Butler Brothers, spring 1907.

The Butler Brothers spring 1906 catalog offered an assortment of "so called" quart-size tankard jugs made by Bryce, Higbee & Company. They actually hold about twenty-four ounces. The patterns are (l. to r.) Anona, Bonair, and *Beautiful Lady*.

a covered cracker jar. The only reference to a cracker jar in any Bryce, Higbee pattern is found in a 1902 trade journal quote of the Monarch pattern. This is not a form typically associated with the company, and the identity of the pattern is still in question. Terminology in period sources is often different from what the modern mind is accustomed. It may be an incorrect assumption that the Monarch cracker jar is covered. The reporter very well may have been referring to a deep, open bowl; indeed, a dish of this description is designated in some J. B. Higbee catalogs as a cracker bowl. By definition, a jar is simply a wide-mouthed vessel.

Individual Creams and Covered Sugars

Though some collectors may think them toy glass for children, these diminutive sets were intended for individual use. Individual creams and sugars are found in two patterns, Ethol and Banquet. They were generally sold as sets; however, the individual cream pitchers were also offered alone for many years by Butler Brothers and other jobbers and are, consequently, much more commonly found than the sugars. Many collectors do not realize there is an individual covered sugar in the Banquet pattern.

Mustard or Horseradish Jars

With only one known exception, mustard or horseradish jars made by Bryce, Higbee have notched lids. In most patterns, the same item without a notch in the lid was sold as a different form. For example, the Bear and Drum sugars that were part of toy sets became "Mustards or Horse Radishes" with the addition of a notch in the lid to accommodate a mustard spoon. The Ethol individual sugar was offered the same way. Other mustards include Alaric, Banquet, and Butterfly. These mustards were offered with notched lids only, but the Banquet mustard without its lid was sold by Butler Brothers as a toothpick. The true Banquet toothpick has a scalloped edge. Many Alaric and Butterfly mustards missing their lids are encountered, which collectors and dealers dubiously call "master salts." A Bonair mustard or horseradish was offered by Butler Brothers as a "utility jar." The base is barrel-shaped and can be easily mistaken for a tumbler when the lid is missing. The high domed cover is not notched but its height allows a small spoon to comfortably sit inside the jar when the lid is in place. Butler Brothers included a small boxwood spoon with this and some of the other mustard jars they sold.

Quart Pitchers

Pitchers of quart capacity are often referred to as milk pitchers by collectors, but originally the term milk pitcher was used interchangeably with cream or cream pitcher in jobber and retail catalogs. Though called quart pitchers in original material, those made by Bryce, Higbee generally hold twenty-four ounces. The form is found in most of Bryce, Higbee's post–1900 patterns, but there are two styles of "quart" pitchers in the Ida pattern that hold twenty to twenty-two ounces.

Syrups

Also called molasses cans, this form is handled and has a metal cap with pouring lip. Syrups are only known in the Admiral and Paris 1900 patterns.

Toothpick Holders

Simply called a toothpick by the manufacturers, these small receptacles were also promoted and used as match holders. The toothpick holder was extremely popular and prolifically manufactured by most glass firms in the late nineteenth and early twentieth century. Small bottles of perfume were often sold inside a toothpick holder. When the contents were consumed the owner had a usable item for the table or mantel. These were very popular goods found at fairs and bazaars. It is a bit unusual that Bryce, Higbee & Company produced so few toothpick holders to match their lines of glassware, unlike the vast majority of their competitors. Bryce, Higbee's first full line including a toothpick is Banquet (1897), followed by Fleur-de-lis (1898) and Anona (c. 1904). There is a Madora toothpick, but it is not certain if it was originally included in the line by Bryce, Higbee or added later by J. B. Higbee when they produced the pattern. Another toothpick holder made by

Fleur-de-lis toothpick holder illustrated in *China, Glass & Lamps*, 1898.

Bryce, Higbee is known as *Swirl and Panel* (c. 1905). It was sold individually as well as a part of *Feathered Medallion* and *Ten-Pointed Star* condiment sets, and it quite likely was intended to be part of the *Feathered Medallion* line.

The remaining toothpick holders known to have been made by Bryce, Higbee were produced as novelties: Our Toothpick, Gatling Gun, and Utility Boot. The Fish spoon holder, part of the Menagerie Toy Set, was offered by Butler Brothers as a toothpick in 1886. Since this was the year the novelty was introduced, it obviously was not old stock being purged. It is not known whether Bryce, Higbee actually marketed this item as a toothpick holder, however.

Toys

Only three toy table sets are known to have been made by Bryce, Higbee & Company: Drum, Menagerie, and *Ten-Pointed Star Variant*. Three ABC plates are also documented. It appears that the company made more toy glassware, however, as evidenced by this report from the October 4, 1883, issue of *Crockery and Glass Journal*:

> Bryce, Higbee & Co. have a good demand for their tableware and toy goods, of which latter they make quite an assortment. They confine themselves to these two alone, and have had a very prosperous year.

To which toy goods this entry specifically refers is unknown, but keep in mind this was before the introduction of the Menagerie and *Ten-Pointed Star Variant* sets. The Emma and Rovers ABC plates are presumed to postdate this report as well. Drum toy sets were mentioned by name in another trade journal about two months prior to this account. Though not referred to as toys on a Bryce, Higbee catalog page, the Acme mugs may have been considered toy glassware by this reporter. The pattern was in production when this account was penned.

Water Bottles

Water bottles were sometimes used instead of half-gallon pitchers and were often sold with tumblers. They resemble decanters, but are larger with wider necks and were not made with stoppers. Water bottles are known in the Oregon and Bonair patterns, but others could certainly exist.

Oregon water bottle. This is one of only two Bryce, Higbee patterns known in this form. $75–$100.

FAVORED FORMS

When one studies the products of the glass companies, it becomes apparent that each company focused on and favored certain things. This may have been to stand out from the others and gain a certain niche of the market. It also could have been governed by the personal preferences and tastes of the designers and management.

A form Bryce, Higbee favored is the cake basket. This term may confuse the modern collector, who tends to call it a banana bowl or banana stand, but original material indicates cake basket was the appellation used by Bryce, Higbee & Company. Just about every pattern produced by them from the mid–1890s to their closing can be found in this form, and most are quite abundant. They generally measure 9" to 10" long, but there are ones a few inches smaller and larger in some patterns. A June 1906 Baltimore Bargain House catalog includes an assortment of Bonair. One item is referred to as a banana stand, but this is the jobber's terminology rather than Bryce, Higbee's. Certainly, it could be used to hold bananas, but the earliest sighting from any glass manufacturer to this form with a specific reference to bananas is Westmoreland Specialty Company's 1905 catalog. One lone example in their No. 180 AKA *Big Wheel(s)* pattern is called a banana stand in this catalog while the same form in the other patterns is called a "fruit stand" or "fruit basket." Most manufacturers called them fruit baskets. Despite what some may think, bananas were not a rare commodity in late nineteenth and early twentieth century America. An article titled "A Bunch of Bananas, and Fifteen Ways of Serving Them," published in the September 1892 issue of *Good Housekeeping,* relates that bananas were inexpensive and so readily available they were becoming a bit cloying:

> It is astonishing that a fruit so delicious, so cheap, and so procurable at all seasons as are bananas, should be seldom served in novel desserts. Bananas *au naturel* are desirable, but like many other good things they grow monotonous by repetition. If "toujours perdrix" pall upon the palate, may not bananas served only in their jackets create satiety, and eventually dislike, in those to whom they are too frequently presented?

Twenty-first century minds seem to have difficulty envisioning how cake was served from this item, but the answer is rather simple. The term cake once referred to any small pastry, some we would now call cookies. There were also larger cakes as we know them today, but some were served differently. A late nineteenth century recipe for "Rose or Clouded Cake" employs cochineal to impart a red color to some of the batter. The baker is instructed to put the batter into a cake mold in alternating layers of red and white and is informed that "this is an ornamental cake to cut for baskets."

The same form is also found on a collar base in sizes ranging from approximately 6" to 12" long. This

Paris 1900 cake basket from a circa 1900 Pitkin & Brooks catalog. *Courtesy of the Rakow Research Library, Corning Museum of Glass.*

version appears to have been called a basket by the company, though there is no handle. To avoid confusion, this form is called a nick nack tray by the author. There are also smaller versions of the high-footed cake basket that measure about 6" to 7" long. Both of these diminutive forms have only been found in patterns introduced 1900 and after. Whether collar-based or stemmed, they are called "child's banana bowls" by collectors and declared to be miniatures, but these are modern designations. One cannot help to think that some people, especially sellers, feel there is an added value by merely calling them such. This small version of the cake basket appears to have been originally called a nick nack. None of these forms were intended or sold as toy dishes for children and were most likely used by housewives for various purposes, even as parlor ornaments. They appear quite liberally and were sometimes designated as bonbon or card dishes in jobber catalogs. The so-called "child's cake stands" are also found in Bryce, Higbee's full lines introduced 1900 and after. They were originally called salvers, and the historian notes that nowhere in their description was there ever any reference to a child. There is a form similar to the small salver that was originally called a wafer stand. The difference is that the rim is upturned on the salver but is flat on the wafer stand.

Another form Bryce, Higbee & Company favored is the square plate. Like cake baskets, these seem to be available in most of their full lines introduced from approximately the mid–1890s until their closing. Though period catalogs usually list them as 7", they actually measure closer to 7.5". Measuring 9.25", the Admiral square plate is much larger than the others. They were designated simply as "square plate" by the company, but some jobber catalogs mention using them for cake or bread. An appealing form to collect, they are quite interesting because the layout of the motifs are slightly altered to accommodate the shape.

The terms found in catalogs issued by J. B. Higbee directly coincide with the same forms for Bryce, Higbee items mentioned in trade journals and shown in Bryce, Higbee catalogs as well as catalogs of Pitkin and Brooks, Wallace & McAfee, and other jobbers issued before Bryce, Higbee closed. Terms such as berry dessert, casserole, nick nack, and comportier are quite unusual and would be much too coincidental to be random, arbitrary uses for these specific forms. In fact, the word comportier is either a misspelling or a corruption of the French *compotier* and regularly appears in reference to the products of Bryce, Higbee and J. B. Higbee. J. B. Higbee Glass Company clearly followed in the footsteps of Bryce, Higbee & Company regarding the forms they favored, as well as those they did not.

Comparison of small salver (left) and wafer stand (right). Note the upturned rim on the salver. The patterns are Anona and Paris 1900. $35–$40 each.

Comparison of *Fine Cut and Fan* nick nack (left) and basket or nick nack tray (right). $30–$35; $15–$20.

6 Colors and Decorations

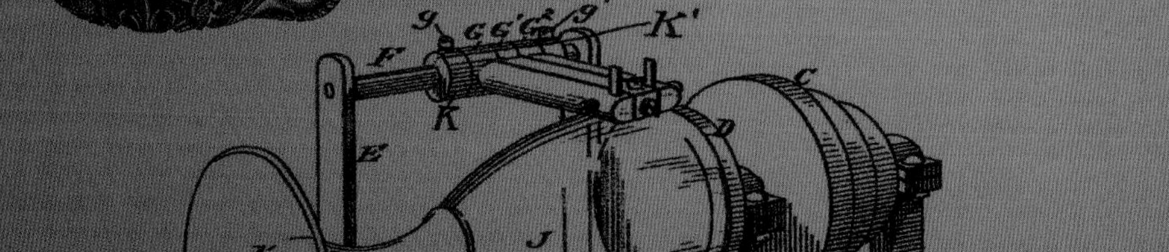

COLORS

During the mid–1880s a burst of color suddenly appeared on the glass market. Prior to this, the majority of tableware was made primarily in clear glass. Shades of amber, sapphire blue, canary, and apple green caught the attention of the public and remained popular for a few years. Bryce, Higbee & Company began making colored glass in 1885, as this quote from the July, 3, 1885, issue of *American Glassworker* indicates:

> BRYCE, HIGBEE & Co., of Homestead, have engaged in the manufacture of colored glassware, and are finding that their patterns, heretofore so much sought and imitated, are meeting with quite a large sale in the new line. We find that chequered, diamond and hob-nail star patterns show to splendid advantage in colors, and that heavy flowered and pillared ware, rather than those patterns of more delicate and finer lines, are best adopted to colored ware.

Jewel-toned colored glassware was very popular in the mid–1880s. This selection of Bryce, Higbee items shows that shades of the same color varied quite a bit. Whether they were intended to be separate colors is not known.

Bryce, Higbee's color production focused primarily on amber and blue. Amber was referred to as "old gold" by the company, a rather common appellation at the time. Some canary was also made, as well as apple green to a much lesser extent. Canary is the original name for the color collectors call vaseline, and apple green is the collector's name for a very pale shade of green. The tableware lines most often found in color are Earl and Ida. The only known apple green items are found in the Earl pattern. Earl (1885), Ida (1885), Fancheon (1885), and Alameda (1886) are found in canary. Note these patterns were introduced in 1885 and 1886 and that no other Bryce, Higbee patterns are known in canary. This indicates a very short time frame for the color, and the scarcity of items certainly supports this limited span of production. Individual items from some of the earlier tableware lines, such as Acme (c. 1882) and Rival (1883), are found in amber and blue, but were made no earlier than 1885. Beginning with the tableware lines introduced in 1887, only individual items were made in amber and blue, such as Persian and Yale. Most of Bryce, Higbee's novelties were made in amber and blue as well. None have been seen in canary or apple green. It is not certain how long the company continued to produce colored wares, but it appears that they were being phased out around 1888.

Clarification must be made concerning the term "tinted amethyst" that the Higbys use throughout their book, *Bryce, Higbee and J. B. Higbee Glass.* They confusingly note it as a separate color in some of the pattern listings and, in at least one case, they state an item found in this hue indicates a "probable reproduction." In the first place, it is possible for any colorless soda-lime glass made approximately prior to World War I to turn amethyst from prolonged exposure to the sun, so any item of Bryce, Higbee glass could potentially be found in a "tinted amethyst" color. Secondly, a sun-colored piece of glass is by no means an indication of a reproduction. The color transformation is due to the presence of manganese dioxide in the glass formula, put there to overcome a greenish tint inherent in the batch for clear glass. Too much of the compound can also cause the glass to be a light amethyst without prolonged exposure to the sun. Some people deliberately expose EAPG to the sun or use UV rays to make it turn amethyst or purple. See chapter 10, Collecting Tips, for more information about sun-colored glass.

Bryce, Higbee is not known to have made any true amethyst glass, despite claims that the Earl pattern is found in this color. The Higbys include *Old Oaken Bucket* (OMN: Bucket) as a Bryce, Higbee pattern, correctly noting the pattern is found in amethyst, but incorrectly stating that John Bryce brought the moulds with him to Bryce, Higbee in 1879. Bryce, Higbee did not make the Bucket set. Trade journal reports written when the company was starting up mention that their patterns were all new, and there is absolutely no mention of *Old Oaken Bucket.* It is a product of Bryce Brothers from the mid–1880s, as mentioned in trade journals from that time.

During the late 1890s when the rich colors of deep blue, emerald green (both often enhanced with lavish gilding), and opalescent colors were being produced by other glasshouses, Bryce, Higbee continued to focus on clear glass. *China, Glass & Lamps* ran an ad for many years declaring the company "manufacturers of crystal glass tableware" and this certainly is what they are best known for.

DECORATIONS

Color staining

Bryce, Higbee's production years directly coincide with the immense popularity of ruby-stained glassware, yet few of their patterns are found with this treatment. Decorating companies such as Mueller Glass Staining Company, Oriental Glass Company, and Pioneer Glass Company bought blanks from the glass companies, decorated them, and sold them as their own product. These decorators were located in Pittsburgh, not far from the Bryce, Higbee factory, but for some reason did not seem to buy much, if any, of their glassware.

The pattern most often found stained ruby (also with the addition of lush gold) is Fleur-de-lis, but it is not known when this was done. It may have been done in the latter part of the company's existence, when wares with heavily applied ruby and gilt were popular. This elaborate treatment is found on many patterns made by Tarentum Glass Company, New Martinsville, and others. It is also possible that old stock of Fleur-de-lis was sold to a decorator when the factory was liquidated in 1908. Because so little Bryce, Higbee glass is found with ruby stain, items were most likely not decorated at the factory. See pattern listings in chapter 9 for individual items known in ruby stain.

Amber-stained glass was also popular in the 1890s (though not as popular as ruby), and some glass factories and decorating companies also employed the use of different colored stains such as green, yellow, blue, and pink in the early 1900s. No examples of Bryce, Higbee glass are known with these decorative colorings. Most companies liberally used gilt to enhance their product, which added considerably to the cost. Comparing prices in catalogs of gold decorated versus plain ware in the same patterns shows that the use of gold nearly doubled the cost. The earliest Bryce, Higbee pattern seen with gold decoration is Banquet (introduced in 1897). Compared to the products of other companies, not much of their glass is found with gilt trim.

Iridescent finish

The Fenton Art Glass Company is credited with being the first company

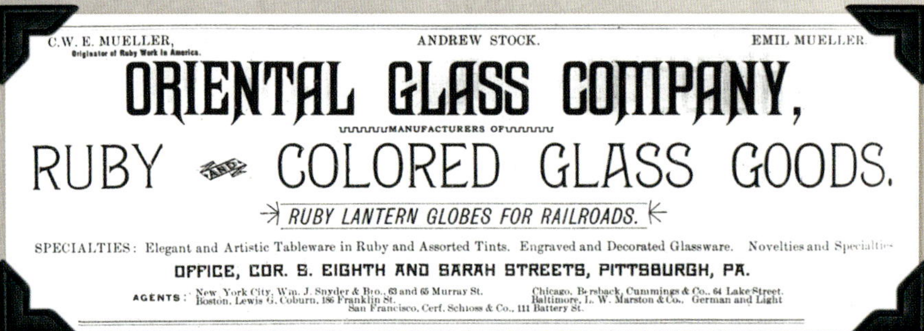

C.W. E. MUELLER,
Originator of Ruby Work in America.

ANDREW STOCK.

EMIL MUELLER.

ORIENTAL GLASS COMPANY,

MANUFACTURERS OF

RUBY AND COLORED GLASS GOODS.

RUBY LANTERN GLOBES FOR RAILROADS.

SPECIALTIES: Elegant and Artistic Tableware in Ruby and Assorted Tints. Engraved and Decorated Glassware. Novelties and Specialties

OFFICE, COR. S. EIGHTH AND SARAH STREETS, PITTSBURGH, PA.

AGENTS: New York City, Wm. J. Snyder & Bro., 63 and 65 Murray St. Boston, Lewis G. Coburn, 186 Franklin St. Chicago, Bersback, Cummings & Co., 64 Lake Street. Baltimore, L. W. Marston & Co., German and Light. San Francisco, Cerf, Schloss & Co., 111 Battery St.

TOP | Ruby-stained New Crescent tumbler engraved "Mother 1900." Value undetermined.

CENTER | Oriental Glass Company ad that ran in *China, Glass & Lamps* in early 1892. One of the firm's partners, C. W. E. Mueller, is noted here as the "Originator of Ruby Work in America."

BOTTOM LEFT | Fleur-de-lis half-gallon pitcher with gold decoration. When made, the use of gilt on pressed glass added greatly to the retail cost. $55–$60.

BOTTOM RIGHT | Admiral 9.75" vase with a poor, uneven amber iridescent finish, which was most likely "water ambered" within the last fifty years. *Photo courtesy of Terry Jondahl.*

to develop and market iridescent pressed glass in late 1907; however, there were some earlier offerings of a light orange or amber iridescent finish done by decorating companies. Examples include items in George Duncan's Sons & Co.'s No. 27 AKA *Block Band* and Riverside's X-Ray (patterns introduced in 1896 and 1897 respectively). As early as the mid–1880s, O'Hara offered their new Bartholdi line in "Rainbow," which was a stain with a very slight, subtle iridescence. A difference in these earlier wares is that the iridescent finish was applied to already-made glass rather than spraying hot glass with metallic salts shortly after it was pressed. A few Bryce, Higbee patterns are known with a golden amber iridescent finish generally called marigold by Carnival glass collectors. There is little doubt it was not done by Bryce, Higbee. Items known to the author are an Admiral mug, tumbler, and vase, Paris 1900 jelly compote, *Fine Cut and Fan* 5.5" nick nack tray, Bonair cruet and 5.5" almond tray, *Ten-Pointed Star* mug, and Anona 9" plate. The color on some of these items is uneven and/or very weak. Certainly other articles and patterns exist as well.

There are two possibile explanations for these pieces: either glassware was acquired and iridized by an outside decorating firm before or after Bryce, Higbee went out of business, or these items of old glassware were much more recently colored, a process which is entirely possible and known to have occurred. In 1967, Clarence Stephens, his wife Janet, and their five children began a business making and selling what they called "water ambered glass." An amber/marigold iridescent finish was obtained by exposing clear glass items to the flowing spring waters on their property in the village of Slaterville Springs, New York. They did not discover this process, however, and Mr. Stephens mentions in a pamphlet published in the early 1970s that the first "water ambered" glass sold commercially was done by a Mrs. Middaugh on her farm in the same village. He does not state when this was done, but does relate it was a profitable and enjoyable undertaking for the elderly Middaugh due to the clientele of the health spas in the area. Since the nineteenth century the waters there were renowned for their beneficial, restorative qualities and attracted many visitors. By the 1920s, the spas seemed to have disappeared, so it appears that Middaugh was "water ambering" glass quite early. An online source states that she was doing this as early as 1871 and that her glass was sold by Rothschild's and Macy's department stores, but no documentation of this has been found by the author.

Many people, including a geologist from Rochester, New York, doubted the waters could color glassware in such a manner. Some of the glass was taken to Rochester and tested by geologists and it was determined that a combination of the minerals in the water flowing over rock or stone caused the transformation. The process the Stephens family used to impart the iridescence was more labor intensive and took much longer than the method used by Middaugh. The Stephens left their clear glassware in the flowing spring water for no less than six weeks. The longer the glass was exposed to the water, the deeper the color would become. They periodically removed the glass to wash and polish it. This, they said, gave the glass its clarity and brought out the iridescence. The Stephens claimed their "water ambered" glass was superior to any Middaugh had made in the past. Clarence Stephens described his own glass as having a "beautiful deep amber color with lustrous iridescence." It was a deeper, richer color and, very importantly, the finish would not wash off. According to Mr. Stephens, Mrs. Middaugh colored her glassware in thirty-six to forty-eight hours, which imparted a lighter tint that was not completely permanent. Antique and new glass was colored by the Stephens operation; in fact, Clarence Stephens mentions becoming so interested in the old glass that he and his wife began coloring and collecting as many different patterns of EAPG as possible to display in their own museum.

As of 2012, Kim Case and her daughter Holly were still making "water ambered" glass in Slaterville Springs under the business Amber Creations. It is not known if new or old glass was used. The author tried to contact the Cases in spring 2015, but was not successful.

The author feels the items of Bryce, Higbee glassware with an amber/marigold iridescent finish were colored by the Stephens family, Mrs. Middaugh, and/or others, either commercially or non-commercially. The Middaugh and Stephens businesses were relatively small. They colored glassware for its novel appearance and chose a variety of EAPG without focusing on specific patterns or makers. These factors would explain why so few items in a random array of patterns are found in the treatment. Sample photos Mr. Stephens included in his pamphlet show thirty-six small items in assorted shapes and patterns, and one is a *Beautiful Lady* 6" nick nack tray. Note that the items of Bryce, Higbee glass found in amber/marigold iridescent are small, individual pieces. The largest example known is a 9.75" Admiral vase, but its size does not convince the author it was originally iridized. Middaugh may have worked in the time frame when EAPG was still being produced, so in some way she could be considered a small-scale private decorator. Though the Stephens colored old glass, they were not unscrupulous and had no intention to deceive anybody. They openly shared their process, stated that antique and new items were used, and marketed the glassware on its own merits. To them, their "water ambered" glass was a novel souvenir and a beautiful testimony of the mysterious ability of nature to color glassware, but many years later the unknowing collector who finds an example mistakenly thinks he/she possesses a rare and valuable piece of Carnival glass.

Cold Painting and Enameling

Cold-painted decoration is not fired on, is not permanent, and can easily flake and wash off. According to period sources, the advantage of this type of decoration was the brightness of the applied colors, which was not obtainable by any other method. Goofus glass is a modern term for a type of cold-painted decoration, often done on the entire under surface of plates and bowls in deep red and gold bronze. A *Feathered Medallion* plate has been seen with this type of decoration, but it is not known when or by whom this was done.

Enameling is a much more durable painting on glass. It is fired on for permanency and is usually highly raised. It is generally done on plain areas of the glass. No Bryce, Higbee glass has been found with this decorative technique.

Engraving and Etching

Bryce, Higbee glass is found with various engravings. It was done at the factory, as this excerpt from the November 25, 1880, issue of *American Pottery and Glassware Reporter* indicates:

> Their [Bryce, Higbee & Co.'s] cutting and engraving shop is now in full blast, and is doing some very artistic and beautiful work.

Yale is mentioned in a trade journal quote as being engraved in "several handsome designs." Other patterns found engraved include Alaric, Butterfly, Earl, Ethol, Fancheon, Flora, Homestead, Mirror, and *Teardrop Row*, but there certainly are others.

A very common error persists in referring to engraving as etching. Etching is a decorating technique achieved through the use of acid, whereas engraving is usually done with a copper wheel. Etching can be in the form of elaborate designs or areas given a frosted appearance. Sandblasting is a mechanical form of engraving.

In January 1881, John B. Higbee was granted a patent for a "Mechanism for Grinding Bands upon the Surfaces of Wine-Glasses, Goblets, and other Articles of Glassware." This type of decoration was not new, but Higbee's desire was to "simultaneously produce [a] series of bands...in a perfect state, and in an expeditious and economical manner." It is the technique that was employed to achieve the clouded surface on items in the Butterfly pattern. At first glance it appears to be acid etching, but close examination proves otherwise. Other items and patterns were likely decorated with Higbee's patented device, especially plain banded goblets as mentioned and illustrated in the patent. For more information, see listings for Butterfly on page 136 and No. 33 on page 203 in chapter 9, Patterns made by Bryce, Higbee & Company.

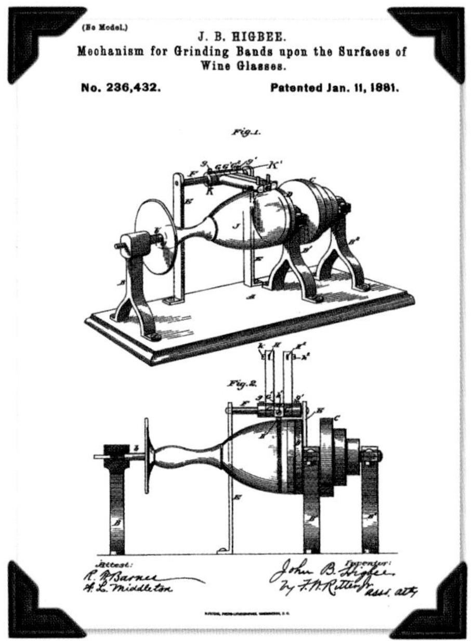

Patent illustration of John B. Higbee's grinding mechanism used to decorate glassware, 1881.

Example of engraving on glass done in the last quarter of the nineteenth century. Note that the design is lightly cut into the glass.

Example of etching on glass by an unknown maker, circa 1880s. Note the smooth, stencil-like design is applied to the surface of the glass.

This wine glass is very similar to the one shown in John Higbee's patent illustration.

7 Common Characteristics of Bryce, Higbee Glass

RETOOLED MOULDS

When closely studied, relationships can be seen in the patterns and shapes produced by Bryce, Higbee & Company. Often the same or very similar mould shapes were used from one pattern to the next. Some patterns utilize the same design in the base, while others share the same handles and/or finials. For example, Yale and Vici contain the identical central design on flat items. The same motif is also found on the Utility Boot inkwell lids. An interesting relationship exists between *Chain*, Rival, Royal, Grand, and Melrose bread plates. The complex star with added elliptical petals is found in the base of the *Chain* bread plate and in the flat bases of Rival and Royal items as well as in the bases of Grand and Melrose. Comparison shows that the same valve was used for the *Chain*, Grand, and Melrose bread plates, clear indication of a common origin. Capitola, *Chain*, Alfonzo, and Butterfly all share the same detailed star design. The same scroll handles (some with slight variation) are found on Capitola, *Chain*, Homestead, and select items of Mirror, New Grand, and Melrose. Covered items in the Mirror, Grand, New Grand, and Melrose patterns all have the same finial and *Prism Bars* and Gem share the same beehive-shaped knobs. The finials of the Charm pattern contain the convex circle found in the main motif and it is rather apparent the finial originated with this pattern. These same finials are also found on Crescent and New Crescent compote lids even though the motif has nothing in common with those patterns. Trade journal reports confirm that Charm was introduced in 1895 and Crescent came along in 1896, followed by New Crescent in 1898.

A common characteristic of many Bryce, Higbee patterns beginning in the 1890s is the use of patterned stems containing elements of the motif found on the body of the piece. Patterns introduced during the late 1890s, such as Banquet, Admiral, and Oregon, display this characteristic, as well as pattern introduced 1900 and after, including Paris 1900, *Fine Cut and Fan*, Bonair, and Anona. It is useful for the researcher to note that many of the earlier compotes and salvers

The same valve was used to impart the elaborate design in the base of the Yale (left) and Vici (right) bread plates, $25–$30 each.

Base patterns (clockwise from top) of *Chain*, Grand/New Grand, and Melrose bread plates show the same valve was used. Note the pattern is not as crisp on the Melrose plate because the well-used valve was about fourteen years old by the time the pattern was introduced in 1894.

The interesting, prismatic finial used on Grand, New Grand, and Melrose originated with the Mirror pattern. New Grand 6.5" covered compote (left), \$40–\$45; Melrose 6.5" covered compote (right), \$45–\$50.

The finials used for Bryce, Higbee's Charm (left) were also used on the Crescent (not shown) and New Crescent (right) patterns. Charm 7" covered compote, \$40–\$45; New Crescent 7" covered compote, \$45–\$50.

Stem of Worlds pattern compote. This same stem is found on six other Bryce, Higbee patterns from the 1890s.

(and in some cases, cake baskets) have pedestals attached to the bowl or plate with a glass wafer. There is a particular pedestal found on no less than seven different Bryce, Higbee patterns from the 1890s, which was originally designed for use with the Worlds pattern, for it contains the motif exclusive to that design only. It can then be deduced that the other patterns that utilize the same pedestal were introduced at the same time as or after Worlds. The patterns found with this pedestal thus far (in estimated order of introduction) are Worlds, *Bowline*, *Teardrop Row*, Charm, Crescent, Surprise, and New Crescent. Beginning with Bryce, Higbee's new patterns for 1899, pedestals were no longer pressed separately and fused to the bodies of cake baskets, compotes, and salvers. These items were exclusively molded in one piece, though the company did utilize this technique earlier with some patterns, including Persian, New Grand, Melrose, and Fleur-de-lis.

Three of Bryce, Higbee's earliest patterns, Capitola, *Chain*, and Alfonzo all utilize the same pedestals applied to items with a glass wafer. The author strongly feels the pattern known as *Chain* is Bryce, Higbee's Vesta, but original catalog proof has not been found to confirm this.

TOP TO BOTTOM

Note that the design motif of Bonair is carried onto the stem of the compote and stopper of the cruet. Cruet, $30–$35; 8" square compote, $25–$30.

The same pedestals were used for the *Chain* (left) and Capitola (right) patterns. Note the similarity in shape of the bowls.

The same pedestals were used for the Capitola (left) and Alfonzo (right) patterns.

RETOOLED MOULDS

Many Bryce, Higbee patterns appear to be retooled from each other or were made with variations in shape. Since the company had a mould shop, it was much easier, more convenient, and more cost effective for them to work their own moulds rather than have an outside firm perform any changes or chip completely new moulds. In late 1879, *American Pottery and Glassware Reporter* mentions that moulds were scrapped for unpopular patterns that did not sell. For companies like Bryce, Higbee, which had skilled mould makers on site, unpopular patterns could be cleverly retooled to create ones that would hopefully prove more successful. Patterns could also be updated and given a fresh new look by changing the shapes. This appears to be the case with the Capitola and Grand/New Grand patterns. The glass market was highly competitive, and many patterns did not win the favor of the buyers. Unpopular patterns would have had a very limited production and may not have had the chance to appear in company catalogs. Some examples of retooled designs are Rival and Royal; Worlds, *Bowline*, and Surprise; Crescent and New Crescent; and some items of New Grand and Melrose.

Bryce Higbee's first known attempt to alter an existing pattern was with Capitola. As early as 1882, items are shown in jobber catalogs with scalloped edges. Plain-edged items are first spotted in 1885. After that, scalloped-edged items are no longer shown. It was not difficult to change the edges to give the pattern a new, more modern appearance. The same forms are found with either plain or scalloped edges, and the cream pitcher and spoon holder are found in three different variations. This suggests reworking of moulds rather than the possibility that these slight variations were offered all at one time.

Capitola items are found with scalloped or plain edges. 5" low-foot compotes, $12–$15 each.

An apparent retooling of moulds occurred with the company's Rival (AKA *Sprig*) and Royal designs. The shapes of these two lines are identical (other than a few items that shall be noted shortly), but some items are found with a leafy sprig design on every other panel. Over sixty years ago, Kamm discussed this variation and came to some incorrect conclusions. She logically assumed the sprig design was added to the moulds, but evidence shows it was actually taken away. Trade journal reviews confirm that Rival was introduced in 1883 and the plain Royal line was new in 1888. Rival is first seen in jobber assortments in 1885, whereas Royal is first observed in mid–1889. The two patterns do not appear together, and after Royal appears, Rival is no longer shown. As noted above, the forms of the two patterns are the same shape, except the Royal celery vase, spoon holder, and covered sugar do not have handles. The moulds could have been altered to incur this change, but it is more likely new moulds were made for those three items. Hands-on comparison of Rival and Royal sugar bases reveals differences to indicate different moulds were used to make them. One might wonder why the handles were eliminated. Anybody who has collected and studied this pattern knows that the handles of the celery vase, spoon holder, and sugar are extremely susceptible to damage due to the nature of their design. Unless it was merely an aesthetic decision, it is reasonable to think the handles were removed because they were very vulnerable and fragile. For further discussion, see individual pattern listing in Chapter 9, Patterns made by Bryce, Higbee & Company.

Rival (left) and Royal (right) were once thought to be the same pattern, but were actually separate lines.

The Worlds pattern is so infrequently found that many people have never seen an actual piece of it. Its scarcity must be due to the fact that it was not popular and the moulds were retooled after a short time. Worlds was very likely named for the World's Fair and introduced 1892/93. By 1895, the moulds had been retooled to become the *Bowline* pattern (OMN unknown). The underlying diamond and cone pattern was retained, but, with the addition of convex spheres or "bubbles," a different design was created. Some alterations were made with the lids and edges as well. This second pattern proved no more popular than Worlds, and the moulds were reworked once more by fall 1896. The final pattern

TOP TO BOTTOM

Comparison of Worlds (left) and *Bowline* (right) patterns. Examination shows *Bowline* was created from the Worlds pattern by adding convex spheres between each diamond.

Detail of Worlds and *Bowline* patterns.

was christened Surprise (formerly known to collectors as *Paneled Diamond Point*), and, indeed, it certainly was and is a surprise, for hardly anybody would know that it was born from two previous unsuccessful designs that are not so obviously related to it. The patterned panels of *Bowline* were carved smoothly away to become plain, convex panels, and the plain, concave panels were carefully chipped with a diamond point design; thus, Surprise was born.

The bread plate is a key indicator of Surprise's parentage because it retained the same mould shape as *Bowline* with very little alteration. Bread plates in the *Bowline* and Surprise patterns were thoroughly and meticulously examined by the staff of the Island Mould & Machine Company of Wheeling, West Virginia. These men are experts in their trade, and even after a long day of work welcomed the opportunity to find some concrete proof that Surprise was tooled from the *Bowline* moulds. Armed with high-powered magnifiers, calipers, and literally decades of hands-on experience in making glassware moulds and working in glass factories, the workers began the investigation. In order to prove that the same mould was used and retooled, they compared measurements between the two items and tried to locate some tiny irregularity in the pattern of *Bowline*, perhaps even a flaw in the original mould that was transferred over to Surprise. After nearly three-quarters of an hour worth of patient study, evidence was found. Bob Roth discovered some tiny, circular marks in a plain area on both plates in the exact same spot and in the same arched configuration. He pointed to this as an indication that the original mould had been repaired at some point in its existence, and the very same mould with the repaired area was used to create the Surprise pattern bread plate.

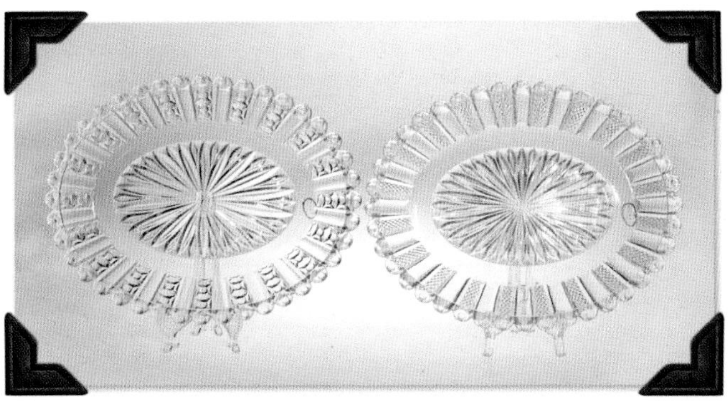

Bowline (left) and Surprise (right) bread plates were made from the same mould. Note the dots drawn in ink show where the original mould was repaired with plugs. *Bowline* bread plate, $45–$50; Surprise bread plate, $25–$30.

It has been this author's belief that the Grand line consisted of fan-edged items, and New Grand was essentially the same pattern (with some slight variation in the size and shape of the diamonds) chipped onto new moulds utilizing simpler, plainer, and in some cases, smaller shapes. Many similarities have been observed between New Grand and Melrose. The Grand/New Grand design consists of plain-centered diamonds against a background of tiny stars. Melrose employs the same or similar diamonds, but the star design is inside each diamond rather than on the background. Smaller diamonds only contain part of the star design. Double fans are placed between each diamond to fill the empty space. At least some Grand/New Grand moulds were reworked to create the Melrose pattern. The mould shapes as well as the shape and placement of the diamonds on many items are the same, but an interesting oddity exists. Out of the entire line, there are three items of Melrose that have fan-and-scalloped-edge borders common to Grand: the bread plate, celery vase, and water tray. This can be logically explained. For whatever reason, these three items were carried over from Grand to New Grand without changing the shape; in fact, the water tray does not have the motif on it at all. It is exactly the same as the Yale water tray. Plain-edged New Grand bread plates and celery vases were apparently not made. The catalog pages of New Grand shown in Kamm 8 clearly contain items of the new shape with plain edges—except for the celery vase and water tray. These were the moulds used to make Melrose, hence the fan edges. The Melrose motif was chipped into the plain body of the water tray mould, which explains why the leafy central design common to Yale is found only on this single piece of Melrose. The bread plate took much more thorough examination to figure out. There are seventeen diamonds on the Grand/New Grand bread plate versus twelve on the Melrose bread plate, so a new block mould must have been chipped—or an old one reworked. The central design and base are the same, indicating the same valve was used. The author painstakingly counted the number of tiny vertical lines on each of the twelve large scallops of bread plates in the Grand/New Grand and Melrose patterns. Each line is about as wide as a pin. The results were eye opening. A total of three scallops contain eighteen lines, seven contain nineteen lines, and

Grand/New Grand (left) and Melrose (right) celery vases, $25–$35 each.

two contain twenty lines. The number of lines on each scallop is as follows (going clockwise): 18–20–19–20–19–19–19–18–18–19–19–19. The sequence is exactly the same between the plates of Grand/New Grand and Melrose, indicating the same ring was used.

When celery vases in Grand/New Grand and Melrose were shown to the staff at Island Mould, they noted many small details indicating the Melrose celery vase was made from an old mould that had been extensively repaired and reworked. After much examination, the conclusion was drawn that the Melrose celery vase was made from a retooled Grand/New Grand mould. When reviewed, all the evidence forms a clear picture. Grand was introduced circa 1886. Around 1888, new, plain moulds were chipped with the same motif and called New Grand, but the earlier Grand celery vase mould with fan edge was still utilized. By fall 1894, the New Grand moulds were retooled and the Melrose pattern was introduced. By that time the mould for the celery vase was about a decade old, which would explain all the wear and repairs to it, and why the Melrose celery vase has a fan-and-scallop edge. New Grand and Melrose do not appear together in any jobber catalogs; in fact, once Melrose appears, New Grand completely disappears.

Crescent, a new pattern for 1896, was given a good, detailed description in *China, Glass & Lamps*. It appears in jobber and retail catalogs from spring 1896 into fall 1897, then is replaced by a very similar, but more ornate pattern beginning in spring 1898. Close examination of the design led the author to belief that New Crescent (AKA *Diamond Point Discs*) was the result of reworked moulds of the Crescent pattern. Celery trays of both patterns were taken to Island Mould & Machine Company and studied with the same fine attention to detail as the other items were. The mould makers marveled at the craftsmanship of the designs, a tangible indication of how perfectly chipped and finished the moulds used to make these items had been. They surmised it likely took up to two weeks to chip the mould for the New Crescent celery tray alone. But could proof be found that New Crescent was made from the same moulds as Crescent? It was very challenging to find some definite indication that the same mould was used for these two patterns. The crew said it was entirely plausible to add the ribs to the plain crescents, but it would have been exceedingly difficult, though not completely impossible for highly skilled workers, to chip the fine diamond point pattern in between the crescents where the star of the Crescent pattern would have been. Finally, with the assistance of another pair of well-trained eyes, a nearly miniscule imperfection was discovered that was carried over to the retooled mould, proving that New Crescent was made from the earlier Crescent moulds.

New Crescent (right) was made from retooled moulds of the Crescent (left) pattern.

8 Production of Bryce, Higbee's Patterns by Other Manufacturers

What Survived the 1907 Flood at the Bryce, Higbee Factory?

Some Insight from Butler Brothers

The John B. Higbee Glass Company *General Catalogue*

The New Martinsville Glass Manufacturing Company 1921 Price List

What Survived the 1907 Flood at the Bryce, Higbee Factory?

Trade journals reported that the flood of March 1907 extensively damaged the Bryce, Higbee & Company factory, which had been closed since John B. Higbee's death in December 1906. In the weeks following the flood, reporters noted an interest on the part of C. K. Bryce to repair the damaged factory and resume operations. The last mention of specific plans to reorganize was mid-June 1907, but, for reasons which are not clear, these proposals were abandoned.

At the end of December 1907, *Crockery and Glass Journal* quoted appraisal figures from the "equity proceedings against Bryce, Higbee & Co.," which give some sort of idea of how much finished glassware existed before the liquidation. The report lists "manufactured goods" valued at $1,212.22. It is difficult to comprehend how much glassware would be appraised at over $1,000.00 in 1907, but one thing to keep in mind is that this was not its retail value. To put this figure into perspective, we can look at the assets of the Millersburg Glass Company, which filed bankruptcy a little over three years later. An appraisal was done that included "manufactured glassware not packed" amounting to $1,733.92. Everything on hand was listed, including quantities of each item. Using this as a rough guideline, even after subtracting $500 worth of product to bring the figure closer Bryce, Higbee's, this still adds up to a staggering sum of nearly 20,000 pieces of glassware. The amount of manufactured goods at the Bryce, Higbee factory could have been even greater than this because Millersburg's glass may have been valued higher and there may have been some inflation in the three-year gap between these appraisals. Still, this gives a bit of a clue to the amount of glassware Bryce, Higbee had when it ceased production. This stock would, naturally, continue to be offered by Butler Brothers and other firms who normally sold their glassware. It is for this reason that the Bryce, Higbee items/patterns offered in jobber and retail catalogs after the company's demise does not warrant that those items were actually being produced. One can only guess how long it might have taken to sell off the previously manufactured stock.

The appraisal figures of Bryce, Higbee & Company also include "machinery and equipment" valued at $2,665. Though no breakdown is given, this figure undoubtedly includes moulds. Moulds were among the greatest assets a glass manufacturer possessed. In late 1879, *American Pottery and Glassware Reporter* mentioned that Campbell, Jones & Co. spent approximately $4,000 for moulds for a single pattern consisting of about fifty items. John and Elizabeth Welker note that, in the early 1890s, moulds would cost upwards of $5,000 for each pattern. By the time of the 1907 appraisal, moulds would have been even more expensive; however, it must be considered that the moulds were undoubtedly appraised below the full value of those that were new. The appraisal amount could have been calculated merely on scrap value.

There would have been some stock of glassware and office equipment in the building on Smithfield Street. This is where the office and showroom were located, and because they were on the second floor, nothing would have been harmed. A Sandborn map from February 1907 indicates a second floor area of the factory was used for storage and engraving. We can only surmise what was stored there, but there logically would have been glassware that had already been engraved as well as glassware that was to be engraved. Obviously some sort of machinery and equipment used in the engraving shop was there as well. The mould room was on the first floor adjacent to an office and a rather large one story warehouse was across the street on the corner of East 2nd and West Streets. When one considers that the $2,665 appraisal figure included all machinery and equipment, it seems likely that there were not a tremendous number of moulds involved.

Lola and Wayne Higby state, "Several of the Bryce, Higbee patterns were continued at J. B. Higbee, indicating that Ollie was able to salvage some of the Bryce, Higbee molds in spite of the flood," but they give no evidence to support this statement. A flood, in itself, would not destroy moulds. If, however, the moulds had not been retrieved in a timely manner, they would have become ruined. At the time of the flood, the factory was reportedly closed, legal battles between the Higbee and Bryce families were unresolved, and the fate of the company was still undetermined. It is not known how many moulds or stock of manufactured glassware J. B. Higbee acquired from Bryce, Higbee & Company, nor is it known how much Bryce, Higbee glass remained in warehouses of wholesalers and retailers when the factory ceased operations.

SOME INSIGHT FROM BUTLER BROTHERS

Other authors have assumed that a great number of the patterns made by Bryce, Higbee & Company were continued by J. B. Higbee. In nearly all cases, there is no evidence whatsoever to corroborate this claim. Butler Brothers assortments from the period between the closing of the Bryce, Higbee factory into the first full year of operations of the J. B. Higbee Glass Company can enlighten us, but this bit of insight involves some speculation. The assortments from this jobber have been thoroughly studied and will be used for many examples because a good number of consecutive catalogs were available to the author and because Butler Brothers consistently sold great quantities of Bryce, Higbee and J. B. Higbee glassware for many years. It must be kept in mind that the presence of items in catalogs of a jobber, a retailer, or even a manufacturer is not a definite indication that those articles were actually being produced at the time the catalogs were issued. The appraisal report leaves us with little doubt that a great quantity of Bryce, Higbee's previously manufactured goods were sold after the May 1908 liquidation.

Butler Brothers was a jobber that sold general merchandise and glassware wholesale. The assortments were made up at the factories, so, theoretically, all items shown in any given assortment should have come from one glass company. For more detailed discussion, see chapter 3, Jobber, Retail, and Company Catalogs.

The catalogs issued by Butler Brothers in the final months of Bryce Higbee's existence and shortly after their demise present some valuable clues. In the spring 1907 catalog (effective February 23 through the end of March), thirty-five different assortments and individual items of Bryce, Higbee glassware were offered. This catalog was issued before the flood. The next issue available for study was mid-spring 1907 (distributed for May). The same assortments and items are shown, but of the thirty-five offered in the spring catalog, twenty-four are noted "Temporarily Out" and one was not offered at all. Half of the Madora items offered in the "Crown Jewel" assortment were also unavailable. This catalog was issued after the flood. In the next catalog, June 1907, three more assortments/items are marked "Temporarily Out" and four more Madora items are unavailable. The mid-winter 1908 issue (December 1907 to January 1908) shows not a single assortment of glass by Bryce, Higbee. Three small, individual items are still illustrated, but each is marked "Out." Except for Madora, very few of these articles were ever offered again. To form a clearer, more concise picture, a timeline of the offerings and events during the final stages of the Bryce, Higbee factory has been compiled.

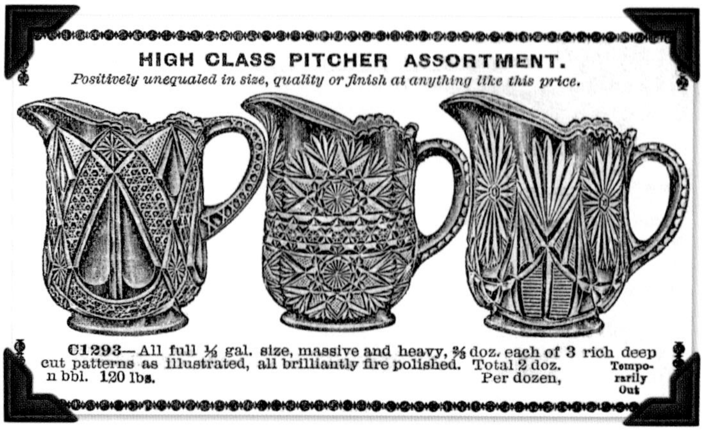

Assortment of pitchers made by Bryce, Higbee shown in a mid-summer 1907 Butler Brothers catalog. Note the annotation "Temporarily Out." Patterns (l. to r.) are Anona, *Ten-Pointed Star*, and *Feathered Medallion*.

December 1906: According to a report published in *China, Glass & Lamps*, the Bryce, Higbee factory closes after the death of John B. Higbee.

December 1906 to spring 1907: Butler Brothers continues to offer assortments and items of Bryce, Higbee glassware without interruption. Either ample stock remained in warehouses or Butler Brothers was being supplied with glassware even though the factory was reportedly shut down.

March 1907: Any hopes of reopening the Bryce, Higbee factory are shattered by the damaging flood, and the factory is no more.

May 1907: A significant amount of Bryce, Higbee glassware previously offered by Butler Brothers on a consistent basis is now unavailable. Stock was dwindling, and there was no way to replenish it.

June 1907: The J. B. Higbee Glass Company is formed and commences operations by fall 1907. Even fewer Bryce, Higbee items are now available from Butler Brothers.

December 1907: Not a single piece of Bryce, Higbee glassware is offered by Butler Brothers, indicating stock was completely exhausted and items were out of production. J. B. Higbee Glass Company was operating but was not manufacturing any Bryce, Higbee patterns.

January 1908: J. B. Higbee's first patterns, Alpha and Laurel, are introduced to the trade. They will appear profusely in the pages of Butler Brothers for the spring 1908 market.

May 1908: Glassware and machinery from the Bryce, Higbee factory go to public sale. Ollie Higbee is reported to have bought the "movable parts." There is no mention of what became of the manufactured goods.

October 1908: Three short-lived assortments composed of Bryce, Higbee glassware in miscellaneous patterns appear in Butler Brothers, suggesting the sale of old stock acquired from the factory liquidation. By this time, the "Crown Jewel" open stock of the Madora pattern is brought back and remains until the first part of 1911. Also by this time, the "Great Victory" assortment consisting solely of Paris 1900 is offered and continues to be offered for about two years.

Many sources incorrectly note that a fair amount of the old Bryce, Higbee patterns was produced by J. B. Higbee in 1907. It is very important to remember that Bryce, Higbee's assets were not sold until May 1908; therefore, none of their moulds could have been acquired before that time.

After the factory liquidation, some assortments have been found that were comprised entirely of Bryce, Higbee patterns. The most comprehensive one was titled "Unmatchable" by Butler Brothers. This assortment is important for the clues it holds. The assortment remained the same (except for a drop in price) between October 1908 and mid-winter 1909 (late December 1908 to January 1909). It did not appear again until mid-winter 1910 (late December 1909 to January 1910), when some items were replaced with patterns introduced by J. B. Higbee: a *Ten-Pointed Star* rectangular dish was replaced by a rectangular dish of the same size in the Banner pattern (introduced 1909) and the table set was replaced by one in the Laurel pattern (introduced 1908). A *Beautiful Lady* 6.5" salver was replaced by one of the same size in the Banner pattern, and *Beautiful Lady* and Bonair patterned bowls were replaced by bowls in the Laurel pattern. These changes indicate that the earlier Bryce, Higbee items were no longer available, so similar items in patterns made by J. B. Higbee were substituted. The Bryce, Higbee items noted do not appear in any known J. B. Higbee catalogs, nor do they appear in other company catalogs issued after J. B. Higbee closed.

There were a few assortments comprised of J. B. Higbee patterns that included one or two older Bryce, Higbee patterns. The "Challenge" and "New Challenge" assortments indicate that J. B. Higbee may have had the mould for the small Bonair vase. The "New Challenge" assortment included said vase and last appeared in the mid-summer (May) 1907 issue. It was the only Bryce, Higbee assortment not shown in the June 1907 issue, but it later appeared in 1908 titled "Challenge." Here all Bryce, Higbee patterns were replaced with like items in J. B. Higbee's Alpha—except for the Bonair vase. This vase was also offered on its own and was marked "Temp-Out" in the June 1907 issue, but was offered again after May 1908. By mid-summer 1911, it was replaced

Butler Brothers' "Unmatchable" assortment of Bryce, Higbee glassware offered in October 1908, after the liquidation of the factory.

The 6.5" Bonair vase (second row from the bottom) was a regular part of Butler Brothers "New Challenge" assortment of J. B. Higbee glassware that ran for about three years.

April 1909 "Bargain Day" assortment from J. B. Higbee. Note the small items of Anona and *Ten-Pointed Star.*

Mid-summer 1909 assortment from Butler Brothers showing J. B. Higbee's Alpha compotes with *Ten-Pointed Star.*

with a vase of nearly identical size and shape in J. B. Higbee's Laurel pattern, and the assortment is titled "New Challenge." J. B. Higbee either acquired the mould or an enormous quantity of vases to offer it in two different assortments in every issue of Butler Brothers' "Our Drummer" for about three years.

By 1910, only a few Bryce, Higbee patterns were seen in quantity with any regularity. Assortments of Madora and Paris 1900 continued to be offered. J. B. Higbee can be documented as producing Madora because trade journals mention it as a new pattern for the company in 1910 and many items are found marked. A small Anona footed berry and custard cup and *Ten-Pointed Star* tumbler and small berry bowl all appear in the "Bargain Day" assortment from April 1909 to mid-winter 1911 (effective December 1910 through January 1911). A *Swirl and Panel* toothpick appears in the mid-summer and fall 1911 issues among items in J. B. Higbee's Banner pattern. The "Bargain Day" assortment seems to have been a way for Bryce, Higbee and J. B. Higbee to purge outdated stock and offer small, miscellaneous items. Between August 1909 and December 1910, *Ten-Pointed Star* compotes and salvers were offered in assortments with compotes and salvers in J. B. Higbee's Alpha pattern.

Lola and Wayne Higby mention a water tray in the Melrose (AKA *Sheaf and Diamond*) pattern marked with the J. B. Higbee trademark bee, and the author can confirm marked examples of the Bijou rectangular dish as well as Emmas, Rovers, and Plain ABC plates. The Bijou dish is not from the same mould used by Bryce, Higbee, however. Paris 1900 ice tubs and celery vases are found with the J. B. Higbee trademark, but these are the only items in the pattern that have been found marked. Homestead square individual salts are sometimes found marked with the bee trademark. J. B. Higbee did not call it Homestead as Bryce, Higbee did; instead, they called it Star. The Plain ABC plate made by J. B. Higbee does not have the beaded design on the scallops and the letters are slightly different. Except for the Star salt, these same items appear in an undated catalog of the New Martinsville Glass Manufacturing Company.

Three small items of Anona (small footed nappy, 3.5" comport, and 5" plate) are shown in a Federal Glass Company catalog dated 1914. A very interesting assortment of small, miscellaneous pieces in a 1906 G. Sommers catalog appears to be an offering of Federal Glass Company. A "5-inch cheese or olive plate" is among the items. There is not enough detail in the cut to be absolutely certain, but it looks to be the same 5" plate labeled Anona in Federal's 1914 catalog. If so, this plate was made by Federal while Bryce, Higbee was still producing the pattern, which would not be too surprising. The central pattern and smooth edge are quite different from other Anona items, so the plate certainly could be a copy. Assortments in G. Sommers catalogs indicate that Federal was simultaneously offering some of the same patterns produced by United States Glass Company. Even more baffling is the fact that Federal used the identical numbers and names given to the patterns by the originating manufacturers. Nearly all of the items shown in Federal's 1914 catalog are older designs that originated at other glass companies. Though some appear in G. Sommers as early as 1906, it is not certain when Federal first offered these items. Many are odd, small items in various patterns with no matching pieces. The 1914 Federal Glass Company catalog illustrates many odd, small items in various patterns with no matching pieces. An illustration of a wine glass that looks like Westmoreland's No. 400 AKA *Wellington* differs enough to state with some certainty that it is a copy. A Federal catalog dated May 1913 shows a photo of a large room filled with machinery. Some very important information is included:

Anona 3.5" comport, 5" plate, and footed nappy shown in Federal Glass Company's 1914 catalog.

> This is a view of our Mold and Machine Shop, which is the largest and most completely equipped shop of its kind in connection with a glass factory, in this country. Here we make all of our own machinery of any and all kinds, as well as all of our molds.

In summer 2014, the author examined a 3.5" Anona comportier that was poorly molded and made from dull, inferior glass, which was nowhere near the quality of glass produced by Bryce, Higbee & Company. It was felt to be a product of Federal Glass Company.

Very few patterns introduced by Bryce, Higbee & Company prior to 1900 are seen in jobber catalogs dating after the 1907 flood. On a page of specials in their mid-winter 1912 (December 1911 to January 1912) catalog, Butler Brothers offered 7.25" covered compotes in Charm and New Crescent patterns (introduced 1895 and 1898, respectively). Though sold at such a late date, these items were undoubtedly old stock. A Fleur-de-lis celery vase (pattern introduced in 1898) is part of a J. B. Higbee assortment in a 1909 G. Sommers catalog and may have been old stock, too. Except for the odd items noted earlier, found with the J. B. Higbee trademark, it is not very likely that Bryce, Higbee's pre–1900 tableware patterns were made by J. B. Higbee.

There are appearances of items that are rather difficult to explain. One such example is the *Feathered Medallion* pattern, introduced by Bryce, Higbee circa 1905. Only a few odd items in this design appeared very sporadically in Butler Brothers assortments after Bryce, Higbee completely ceased to exist in 1907. Beginning in 1909, it appeared even less, or not at all.

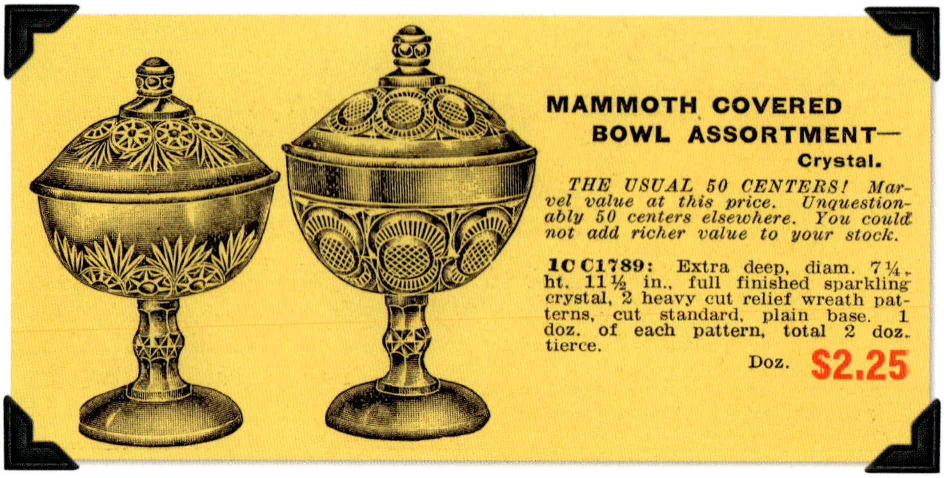

Bryce, Higbee's Charm and New Crescent covered compotes were included on a page of specials in a mid-winter 1912 Butler Brothers catalog. This late, random appearance of these patterns introduced in the 1890s indicates old stock.

Fast forward six years, and we find an assortment of 10" open compotes in the August 1915 Butler Brothers catalog; the patterns are *Feathered Medallion* and J. B. Higbee's Alpha. The assortment was offered for at least eight months.

There are many other mysteries concerning the final stages of the Bryce, Higbee factory. The author's research indicates *Ten-Pointed Star* was a new pattern for 1906. The Bryce, Higbee factory reportedly shut down in December 1906. This would mean the pattern was produced for only about a year; however, most pieces are quite abundant on today's market. There is no documentation that J. B. Higbee ever produced it. Could Bryce, Higbee alone have manufactured such huge quantities of *Ten-Pointed Star* in such a short amount of time?

Another mystery is the timing of Butler Brothers offering the Madora pattern as their "Crown Jewel" stock pattern. It was not offered while the factory was operating, so we are left to believe that Butler Brothers must have had a supply of the glassware in their own warehouses. But why was it not presented until after the Bryce, Higbee factory was reported shut down in late December 1906? After the March 1907 flood, some items are gradually marked "Temporarily Out." Is it mere coincidence that Butler Brothers began running out of items only after the flood destroyed the Bryce, Higbee factory? This may indicate Bryce, Higbee was operating until the flood even though *China, Glass & Lamps* reported the factory shut down in December 1906.

There is little doubt Bryce, Higbee was planning to introduce new patterns to the trade for the 1907 market. John B. Higbee died suddenly on December 9, 1906, less than a month before the unveiling of new patterns at the annual glass show in Pittsburgh, so there is no reason to think samples would not have been ready for presentation. Certainly by that late date moulds would have been prepared, if nothing else. As a rule, two new patterns—sometimes more—were introduced each January for the spring market. There is no record of what Bryce, Higbee had planned to unveil at the January show. Since the patterns were apparently not presented to the trade in January 1907, it is tempting to wonder if they were later introduced by J. B. Higbee. Could Madora have been planned as one of Bryce, Higbee's spring patterns for 1907, and since it was not introduced to the trade, did Butler Brothers present it as a pattern made "especially" for them?

We may never have a definitive explanation to these and other similar questions, but an enigma is a great force to reckon with and considered a welcome guest to the assiduous researcher.

THE JOHN B. HIGBEE GLASS COMPANY *GENERAL CATALOGUE*

Among the vast resources at the Rakow Research Library at the Corning Museum of Glass is a catalog issued by J. B. Higbee with a large bee on the cover and simply titled *General Catalogue*. Though undated, Corning places it between 1907 and 1911. It is uncertain how they came about this range, but it is not accurate. After thoroughly studying the catalog, I feel the date of circa 1917 is more plausible. The latest tableware pattern shown is Iris (patented March 7, 1916, and introduced to the trade in January 1917); therefore, the earliest this catalog could date is 1917. The catalog could possibly be later still, for the August 22, 1918, issue of *Pottery, Glass & Brass Salesman* mentions some new items that seem to be shown in the *General Catalogue*. If this were the case, the catalog may have been compiled to sell what the company had on hand shortly before going into receivership in late 1918. At any rate, the catalog dates quite late in the company's history.

The earliest patterns shown, Laurel and Alpha, were introduced to the trade in January 1908. Forty-three pieces of Laurel are shown, but only seven pieces of the Alpha line, which at one time was very extensive. None of the latter pattern is listed by name. Lola and Wayne Higby use the spelling "Alfa" for dubious reasons. The pattern is listed as Alpha in trade journal reports and on the New Martinsville Glass Manufacturing Company's list of moulds acquired from J. B. Higbee. An interesting side note is that, among the pieces clearly labeled Laurel in the *General Catalogue* is one piece of Alpha (an individual salad bowl), and six pieces of Madora (5" plate, 5" belled footed jelly, 5" sweetmeat, 6" salver, wafer stand, and olive tray). It is unlikely any of this is in error, as each item is given a catalog number consisting of a different digit preceded by a letter that corresponds with the first character of the pattern's name (for example, all items of Laurel are prefixed by "L," all of Iris are prefixed by "I," and so on). The digits begin at number 1 and correspond to the form of the item, regardless of the pattern. The numeric code for a celery vase is 100, so one in the Colonial pattern is designated C–100; one in the Gala pattern is G–100. The only pieces of Madora shown with an M-prefix are two styles of wines. Oddly enough, the Alpha condiment set is also given the M-prefix for Madora. It is not known why this set or the other items noted were included as part of other patterns. This type of anomaly also appears with Bryce, Higbee and J. B. Higbee items found in original documents of the New Martinsville Glass Manufacturing Company.

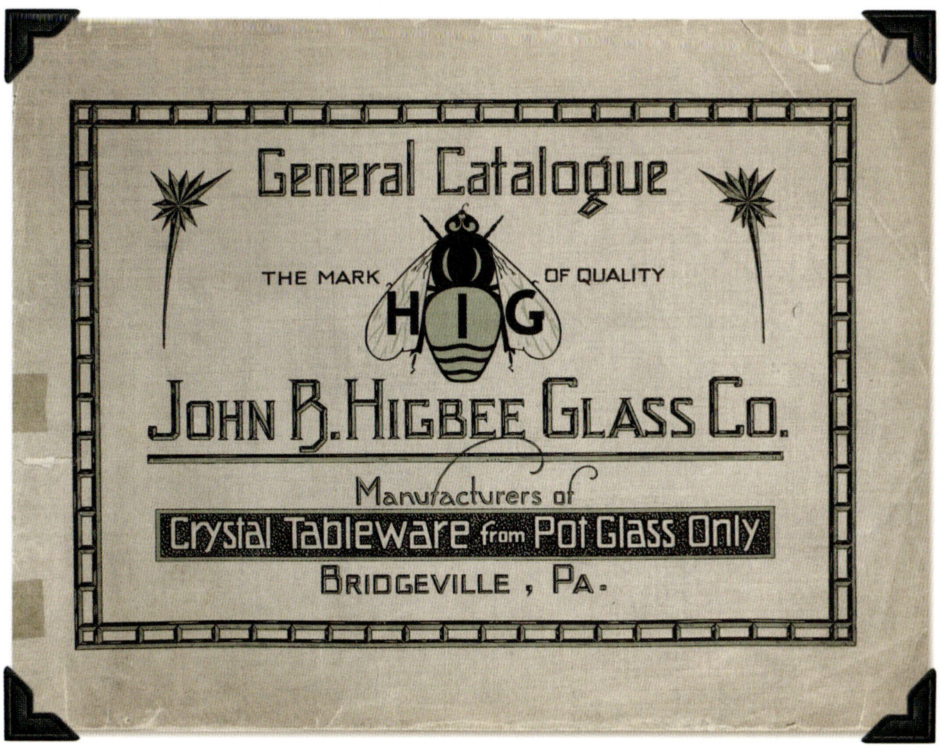

Cover of the circa 1917 J. B. Higbee *General Catalogue* boldly displays the company's bee trademark. *Courtesy of the Rakow Research Library, Corning Museum of Glass.*

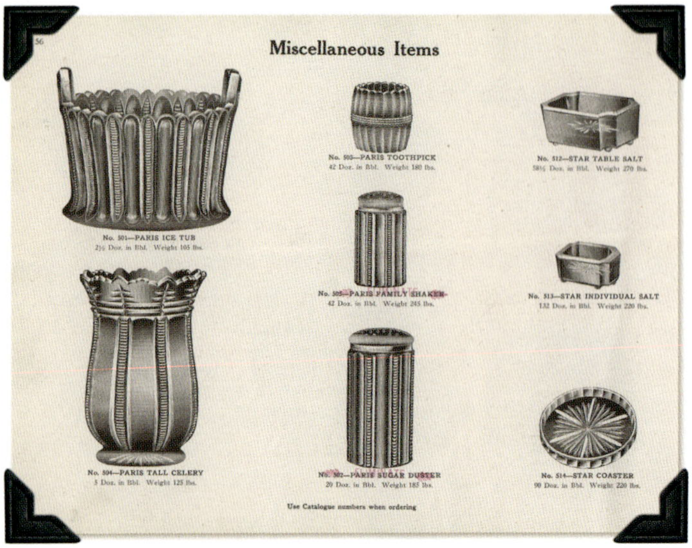

TOP LEFT | Star salts (originally part of Bryce, Higbee's Homestead line) and Paris 1900 items (simply called "Paris") in the J. B. Higbee *General Catalogue*. Note Bryce Higbee's Our toothpick was renamed "No. 503—Paris Toothpick" even though it does not match and was not originally part of the Paris 1900 line. *Courtesy of the Rakow Research Library, Corning Museum of Glass.*

TOP RIGHT | Mirror, Optic, and Plain items from J. B. Higbee's *General Catalogue*. The Plain items may not have originated with Bryce, Higbee. *Courtesy of the Rakow Research Library, Corning Museum of Glass.*

Star ABC plate shown in an undated New Martinsville Glass Manufacturing Company catalog. This same illustration was used in circa 1917 J. B. Higbee's *General Catalogue*, but they called it Plain.

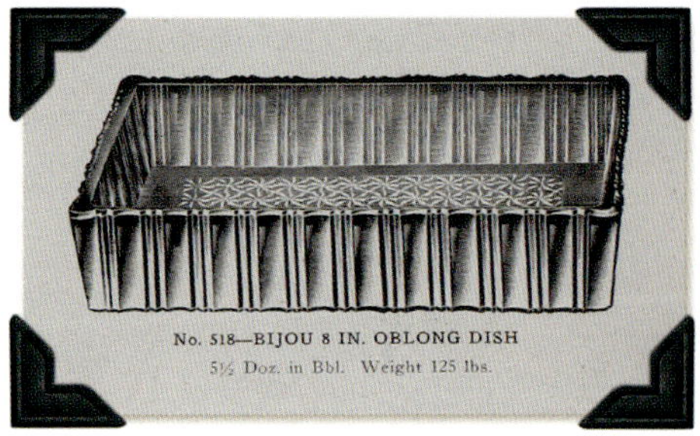

Bijou oblong dish from the circa 1917 J. B. Higbee *General Catalogue*. It was also shown in an undated New Martinsville Glass Manufacturing Company catalog. *Courtesy of the Rakow Research Library, Corning Museum of Glass.*

The last eleven pages of the catalog are labeled "Miscellaneous Items" and include patterns that originated at Bryce, Higbee & Company: four pieces of Paris 1900 (simply called "Paris" in this catalog), a Highland celery vase, a Melrose (AKA *Sheaf and Diamond*) water tray, and Homestead table and individual salts (called "Star" in this catalog). Also shown are three ABC plates, one called "Plain" (shown with a beaded border on a Bryce, Higbee & Company catalog page with the caption "ABC Plate"), one called "Boy" (originally called Emmas by Bryce, Higbee), and the last called "Dog" (originally called Rovers by Bryce, Higbee). A toothpick labeled "Paris" is shown, but it is not the same as the Paris 1900 pattern. It was called Our Toothpick by Bryce, Higbee and was not originally part of the Paris 1900 line.

Due to their plainness, there are several items in the catalog that are difficult to ascertain if they truly originated at Bryce, Higbee & Company. These are wines and cocktails in Mirror and Optic patterns, as well as two compotes and a salver labeled "Plain."

Another item shown that originated with Bryce, Higbee is labeled "Bijou 8 in. oblong dish." Bryce, Higbee & Company introduced their Bijou pattern nearly thirty years earlier. Though this rectangular dish does not contain the fan and acanthus motif associated with this design, it was a part of this line. The Bijou 8" oblong dish appears in

Butler Brothers assortments with other Bryce, Higbee products before 1907, so we can be sure it originated with them. There are differences between the Bijou dishes made by Bryce, Higbee and J. B. Higbee (see discussion on page 129). This item had quite a long life and appears in a July 1924 Butler Brothers catalog, no doubt as an offering from the New Martinsville Glass Manufacturing Company since it is shown and mentioned in company material dating from this time frame.

None of the miscellaneous items that originated with Bryce, Higbee follow the numbering system used in the rest of the *General Catalogue*. Nearly all of them appear in a later, undated catalog of the New Martinsville Glass Manufacturing Company with the same numbers as shown in the J. B. Higbee *General Catalogue*, but with slightly different captions (other than the Boy and Dog ABC plates, which remain the same). In addition to the items noted, a mug in the Paris 1900 pattern is shown by New Martinsville, labeled "No. 116—Mug," but does not appear in the J. B. Higbee *General Catalogue*. It does, however, appear in Butler Brothers assortments during the years J. B. Higbee operated.

THE NEW MARTINSVILLE GLASS MANUFACTURING COMPANY 1921 PRICE LIST

Also at the Rakow Research Library in Corning, New York, is a type-written price list of items headed "Higbee Glass Company's Moulds" with the notation on the cover "Effective Dec. 20, 1921." Each item is given a number, description, and price per dozen. The majority of the sixty-four items on this list are illustrated in the J. B. Higbee *General Catalogue*, in an undated New Martinsville company catalog, or both. With only a few exceptions, the numbers and descriptions correspond with entries in the above-mentioned catalogs. Many of the patterns on the list are known to have originated with Bryce, Higbee & Company, though the names of some were changed by J. B. Higbee. The numbering system appears to have originated with J. B. Higbee as well. Annotations in brackets are by the author.

Melrose water tray from the circa 1917 J. B. Higbee *General Catalogue*. This is one of four different original sources that use the Melrose name for this pattern, formerly known only by its AKA of *Sheaf and Diamond*. The tray was also sold by New Martinsville. *Courtesy of the Rakow Research Library, Corning Museum of Glass.*

116 Paris Mug
130 Star Ind. Salt [originally part of Bryce, Higbee's Homestead line]
501 Paris Ice Tub
502 Paris Sugar Duster
503 Paris Beauty Toothpick [originally called Our Toothpick by Bryce, Higbee]
507 Plain 5" Ftd Bowl [the J. B. Higbee *General Catalogue* shows a 507 "Plain 8 in. bowl, flared" (compote) which may be the same pattern]
511 Mirror Wine—Optic or Plain
517 Highland Tall Celery
518 7" Bijou Oblong [listed as 8" in the J. B. Higbee *General Catalogue*, though it actually measures closer to 7".]
518 Paris Tall Celery [shown in the J. B. Higbee *General Catalogue* as No. 504—Paris Tall Celery]
520 Cocktail 2 oz [shown in the J. B. Higbee *General Catalogue* as No. 520—Mirror Cocktail]
523 Melrose Water Tray
593 Star Table Salt [originally part of Bryce, Higbee's Homestead line]
600 Mirror Short Stem Wine or Egg Cup [shown in the J. B. Higbee *General Catalogue* as No. 600—Single Egg Cup]
613 Highland Butter
614 Anona Butter & Cover
615 Monarch Butter
616 Bonair Butter

It is uncertain if the 507 Plain 5" footed bowl originated with Bryce, Higbee. The Plain items numbered 507, 509, and 510 in the J. B. Higbee *General Catalogue* (there is nothing with the number 508 shown) share characteristics of the Mirror and Vici lines.

The 518, 7" Bijou Oblong differs slightly from the version made by Bryce, Higbee and is not from the same mould.

In addition, there is an entry "548 ABC Plate 3 Mlds–1R & P," which may be for the Plain (called Star by New Martinsville), Boy, and Dog ABC plates originally called ABC, Emmas, and Rovers by Bryce, Higbee, but they are shown in the J. B. Higbee and New Martinsville catalogs as numbers 530, 531, and 532 respectively.

The "524 Royal Spl Cov'd Jelly" [524 Royal Special Covered Jelly] may have been originally produced by Bryce, Higbee & Company. For detailed discussion, see Royal Special Covered Jelly on page 269.

Numbers 613 through 616 are of great interest because these patterns and/or items were not previously known to have been produced by a factory other than Bryce, Higbee. This indicates J. B. Higbee acquired these moulds, which were then sold to New Martinsville. The butter dishes are not illustrated in any known catalogs by J. B. Higbee or New Martinsville, but the price list titled "Higbee Glass Company's Moulds" indicates that New Martinsville did produce them.

In conclusion, it is extremely difficult to know whether late offerings of earlier patterns were part of the stock of manufactured goods from Bryce, Higbee or were made by J. B. Higbee from moulds acquired from Bryce, Higbee. Random, short-lived appearances of items in jobber catalogs certainly indicate previously manuactured goods, but there are really only two ways to know for certain if J. B. Higbee actually produced the glass: 1) if items are marked with J. B. Higbee's trademark bee; and 2) if the item appears on the New Martinsville 1921 list of "Higbee Glass Company's Moulds." Of course, J. B. Higbee may have had Bryce, Higbee moulds that they did not add the bee mark to and ones that did not make their way to New Martinsville, but at present there is nothing to document these possibilities

9

Patterns made by Bryce, Higbee & Company

TABLEWARE

NOVELTIES

Patterns are presented alphabetically by their OMN when known. Some OMNs are documented here for the first time, so, to avoid confusion between these patterns, others that have been incorrectly named by previous authors, and those that may not be commonly referred to by their OMN, a pattern index is included as a cross reference. OMNs appear in regular text, common collector's names (AKAs) appear in *italics*. Sometimes the same names were used by more than one company. In these instances, the company name should precede the pattern name when speaking of EAPG in general, i.e.: Bryce, Higbee's Oregon versus United States Glass Company's Oregon.

Exact years of introduction are given when directly noted in trade journals. The years presented refer to when the patterns were put on the market, not necessarily when they were first mentioned in the trade journals. Circa (c.) dates are used when trade journal descriptions are not as definitive, and, in some cases, are based on when a pattern is first spotted in jobber catalogs. This may not be the first time it actually appeared in the catalogs. I have studied hundreds and hundreds of catalogs, but not every single catalog that was printed is known or has been observed by me. When this was the only way to date a pattern, I tried to ensure that consecutive issues of the same catalog were observed so as not to miss an earlier appearance. It will be seen that most patterns appeared for sale shortly after their known introduction dates. This is especially true during the late 1800s and early 1900s, when new patterns were constantly being offered to capture the eye of the buyers and catalogs were being issued with greater frequency due to the larger volumes of wares being offered. These catalogs have, naturally, survived in larger quantities than the earlier catalogs from the 1880s to early/mid–1890s.

In most cases, it is nearly impossible to state with a high amount of certainty exactly when the production of a particular pattern ceased. Each glass company had its stand-by or staple items, and some popular items may have been made after production for the rest of the line was discontinued; random appearances of odd, earlier items in jobber and retail catalogs are not an absolute indication that the item was still in production. Warehouses were periodically purged of old stock and in assortments these pieces were sometimes included among new and recent patterns. An indication that patterns may have been discontinued is when items are replaced by the same items in different patterns in the same assortment and/or completely disappear from assortments for an extended period of time. It is still not possible to pinpoint an end date with a high level of accuracy because there is no way of knowing how much product was in the warehouses of the distributors or the factory after a pattern was discontinued. Greater accuracy is assured in the case of patterns made from retooled moulds. When there is not enough information available to closely date a pattern, a broader range or "year unknown" is given. Future discovery of additional catalogs, trade journal reports, and other documents may help to assist in more precise dating in these instances.

For each entry, supporting sources that existed at the time of manufacture are given to document or attribute the pattern to Bryce, Higbee & Company. Modern references have not been used for this purpose. Though information presented by other authors may be correct and complete, it also may not be. Too many inaccuracies and inconsistencies have been encountered, so I consider it all hearsay and prefer to go straight to the source whenever possible. Some patterns were shown for many years by the same jobber, usually Butler Brothers, and when this occurs I list the catalog where the pattern has first been seen. Appearances in other catalogs and trade journals are given to support the attribution, OMN, and/or year of production/introduction, to show how quickly many patterns were offered in jobber and retail catalogs, and to document items made later by other companies. In many respects, researching this company's products is a bit unique, so different approaches must be taken. It is most ideal to use company catalogs to document patterns, but in the majority of cases this is impossible with Bryce, Higbee glassware.

Bryce, Higbee advertised themselves as manufacturers of crystal tableware and this is the product on which they predominately focused. Remember that "crystal" referred to colorless glassware at the time and had nothing to do with quality or the presence of lead in the formula. During the mid–1880s the company produced some patterns and novelties in colors as most factories at the time did. It is difficult to say when color production was terminated, but it appears that colored table wares, novelties, and individual items were being phased out by the late 1880s. Under each entry, known colors are listed, including decorative treatments. It is possible that colors and treatments other than those listed for each pattern may be found.

Reproductions and look-alikes are listed under each entry. For the purpose of this book, a reproduction is defined as an item issued at a much later date from new or original moulds in a conscious attempt to closely replicate the original. This is usually done with collectors in mind and there is often intent to deceive, but not always. A look-alike is a similar pattern issued by a competing company in the same general time frame, which may be confused for another pattern. The intent was to capture some of the market of successful designs by either copying or emulating them. Patterns that were later made in the same general time frame by another company from the original moulds are noted. These are considered reissues, and the intent was merely to make salable product from moulds that were still useable. The collector who shies away from collecting EAPG due to the threat of reproductions will do well to notice how very few Bryce, Higbee patterns have been reproduced. Confusing mould transfers are not much of a factor either, for the company remained independent and never joined a conglomerate like so many others during this era. The majority of moulds were used only by them.

Because very few original Bryce, Higbee company catalog pages are known, a definitive list of items made in each pattern is not possible. Listings are compiled from catalog pages, trade journal reports, jobber and retail catalogs, and actual items owned and seen. As in the time the glassware was made, different terms for the same form appear in the listings. Whenever possible, original terms are retained; however, modern terms are sometimes substituted. For example, the original term for a compote was simply "bowl." The term compote is used here to avoid confusion and superfluous description.

Measurements often vary from original catalog listings and are approximate to the nearest quarter inch. Measurements do not include handles. Size of actual items can and does vary, especially for those that were hand-tooled. Too many collectors become bogged down with listed measurements and think they have a "rare" item because theirs varies by a fraction of an inch. Any deviation in size of approximately a quarter of an inch up to a half of an inch should be considered insignificant. As an example, cake baskets of the same pattern were measured and some vary by a quarter of an inch or more in length. They were not intended to be different sizes; the variation occurred because the items were tooled by hand. Hand-tooling was a common practice at the time. Labor was cheaper than moulds, and hand-tooling was an economical way to extend the number of items produced from a single mould. While the glass was still malleable, the edges of bowls and compotes were ruffled, flared, squared, or brought inward to create different shapes. Salvers and cake baskets were formed from compotes in most patterns. These are just a few examples. Quite often there was more than one mould for popular items or those that required heavy, continual production; consequently, those moulds could vary slightly in size from each other. The fact that something is not listed does not necessarily mean the item is rare or even unusual; it only means that the author has not observed it or has inadvertently omitted it from the listings. If an item should be found that is not listed, refer to the Forms section in chapter 5. There are many patterns presented here for the very first time as products of Bryce, Higbee & Company, but there are undoubtedly more patterns, forms, and colors unknown to us. Who knows what might be discovered around the next corner? This is just one aspect that makes collecting Bryce, Higbee glass so exciting. Anything is possible!

Note: If the collector knows of additional items (in only the Bryce, Higbee patterns presented here), please contact the author at FiddlerPaul71@gmail.com so future listings can be as complete as possible.

List of Patterns Commonly Known by Their Collector Names:

Arched Fleur de Lis see Fleur-de-lis

Arrowhead in Oval see Madora

Barley see Capitola

Block and Pleat see Persian

Butterfly Ears see Alaric

Butterfly Spray see Acme

Button and Star Panel see Anona

Coarse Zigzag see Highland

Cut Log see Ethol

Diamond Medallion see Grand and New Grand

Diamond Point Discs see New Crescent

Fan Band see Yale

Fan with Acanthus Leaf see Bijou

Florida Palm see Tidal

Heavy Heart see Oregon

Medallion Sunburst see Banquet

Nailhead see Gem

Opposing Pyramids see Flora

Palm Leaf Fan see Bonair

Paneled Diamond Point see Surprise

Ribbed Ellipse see Admiral

Rosette and Palms see Charm

Sheraton see Ida

Sheaf and Diamond see Melrose

Spirea Band see Earl

Sprig see Rival

Three Stories see Persian

Twin Teardrops see Anona

V-in-Heart see Beaunot

Zipper Cross see Paris 1900

KEY TO ABBREVIATIONS USED IN THIS CHAPTER:

Trade Journals:

AG: American Glassworker
AP&GR: American Pottery and Glassware Reporter
CG&L: China, Glass & Lamps
C&GJ: Crockery and Glass Journal
G&PW: Glass and Pottery World
P&GR: Pottery and Glassware Reporter
(formerly American Pottery and Glassware Reporter)

Company Catalogs:

BH: Bryce, Higbee & Company
FG: Federal Glass Company
JBH: J. B. Higbee Glass Company
JG: Jefferson Glass Company, Ltd, Toronto, Canada
NM: New Martinsville Glass Manufacturing Company
NMPL: New Martinsville Glass Manufacturing Company Price List

Jobber and Retail Catalogs:

BB: Butler Brothers
BS: B. Sommers & Co.
FP&W: French, Potter & Wilson
GS: G. Sommers & Co.
HB&F: Hollander, Bradshaw & Folsom
HLS: H. Leonard's Sons & Co.
HRE: H. R. Eagle & Co.
MW: Montgomery Ward
OM&G: Ogden, Merrill & Greer
P&B: Pitkin and Brooks
SB: Spelman Brothers
SR: Sears, Roebuck
TE: T. Eaton Co. Limited (Toronto, Canada)
W&M: Wallace & McAfee

TABLEWARE

Acme, c. 1882

References: BH, undated; *C&GJ*, 1/11/1883; BB 83rd Trip, 1885
Colors: clear; amber and blue (mugs only)

The January 11, 1883, issue of *Crockery and Glass Journal* reports:

> Among the patterns lately produced by this house [Bryce, Higbee & Co.] are the "Acme" and "Rival" sets, the latter just out. Both are very pretty, and will, no doubt have a large sale.

Since Acme is mentioned as "lately produced" as opposed to "just out" in January 1883, the date circa 1882 has been assigned to it. The pattern obviously remained popular for some years to follow, for the table set was offered by Butler Brothers in 1885 and 1886, and a mug (available in three sizes) is shown on an undated, circa 1888 Bryce, Higbee catalog page. By that date it is likely that only mugs were being produced. Mugs are the only items of Acme found in amber and blue, though the catalog makes no mention of colors. Colored items do not date before mid–1885, for this is when the company began producing colored glass.

Past authors have mistakenly reported the handles and finials of Acme items are in the shape of butterflies. This is true of the Butterfly pattern, but not of Acme. Kamm surmises items might be found without the leaf design above the butterflies, but no such variation has come to light and it is highly doubtful it ever will.

Acme mugs are found with slight variations in the pattern due to the use of different moulds. They are rather common.

Acme spoon holder, $30–$35; butter $70–$75.

Acme mugs, 3.25" tall, $20–$30 each. Note the slight variation in the butterflies.

The cream and spoon holder are frequently found as well, but other items are more challenging to find.

Acme means "the point at which something is at its best," a reference to the pattern being the highest achievement on the market.

Items Noted:

butter, covered, handled
cream
mug, three sizes, 2", 2.5", and 3.25" h.
pickle jar, glass lid
spoon, plain edge, handled, 3.5" w.
sugar, covered, plain edge, no inner ledge, handled, 4.5"w.

Acme may have been a full line. Items common to glassware lines of this period, such as bowls, covered compotes, salvers, water pitchers, and goblets have not been found, but they could exist.

Acme table sets were offered by Butler Brothers for 83¢ per dozen in 1886.

Reproductions and Look-alikes: None known. The Higbys state that the cream pitcher and smallest size mug may have been reproduced, but give no reason as to why they think this. There is no evidence to confirm their claim.

Admiral, 1899

References: *C&GJ*, 12/22/1898; P&B, 1899; MW, spring and summer 1899; BB, October 1899
Colors: clear

Admiral is first mentioned in *China, Glass & Lamps* in late 1898 as one of three new patterns for the 1899 spring trade done in the "beaded cut style." No images appeared in the trade journals, but a Pitkin & Brooks 1899 catalog lists and illustrates many items labeled Admiral. Montgomery Ward first offered Admiral by name in Catalog No. 65, spring and summer 1899. Ward used the same unusual terms to describe specific forms (such as cake basket and comportier) that the trade journals and Pitkin & Brooks used, strengthening the conclusion that these terms originated with Bryce, Higbee. Admiral is first observed in Butler Brothers October 1899 catalog and appears quite a bit until 1907.

Some sources list Admiral as a product of J. B. Higbee in 1905. The origin of this misinformation is unknown, but it is completely impossible because J. B. Higbee did not exist until 1907. Other sources say the pattern was made by Bryce, Higbee and continued by J. B. Higbee. There is absolutely no evidence that any factory other than Bryce, Higbee produced Admiral.

The name Admiral is a direct reference to the naval hero of the Spanish American War, Admiral George Dewey

Admiral celery vase, $40–$45; spoon holder, $35–$40; sugar, $50–$55; butter, $65–$70.

Admiral 10" cake basket, $40–$45; 8" compote, $25–$30.

(December 26, 1837–January 16, 1917). Dewey secured the U.S. victory over Spain at the battle of Manila Bay on May 1, 1898. All types of souvenirs were issued to commemorate this celebrated event, and many glass companies paid tribute by naming new patterns after Dewey and other things related to the war.

Admiral 10" salver, $40-$45; 5.5" shallow bowls, $15–$18 each.

Admiral 7" round plates, $20–$25 each; 9.25" square plate, $45–$50; 11" flat celery, $35–$40.

Admiral syrup, $75–$100 (complete); 12" plate, $35–$40; 4.5" square comportier, $12–$15; 9.25" square comportier, $25–$30.

Though Admiral was originally described as a medium weight glass, items are rather brilliant and substantial. It is not known how many different articles were made, but Admiral is quite an extensive line. The list presented here is compiled from jobber catalogs and actual pieces owned and seen.

Items Noted:

bowl, collar base, round, square, various depths and sizes (some originally termed "comportier")
bowl, flat, round, square, various depths and sizes
bowl, flat, oval, 8.5"
butter, covered
cake basket, 10" l.
celery tray, 11" l.
celery vase, 6.75" h.
compote, high-foot, round, square, 8" w.
cream, applied handle
cruet, stopper #1
mug
nick nack tray, 10.75" l.
olive tray, oval, 8"
pitcher, half-gallon
plate, round, 5.5", 8", 12"
plate, square, 9.25"
rose bowl, collar base, globe-shaped with smooth edge, 4", 7" w.
salver, 9"
shaker, salt and pepper
spoon, scalloped edge
sugar, covered, scalloped edge, inner ledge
syrup, metal lid
tumbler
vase, trumpet-shaped, cupped, flared, various sizes
wine

Reproductions and Look-alikes: No reproductions known. New Martinsville's No. 700 AKA *Pleated Oval* (1906) is quite similar to Admiral. The most notable difference is that the oval medallions are framed by diamonds on No. 700. United States Glass Company's No. 15,100 AKA *Gloved Hand* (1907) could be confused for Admiral, but there is a diamond pattern between the ribbed medallions. More than casual inspection will reveal other differences.

Admiral (left) is often mistaken for New Martinsville's No. 700 AKA *Pleated Oval* pattern (right).

United States Glass Company's No. 15,100 AKA *Gloved Hand* shows similarities to Admiral.

Alameda, 1886

References: *P&GR*, 2/11/1886; BB, c. 1886; P&B, c. 1887; HLS, 1888
Colors: clear, amber, blue, canary

Alameda butter, $60–$65.

Alameda clear celery vase, $35–$40; canary 4" footed fruit dessert, $45–$50; blue salt & pepper, $40–$45.

Bryce, Higbee's Alameda is a good example of using period sources to attribute a pattern to its maker when original company catalogs are not available. We know Bryce, Higbee made a pattern called Alameda by a report in the February 11, 1886, issue of *Pottery and Glassware Reporter*:

> Bryce, Higbee & Co. are running as full as possible and have big orders coming in every day. Their new Alameda line, complete, is ready for the market this week. It is an elegant round shape, handsomely figured and comprises set, bread plates, bowls, comports, pitchers, celeries, shaker salts, etc. Dealers will find this a very neat and good selling pattern, entirely new and of clear brilliant glass.

Characteristic of many trade journal reports of the time is the lack of detailed description of the pattern. It was deemed sufficient to concisely mention new patterns to entice buyers to inspect them in person.

Alameda amber 8" bowl. Note the raised, patterned disc in the center of the underside, $40–$45.

A catalog of H. Leonard's Sons & Co. dated to summer 1888 offers Alameda salvers and salt and pepper shakers by name with brief descriptions, though without illustrations. The entry for the shakers reads: "Alameda. Assorted color Salts...Low shape, deep cut stars in glass." A circa 1887 Pitkin & Brooks catalog illustrates a shaker that exactly fits this description labeled "Alameda." Both jobber catalogs are known for their use of OMNs. Finally, a circa 1886 Butler Brothers catalog shows "Our New '5 CENT' Colored Ware Assortment," which includes a tumbler in this same pattern in amber and blue. This grouping completely ties the pattern to Bryce, Higbee, for other patterns made by the company are clearly shown in the assortment.

An amber Alameda tumbler is shown in *Glass Tumblers, 1860s–1930s* by Tom Bredehoft, but is misidentified as "Hanover." Arthur Peterson shows an Alameda shaker in *Glass Salt Shakers* that he calls *Star and Bar*. To avoid confusion with Bellaire Goblet Company's No. 600, commonly known as *Stars and Bars*, Peterson's name should be abandoned in favor of the OMN, Alameda.

The crisply molded, multi-rayed stars are a distinguishing feature of Alameda, and many pieces also have interesting architectural arches at the base. There are items that do not have this, however. The pattern does not seem too plentiful, but since it is now properly identified perhaps more items will be discovered.

Alameda means "tree lined avenue" in Spanish and is a city in the San Francisco Bay area. Bryce, Higbee referenced the state of California in at least one other pattern, Capitola; the significance, if any, is not known.

Items Noted:

bowl, six rounded feet, 8"
butter, covered
celery vase, cylindrical, 7.5" h.
compote, high foot, covered 6" w.
cream
footed fruit dessert (low-foot compote), 4" w.
shaker, salt and pepper, squat
salver, 10"
spoon
sugar, covered, plain edge, no inner ledge
tumbler

Pottery and Glassware Reporter enumerates specific forms including the bread plate, bowls, comports, and pitcher, so obviously other items are to be found.

Reproductions and Look-alikes: No reproductions known. O'Hara's No. 725 AKA *Daisy in Diamond* is similar, but the star motif is slightly different. On Alameda, there is a point of the star at the north, south, east and west positions, but on No. 725, there is a V in these locations (see photo). Many pieces of No. 725, though not all, have a vertically ribbed band at the midsection not present on Alameda.

31395 Glass Individual Salt Bottles in assorted colors, Britannia tops.

Alameda shakers were offered by Montgomery Ward in assorted colors for several seasons.

O'Hara's No. 725 pattern (right) shows many similarities to Bryce, Higbee's Alameda (left).

Alaric, c. 1880s

References: BH, undated; BB 85th Trip, 1886; FP&W, April 1886
Colors: clear, clear with engraving

An Alaric mustard appears on a Bryce, Higbee & Company catalog page shown in Kamm's *An Eighth Pattern Glass Book*. Though undated, the page likely dates to circa 1888 (see discussion of plates 31–33 on page 43). Kamm only knew of the mustard, but it appears to have been a full line. For about three years, Butler Brothers offered various pieces of Alaric in their Perry and New Perry assortments, including a bread tray, butter dish, salver, cream pitcher, and open compotes. Though first observed in 1886, this odd mélange of items may suggest it was a slightly earlier line. By the time the circa 1888 Bryce, Higbee catalog was issued, the rest of the line was undoubtedly discontinued and that is why only the mustard was offered. It is highly unlikely that Alaric dates before 1882 because it borrows the main pattern motif from T. G. Hawkes & Company's Russian pattern, which was patented June 20, 1882. Many claim that the Russian pattern, now commonly called *Daisy and Button*, originated at the 1876 Centennial Exhibition. This is a myth that has been repeated for too long and must be laid to rest. Many companies were producing patterns based on the daisy and button design in great profusion and variety during the 1880s, much of it made in the popular colors of amber, blue, canary, and apple green. Curiously, Alaric is the only pattern known to have been made by Bryce, Higbee that incorporates the daisy and button motif and it has not been found in color.

An interesting item found in the Alaric pattern is the Grand Army of the Republic bread tray. It is not known when this was produced, but no doubt it was sometime during the 1880s. The motif in the base of the standard Alaric bread tray is nearly identical to the design in the ellipses of the *Chain* pattern and the base of the *Boat Covered Dish*. The only difference is that some of the diamonds do not contain a star on Alaric.

Alaric is a masculine Germanic name that loosely translates to "ruler of all" and may be a metaphor that the pattern would take lead over all others in the market. Many

Alaric 6" open compote, $25–$30; bread tray with standard center, $40–$45; butter, $50–$55.

Alaric 9" salver, $35–$40; covered mustard, $20–$25; 6" covered compote, $40–$45.

Alaric Grand Army of the Republic bread tray, $125–$150.

O'Hara's Bartholdi (left) and Richard's & Hartley's Tremont (center) could be mistaken for Bryce, Higbee's Alaric (right).

forms of Alaric are the same mould shape as Butterfly, but with different handles (where applicable).

Items Noted:

bread plate, rectangular, checkered center, 11.25"
bread plate, rectangular, Grand Army of the Republic center, 11.25"
butter, covered, low-foot, handled
compote, high and low-foot, open and covered, various sizes
cream
mustard, covered, handled, 2.75" w.
salver, 8", 9"
shaker, salt and pepper, handled (do not have band of daisy and button)
spoon, scalloped edge
sugar, covered, plain edge, no inner edge

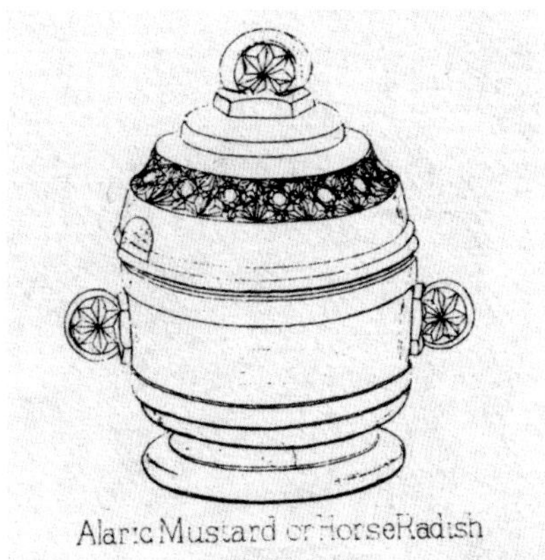

Alaric mustard illustrated in a Bryce, Higbee & Company catalog. Note that the handles match the finial. Actual examples with this variation have not been found.

Reproductions and Look-alikes: No reproductions known. Could be confused for the multitude of daisy and button variations, but Alaric has a single row of the motif contained within a band. The octagonal "buttons" are slightly elongated. Richards and Hartley's Tremont (1887) is similar, but there are flutes and zippered flutes below the band of daisy and button not found on Alaric. O' Hara's No. 650, Bartholdi (1885) is also similar, but has a band of daisy and button at the top and usually at the base as well.

Alfonzo, c. 1880

References: BH, undated; *C&GJ*, 12/2/1880; *AP&GR*, 11/25/1880; BS, spring 1885; BB, c. 1886; P&B, c. 1887; W&M, c. 1891
Colors: clear; undoubtedly clear with engraving

Alfonzo 6" compote, $25–$30.

Alfonzo goblet from a circa 1888 catalog and an unidentified Bryce, Higbee goblet offered by Butler Brothers circa 1886 that seems to match the rest of the set more closely.

Alfonzo was mentioned in *American Pottery and Glassware Reporter* along with Bryce, Higbee's Butterfly and Capitola on November 25, 1880t, with only a brief description:

> Their "Alphonso" table set is a capital imitation of cut ware.

Interestingly, the December 2, 1880, issue of *China, Glass & Lamps* enumerates the same patterns and items and uses much of the same sentence structure and language. This journal reports:

> The "Alphonse" is a handsome imitation of cut ware.

A Bryce, Higbee catalog page of stemware, shown in Kamm 8, includes a goblet completely void of pattern labeled Alfonzo. It appears to be the same as the No. I Plain goblet shown on the same sheet, but without a line nearly halfway down the bowl. This catalog page must date 1888 or after, as a Royal goblet is shown, and Royal was mentioned as a new pattern in a July 1888 trade journal report. B. Sommers included a "4-in Nappie or Sauce Dish, plain fire-polished" in their "'Rival' Assortment" in spring 1885. "Our Modern 'Leader' Assortment" offered by Butler Brothers circa 1886 shows an Alfonzo 6" bowl described as having plain high sides and a "fancy bottom." A circa 1887 Pitkin and Brooks catalog shows a 4" round bowl, 8" oval bowl, and a celery vase labeled "Alfonso," which are completely plain, though one of the illustrations reveals a star with wide rays in the base of the 4" bowl. The shape of the celery is quite similar to one in the Homestead pattern, but without the distinctive handles that characterize that pattern. Beginning in spring 1888, Montgomery Ward offered the 4" bowl for a few years and called it a "sauce nappie," an interesting parallel with the distinctive spelling used by B. Sommers. A circa 1891 Wallace & McAfee catalog presents the Alfonzo celery vase with items of

Mirror and Homestead, all referred to simply as "No. 3." These plain lines were combined and sold together by jobbers, but whether they were offered this way by Bryce, Higbee is not completely certain.

The goblet labeled Alfonzo on the Bryce, Higbee catalog page is not the same shape as the items with angled sides identified as "Alfonso" by Pitkin & Brooks; however, the Butler Brothers assortment noted above shows a goblet that is a perfect match. It has sloped sides and is the same shape as the Alfonzo celery vase. This goblet is nearly identical to the Bryce, Higbee catalog illustration of the Homestead goblet, but the sides are sloped at a steeper angle and it appears to be thinner and more graceful.

Alfonzo high-foot compotes have the same applied pedestals used on Capitola and *Chain* compotes. Alfonzo salvers very likely exist and ostensibly employ the same pedestal as well. Like the small bowls shown by Pitkin and Brooks and Montgomery Ward, compote bowls also have sloped sides with a star in the base. The star is composed of wide rays, each of which has a raised line in the center. This is the same type of star found on Acme, Butterfly, Capitola, *Chain*, Grand, New Grand, and Melrose. The flat-bottomed Mirror bowls with the fine cut design in the base are identical in shape to Alfonzo bowls and the same moulds were most likely used. It is not known what the handles of Alfonzo pitchers or finials and lids of covered items look like.

It is perhaps a bit perplexing that the trade journals describe Alfonzo as being an imitation of cut ware when in actuality it is completely or almost completely plain; however, a few things must be considered. Firstly, our twenty-first century minds have been subjected to different stimuli and influences, and we think quite differently than people did in the nineteenth century. We often would not describe things the same way as our predecessors did. Secondly, most people associate cut glass with ornate American Brilliant Period designs, but in 1880 this style had not reached its zenith. When Alfonzo was made, cut glass was less ornate and often downright plain to enhance and draw attention to the quality of the glass itself. The detailed, crisply-molded

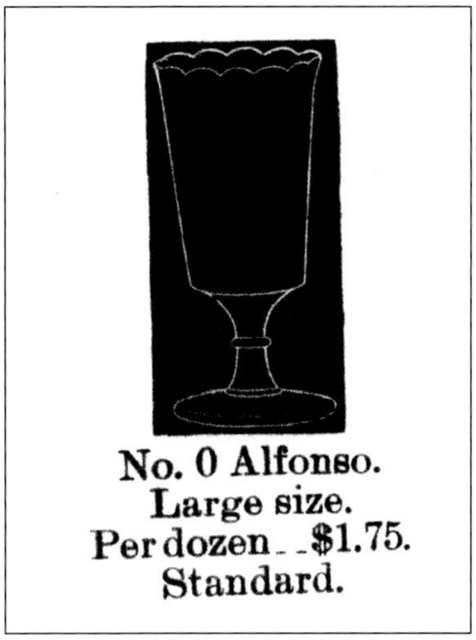

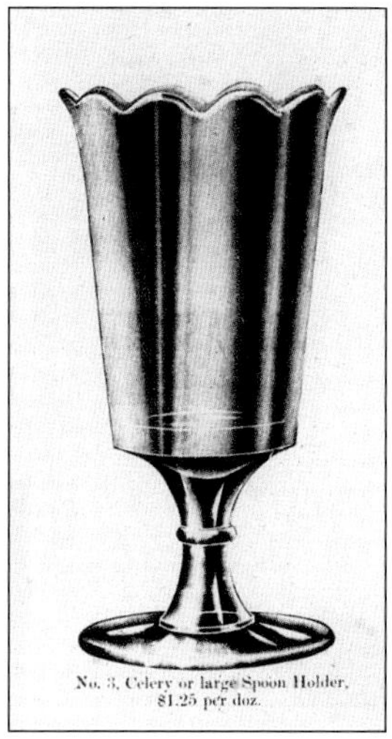

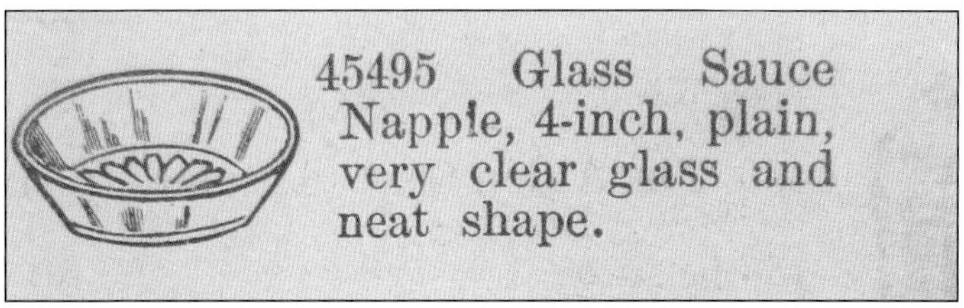

Alfonzo items offered by Pitkin & Brooks, Wallace & McAfee, and Montgomery Ward in the 1880s.

star in the base of some items, as well as the brilliant finish, were likely enough for Alfonzo to have been considered an imitation of cut ware.

Alfonzo has alternate spellings including Alfonso, Alphonso, or Alphonzo and is an Italian or Spanish variant of Alphonse, thus explaining the different spellings found in the company catalog, the two trade journals, and the

Pitkin and Brooks catalog. Company catalogs are the most definitive source in research, so we must believe the spelling "Alfonzo" is what Bryce, Higbee intended. The name is of Old German origin meaning "ready for battle" and may be a metaphor for the pattern being a fit choice to compete in the glass market.

Items Noted:
bowl, flat, 4", 6"
bowl, oval, 8"
celery vase, stemmed
compote, high-foot, star in base of bowl, 6" w.
goblet

Though this is all that can be confirmed, the selection of items indicates Alfonzo was a full line. Articles common to glassware sets of this period, such as the table set, salver, pickle dish, as well as a variety of open and covered compotes, must exist. There is little doubt flat 5", 7", and 8" bowls like those found in the Mirror pattern were made also.

Reproductions and Look-alikes: Since Alfonzo is so plain and so few catalog images are known, confirming items can be an arduous task. Most, if not all, the glass companies offered plain lines for home as well as hotel and public use, sometimes enhanced with etching or engraving. Glassware with little or no pattern is quite challenging to distinguish and properly identify, but the common components and design elements mentioned above could assist in recognizing other pieces of Alfonzo.

Anona, c. 1904

References: BB, spring 1904; FG, 1914 (only 3 small items, see below); NMPL, 1921 (covered butter)
Colors: clear, clear with gold trim, clear with ruby stain (belled ice cream cup and toothpick known)

Anona is first noted in Butler Brothers spring 1904 catalog, and it was most likely a new pattern that year. By this time, most Bryce, Higbee patterns appeared in Butler Brothers catalogs not long after they were introduced. The author's research indicates the four items known as *Button and Star Panel* were part of the Anona line: salt and pepper shakers, individual salts, toothpick holders (sometimes found with ruby stain on the upper rim), and swung vases. The intricate design is identical to the patterned bands within the Anona pattern.

The Anona cruet was sold with the same stopper that originated with Bonair; in fact, this stopper was used with all Bryce, Higbee cruets introduced after Bonair. This stopper can be considered a "universal" stopper for the company. An Anona cruet has been seen with the "J. B. Higbee universal stopper" commonly found with many of that company's cruets beginning with their first patterns for 1908, Alpha and Laurel. It appears this stopper was originally designed with Alpha in mind because it is the same as finials in that pattern, but if one looks closely, the elongated star design is found horizontally placed in the pattern of Anona. That alone does not validate its authenticity, however. The "J. B. Higbee universal stopper" is not seen in Butler Brothers catalogs while Bryce, Higbee was in existence. It first appears in J. B. Higbee assortments.

There is no *Twin Teardrops Variant*, despite other authors listing a separate pattern under that name. There is not enough surface area on small items to display the pattern in the same exactness as the larger items, hence the differences. If one looks closely, it will be seen that there is a tiny division

Anona 9" bowl, \$20–\$25; 10" shallow bowl, \$20–\$25; cake basket, \$40–\$45.

Anona high-foot lily vases or rose bowls, \$30–\$35 each; 6" nick nack tray, \$18–\$20; 6" salver, \$35–\$40; flat lily or rose bowl, \$25–\$30.

in the area where the double teardrops would be on the smaller items. The space is so miniscule that the teardrops would not fit into this triangular area. The design is like this on smaller items such as the 3.5" comportier, 3.5" bowl, custard and ice cream cups, as well as some of the larger items like the condiment tray, handled jelly, and 7.25" oval bowl. For whatever reason, the quart pitcher only contains one large teardrop even though there is enough space to display two narrow teardrops together. Despite these slight differences, they are all the same pattern and Bryce, Higbee intended them as such. There is no need to complicate the matter by adding the term "variant" to differentiate a few items of the set that deviate so insignificantly. Besides, the name Anona is superior to any made-up name that could be given to this pattern.

The only items shown in Federal Glass Company's 1914 catalog are a small nappy, 3.5" comport (the same form Bryce, Higbee called a comportier), and 5" plate. No size is given for the nappy, but it is estimated to measure approximately 4" to 5". All three items contain the single teardrop due to their size. It is not known when Federal first staring offering these items, however, this plate may be shown in a Federal Glass Company assortment in a G. Sommers catalog for 1906. Unfortunately, the quality and angle of the illustration prevents a high level of certainty. If this is the 5" Anona plate shown in Federal's 1914 catalog, it must have been a copy made from a new mould because Bryce, Higbee was still in business and making the pattern in 1906. The plate has a plain edge and a spoke-like pattern in the center, characteristics quite different from all other items in the set. It is likely that this variation was not made by Bryce, Higbee at all. A 3.5" comport was observed by the author that was not crisply molded and was made from grayish glass of inferior quality. It was felt to be a product of Federal rather than Bryce, Higbee. Indeed, the quality of glassware made by Federal in this era is rather mediocre.

The majority of patterns Federal offered in their 1914 catalog originated from other factories. Because of this it has been assumed Federal acquired moulds from various companies, but this does not appear to be the case, for a 1913 Federal catalog states that the company made all of

Anona 9" plate, \$25–\$30; 7" shallow bowl, \$12–\$15; half-gallon pitcher, \$50–\$55.

their own moulds. Oddly, nearly all of the patterns are labeled with the OMNs the issuing companies gave them, even the United States Glass Company patterns in the 15,000 series. It appears that Federal offered these patterns concurrently, and the reason they went so far to use the same names as the issuing companies is a mystery.

The fact that the pattern appears as Anona in the Federal Glass Company catalog allows a high level of assurance that this is the OMN Bryce, Higbee gave the pattern. An additional source with a much closer connection to Bryce, Higbee has been discovered. A type-written page pasted inside a New Martinsville Glass Manufacturing Company price list dated 1921 enumerates a list of items headed "Higbee Glass Company's Moulds." Many of the moulds on this list originated at Bryce, Higbee and are itemized by their OMNs. Any numbers included with the names appear to have originated with J. B. Higbee. On the list is the entry "614 Anona Butter & Cover." This, along with the Federal Glass Company catalog, is proof enough to the author that Anona is the name Bryce, Higbee gave the pattern.

Through this price list we now know that New Martinsville produced the Anona covered butter dish. Although the mould came from J. B. Higbee, we have no proof of when, or even if, J. B. Higbee actually utilized it.

Anona is a feminine name of Hebrew origin which means "favor" or "grace." It may be derived from *Anonna* (Latin: "means of subsistence"), the divine personification of Rome's grain supply.

Anona ice cream cups. Note hand-tooled flared edges. $12–$15 each.

Anona 14.75" swung vase with detail $25–$30.

Items Noted:

bowl, collar base, various edge treatments, depths, and sizes
bowl, flat, 3.5"
bowl, flat, oval, 7.25"
butter, covered
cake basket, 9.75" l.
celery vase, 6" h.
comportier, low-foot, 3.5" w.
comportier, low-foot, flared, 4.25"
compote, jelly, high-foot, round, flared, square, 5"–5.5" w.
compote, high-foot, round, square, 8" w.
compote, high-foot, round, 10" w.
cream
cruet, stopper #3
cup, custard or ice cream, straight, belled
jelly, handled, 5.5"
nick nack, 6.5" l.
nick nack tray, collar base, 6", 7.25", 9.75", 11" l.
pitcher, quart, half-gallon
plate, round, various sizes
plate, square, 7"
rose bowl, high-foot, 8" h.
salt, individual, 1.5"
salver, 6", 9.5"
shaker, salt and pepper
spoon, scalloped edge
sugar, covered, scalloped edge, inner ledge
toothpick
tray for cruet set, three feet, 6.5"
vase, swung, 14.75" (height varies)
wine

Reproductions and Look-alikes: See text.

Anona cruet, \$30–\$35; cruet tray, \$25–\$30; toothpick, \$20–\$25; individual salt, \$12–\$15; cream, \$25–\$30; spoon, \$25–\$30; celery vase, \$30–\$35.

"COLUMBIA" ASSORTMENT.

A128"Columbia" Glass Assortment—Brilliant crystal, fire polished, all large pieces; to **retail at** 5c, 10c, 15c and 25c; new patterns; contains the following pieces:

½ doz. Sugar Bowls.
½ doz. Butter Dishes.
½ doz. Cream Pitchers.
½ doz. Spoon Holders.
½ doz. ½-gal. Water Pitchers.
½ doz. Tall Celeries.
½ doz. 8-inch Bowls.
½ doz. 9-inch Celeries.
½ doz. 8-inch Compotiers.
½ doz. 9-inch Compotiers.
½ doz. 8-inch Fruit Bowls, high foot.
½ doz. 18-inch Vases.
½ doz. 7½-inch Preserve Dishes.
½ doz. 7½-inch Compotiers.
½ doz. 9-inch Plates.
½ doz. 7-inch Square Plates.
½ doz. 6-inch Salvers.
½ doz. Footed Jellies.
½ doz. 6-inch Compotiers, square.
½ doz. 8-inch Compotiers.

Total, 20 styles, 10 dozen pieces ....per doz., **85c**

Assortment of Anona from Baltimore Bargain House, June 1906. Note the swung vase.

B Goblet, year unknown

References: BH, undated
Colors: undoubtedly clear, possibly clear with engraving

A rather plain goblet with a paneled stem is shown on a circa 1888 Bryce, Higbee catalog page of stemware as "B Goblet." The designation causes one to wonder if the company also made an "A Goblet." Bryce, Higbee's B goblet is similar to other wares of the time. This type of plain stemware was made by many manufacturers and was commonly used in public establishments such as hotels, restaurants, and taverns. Stemware such as this is often found engraved.

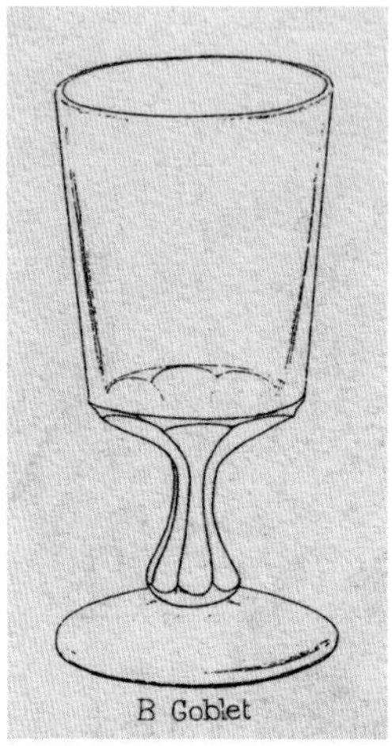

Bryce, Higbee's B Goblet from a circa 1888 company catalog.

Reproductions and Look-alikes: Unknown. It would be difficult at best to distinguish Bryce, Higbee's B Goblet from similar wares made by other companies.

Banquet, 1897

References: *CG&L*, 1/6/1897; BB, fall 1897
Colors: clear, clear with gold trim

> The Banquet is an imitation cut pattern, a series of fine cut rings, which cross each other at the horizontal center line, forming a chain around the article...

This quote from *China, Glass & Lamps* is a clear and accurate description of Bryce, Higbee's Banquet. The pattern is first noted in the Butler Brothers fall 1897 catalog where a 4.5" bowl is labeled "Extra Deep Bonbon Dish—Banquet pattern." A quart jug is given the description "Brilliant banquet pattern" in a 1901 Butler Brothers catalog. It is quite unusual for Butler Brothers to use an OMN, and a correct one at that. These are the only period catalogs known that refer to the pattern by name accompanied by an illustration. This, along with the detailed trade journal description, is enough to ensure correct assignation of the OMN.

Banquet was offered in assortments along with many other patterns, but a grouping that first appeared in 1897 titled "Our Wedding Table Outfit" included eighty-five pieces exclusively of this pattern for $2.95. By 1900, the last year this particular assortment was offered, the price was raised to $3.35—quite a significant increase for the time. Banquet is shown up to 1907, though by that late date not as many items were offered.

Banquet tumbler, $25–$30; 7" square plate, $25–$30; 8.25" olive or pickle, $15–$20; 7" round plate, $20–$25; 10" vase, $30–$35.

Banquet water goblets, $25–$30 each.

Large covered compotes and bulbous quart and half-gallon pitchers with applied handles are from an early issue and do not appear in Butler Brothers catalogs after spring 1900. The straight-sided water pitcher with applied handle was last offered in the January 1904 issue. Beginning in spring 1904 only pitchers of cylindrical shape with small molded handles are shown. The applied handle quart pitcher looks to be tooled from the celery vase. The covered individual handled sugar is from this early issue as well. The individual cream pitcher was offered on its own for many years after the individual sugar ceased to appear and is much more common. This small pitcher, along with the mug, was called "Tiffany" by Butler Brothers, causing some to believe this is the pattern Bryce, Higbee introduced as Tiffany in 1901. This cannot be so, because Butler Brothers called these items "Tiffany" as early as 1897. Pitchers with applied handles and covered compotes are difficult to find. The true toothpick has a scalloped rim, but the mustard was sold without a cover as a toothpick as well. An interesting variation of the 8" open compote has been found. The usual compote has the Banquet pattern on the underside of the base, but one has been found that has a star with twenty-four points instead. It is possible that salvers and cake baskets exist with this base variation, since these forms were tooled from the 8" open compotes.

Banquet was made in a full line, though it is unknown how many pieces are in the set.

Banquet 10" shallow bowl, $30–$35.

Banquet cake basket, $40–$45; 8" compote with unusual base pattern variation, value undetermined.

Items Noted:

bowl, round, square, oblong; various depths and sizes
butter, covered
butter pat, 3"
cake basket, 9.5"–10" l.
celery tray, oval, 11"
celery vase, 7" h.
compote, high-foot, open, scalloped rim, rayed or patterned base, 8"- 8.5" w.
compote, high-foot, plain edge, covered
cream, individual
cream, applied handle, table size
cruet, stopper #1
custard cup, small looped handle (appears applied, but is molded)
goblet
jelly, handled, 5"
mug
mustard, barrel shape, notched glass lid
olive tray, oval, 8.25"
pickle jar, glass lid, cylindrical
pitcher, quart, applied handle, bulbous
pitcher, quart, small molded handle, cylindrical
pitcher, half-gallon, applied handle, bulbous
pitcher, half-gallon, large applied handle, scalloped top, cylindrical
pitcher, half-gallon, small molded handle, cylindrical
plate, round, various sizes
plate, square, 7"
salt dish, individual
salver, 9.5"–10"
shaker, salt and pepper
spoon, scalloped edge
sugar, covered, table size, plain edge
sugar, covered, individual size, handled
toothpick, scalloped edge
tumbler
vase, trumpet shape, swirled stem, 10"
wine

Banquet individual butter plates, $15–$20 each; individual salts, $10–$15 each; tumbler, $25–$30; toothpick (or mustard base), $20–$25; individual cream, $15–$20.

Large assortment of Banquet offered by Butler Brothers as "Wedding Table Outfit," May 1898. Note the large covered compote and pitcher with applied handle.

Reproductions and Look-alikes: No reproductions known. Westmoreland's No. 180 AKA *Big Wheel(s)* (circa 1899) is clearly based on Banquet and could be confused. There are numerous differences, but the most obvious is the design in the center of each ring. On No. 180 this alternates between a hobstar and a cane figure. On Banquet this area is composed of rays. Though less ornate than Banquet, New Martinsville's No. 713 (circa 1910) AKA *Pleated Medallion* is also similar. See photos for comparison.

Two patterns similar to Bryce, Higbee's Banquet, (l. to r.) Westmoreland's No. 180 and New Martinsville's No. 713 AKA *Pleated Medallion*.

Beaunot (or Bow-knot), 1899

References: *CG&L*, 12/22/1898; BB, fall 1899; P&B, c. 1900
Colors: clear

Beaunot cake basket, $40–$45; 9.25" salver, $35–$40; 8" compote, $20–$25.

Beaunot is first mentioned in the December 22, 1898, issue of *China, Glass & Lamps*:

> Bryce, Higbee & Co. are out with three entirely new patterns in brilliant crystal glass which they will offer the trade the beginning of the new year. The shapes are very handsome and the figured patterns of each are artistic and attractive and produce a very pretty effect. They have named them the Admiral, Oregon and the Bow-knot—the name of the latter being given it from the resemblance of the figure pattern to a bowknot. The figured pattern of each is of the beaded cut style and they are very neat.

A butter dish appeared in a fall 1899 Butler Brothers catalog, among other Bryce, Higbee patterns, noted as "Bow-knot pattern." It is rather uncommon for Butler Brothers to use an OMN, but several instances are known. A circa 1900 Pitkin and Brooks catalog shows a salver in the same pattern labeled "Beaunot." The unusual spelling is notable and most likely what Bryce, Higbee intended, despite the expected spelling given in *China, Glass & Lamps* and Butler Brothers. Things Parisian were *de rigueur* in modish circles during the late 1890s, and the Beaunot spelling alludes to something French. The main motif is certainly a stylized bow knot, but the overall look of the design is influenced by *L'art Nouveau*, a style movement quite popular in France at the time, characterized in part by flowing lines and organic forms. Remember that Bryce, Higbee used a French theme for their Fleur-de-lis pattern the previous year, which proved a smashing success. Indeed, other companies used French names for their patterns in the same period of time as well, such as Northwood's Louis XV (1898), Dithridge and Company's Versailles (1900), and National/McKee's Navarre (1900). An even greater number of French names were used for china and porcelain patterns. One must wonder how Pitkin & Brooks would come up with the unusual spelling of Beaunot if it had not come directly from the manufacturer. This jobber did use OMNs, and even the Jeannette pattern made by McKee is spelled in Pitkin & Brooks catalogs as the company intended rather than the usual spelling of the feminine name "Jeanette." Though there is no Bryce, Higbee catalog known that shows Beaunot, the image of the salver noted above certainly appears to be from a company catalog, as do other illustrations shown by Pitkin & Brooks. They also used company terms for items they sold.

This is the first time this pattern, formerly known as *V-in-Heart*, has been published under its correct title. Beaunot is a colorful and charming name that deserves to be used. The pattern was probably made in a large line, but forms usual for Bryce, Higbee, such as a square plate, salt and pepper shakers, mug, celery vase, celery tray, and flower vase have not been found. The Higbys give the superfluous name *V-in-Heart Variant* to a footed cream and spoon holder of the same design. Despite the slight variation, these items were undoubtedly intended to be part of the same line and are included here as Beaunot.

Beaunot half-gallon pitcher, $50–$55; butter, $55–$60; spoon, $25–$30.

Beaunot salver from a circa 1900 Pitkin & Brooks catalog. *Courtesy of the Rakow Research Library, Corning Museum of Glass.*

Items Noted:

bowl, collar base, round, square, approximately 9"
butter, covered
compote, high-foot, round, square, 8" w.
cake basket, 10" l.
cream, flat
cream, footed
pickle dish, boat-shaped, four points on edge, 7.75"
pitcher, half-gallon
salver, 9.25"
spoon, flat, scalloped edge, inner ledge (not made to accept a lid)
spoon, footed, scalloped edge (possibly intended as an open sugar)
sugar, flat, covered, scalloped edge, inner ledge
tumbler

Reproductions and Look-alikes: None known.

Beautiful Lady, c. 1903

References: BB, spring 1903
Colors: clear, clear with gold trim

Beautiful Lady 8.5" vases (note different edges) and 6.5" cupped vase, $18–$20 each; 6.5" bowl, $12–$15; spooner, $25–$30; 7.5" rose or lily bowl, $30–$35.

Beautiful Lady 10.25" plate, $30–$35.

Kamm bestowed the name *Beautiful Lady* to this pattern and guessed it to date from 1885–1890. The pattern is clearly much later, but this error has been continually repeated by some to this day. The design is indicative of pressed glassware from the early part of the twentieth century, and the forms are typical of Bryce, Higbee's post–1900 production. Though the year of introduction and OMN are both uncertain, the pattern is first noted in a Butler Brothers catalog dated spring 1903. *Beautiful Lady* consistently appears in many assortments with other Bryce, Higbee patterns over the course of about four years.

The pattern must have been popular and made in great quantity, for it is readily found today. Vases, bowls, and compotes are especially prevalent, but the table set is a bit more challenging to find. The usual covered butter dish has a flange edge with rounded serrations. A variation is found with a smaller base that has large, broad scallops. It appears that no covered compotes were made in this design, a characteristic common to Bryce, Higbee's later lines of glassware. Also characteristic of this period are the small salvers and nick nacks (mistakenly referred to as children's items), as well as an abundance of bowls of all shapes and sizes. There may even be smaller stemmed rose bowls like those found in the Bonair pattern. *Beautiful Lady* is one of many patterns that cannot be documented by company catalogs. If it were not for Butler Brothers assortments, we might have no idea it was manufactured by Bryce, Higbee & Company.

A *Beautiful Lady* half-gallon water pitcher appears in the "Big 'Beauty' Jug Asst." offered by Butler Brothers in October 1908, but it may have been previously-manufactured stock and not produced by J. B. Higbee. The other pitchers in the assortment are Paris 1900 and *Feathered Medallion*. Though the smaller pitcher was classified as a quart size, the capacity is only twenty-four ounces.

Beautiful Lady 8.25" square compote, $25–$30; quart pitcher, $35–$40.

Items Noted:
almond tray, one side up, 5.5"
bowl, collar base, round and square, various depths and sizes
bowl, flat, oblong, deep, 7.5" and 10"
butter, covered, two base styles:
  flanged with tiny scallops, 7.25"
  not flanged with large scallops, 6.25"
cake basket, 9.5"–10" l.
celery tray, 11"
celery vase, collar base, 6" h.
compote, jelly, high-foot, round, square, 5" w.
compote, jelly, high-foot, slightly cupped, 4" w.
compote, high-foot, round, square, 8" w.
cream
cruet, stopper #3
nick nack, high-foot, 6.5" w.
nick nack tray, collar base, 6"–12"
pitcher, quart, half-gallon
plate, collar base, round, 5.5"–12"
plate, square, 7"
rose bowl, high-foot, 7.5" h. with 3.75" opening
salver, 6", 9"
spoon
sugar, covered, inner ledge
vase, pedestal, cupped, flared, straight, various sizes
wafer stand, 6.5" w.
wine, 4" h.

Beautiful Lady 6.5" nick nacks (note the pattern faces differently on each), $25–$30 each; 8" round compote, $20–$25.

Beautiful Lady 10" cake basket, $45–$50; 9" bowl, $20–$25; 9" salver, $40–$45.

Reproductions and Look-alikes: No reproductions known. Similar to Cambridge's No. 2579, the most notable difference being the eight-pointed stars found in that design. *Beautiful Lady* contains rays in the shape of a fan instead. The pattern could also be mistaken for Westmoreland's little-known No. 98 berry set. The fan motif is very similar, but the rest is quite different.

No. 98. 9 in. Berry

Westmoreland Specialty Company's No. 98 bowl shown in the company's 1905 catalog is clearly based on *Beautiful Lady*.

Cambridge Glass Company's No. 2579 pattern (right) is similar to *Beautiful Lady* (left).

Beveled Cube and Diamond, year unknown

References: SB, February 1891; BB, May 1898
Colors: clear offered in jobber catalogs

Beveled Cube and Diamond tumbler illustrated in a May 1898 Butler Brothers catalog.

A tumbler is shown in Butler Brothers fall 1899 and spring 1900 Mission catalogs in "Our 'LEADER' 3c Asst." and noted as "Daisy Pattern Tumbler," though it is first noted in "Our 'Furore' 5-cent Assortment" in May 1898 listed as "rich table tumbler." Butler Brothers is not known for their use of OMNs, but they do correctly include them in Bryce, Higbee assortments on occasion. This tumbler appears to be shown much earlier in a February 1891 Spelman Brothers tumbler assortment with Bryce, Higbee's Persian pattern, but the illustration is not as detailed and the cubes and central row of diamonds are shown plain with no diamond point.

Pottery and Glassware Reporter mentioned a butter dish named Daisy in January 1885, but it is unlikely that it was the same pattern as this tumbler called "Daisy" by Butler Brothers. The journal makes no mention of additional items and the first appearance of this tumbler is six years after the trade journal quote.

The name *Beveled Cube and Diamond* has been assigned to this tumbler, since it has not been shown in any reference, to the author's knowledge. It may have been called Daisy by Bryce, Higbee, but until proof is found, the temporary descriptive name should prove adequate. Like the *Scroll* dish, it is possible there are two versions of this tumbler, one with diamond point in the pattern and another without.

Reproductions and Look-alikes: Unknown.

Bijou, 1888

References: BH, undated; *P&GR*, 7/12/1888; BB, September 1889; SB, February 1891; JBH, c. 1917 & NM, undated (rectangular dish only—see below)
Colors: clear; possibly amber and blue (mug)

> The firm [Bryce, Higbee & Co.] have now ready no less than three entirely new lines of tableware for the fall trade. The first of these, which they have styled the "Bijou," is a most elegant one, and it comprises several different varieties of shapes and patterns, which enhances its merits as a selling line considerably. It is very extensive, including orange bowls, (three different styles) berry dishes, casseroles, footed and unfooted, pickles, salad dishes, mugs, bread dishes and plates (shell pattern) ice cream and berry sets, (4 kinds), pitchers, celeries and several more pieces. The patterns are altogether original, the glass bright and clear and the line is entirely out of the common run of things and is sure of a big sale.

Bijou half-gallon pitcher, \$50–\$55; 6.75" low-foot compote, \$25–\$30.

The researcher certainly is grateful for this lengthy description of Bryce, Higbee's Bijou from the trade journal *Pottery and Glassware Reporter.* The quote is extremely important because it establishes that the Bijou line consists of different patterns that were once thought to be items from other lines. Note the report states that Bijou "comprises several different varieties of shapes and patterns" and the specific mention of shell pattern plates.

The Higbys include the shell-shaped items (they refer to them as fans) with the *Prism Bars* pattern, but we can now rightfully place them with Bijou. Kamm erroneously credits the Greensburg Glass Company with Bijou and reprints three catalog pages showing the pattern in *An Eighth Pattern Glass Book.* Plate 54 is especially notable because it illustrates some of the different patterns, which were meant to be part of the line. For detailed discussion see page 48 (pages from Kamm 8.)

Bijou (*Star & Pinwheel*) 10" ruffled bowl, \$40–\$45.

A 10" shell-shaped Bijou plate is first noted in Butler Brothers 1888 Santa Claus catalog. The September 1889 issue offers a Bijou mug, 7" and 10" shell-shaped plates,

Bijou 6.75" low-foot compote, \$25–\$30; *Shell* 8.5" pickle dish, \$15–\$20; *Shell* 12" oblong bowl, \$45–\$50. Though these items seem quite dissimilar at first glance, they do incorporate the same motifs. Note the fan design on the compote is used to separate the large shells on the oblong bowl.

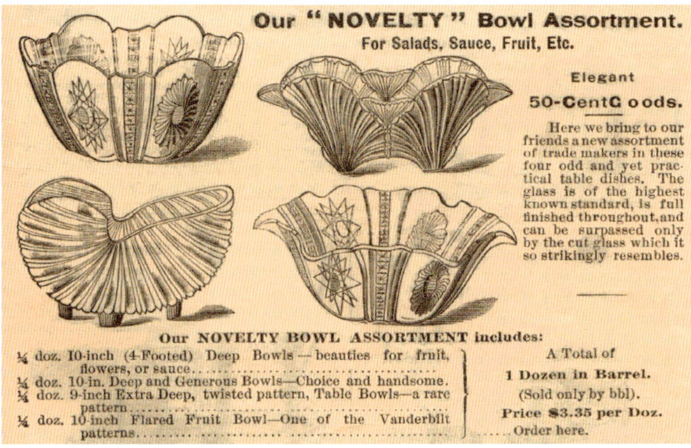

Our "NOVELTY" Bowl Assortment.
For Salads, Sauce, Fruit, Etc.

Elegant
50-CentG oods.

Here we bring to our friends a new assortment of trade makers in these four odd and yet practical table dishes. The glass is of the highest known standard, is full finished throughout, and can be surpassed only by the cut glass which it so strikingly resembles.

Our NOVELTY BOWL ASSORTMENT includes:

¼ doz. 10-inch (4-Footed) Deep Bowls — beauties for fruit, flowers, or sauce........
¼ doz. 10-in. Deep and Generous Bowls—Choice and handsome.
¼ doz. 9-inch Extra Deep, twisted pattern, Table Bowls—a rare pattern........
¼ doz. 10-inch Flared Fruit Bowl—One of the Vanderbilt patterns........

A Total of
1 Dozen in Barrel.
(Sold only by bbl).
Price \$3.35 per Doz.
.....Order here.

Assortment of large Bijou bowls, Butler Brothers, summer 1891. Note the different patterns represented, yet all were part of the same line.

and a small shell-shaped sauce dish. This particular catalog also shows an interesting grouping titled "Our 'Novelty' Bowl Assortment" and comprising large bowls of three different patterns, which are very likely the different styles of Bijou orange bowls mentioned in the trade journal quote. One bowl is the same shell design shown on plate 54 of Kamm 8, one is shaped like a full nautilus shell on stubby feet, and the third is an imitation cut pattern consisting of stars and pinwheels. It incorporates the small eight-pointed star motif found in many other known Bryce, Higbee patterns including Grand, Melrose, Admiral, Oregon, as well as attributed patterns such as *Chain* and the *Boat Covered Dish*. The design on the nautilus shell bowl is the same wide, convex rib separated by two flutes found on the shell patterned bowl shown as part of the Bijou line in Bryce, Higbee's catalog.

The Bijou line is a perfect example of why OMNs should be used, for the seemingly-descriptive AKA *Fan With Acanthus Leaf* does not apply to each item in the set. As noted in the discussion of Bijou in chapter 4 on page 48, the Bryce, Higbee catalog pages differentiate the separate patterns with initials. Calling all these different designs Bijou, as the company intended, might prove confusing to some, though it would be even more confusing referring to them by the AKA *Fan With Acanthus Leaf*. In order to keep the integrity of the OMN, descriptive words can be added to the items that differ. *Bijou Shell* can be used for items with the shell motif, *Bijou Fenced Diamond* for the design on the rectangular sauce dish, *Bijou Star and Pinwheel* for the ornate imitation cut glass pattern, and *Bijou Nautilus* for the full-figured nautilus shell bowl. These variations are noted in the list of items. Items with the standard fan and acanthus leaf motif are given no additional description here.

The shallow rectangular dish labeled "Bijou 8 in. oblong dish" in the J. B. Higbee *General Catalogue* was part of the original Bijou line as well, though it is not shown in the pages Kamm chose to reprint. It also appears in an undated New Martinsville Glass Manufacturing Company catalog as "No. 518—Bijou 8 inch Candy Tray" and has been seen in Butler Brothers catalogs as late as 1924. There are three versions that are slightly different. The following details are best observed when viewed from the top looking straight down at the dish.

> Version 1: The wide vertical ribs on the edge are convex and there are two points between each rib. Observe the star pattern in the base. The stars in each corner have the point closest to the edge slightly cut off.
>
> Version 2: The wide vertical ribs on the edge are concave and there is one point between each rib. Observe the star pattern in the base. The stars in each corner have the point closest to the edge slightly cut off. This tray has been seen with J. B. Higbee's bee mark.

Version 3: The wide vertical ribs on the edge are concave and there is one point between each rib. Observe the star pattern in the base. The stars in each corner do not have the point closest to the edge cut off at all.

Version 1 is the earliest and is clearly illustrated in Butler Brothers catalogs dating as early as September 1895. On the example in the author's collection, there is a molded ⅝" circle on the inside center. Lola and Wayne Higby state that Bijou trays with this circle are reproductions, but give absolutely no evidence to support their observation. The flat Mirror bowls with star-patterned bases, the Capitola pickle jar, and the Persian sugar bowl also have this. This circle is merely a mark left from the use of a plunger vent and is by no means any indication of a reproduction. The purpose of the plunger vent is to allow trapped air to escape during pressing. It is also used to assist in releasing the set glass from the plunger after it is molded. This version appears to have been made only by Bryce, Higbee.

Version #2 or #3 is first noted in the Butler Brothers mid-winter 1909 (December 1908 to January 1909) catalog. The edge visibly has concave panels, but the star pattern in the base is not drawn clearly. This is the version shown in J. B. Higbee's *General Catalogue*. The same illustration appears in an undated New Martinsville catalog. As in the Butler Brothers illustrations, it is difficult to see the star pattern in the base. Though listed in catalogs as 8", the dish actually measures about 7.5" long.

The design on the Bijou rectangular dish seems to have nothing in common with any of the other motifs included in the line, but more than casual inspection reveals that the vertical design on the edge of version 1 actually matches the *Bijou Shell* items. This is especially evident when the contours of the edges are viewed from above. Note that this is the earliest version, and was most likely produced only by Bryce, Higbee. They were often sold as candy trays and despite the dimension given in catalogs, actually measure closer to 7.75". Since this is also a variation of the Bijou pattern, it might be more descriptively called *Bijou Rib and Star*.

The items of Bijou with the fan and acanthus leaf design actually have quite an Egyptian look about them. This variation of the pattern is labeled "(C.)" in Bryce, Higbee's catalog. It is unknown what designation that abbreviation stands for. The catalog illustration of the table set varies slightly from actual items found, especially in the details on the domed bases. Interestingly, lids employ the identical ribbed design found on the *Prism Bars* pattern. A March 1891 catalog of the American Merchandise Company, a New York City jobber, offered Bijou mugs in assorted colors. None have been found, but if they truly do exist the colors would certainly be amber and blue.

Bijou is a French word meaning "a small exquisitely wrought trinket."

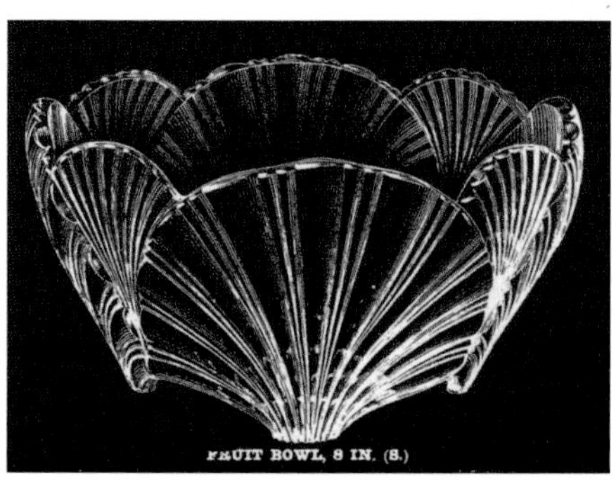

Bijou (F.D.) *Fenced Diamond* sauce dish, Bijou (S.) *Shell* fruit bowl, and Bijou (C.) butter from an undated Bryce, Higbee company catalog. Note the different abbreviations after each item.

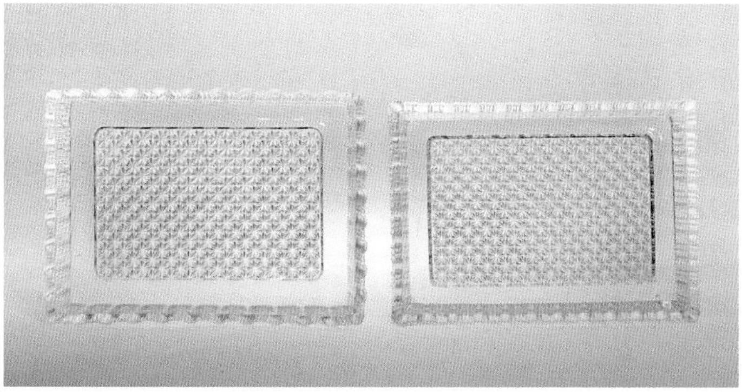

Bijou (*Rib & Star*) rectangular dishes, $15–$20 each. The dish at left is by Bryce, Higbee (note the convex ribs), whereas the smaller dish at right is by J. B. Higbee (note concave ribs) and is marked with the bee trademark.

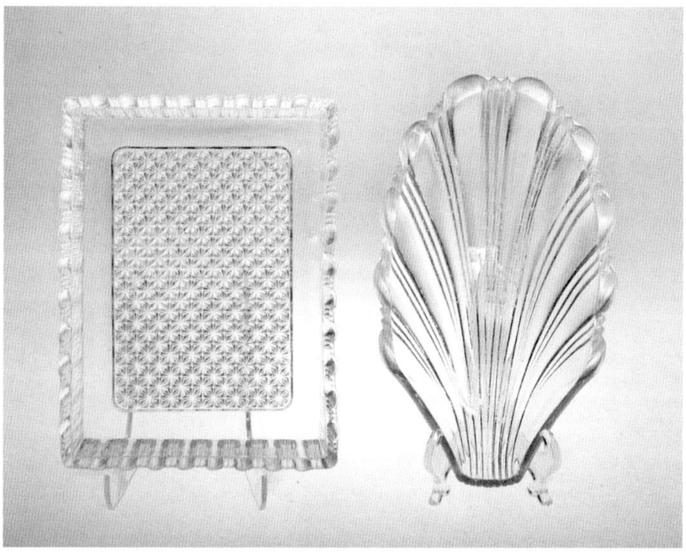

Comparison of Bijou (*Rib & Star*) dish with the Bijou (*Shell*) pickle. Notice the contour of the edges is the same.

Items Noted:
berry bowl, deep, 9"
berry dessert, deep, 5"
berry dessert, *Shell*, shallow, four feet, 4.5"
berry bowl, *Shell*, flared, four feet, 10"
bowl, *Shell*, shallow, small (size unknown)
bowl, *Nautilus*, four stubby feet,10"
bowl, *Shell*, ruffled, four feet, 10"
bowl, *Shell*, oblong, four feet, 9" x 12"
bowl, *Star and Pinwheel*, deep, 9"
bowl, *Star and Pinwheel*, ruffled, 10"
butter, covered, 6" w.
celery vase, footed
compote, low-foot, open, shallow, 6.75"
cream
dish, *Rib and Star*, rectangular, 7.5"–7.75"
fruit bowl, *Shell*, four feet, 8"
fruit bowl, flared, 10"
mug
pickle dish, *Shell*, 8.5"
pitcher, half-gallon
plate, *Shell*, 7", 10"
sauce dish, *Fenced Diamond*, rectangular, sloped sides, 7"
spoon
sugar, covered, inner ledge

The 6.75" low-foot compote in the listing has a very shallow ledge and most likely was made to accept a lid. No high-foot compotes have been seen, but like the low-foot compotes, they should exist in various sizes (covered and uncovered) as well. Kamm mentions a salt shaker, tumbler, and flat cake plate. Since she was not aware of the variations in the pattern, those items may employ the fan and acanthus leaf motif. This is a tenuous assumption, however, because Kamm can be rather inconsistent in her classifications and reporting.

Reproductions and Look-alikes: No reproductions known. The author has encountered stemware of two sizes with a design very much like *Bijou Shell*, but with rayed, octagonal bases. Their origin is not known, but these stems were not made by Bryce, Higbee.

Bonair, c. 1903

References: *G&PW*, May 1903; BB, spring 1903; MW fall and winter 1903–1904; NMPL, 1921 (covered butter only)
Colors: clear, clear with ruby stain (goblet known)

> Mr. R. G. West, representing Bryce, Higbee & Co., 623 Smithfield St., Pittsburg, Pa., spent a week at the Palmer House up to the 23rd of April.
>
> Mr. West carried an entirely new line of pressed glass table ware, which he was presenting to the western trade for the first time. The line consists of many original designs and shapes, and is proving a "winner."
>
> Everyone has heard of Bryce, Higbee & Co.'s Bonair, and Mr. West had his entire line tastefully arranged, showing off each piece to the best advantage.

Bonair cake basket, $40–$45; 5" square bowl, $12–$15; 8" square compote, $25–$30.

This enticing quote from the May 1903 issue of *Glass and Pottery World* gives an undocumented pattern name, but, unfortunately, still leaves us with some questions. It is not clear if the entry is describing one or two separate lines of glassware. The reporter may be saying that Mr. West brought an entirely new line (without giving its name) to show along with the well-known Bonair. It is also possible the reporter may be talking about one pattern, the new Bonair, implying that everyone but those in the west has heard of it, or he may be saying everyone has heard of it now that the western trade has become acquainted with it. The use of a separate paragraph to first mention the Bonair name makes it all the more confusing. If the reporter is referring to only one pattern, Bonair probably made its debut at the annual Pittsburgh glass show in January 1903 where new spring patterns were typically shown for the first time.

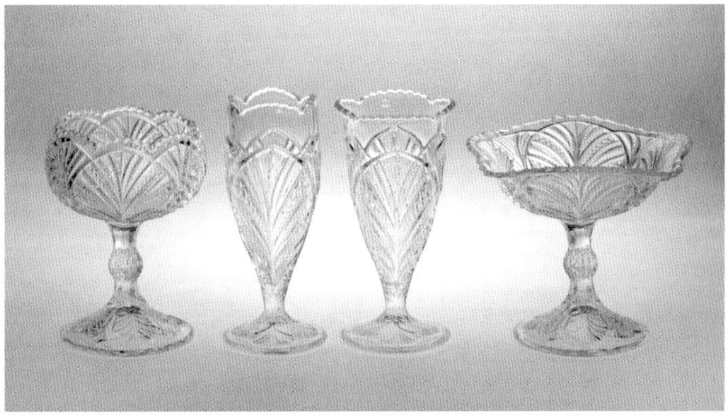

Bonair stemmed rose bowl or footed jelly, $25–$30; 6" and 6.25" vases, $15–$20 each; 5.75" square jelly compote, $18–$20.

It was a great pleasure to discover that the pattern known as *Palm Leaf Fan* is actually Bryce, Higbee's Bonair. A berry set, jelly compote, and water bottle are shown in Montgomery Ward catalog No. 72 for fall and winter 1903–1904, all labeled Bonair. The same items are also shown in the company's catalog No. 73 for fall and winter 1904–1905. Bonair first appears in Butler Brothers spring 1903 catalog in "Our 'Sunrise' 5-cent Assortment."

Bonair 10.5" plate, $30–$35.

Bonair 8" bowl, $20–$25; individual salt, $10–$12; cruet, $35–$40; nick nack, $25–$30.

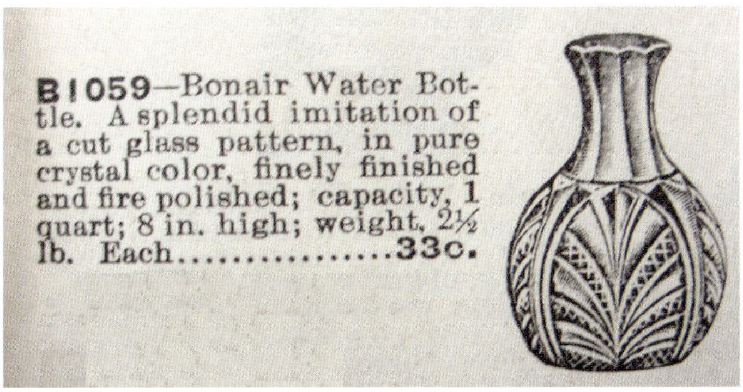

Bonair berry set, water bottle, and jelly compote, Montgomery Ward catalog No. 72, fall and winter 1903–1904.

Small salvers, wafer stands, and nick nacks are erroneously referred to as toy glassware made for children and are not too difficult to find. Nick nacks were tooled from the same mould used to make wafer stands and small salvers. The wafer stand is flat, has a round edge, and is smaller than the salver. The salver has an upturned rim and a scalloped edge. Both forms have small pointed teeth on the edge.

The Bonair stopper contains motifs found in the pattern and was used with cruets of other patterns including Anona, Paris 1900, *Fine Cut and Fan*, *Beautiful Lady*, *Feathered Medallion*, *Ten-Pointed Star*, and Madora. It can be thought of as a "universal" stopper used by the company.

Bonair must have been quite popular in its day, for it was made in a vast number of shapes and is readily found today. Bowls were made in a seemingly endless variety of shapes, sizes, and depths. A 6.25" Bonair vase consistently appears in Butler Brothers "New Challenge" assortment for about three years among items in J. B. Higbee's Alpha pattern. The vase was offered alone as well. By mid-summer 1911 it was replaced by a vase of the same size and shape in J. B. Higbee's Laurel pattern. The late, extended, and continuous offering of this vase implies production by J. B. Higbee from a mould acquired from Bryce, Higbee. Indeed, many of them lack the crisp detail found on other items and appear to have been made from a well-used mould. A Bonair butter dish is on a price list from the New Martinsville Glass Manufacturing Company enumerating items made from moulds acquired from J. B. Higbee. It has not been seen in any New Martinsville catalogs, and it is not known what became of the mould.

Bonair is yet another French name used by the company. It means "gentle, courteous, and complaisant."

Items Noted:

almond tray, one side up, 5.5"
bowls, round, square, oval, various depths and sizes
butter, covered
cake basket, 9.5" l.
celery tray
celery vase
compote, jelly, high-foot, round, square, 5" w.
compote, high-foot, round, square, 8" w.
cream
cruet, stopper #3

goblet
mug
mustard or horseradish, high domed lid, barrel-shaped, 6" h.
nick nack, high-foot, 5.75", 6.5" l.
nick nack tray, collar base, 6", 10.75" l.
pitcher, quart, half-gallon
plate, collar base, round, various sizes from approximately 5.5"–12"
plate, square, 7"
rose bowl, collar base
rose bowl, high-foot, 5.75" h.
(may have been intended as a footed jelly)
rose bowl, high-foot, 7.5" h.
salt, individual
salver, 5", 6.5", 9.5"
shaker, salt and pepper
spoon
sugar, covered, inner ledge
vase, 5.5", 6.25"
vase, swirled stem, 9", 9.75"
wafer stand, 5.75" w.
water bottle
wine

Reproductions and Look-alikes: None known. Be aware that Tidal has been confused for Bonair by Kamm and others.

Bowline, c. early– to mid–1890s

References: BB, September 1895; TE, spring & summer 1896
Colors: clear

The only known reference in the glass literature for this design is Arthur G. Peterson's *Glass Salt Shakers*, shown as photo H on page 23. Peterson assigns the name *Bowline* and notes "Corners resemble a line of bow ties. Sides have concave panels." Since he was the first to photograph and adequately name the pattern, the designation *Bowline* is endorsed until the OMN is discovered.

This is a pattern few collectors know about. The author discovered items in this design many years ago and noted their similarity to other Bryce, Higbee patterns. After much study and comparison, it was determined to be an undocumented Bryce, Higbee product. As strong as the conviction was, any bit of period proof was still lacking. A connection finally made itself known. *Bowline* is shown in a September 1895 Butler Brothers catalog in "Our 'Sparkling Jewel' Assortment" along with items of Ethol. In the same catalog is a *Bowline* shaker offered for 39¢ per dozen. Interestingly, the identical image is shown in the spring and summer 1896 catalog of T. Eaton Co. Limited of Toronto, Canada. Here the shakers were retailed for 5¢ each.

Bowline is the result of retooled moulds of the Worlds pattern. The underlying pattern is identical to Worlds with the addition of convex spheres. Pedestals of compotes and cake salvers are attached by glass wafers and are also the same as used on Worlds, minus the base pattern. *Bowline* obviously came after Worlds and it is believed to have been introduced sometime between 1893 and 1894. For more information on retooled moulds, see page 85.

Bowline, like Worlds, is very heavy, brilliant, and well made from good quality glass. Since this is the first time the pattern is presented in an EAPG reference book as a Bryce, Higbee product, only time will tell how common or uncommon it is. As the discussion in chapter 7 indicates, at least some of the *Bowline* moulds were later retooled to become the Surprise pattern (formerly known as *Paneled Diamond Point*), so it likely was not popular. The known

Bowline 8" high-foot covered compote, $100–$125; 8.25" high-foot open compote, $60–$65.

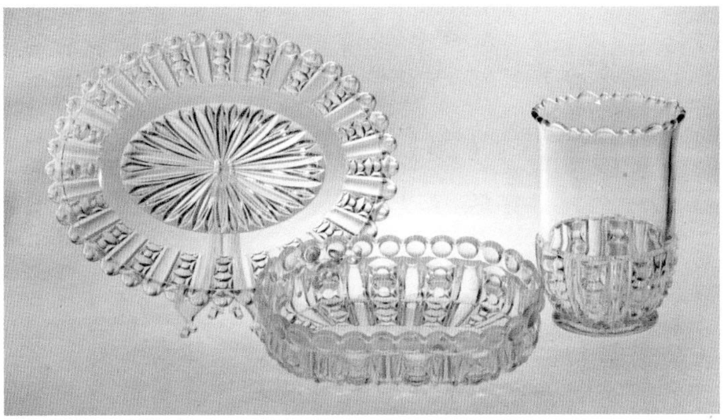

Bowline 10" oval bread plate, $45–$50; 8" oblong bowl, $40–$45; celery vase, $50–$55.

The "Sparkling Jewel" assortment offered by Butler Brothers in September 1895 included two compotes and a bowl in Bryce, Higbee's *Bowline*.

forms imply it was made in a full line and, theoretically, any item found in Worlds should be found in *Bowline*.

Items Noted: *This list includes actual items found and those shown in the September 1895 Butler Brothers catalog.*

bowl, round, flat, point and scallop edge, 7.25"
bowl, oblong, scalloped edge, 8"
bread plate, oval, scalloped edge, 10"
celery vase, point and scallop edge, 6.5" h.
compote, high-foot, covered (scallops are on edge of lid), 5", 8" w.
compote, high-foot, open, point and scallop edge, 6", 8.25" w.
salver, scalloped gallery edge, 10"
shaker, salt and pepper

Reproductions and Look-alikes: None known.

Bowline 10" salver, $125–$150.

Butterfly,
late 1880 for the 1881 market

References: *AP&GR*, 11/25/1880 & 1/6/1881
Colors: clear, clear with ground bands, clear with engraving

Bryce, Higbee's Butterfly has been wrongly attributed to Ætna Glass and Manufacturing Company of Bellaire, Ohio for many years. This stems from a trade journal quote from late 1883 briefly mentioning a Butterfly tableware pattern made by Ætna. No illustration or description was given. *American Pottery and Glassware Reporter* mentions Butterfly on November 25, 1880, noting it is one of Bryce, Higbee's newest patterns. Though no illustration is included, the reporter describes in detail some key elements in the January 6, 1881, issue:

> A perfectly plain set of ware of the "Butterfly" pattern is taken, and the bands are ground on each piece, giving the effect of etched ware, with the difference in favor of the grinding that the bands are uniform in appearance and accurate in outline—something difficult if not impossible of accomplishment in acid etching. The set has not been named yet, but is worthy the attention of the trade. To do this work a special machine has been constructed, which does its duty rapidly and well.

Note the description of the grinding often found on the pattern. Remember, the term etched refers to what most collectors now call "frosted." The clouded areas found on the Butterfly pattern are rougher than acid etching and are clearly ground when observed under magnification. The mention of the special machine used to impart the grinding is significant. John Higbee applied for a patent for such a device on November 8, 1880, and the patent was granted on January 11, 1881. These dates directly coincide with the trade journal descriptions of Butterfly. See page 80 for patent illustration and discussion of etching.

It is interesting that the journal states the set had not been named at the time of the report, so it is possible that Bryce, Higbee called the pattern something other than Butterfly. Unless documentation to the contrary is found,

Butterfly frosted cream, $50–$55; frosted shaker, $35–$40; plain shaker, $30–$35; plain mustard, $40–$45; plain butter, $55–$60.

Butterfly 8" plain covered compote, $60–$65.

TOP TO BOTTOM | Popular designs were freely borrowed and produced in different mediums. Haviland & Company's Papillion cup and saucer and a silver-plated mug from an early 1880s Montgomery Ward catalog illustrate that Bryce, Higbee's Butterfly pattern was clearly inspired by such wares.

it will be believed that Butterfly is the OMN, for this is the only report mentioning this discrepancy.

Additional evidence that Butterfly was made by Bryce, Higbee is the fact that many of the mould shapes are the same as Alaric, with the substitution of butterfly handles and finials, of course. This includes the butter dish, compotes, mustard, and salt and pepper shakers. The bodies of the shakers are, incidentally, also the same shape as Homestead. Since trade journals mention Butterfly was a full line of tableware, there must be some items in the set, such as salvers and bowls, that do not have the distinctive butterfly handles. Indeed, small footed bowls are known that are the same shape as Alaric, but are ground on the plain area at the bottom of the bowl. Presumably the Butterfly salver would have the same mould shape as the Alaric salver as well.

The idea of implementing a full-figured butterfly for handles was also done on silver-plate and porcelain in the same era. Haviland & Company's Papillion very well could have been the inspiration for Bryce, Higbee's creation in glassware.

Items Noted: *Butterfly has not been found in any period catalogs, so this listing is by no means complete.*

bowl, footed, 4" w.
butter, covered, footed, 6" w.
celery vase, 8.5" h.
compote, high-foot, covered, 6", 7", 8" w.
cream, two styles: open butterfly handle, solid butterfly handle
mustard, covered
pickle dish, oval
pickle jar, flat, glass lid, 4.25" h.
shaker, salt and pepper
spoon, 5" h. x 3.5" w.
sugar, covered, inner ledge, footed, 5" h. x 4.75" w.

Reproductions and Look-alikes: No reproductions known. Items in Alaric are sometimes confused for Butterfly, no doubt due to the strange AKA *Butterfly Ears* some use for Alaric. This inept name implies that all pieces of Alaric have handles or "ears," but they do not.

Capitola,
late 1879 or early 1880

References: *AP&GR*, 2/19/1880; *C&GJ*, 3/4/1880; SB, February 1882; GS, 1885; FP&W, April 1886
Colors: clear, light amber (6" plate noted by Ruth Webb Lee)

Though Capitola is first mentioned in February 1880, it is not clear if the pattern was new for that year. It appears to have been one of the first patterns introduced by Bryce, Higbee & Company when they began producing glass in late September 1879, but this was likely targeted for the spring 1880 market. A pleasantly lengthy review of the recently built Bryce, Higbee factory appeared in *American Pottery and Glassware Reporter* on May 6, 1880. In part it states:

> Their latest novelty is an imitation of engraved ware, which would require no great stretch of the imagination to be mistaken for the real thing. They are now making a full line of this ware, and have more orders for it than they can fill.

It is worthy to note this was before the company's engraving shop was up and running, so it would make sense for them to offer an imitation of the desirable engraved wares. Capitola remained a good seller throughout the year and is still mentioned in early December 1880, described as a full line in a "clever representation of engraved ware."

Assortments and individual items of Bryce, Higbee glassware offered by French, Potter & Wilson in the April 1886 issue of *American Potter & Illuminator* have confirmed the author's long-held belief that Capitola is the pattern collectors have misnamed *Barley*. Though the Chicago-based jobber consistently used the name "Capital" throughout the catalog, there is no doubt this is Bryce, Higbee's Capitola. In an assortment of table sets, another pattern name was slightly altered as well; here an Ida sugar bowl appears as "Ada." The similarity in names is obvious.

Capitola 5" low-foot compote with plain edge, $12–$15 each; spoon with plain edge, $20–$25.

Capitola covered pickle jar, $50–$55; butter, $40–$45; 4.5" bowl with scalloped edge, $8–$10; 5" footed fruit dessert with scalloped edge, $12–$15.

Capitola 8" pickle dish with scalloped edge, $18–$20; 11.5" oval bread plate with scalloped edge, $30–$35; 4.25" footed fruit dessert with scalloped edge, $10–$12; 7.5" low-foot compote with scalloped edge, $25–$30.

Capitola 8", 6.5", and 7.5" covered compotes with scalloped edge, $60–$65; $45–$50; $55–$60.

Early offering of Capitola by Spelman Brothers, February 1882. The unidentified plain goblet (with engraving) appears in an 1881 patent illustration assigned to John B. Higbee (see page 80).

Capitola and Ida sugar bowls offered in a wholesale assortment, April 1886. Note how the pattern names were slightly altered.

Capitola is quite typical of the fanciful, botanically incorrect engravings that were enormously popular during the Victorian era. The low-relief molded design has a frosted appearance and at first glance is easily mistaken for engraving. It does not represent barley by any stretch of the imagination, so, since the OMN is now known, its use is highly encouraged. Most sources list the pattern as maker unknown or wrongly attribute it to Campbell, Jones & Company. This error is based on a wheelbarrow with a leafy design patented by James Dalzell on January 3, 1882. Close inspection reveals that the patterns are only similar to each other.

Capitola is sometimes found with a weak impression. Many believe this is due to old, worn moulds, but there are other factors that can cause this. Moulds had to be scoured and buffed periodically and, if not perfectly clean, could impart weak impressions. Poor mould design, insufficient pressure exerted in the pressing process, and temperature of the mould at the time of pressing are additional factors.

The Capitola cream pitcher and spoon holder have each been noted in three distinct variations, and the pickle dish is found with and without handles. The handles are the same intricate scroll shape as the same forms in the *Chain* pattern and are quite reminiscent of handles found on Homestead. Lids are found with the design molded on the inner or outer surface. Nearly all items can be found with a beaded, scalloped edge as well as a plain edge with the beaded scallops molded into the glass on or near the rim. Items with scalloped edges are earlier and are first seen in jobber catalogs in 1882. The plain-edged items are first noted beginning in 1885. After that year, Capitola items with scalloped edges no longer appear. Whether or not the company classified the plain-edged items as a separate line with an alteration in name is not known.

Ruth Webb Lee notes a 6" plate in light amber, but does not definitively state whether the plate has a scalloped or plain edge. Blue should also exist since a spring 1886 B. Sommers catalog offered plain-edged 6" plates in "assorted colors." The time frame is also correct for canary, though Bryce, Higbee's production of the color was rather limited.

Collectors and researchers once believed that any variation of a particular pattern indicated production by more than one factory. Although this may be the case with some patterns, it is not always true. Despite the variations noted, it is very unlikely that any factory other than Bryce, Higbee produced Capitola. It can be deduced that the pattern was quite popular, for items are in good supply despite being well over a century old.

Capitola is a city in California on the coast of Monterey Bay. The significance of Bryce, Higbee using this name is not known, but at least one other pattern by the company, Alameda, also references the state of California.

Items Noted:

bowl, flat, round, plain edge, scalloped edge, 3.5" to 8"
bowl, flat, oval, plain edge, scalloped edge 7.5", 8.5", 9.5", 10"
butter, covered, plain edge, scalloped edge
celery vase, stemmed, scalloped edge with no beads
compote, high-foot, covered, plain edge, scalloped edge, 6.5", 7.5", 8.5"
compote, high-foot, open, plain edge, scalloped edge, 8.5"–10.25"
compote, low-foot, covered, plain edge, scalloped edge, 6.5", 7.5", 8.5"
compote, low-foot, plain edge, scalloped edge, open, 4"–8"
cream, three styles:
  flared rim with three points
  straight rim, smooth edge, plain handle
  straight rim, smooth edge, textured handle
goblet
pickle dish, oval, scalloped edge, handled, 8.25"
pickle dish, oval, plain edge, no handles (also handled)
pickle jar, glass lid, flat, cylindrical
pitcher, half-gallon
plate, plain edge, scalloped edge, 6"
plate, bread, oval, plain edge, scalloped edge, 11"–11.5"
salver, plain edge, scalloped edge, 8"–10"
spoon, three styles, 3.5" w.:
  scalloped edge
  plain edge with beads in arches below rim
  plain edge with row of beads on thick rim
sugar, covered, three styles:
  plain edge, inner rim
  plain edge, no inner rim
  scalloped edge, inner rim
wine

Reproductions and Look-alikes: No reproductions known. The pattern on the wheelbarrow dishes previously noted is only similar to Capitola. They are not the same pattern.

Chain, c. late 1879 or early 1880s

References: SB, c. 1885
Colors: clear

A wine glass in the pattern known as *Chain* is shown in a circa 1885 Spelman Brothers assortment with other Bryce, Higbee products. Like Butler Brothers and other jobbers, Spelman Brothers offered unopened assortments put together by the glass factories, so all items shown in an assortment should have come from the same company. It must be noted, however, that Spelman Brothers catalogs are not infallible, and errors have been spotted in a few assortments from other companies.

There is no conflicting documentation for *Chain*, and there has never been any attribution for the pattern. Its maker has been unknown since it was first classified by Ruth Webb Lee over eighty years ago. I have thoroughly studied the pattern and have absolutely no doubt it is a product of Bryce, Higbee & Company.

When examined closely it becomes apparent that *Chain* shares many similarities with other known Bryce, Higbee products. The handles on bread plates are the

Chain 7" flat bowls, $20–$25 each; 8" high-foot covered compote, $55–$60; 8" low-foot compote, $25–$30; 9" open high-foot compote, $30–$35.

Chain sugar, $45–$50; 11.5" bread plate, $35–$40; 10.25" oval bowl, $25–$30; spooner, $30–$35.

Chain 10" salver, $45–$50; 5.75" low-foot compote, $15–$20; 9" high-foot compote, $60–$65 (with lid).

same shape as handles on pickle dishes in the Capitola pattern. Nearly identical scroll-shaped handles are found on the New Grand pickle and items of the Homestead pattern as well. The intricate design in the ellipses of the *Chain* pattern is found in the bottom of the Alaric bread tray in a slightly different configuration and is so strikingly like the design in the bases of the full-sized Drum items that the possibility of a common origin cannot be ignored. The same tiny star motif is found in the background design of Grand and New Grand and is found within the Melrose and *Bijou Pinwheel and Star* patterns.

It is risky to attribute a pattern to a certain maker based on shape or design alone, but the risk is lessened when there are other factors to firmly tie it to that company. There are some very important physical features that link *Chain* to Bryce, Higbee. The pedestals of the high-foot compotes and salvers are identical to those of the Capitola and Alfonzo patterns. These items all employ a glass wafer connecting the bowls or plates to the pedestals. The pedestals of the three patterns are not merely similar, they are the same. The ornate star design found in the center of the *Chain* bread plate is also found on flat items of Rival and Royal, but more importantly, it is identical to the central design of the Grand and Melrose bread plates. No other items of Grand or Melrose include that distinctive star design. Not only is it the same design, but close examination indicates that the same valve was used for all three bread plates. A valve is the bottom part of a block mould and is easily reused. The intricate star found in the bottom of flat bowls matches the star found on Butterfly, Alfonzo, and Capitola. In addition, it appears that the mould for the base of the *Chain* sugar bowl was later used to make the Grand sugar bowl.

Like Grand and Capitola, the *Chain* salvers and high-foot, shallow, open compotes have a ridge close to the edge because the bases of the covered compotes (which have a ledge for the lid to sit on) were flattened and hand-tooled to make these items. The usual salver is about 9.5" wide and has the same pedestal (measuring 3.5" tall and 4.5" at the base) found on the 8" high-foot compotes, but a 10" salver has been found with a pedestal measuring 4.25" tall and 4" wide at the base.

Chain is notably quite similar to Bryce, Walker's No. 79 AKA *Chain with Star,* introduced circa 1880. This is very interesting because John Bryce was formerly a partner and designer at Bryce, Walker before becoming a founder, manager, and designer for Bryce, Higbee. *Chain* is undoubtedly one of Bryce, Higbee's earliest patterns. It could very well be Vesta, mentioned in trade journals alongside Capitola with little description during the early part of 1880.

Chain goblet, \$25–\$30; wine, \$20–\$25; 4.5" flat bowl, \$10–\$12.

Items Noted:

bowl, flat, round, 4.5" , 5.75", 7"
bowl, oval, 10.25"
bread plate, handled, 11.5"
butter, covered
compote, high-foot, open, shallow, 9" w.
compote, high-foot, covered, 8", 9" w.
compote low-foot, 5.75", 8"
cream
goblet
pickle dish, oval, 7.5"
salver, 9.5" w., 4.75" h.
salver, 10" w., 5.5" h.
spoon, scalloped edge, 3.75" w.
sugar, covered, inner ledge, 5.5" w.
wine

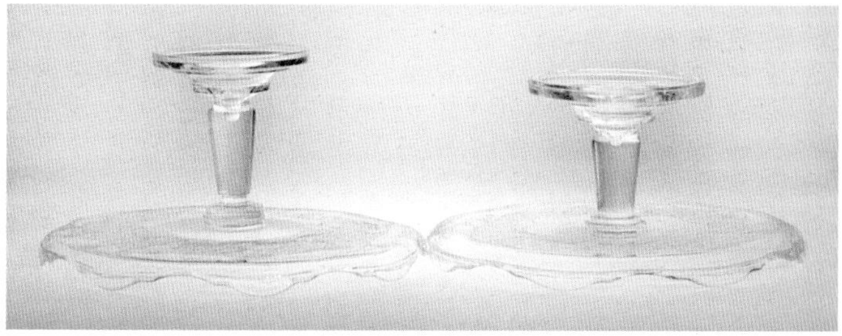

Chain salvers showing different pedestals used. Left, 5.5" h. by 10" w., \$45–\$50; right, 4.75" h. by 9.5" w., \$40–\$45.

Other items likely exist, including a celery vase as well as bowls, compotes, and salvers in other sizes. Lee lists a half-gallon water pitcher, cordial, 7" and 11" plates, but these have not been confirmed. She refers to wine glasses as cordials in many of her classifications. This may also be the case with *Chain*, though she does list both. A quart pitcher may also exist.

Comparison of *Chain* and Grand sugar bases shows that the same mould was likely used.

Reproductions and Look-alikes: No reproductions known. *Chain* is easily confused for Bryce Walker's No. 79 AKA *Chain with Star*. One is clearly a copy of the other, but at this point it is uncertain which pattern came first.

Bryce Brothers' No. 79 AKA *Chain With Star* (right) is extremely similar to Bryce, Higbee's *Chain* (left), but is a bit more ornate.

Charm, 1895

References: *CG&L*, 1/9/1895; MW, spring & summer 1895; BB, September 1895; P&B, 1897
Colors: clear

Charm 7" and 5.5" high-foot covered compotes, \$40–\$45; \$30–\$35; 9" salver, \$40–\$45.

> Bryce, Higbee & Co., sample rooms at 623 Smithfield street, have every reason to feel proud of and satisfied with their new and beautiful pattern for 1895, the "Charm," which is happily and appropriately named. The designer made a palpable hit in it, and it works out well in the brilliant metal used, and is not only original in conception but very artistic in shape and ornamentation...
>
> —*China, Glass & Lamps*, 1/23/1895

Bryce, Higbee's Charm was lauded in many trade journal reports throughout 1895, the year it was introduced. *China, Glass & Lamps* mentions the line consisted of seventy pieces, and a later issue notes: "They have just added to this line five comportiers in sizes 4½, 7, 8, 9 and 10 inches." Charm continued to be favorably mentioned into 1896, indicating that it was a good seller.

Unfortunately, Lola and Wayne Higby misidentify the Charm pattern in their book *Bryce, Higbee and J. B. Higbee Glass*. They give this title to a plain pattern with a star border based on a rather absurd personal observation that "it is a delicate and charming pattern." Charm is actually the pattern that has been known as *Rosette and Palms*.

Charm appears by name in Montgomery Ward Catalog No. 57, spring and summer 1895. This is quite notable because it dispels the theory that this retailer offered only old goods. Several items are shown in Pitkin and Brooks's 1897 and circa 1900 catalogs, all correctly labeled as Charm.

The first appearance of Charm found in Butler Brothers is the September 1895 issue. The 1896 Santa Claus issue shows a "New Pattern Glass 'Table Outfit'" of eighty-five pieces for \$3.38; by fall 1897 it was reduced to \$2.95. After 1900 fewer items are shown. It seems that Charm

Charm 10" bread plate tooled from 8.25" bowl, \$25–\$30; 8.25" bowl, \$25–\$30; 10" cake basket, \$40–\$45.

was being phased out by 1905, for between February and September of that year only a few items (8" oval dish, goblet, tumbler, and half-gallon pitcher) are randomly included in assortments with no consistency. By spring 1906, Charm does not appear at all. There is nothing to prove it was also produced by J. B. Higbee as Lola and Wayne Higby and others have claimed. For more detailed discussion see chapter 8, Production of Bryce, Higbee's Patterns By Other Manufacturers

Charm compotes, cake baskets, and salvers have pedestals attached with a glass wafer. There are three different stems found that originated with other patterns:

1: Worlds, found on compotes and cake baskets. This seems to be the most common pedestal found on Charm.
2: Crescent, sometimes found on compotes and cake baskets. A Charm 9.5" salver, located in Australia, has been seen with this pedestal as well.
3: Mirror, found only on salvers.

Since the pedestals are applied, any combination of top and bottom is within the realm of possibility, i.e.: Charm compotes and cake baskets with plain Mirror stems and Charm salvers with Worlds stems.

There are two styles of Charm compote lids. One is more rounded and higher domed than the other, and, when in place, gives the compote a ball shape. Two styles of bread plates are found as well. One has a star impressed in the center with the pattern placed close to the edge. Its form and center are very much like the Gem bread plate. The other style plate has the pattern placed close to the center. These were flattened from the bowls used to make the scalloped-edge compotes. In the center is a ground and polished circle, slightly raised. This is the area where the pedestals would have been attached to make the open compotes and cake baskets, which were also tooled from the compote bowls. Bowls are also found with the ground and polished circle; they are essentially compotes without the pedestals. The same type of plates and bowls with the ground and polished circle were also made in the *Teardrop Row* pattern.

See Vici for the pattern the Higbys mistakenly call "Charm."

Charm 9" open high-foot compote, \$30–\$35; 7" bowl, \$20–\$25; 8.5" cake basket, \$35–\$40.

Charm wines, \$15–\$20 each; 9.25" bread plate with star center, \$25–\$30; goblet, \$25–\$30; celery vase, \$30–\$35.

Items Noted:

bowl, flat, round with scalloped edge, various depths and sizes from 4.5"
bowl, collar base, round with scalloped edge, various depths and sizes
bowl, flat, oval, 7", 8", 9"
butter, covered
cake basket, 8.5", 9", 10" l.
celery vase, 6.5" h.
compote, high-foot, open, scalloped edge, 5.5", 7", 8", 9", 10" w.
compote, high-foot, covered, plain edge, 5.5", 6.25", 7", 8" w.
compote, low-foot, open, scalloped edge, 9", 10"

Charm items offered by Pitkin & Brooks and Montgomery Ward in the 1890s. Note the use of the OMN and the original term "cake basket." Though the Montgomery Ward illustrations of the cake basket and compote are somewhat crude, the use of two different stems is apparent.

This large assortment of Charm was offered by Butler Brothers in their 1896 Santa Claus catalog. Note the name "New Pattern Glass Table Outfit."

cream
goblet
pickle dish, oval, handled
pitcher, half-gallon
plate, bread, round, scalloped edge, plain center with ground and polished circle, 10"
plate, bread, round, scalloped edge, star center, 9.25"
salver, 8", 9", 10", 11"
shaker, salt and pepper
spoon, scalloped edge
sugar, covered, plain edge
tumbler
wine

Since plates with the ground and polished circle in the center were made from the same mould as the bowls used for the high-foot open compotes, other sizes potentially exist.

Reproductions and Look-alikes: None known.

Three different stems found on footed Charm items that originated with different patterns: (l. to r.), Mirror, Worlds, and Crescent.

Crescent, 1896

References: *CG&L*, 1/9/1896; BB, 1896 Santa Claus; MW, spring & summer 1896; P&B, 1897; SR, 1897; HRE, November 1897
Colors: clear

Bryce, Higbee's Crescent was first mentioned in the January 9, 1896, issue of *China, Glass & Lamps*. On January 15, 1896 the same journal reported:

> The rooms of this old reliable firm [Bryce, Higbee & Co.] at 623 Smithfield street, are filled with good honest conservative patterns, which have held the favor of the trade for years. But the firm are not resting on their laurels and show their new "Crescent" tableware set, a bright star surrounded by the Oriental crescent, which cannot be strictly classed as an imitation cut pattern, but has the roundness and wearing quality of the best pressed shape, with the light diffracting effect of cut glassware.

Other authors have identified the pattern known as *Diamond Point Discs* as Crescent, but that pattern does not fit the above description at all. A pedestal vase that perfectly matches the trade journal descriptions is first noted in Butler Brothers 1896 Santa Claus issue. H. R. Eagle & Company and Pitkin & Brooks both show a pitcher in this pattern labeled Crescent. The same image was used in Sears, Roebuck's 1897 catalog and H. R. Eagle & Company's November 1897 catalog. The woodcut engraving shown by Pitkin & Brooks is larger and more detailed than the others noted, and comparison of other images in their catalogs reveals that they match the illustrations in company catalogs of other glass manufacturers.

Montgomery Ward presented seventeen pieces of Crescent in their spring and summer 1896 and fall and winter 1896–1897 catalogs under the name "Sultana." Montgomery Ward generally used OMNs, but sometimes different names were used for unknown reasons. Again, this is significant because Crescent was a new pattern for spring 1896 and this is when it was first offered by Montgomery Ward.

Crescent 4.5" fruit dessert, $18–$20; 8.5" cake basket, $40–$45; 8" olive tray, $20–$25; 6.5" covered compote, $50–$55.

Crescent oval cream, $25–$30; 9.5" vase, $30–$35; butter dish base, $55–$60 (with lid); 7" square plate, $45–$50.

Crescent 8.5" cake basket, $40–$45; 4.5" fruit dessert, $18–$20; 7" open compote, $40–$45.

Crescent 11.5" celery tray, $25–$30.

CRESCENT, ONE-HALF GALLON.
$2.50 per doz.
Less 10 per cent. in barrel lots of 2 dozen.

Crescent half-gallon pitcher, Pitkin & Brooks catalog, 1897.
Courtesy of the Rakow Research Library, Corning Museum of Glass.

The bowls of cake baskets and compotes are applied to the pedestal bases. The stem contains the star motif found inside each pair of crescents. These same pedestal bases were used for the New Crescent pattern, and, interestingly, are also found on some Charm cake baskets, compotes, and salvers as well. Charm items found with the Crescent-patterned stems were obviously made after 1896.

Crescent was a relatively short lived pattern. By 1898 the moulds were retooled to become New Crescent, the pattern collectors have known as *Diamond Point Discs.* For a discussion of that pattern see New Crescent on page 195.

Items Noted: *This listing is compiled from actual items as well as those shown in jobber and retail catalogs and is by no means complete.*

bowl, flat, scalloped edge, 4.5", 8", 9"
butter, covered
cake basket, 8.5", 10" l.
celery tray, 11.75"
celery vase
compote, high-foot, covered, 6.5", 8" w.
compote, high-foot, open, scalloped edge, 7", 8", 9" w.
cream, oval, 4" l.
cream, table size
fruit dessert, thick collar base, 4.5"
jelly, handled, round, 5.25"
mug
olive dish, oblong, scalloped edge, 8"
pickle dish, boat-shaped, four points on edge, 7.75"
pitcher, half-gallon
plate, round, 6.25"
plate, square, 7"
salver, 9.5", 10.5"
shaker, salt and pepper
spoon, scalloped edge
sugar, covered, plain edge
tumbler
vase, swirled stem, 9.5"

Reproductions and Look-alikes: No reproductions known. McKee's Britannic (1895) is quite similar at first glance, but the areas containing the eight-pointed stars are pointed ovals, whereas on Crescent these areas are round. The star on McKee's Britannic is not as complex. Upon casual inspection, Crescent could be confused for United States Glass Company's No. 15038, Electric (1896). The most obvious difference is that Electric has plain circles between the crescents. These three designs date from the same time period and are clearly based on each other, confirming that a lot of copying went on in the business.

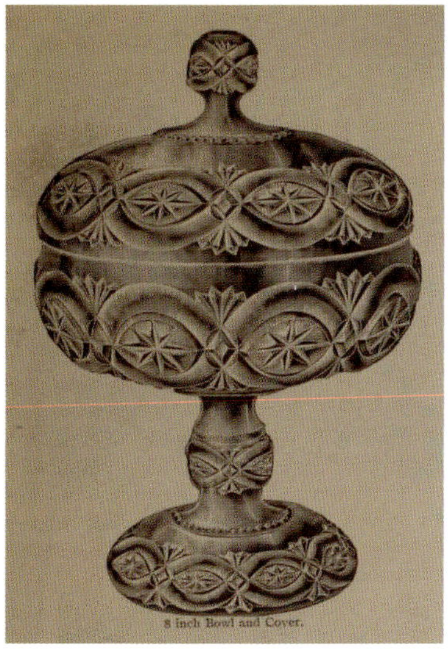

McKee & Brothers' Britannic and United States Glass Company's Electric are similar enough to Bryce, Higbee's Crescent to cause confusion until closely inspected.

Curlicue, c. 1901

References: BB catalog No. 354, 1901
Colors: clear, clear with gold trim

Lola and Wayne Higby refer to this very distinctive pattern as "Surprise" based on fallacious personal beliefs and their misinterpretation of trade journal descriptions. This is not the pattern Bryce, Higbee called Surprise. There are some important details mentioned in trade journal reports which must be noted. Surprise was described as a combination of plain and figured pattern. This terminology is repeatedly used by reporters in the trade journals of this era and refers to a specific type of pattern; namely, one that has a patterned lower section and plain top, or one that contains alternating plain and patterned sections. Patterns described this way in period journals include Heisey's No. 1220 (AKA *Punty Band*) and Riverside's No. 420 (AKA *Box in Box*), which both have plain top sections and patterned bases; Fostoria's Carmen and Indiana Tumbler and Goblet Company's No. 140,

Curlicue 9.75" cake basket, $45–$50; 5.5" plate, $15–$20; 7" shallow bowl, $15–$20; 8" nick nack tray, $20–$25.

Curlicue 9" square bowl, \$25–\$30; 7" shallow bowl, \$15–\$20; 8" compote, \$35–\$40.

Curlicue 9.5" salver, \$45–\$50.

Columbia (AKA *Herringbone Buttress*), which both have alternating plain and patterned panels. *China, Glass & Lamps* mentions Surprise is a tableware pattern made in a complete line. The pattern the Higbys identify as Surprise is not found in a complete line; only plates, bowls, compotes, salvers, and cake baskets have been found. Bowls were hand-tooled in various ways. It was a standard practice of the day to expand a line of glassware through the use of hand-tooling. Labor was cheaper than moulds, so the more items that could be produced from a single mould, the better.

Since this pattern is not Surprise, the temporary name of *Curlicue* has been assigned until the OMN is discovered. It is quite likely this pattern is either the Waldorf or Oxford pattern described in *China, Glass & Lamps* on January 10, 1901, as short lines "comprising bowls, compotiers, berries, salvers and a few other articles." *Curlicue* is found only in these shapes and is first noted in Butler Brothers catalog No. 354 dating to 1901. The pattern is shown in assortments into 1907 and was produced by no other factory.

Despite the Higby's claim that this pattern is rare, it does not seem too difficult to find, especially the 8" nick nack trays. Since they were tooled from plates, 5.5" nick nack trays and 11" plates are possible. A greater variety of bowls may be found than listed due to hand-tooling.

For more discussion and further documentation, see Surprise on page 224.

Items Noted:

bowl, collar base, round, shallow, 7"
bowl, collar base, round, deep, 8.5"
bowl, collar base, square, 6", 9"
cake basket, 9.75" l.
compote, high-foot, round, square, 8" w.
nick nack tray, collar base, 8", 11"
plate, collar base, round, 5.5", 8"
salver, 9.5"

Reproductions and Look-alikes: None known.

Daisy, 1885

References: *P&GR*, 1/1/1885; possibly BS, spring 1885
Colors: unknown, but undoubtedly clear

The January 1, 1885, issue of *Pottery and Glassware Reporter* mentions a butter dish by the name of Daisy:

> Bryce, Higbee & Co. ...have ready now, among other new goods, an exceedingly pretty butter dish named the "Daisy," which is a daisy in name as well as in fact.

It was quite common in this time period to describe something appealing as "a daisy," but the trade journal reporter makes it evident that the butter dish was actually named Daisy. Unfortunately, no description of the pattern was given. Since the report dates prior to Bryce, Higbee's manufacture of colored wares, it may be deduced the butter dish was made in clear glass. Amber, blue, and perhaps canary is within the realm of possibility since color was introduced shortly before July 1885.

Crude image of an unidentified butter dish sold in an assortment of Bryce, Higbee glassware by B. Sommers that could be the Daisy butter dish mentioned in *Pottery & Glassware Reporter* in 1885.

An unidentified butter dish is shown in "Our 'Rival' Assortment" in B. Sommers & Co.'s 1885 Spring Edition catalog. Sadly, the illustration is rather crude, but there appears to be beads near the top and rim of the lid and at the rim and base of the bottom. The top portion of the finial looks to be the same or similar shape as finials of the Capitola pattern, and the overall shape of the bowl appears to be the same as the earlier Alfonzo pattern. Even the lid is illustrated with very sloped sides, which is typical of Alfonzo. Vertical ribs are shown on both lid and base, which may be molded into the glass, but these could be plain areas drawn with lines to show highlights of shimmering glass. Among the other items in the Sommers assortment is an Ida bread tray, a new pattern mentioned in the same January 1, 1885, quote with Daisy. The identical assortment was offered in B. Sommers 1885–1886 catalog (presumably fall to winter), but the spring 1886 issue offers "Our New 'Rival' Assortment" and the odd butter is replaced by one in the Ida pattern. Could this odd butter be the Daisy butter dish mentioned in *Pottery and Glassware Reporter*? More research is definitely needed.

Reproductions and Look-alikes: Unknown.

Diamond Point Swag and Fan, c. 1901

References: BB catalog No. 354, 1901
Colors: clear

Diamond Point Swag and Fan 5.25" plates, $15–$20 each; 8.25" plate, $20–$25; 6" bowl, $15–$20.

Diamond Point Swag and Fan 9.5" cake basket, $40–$45; 9.75" salver, $40–$45.

Diamond Point Swag and Fan 11.25" and 8.25" nick nack trays, $35–$40; $20–$25.

Though this pattern is very typical of Bryce, Higbee glassware in form, design, and quality, the only documents that link it to them are Butler Brothers catalogs. The pattern is first noted in catalog No. 354 from 1901 and appears in assortments up to 1907, the year Bryce, Higbee forever closed its doors.

Lola and Wayne Higby identify this pattern as "New Crescent," but this is incorrect. The January 5, 1898, issue of *China, Glass & Lamps* mentions that New Crescent was made in a "very full line" of tableware, but the pattern in question is only found in miscellaneous items. It was offered by Butler Brothers for a full six years and only compotes, salvers, plates, and various bowls are shown by them and other firms. It is more than likely either the Waldorf or Oxford pattern, two new designs mentioned in *China, Glass & Lamps* in early 1901:

> The Waldorf and Oxford are short lines, comprising compotiers, berries, salvers and a few other articles.

Indeed, this pattern is found in a wide range of bowls tooled in various ways as well as salvers, cake baskets, and plates. A catalog page from the M. S. Benedict Manufacturing Company shows several interesting dishes mounted on quadruple silver-plated bases. Though the catalog is undated, it must be prior to 1906, when the company's name was changed to T. N. Benedict Manufacturing Company. One can see that the silver-plated bases added greatly to the price of the items. At $12 per dozen wholesale, these dishes retailed approximately $1.25 each as opposed to a retail price of approximately 10¢ each without the metal bases—quite a significant difference in price. This is just one example of how the silver manufacturers mounted glassware purchased from various companies with their own fittings. A small investment of inexpensive, fancy pressed glassware added much to the look, appeal, and cost of the final product.

The temporary descriptive name of *Diamond Point Swag and Fan* has been assigned and should prove adequate until the correct OMN is confirmed.

Items Noted:

bowl, collar base, round, square, cupped, various edge treatments, depths, and sizes
cake basket, 9.5" l.
compote, high-foot, round, square, 8" w.
nick nack tray, collar base, 8.25", 11.25"
plate, collar base, round, 5.25", 8.25", 11.25"
salver, 9.5"–9.75"

Diamond Point Swag and Fan 8" square compote, $25–$30; 6.5" square bowl, $18–$20; 8" round compote, $20–$25.

Since nick nack trays were tooled from plates, it is very likely that trays measuring approximately 5.25" exist as well. It was a very standard practice of the time to expand a line of glassware by the use of hand-tooling, as evidenced by the great variety of bowls found.

Reproductions and Look-alikes: None known.

M. S. BENEDICT MANUFACTURING COMPANY.

NO. 425. ASSORTED DISHES.

Crystal Glass, Burnished Base, Quadruple Plate, - - Per dozen, $12 00
Cuts One-third Size.

Interesting assortment of *Diamond Point Swag and Fan* dishes mounted on quadruple-plated bases from an undated catalog of M. S. Benedict Manufacturing Company.

Drum, year uncertain

References: BH, undated; *AP&GR*, 8/16/1883; SB, c. 1885; BB 86th Trip, c. 1886; HB&F, c. 1888
Colors: clear; amber and blue (covered mustard known)

Most collectors are not aware that this charming pattern can be found in anything other than the toy table set and mugs. Full-sized table items were also made. The August 16, 1883, issue of *American Pottery and Glassware Reporter* mentions only "toy 'drum' sets," but does not give any clues as to when the set was introduced. A circa 1885 Spelman Brothers assortment shows a 6" deep bowl, a circa 1886 Butler Brothers catalog illustrates a

Drum table-size cream and sugar, $45–$50; $60–$65 (with lid).

The design in the base of the full-sized Drum items is very similar to the motif found in the *Chain* pattern.

BELOW | Drum 6" bowl from a circa 1885 Spelman Brothers assortment may be a butter dish without lid. *Courtesy of the Rakow Research Library, Corning Museum of Glass.*

"Drum Design Mustard Pot with Cover," and a circa 1888 spring-summer catalog of Hollander, Bradshaw and Folsom shows a toy table set. The only item of Drum shown on a circa 1888 Bryce, Higbee catalog page is the covered mustard, so it is probable that the other items were discontinued by then. Drum is the OMN.

The toy sugar bottom is easily mistaken for the toy spoon, but the sugar is 2.5" wide whereas the spoon is only 2" wide. The covered mustard or "Horse Radish" (as it is designated on the Bryce, Higbee catalog page) is the same as the toy sugar, but with the addition of a slot in the lid to accommodate a spoon. So far the only item found in amber and blue is the covered mustard. In their book, *Collector's Encyclopedia of Children's Dishes,* authors Margaret and Kenn Whitmyer list mugs in three sizes.

In addition to the 6" bowl offered by Spelman Brothers, full-sized cream pitchers and covered sugars are known. Surely spoon holders were made, too. It is very possible the 6" bowl is actually a butter dish base. The handle on the full-sized cream differs from those on the toy cream and mugs. Full-sized items have a complicated diamond design in the base (also found on the underside of the sugar lid) that bears a striking resemblance to the motif contained within the ellipses of the *Chain* pattern.

Items Noted:

bowl, deep, 6" w.
butter, covered, toy-size
cream, full-size
cream, toy-size
mug, 2", 2.25", 2.5"
mustard, covered, slotted lid, 2.5" w.
spoon, toy-size, 2" w.
sugar, covered, full-size, 4" w.
sugar, covered, toy-size, 2.5" w.

Reproductions and Look-alikes: Margaret and Kenn Whitmyer mention the 2.25" mug has been reproduced, but no evidence of this has been found. Portieux/Vallerysthal made a very similar drum design. There are differences in the ropes on the side, and finials are either a cat, pig, or large cannon, unlike the small cannons on Bryce, Higbee's covered items. The P/V items are often marked and are found in many transparent and opaque colors as well as clear. The drum mug with a design of an eagle with outstretched wings (often found gilded) was made by Westmoreland and is not part of Bryce, Higbee's Drum set.

Toy Drum Set.

No one has ever been able to offer this splendid toy less than a 25-cent article. By purchasing a very large quantity it enables us to offer them as a big 10-cent leader. Packed 3 doz. sets in case, per doz. sets 88

Drum toy set sold by Hollander, Bradshaw & Folsom in their spring and summer 1888 catalog. *Courtesy of the Rakow Research Library, Corning Museum of Glass.*

Look-alike items often confused for Bryce, Higbee's Drum. Left to right: Portieux amber drum box with cat finial, Portieux blue opaque drum mustard base, and *Drum with Eagle* mug made by Westmoreland Specialty Company in the early 1900s. Bryce, Higbee's Drum cream is shown at far right for comparison.

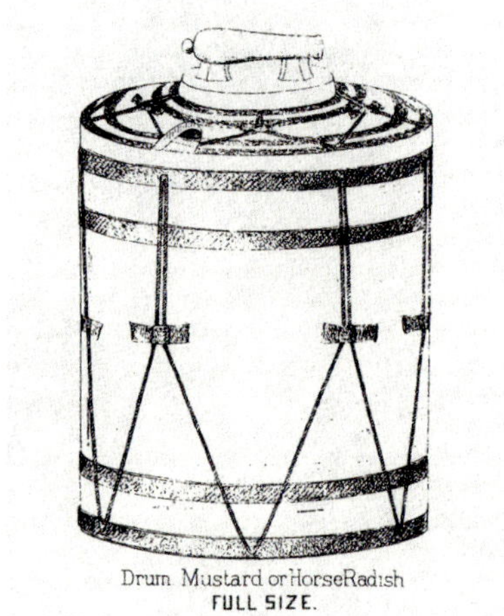

Drum mustard or horseradish from a circa 1888 Bryce, Higbee company catalog.

Earl, 1885

References: BH, undated; *P&GR*, 7/16/1885; BB 83rd Trip, 1885; BS, 1886
Colors: clear, clear with engraving, amber, blue, canary, some apple green

They [Bryce, Higbee & Co.] have just ready a new engraved and figured line, comprising set, comports, salvers, covered and uncovered bowls, pitchers of all sizes, tumblers, wines, goblets, clarets, etc. This set will be known as the Earl, and it is one of the handsomest got out by them. The shape is round with some oval pieces. There is a ring of neat figured work just above the foot, and another at the lower edge of the cover, and the remainder plain glass...the whole line contains 55 pieces, all of which are now ready for the market...

–*Pottery and Glassware Reporter*, 7/16/1885

Earl cream, $25–$30; sugar, $35–$40; spoon holder, $25–$30.

Earl blue butter and clear pickle jar, $60–$65 each.

Earl clear 10.75" oval bread plate, $25–$30; blue 4.5" fruit dessert, $12–$15; blue 10.75" oval bread plate, $35–$40.

Fortunately, there are period sources illustrating Earl by name. A goblet is included on circa 1888 Bryce, Higbee catalog page of miscellaneous stemware, the only company-issued illustration to fully document the pattern. A table set is shown in B. Sommers 1886 catalog, correctly called Earl. The name is very fitting, for items have a solid, regal presence, especially the covered pieces, which are topped with a plume-shaped finial.

Clear items are found with engraving, and according to the report in *Pottery and Glassware Reporter*, there were several designs available. Along with Ida, Earl is the Bryce, Higbee pattern most extensively issued in color. No colored items have been found engraved. It is a bit perplexing that J. Stanley Brothers mentions in his personal notes that Earl is also found in amethyst. This is not a typical Bryce, Higbee color and items have not been seen by the author. Brothers does not mention canary or apple green, however, and items are known in these colors. Only two oval bread plates are documented in apple green, a color not seen in any other Bryce, Higbee pattern. Amber and blue are by far the most common colors found in Earl. The shades often vary from piece to piece.

Pitchers are found in two variations. One is wider and shorter and has an ear-shaped handle like that found on the cream. The other is slightly taller and narrower, and the vertical part of the handle runs nearly parallel with the body of the pitcher. The goblet is found with the usual "beehive" stem found on other stemmed items, but some have a single ring around the stem. The claret and wine may exist in this variation as well.

Earl is an Anglo-Saxon title for a British nobleman who ranks between a marquess and a viscount. This meaning is extended to the male name Earl, which translates to "nobleman or prince."

Items Noted:

bowl, oval, 7", 8", 9.5", 11"
bowl, round, 4", 6"
bread plate, oval, 10.75"
butter, covered, flat or footed, hexagonal flange
celery vase, pedestal, scalloped edge
compote, high-foot, covered, 7", 8" w.
compote, high-foot, open, flared, 8", 10"
compote, fruit dessert, low-foot, open, flared, beaded edge, 4.5"
compote, low-foot, open, covered, 8"
claret
cream

Earl apple green 10.75" oval bread plate, value undetermined; blue 6" bowl, $20–$25; amber 7" oval bowl, $15–$20; amber 8" high-foot covered compote, $55–$60; amber wine, $25–$30.

goblet
pickle dish, oval, plume handles, 7"
pickle jar, flat, cylindrical, glass lid
pitcher, half-gallon, "ear"-shaped handle, 7.75" h.
pitcher, half-gallon, handle runs nearly parallel to body, 8.25" h.
salt, table, 2.75" h. by 3" w.
salver, 8.5", 9.5", 10.5"
shaker, salt and pepper, footed
spoon, plain edge, 3.5" w.
sugar, covered, plain edge, no inner ledge, 4.25" w.
tray for water set, octagonal
tumbler, pattern covers lower half
waste bowl, belled, approximately 5.25" w.
wine

Earl 8" high-foot engraved covered compote, $50–$55.

Earl goblet from an undated Bryce, Higbee catalog.

Reproductions and Look-alikes: No reproductions known. A flat shaker shown in Peterson's *Glass Salt Shakers* as "Spirae Band, Tall" is similar, but definitely not Earl. See Fancheon on page 163.

Earl table set offered by B. Sommers & Co., spring 1886.

Era, 1891

References: BH, undated; *CG&L*, 12/31/1890; BB, September 1895
Colors: clear, clear with ruby stain (spoon holder known)

Though Kamm states in her fifth book that Bryce, Higbee's Era was first introduced in 1880, there is nothing to prove that it was, and everything to prove that it was not. The pattern is in no way typical of American pressed glass of that period. The square shapes are quite distinctive, and for a new company to put out such an original pattern in such brilliant glass would surely have attracted the attention of the reporters, yet there is absolutely no mention of it in any trade journals from late 1879 or 1880. Kamm then states in her eighth book that Era was made in the mid–1880s and "reproduced or else kept in stock until at least 1891 when the 'New' was added to the name." This is incorrect

Era butter, $55–$60.

Era celery vase, $40–$45; covered pickle jar, $70–$75.

Era bread plate illustrated in an ad in *China, Glass & Lamps* in April 1891.

as well. The first mention of Era is in the December 31, 1890, issue of *China, Glass & Lamps*:

> Bryce, Higbee & Co. are in full operation, having closed on Christmas day only. They have two new patterns ready for the spring trade, both of which are exemplifications of new ideas in design and which the trade will undoubtedly be pleased with. One of these is the "Era," a very extensive line of 74 pieces, comprising set, bowls, dishes, lemonade set, salvers, nappies, salads, comportiers both covered and uncovered and a number of other articles. The shapes are altogether out of the common rut, the lids are high and massive and the general effect pleasing.

Note the reporter states the new patterns are "exemplifications of new ideas." Other journals describe Era as a new departure and "strictly original."

There is also confusion over the name because some sources list it as "New Era." This discrepancy comes from a Bryce, Higbee ad that mentions their Era pattern is new. The January 15, 1891, issue of *Pottery and Glassware Reporter* calls the pattern "New Era," but this is the only report that refers to the pattern this way. All others simply call it Era. Most important, original Bryce, Higbee catalog pages show the pattern as Era.

The pickle jar was made with a matching glass lid, which is very flat. The base appears to be the same as the spooner. Barret illustrates this item, with no lid, in *Popular American Ruby-Stained Pattern Glass*. This is the only item of Era noted with ruby stain.

Era items are square or rectangle-shaped and made from heavy, good quality glass. The pattern does not seem to be very abundant.

Items Noted:

bowl, covered, open, 6", 7", 8"
bowl, open, 4", 4.5"
bowl, oblong, 8"
butter, covered, flange edge
celery vase, 6.5" h.
compote, high-foot, covered, open, plain rim, 6", 7", 8" w.
cream
pickle dish
pickle jar, flat glass lid, 4.5" by 3" w.

pitcher, quart, half-gallon
plate, bread, square
salver, 10"
shaker, salt and pepper
spoon, plain rim
sugar, plain rim, no inner edge
tray for water set, square
tumbler

Era cream pitcher from a Bryce, Higbee & Company catalog.

There are obviously more items to the set because trade journals reported Era was an extensive line of seventy-four items. Kamm mentions compotes with stems of medium height, stemmed covered jelly dish, olive dish, covered olive jar, covered honey dish, square salad plate, and salt dip. The covered honey dish could simply be the covered butter dish since it is square. It is not known if any of these forms overlap with those listed above, or if these terms came from the Bryce, Higbee catalog Kamm saw.

Reproductions and Look-alikes: No reproductions known. There are some patterns with similar paneled star/fine cut designs. George Duncan & Sons' No. 800 AKA *Heavy Paneled Fine Cut* (1883) utilizes a similar paneled pattern on square shapes, but the star (or fine cut) motif is much smaller than that found on Bryce, Higbee's Era.

George Duncan & Sons' No. 800 pattern (left) is similar to Bryce, Higbee's Era (right), but the fine cut design on No. 800 is smaller and quite different.

Estoria, 1901
(pattern unknown)

References: *CG&L*, 1/10/1901
Colors: unknown, but undoubtedly clear

Estoria was one of five new patterns mentioned in the January 10, 1901, issue of *China, Glass & Lamps* without much description:

> Bryce, Higbee & Co. are showing five new patterns at their sample room, 623 Smithfield street, and they are eminently worthy of the attention of buyers...Next is the Estoria, also imitation cut. This has about 50 pieces and is a clear and brilliant pattern.

It may be that "Estoria" should be "Astoria." The two words sound much the same, and the reporter may have simply written it phonetically. This is the only reference for this pattern name, so there is nothing else to compare. *Estória* is a Portuguese word meaning "story or fable." Astoria could refer to a U.S. city by that name or to the famed New York City Astoria hotel built in 1896 by John Jacob Astor IV next to his cousin's Waldorf Hotel (built 1893). The hotels were connected by Peacock Alley and became known as the Waldorf-Astoria. It was the largest hotel in the world at the time and well known in its day for its size and grandeur. Women were admitted singly without escorts, which was unusual at the time, and this led to the hotel becoming a social center of the city. Prior to this, hotels were generally for transients. Bryce, Higbee also introduced its short Waldorf line in 1901, so Astoria may be what was intended. Is it mere coincidence that in the same year Heisey introduced a line of tableware they called Waldorf-Astoria? See Waldorf on page 245 for additional discussion.

Reproductions and Look-alikes: Unknown.

Ethol, 1890

References: BH, undated; *P&GR*, 12/26/1889, 1/2/1890; BB, 1890 Santa Claus
Colors: clear, clear with engraving, clear with ruby stain (champagne tumbler known)

Ethol 10" salver, $75–$100; handled olive, $15–$20; 9" salver, $60–$75.

Ethol is first mentioned by *Pottery and Glassware Reporter* on December 26, 1889, as a new line for the approaching season. On January 2, 1890, the journal reports:

> The new "Ethol" pattern of Bryce, Higbee & Co., noticed last week, is now complete, and on exhibition at their sample rooms, 623 Smithfield street.

Many items are specifically mentioned in the December quote noted above. The reporter states "this is the biggest line they have ever got out." Though a count is not given, it must be greater than fifty-five because the same journal reported in July 1885 that the Earl pattern included that many items.

A half-gallon Ethol pitcher is shown in an undated Bryce, Higbee & Company catalog with the very interesting appellation "Brazilian Pitcher." *Pottery and Glassware Reporter* uses the same name and states that the Brazilian pitcher was made in "all sizes" and that they "are of the exact shape of the pitcher used by Dom Pedro, late Emperor of Brazil," hence the name. Other interesting items noted in the journal report are table salts, claret and champagne glasses, tankards and handled jellies of "all sizes," and hotel sugar. The last-mentioned item has not been identified, so its form and size are unknown. Another entry in the same journal on April 17, 1890, reports on Ethol and makes reference to the square covered honey dish, mustard, individual cream and sugar as well as "a line of hotel sugars and creams of the same pattern." Kamm notes that among the items illustrated on catalog pages she did not show are a hotel sugar and cream. One would surmise the referenced hotel sugar and cream are not the same as the table or individual sugars and creams, for those are also mentioned in the reviews. Items designed for hotel use generally had broad bases and were shorter than standard articles so they were not easily upset.

A swung vase is shown in an assortment offered in a January 1905 Butler Brothers catalog. This is quite a late offering for Ethol, which seems to disappear from the pages of Butler Brothers in the late 1890s. It was most likely made from a revived (and possibly slightly retooled) spooner mould since swung vases did not exist in the early 1890s when Ethol was introduced. An early assortment of swung vases in the Butler Brothers fall 1902 catalog shows United States Glass Company's No. 15042 pattern AKA *Zippered Swirl and Diamond* (introduced 1895) in four sizes ranging from 15" to 28". They seem to be an innovation of the early 1900s, for the description states the vases are "everywhere the rage," a strong implication they were something new and novel. Within the next decade swung vases appear in much greater abundance and were also produced in great quantities in opalescent and iridescent glass.

A large assortment of sixty-one items of Ethol was offered by Butler Brothers in October 1894. Each item is listed and described in rather good detail. The terms used undoubtedly came directly from the company, for they match those given by *Pottery and Glassware Reporter* as well as those found on Bryce, Higbee catalog pages, including the unique designation of the Brazilian pitcher. Ethol is found in a great variety of open bowls as well as high and low-foot compotes. Bowls and compotes are found with plain flared edges or with scalloped edges that are flared. Bowls and compotes with straight sides accept lids, though they were not always sold with them. The numerous compotes available with various edge treatments were originally called bowls, but the term compote is used in the listing to avoid confusion. It becomes challenging to match up catalog descriptions with actual items, for dimensions vary, especially for items that were flared by hand. The individual sugar is the same as the mustard/horseradish, though the latter has a notched cover. There is no marmalade jar; it is properly called the mustard/horseradish. The table sugar is on a short pedestal. It is rather large and is often confused for a compote. Darryl Reilly said he once saw an Ethol cake basket and told the author that it was

Ethol 5.25" high-foot covered compotes, $30–$35 each; 6.5" high-foot scallop-edge compote, $25–$30.

Ethol tumbler, $25–$30; salt shaker, $40–$45; individual cream, $15–$20; individual sugar, $45–$50; mug, $10–$15.

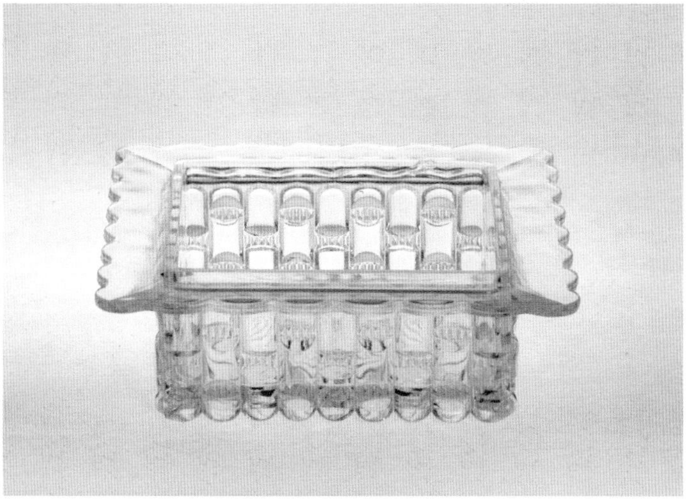

Ethol honey dish base, $100–$125 (with lid).

Ethol table cream, $25–$30; celery vase, $35–$40; butter lid ($60–$65 complete); table sugar, $40–$45.

Ethol half-gallon tankard pitcher from a Wallace & McAfee catalog next to an engraved example.

tooled from either the 9" or 10" salver. The camphor (frosted) items mentioned by other authors were more recently fabricated through the use of acid and were not originally made this way.

It appears that Bryce, Higbee's Ethol line did not include cruets. Though there are cruets found that look to be the same pattern, the author feels they are copies by Westmoreland, called No. 15 by the company. Oddly, of all the items of No. 15 shown in a 1902 Westmoreland Specialty Company catalog, only the cruets (offered in 4 oz. and 8 oz. sizes) have notches on the cuts between the "logs." This single form alone appears identical—or nearly identical—to Ethol. One apparent but subtle difference is the beveled band of "logs" at the top of the design on the No. 15 cruets. This detail is not noted on any item of Ethol. A definitive, complete company listing of Ethol is not known, but of those compiled from original sources, not one mentions or illustrates any cruets. These sources are: 1) jobber catalog assortments; 2) the list of items enumerated in *Pottery and Glassware Reporter* on December 26, 1889, and April 17, 1890; 3) the sixty-one pieces itemized in the October 1894 Butler Brothers assortment; 4) the Ethol catalog pages Kamm reprinted; and 5) the list of items Kamm names from the Ethol catalog pages she did not reprint. The April 17, 1890, issue of *Pottery and Glassware Reporter* mentions new items added to the line. They are all included in the October 1894 Butler Brothers assortment, but again, not one mention of a cruet is found. Ethol was introduced for the 1890 spring market. No other cruet appears in any of Bryce, Higbee's lines until 1897 with the Banquet pattern. From that point forward at least one of their full lines each year for the next ten years of their existence included a cruet. If the Ethol line included a cruet, surely the company would have included this form in the many other lines made in the seven year gap between 1890 and 1897, but this does not appear to be the case.

The spelling of Ethol is a bit strange. One cannot help but think of the famous (but later) 1907 painting *Ethol with Roses* by Edmund W. Greacen. Presumably, Ethol was intended to be the feminine name Ethel, of Old English origin meaning "noble." There is a remote possibility the name refers to Athole (also spelled Atholl), a large historical division in the Scottish Highlands. Athole is pronounced much the same as "Ethel."

Items Noted:

berry dessert, footed, scalloped edge, 4.5"
berry dish, flat, scalloped edge, 5", 6", 7", 8"
bowl, flat, open, flared; plain or scalloped edge
bowl, flat, covered, straight sides, 7", 8"
bowl, flat, open, straight sides, 7", 8"
butter, flanged edge with dome cover
cake basket (not confirmed by author)
celery vase, scalloped edge, 6" h.
champagne tumbler, narrow, 3.5" h.
comport, 4.5" w. (per catalog description; may be berry dessert with plain rim)
compote, high and low-foot, covered, plain edge, 5", 6", 7", 8" w.
compote, high and low-foot, open, plain edge, 5", 6", 7", 8" w.
compote, high and low-foot, open, flared; plain or scalloped edge, 6", 7", 8", 9" w.
cream, individual
cream, table, shaped as Brazilian pitcher
fruit bowl, low, low-foot, and high-foot, scalloped edge, 10" (per catalog description)
goblet
honey dish, covered, square, 7" w.
jelly, handled, 5"
mustard or horseradish, notched lid, 3.5" w.
nappy, flat, flared, plain edge, 6", 7", 8", 9"
nut bowl, rectangular, sloped sides, 8" x 5.5"
pickle, oblong, 9.25"
pitcher, Brazilian, half-gallon
pitcher, tankard, applied handle, half-gallon
salver, plain gallery edge, 9", 10"
salt, table, 3.5" w.
shaker, salt and pepper
spoon, scalloped edge, 4.5" h.
sugar, covered, individual, 3.5" w.
sugar, covered, table, pedestal, plain edge, 5.5" w.
tumbler, 4" h.
vase, swung, ribbed upper section, approximately 14"–17.5" (height varies)
wine

Reproductions and Look-alikes: No reproductions known. Westmoreland's No. 15 is a copy. The most noticeable difference is that the cut areas in the "logs" are patterned on Ethol, but left plain on No. 15. The No. 15 cruets shown in Westmoreland's 1902 catalog, however, have patterned cuts and appear nearly identical in every detail to Ethol. This is quite interesting because the rest of the items are not illustrated like this.

Westmoreland's No. 15 (left) is a copy of Ethol (right). Note the "cuts" on Westmoreland's No. 15 are plain on all items but the cruets.

Westmoreland's No. 15 cruets differ from the other items in the line and appear nearly identical to Ethol. There is no evidence Bryce, Higbee ever made cruets in the pattern.

Fancheon, 1885

References: *AG*, 6/5/1885; BB 83rd Trip, c. 1885; SB, c. 1885; FP&W, April 1886; GS, 1888
Colors: clear, clear engraved, blue, canary; undoubtedly amber

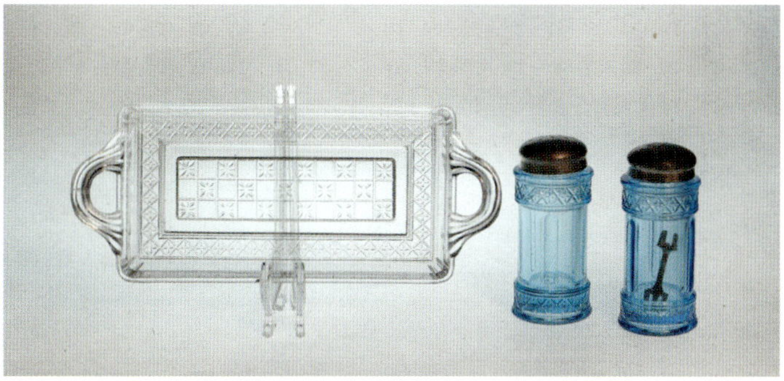

Fancheon 7.25" handled pickle, $18–$20; blue salt and pepper shakers with metal agitator, $50–$55.

Comparison of Fancheon and New Grand shakers show they were made from the same mould.

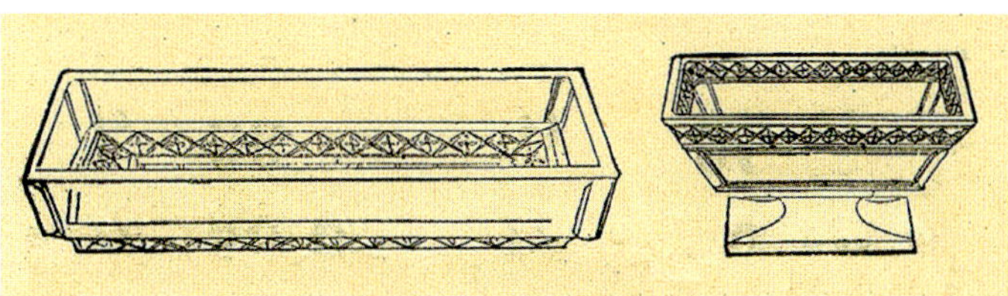

Fancheon pickle and low-footed nappy from a circa 1885 Spelman Brothers catalog. *Courtesy of the Rakow Research Library, Corning Museum of Glass.*

American Glassworker gave a brief description of Bryce, Higbee & Company's new Fancheon pattern on June 5, 1885:

> Bryce, Higbee & Co. have started to make a new line of ware called "Fancheon." Six and seven inch bowls have been made, and a large run is anticipated, as it is a plain but pretty pattern, with a chequered rim at the base.

A few items in a pattern that matches this description are shown in Butler Brothers and Spelman Brothers assortments dating circa 1885. An engraved half-gallon water pitcher has also been seen. In *Glass Salt Shakers*, Arthur G. Peterson shows a shaker in this pattern, which he labels "Spirae Band, Tall." It is similar, but definitely not Bryce, Higbee's Earl (AKA *Spirea Band*). There is no doubt the shaker Peterson shows is, indeed, a product of Bryce, Higbee. The checkered bands at the top and bottom and ribs on the body are also found on the New Grand shaker; in fact, close comparison of shakers reveals that the same mould was used for both patterns. The Fancheon shakers are known in canary and blue, so the possibility of amber is very high. These are the only items seen in color, but others were likely made.

A Fancheon four-piece table set was sold wholesale by the Chicago jobber French, Potter & Wilson and appeared in their illustrated price list published in April 1886. Here they were offered for $4.25 per dozen sets when a full barrel of twelve sets was purchased. Lesser quantities were sold for $4.50 per dozen sets, presumably because the jobber would then have to open the barrels of glass sent by the manufacturer and repack the goods at their own expense.

Fancheon is another obscure pattern that only time will tell how available it is. Most items are square or rectangular, and some are found with interesting engravings not encountered on other Bryce, Higbee patterns. The known forms indicate it was a full line, though how extensive the line was is uncertain. Surely items common to sets of glassware made in the 1880s exist, such as high and low-foot compotes in various sizes (covered and uncovered), bread plate, and perhaps even a goblet or salver.

Though the spelling differs slightly, Fanchon is a French feminine name, which is the equivalent of Frances. The significance of Bryce, Higbee using the name is not known.

Items Noted:
bowl, low-foot, flat, square, 4"
butter, covered, low-foot, square
cream, square
pickle, rectangular, with or without handles, 7.25"
pitcher, half-gallon, rectangular
shaker, salt and pepper, cylindrical, about 3.5" h.
spoon, plain edge, square
sugar, covered, square, plain edge, no inner ledge

Reproductions and Look-alikes: None known. Note the similarity of Fancheon to Earl.

Feathered Medallion, c. 1905

References: BB, spring 1905
Colors: clear, clear with gold trim, clear with red and gold cold painted "goofus" decoration

This is one of many instances where, if it were not for Butler Brothers assortments, we would not know that Bryce, Higbee made this pattern. *Feathered Medallion* is first noted in Butler Brothers spring 1905 catalog and appears in many groupings for at least two years. Despite Lola and Wayne Higby's claim that the pattern is fairly rare, it seems to be rather abundant, especially cake baskets and bowls of various sizes. *Feathered Medallion* appears very sporadically in only a few items in jobber catalogs after 1907. Those items may have been previously manufactured stock from Bryce, Higbee. A large open compote appears in Butler Brothers catalogs between August 1915 and April 1916.

Feathered Medallion 9.5" tall rose bowl, $35–$40; 7.25" tall rose bowl, $25–$30; 9.25" tall tulip-shaped vase, $35–$40; 7" tall tulip-shaped vase, $25–$30; tall compote with square bowl, $30–$35.

In November 2015, an 11" salver was discovered with what appeared to be the mark of the New Martinsville Glass Manufacturing Company (see page 264). The author was, unfortunately, not able to examine the salver in person. Some uncertainty exists because a very similar mark is said to have been used by Mirror Images on various items of reproduction glassware. There is no record that *Feathered*

Feathered Medallion 11.5" plate, $25–$30; 9" deep bowl, $20–$25; 10" plate, $20–$25; 8.5" bowl, $15–$20. The plates were tooled from the same mould as the bowls.

Feathered Medallion 11" nick nack tray, $25–$30; 7.5" plate, $15–$20; 5" deep bowl, $12–$15. The 7.5" plate was tooled from a 5" deep bowl.

Feathered Medallion spoon, $25–$30; sugar, $35–$40 (with lid); cream, $25–$30.

Medallion was made by New Martinsville, but the possibility cannot be discounted. More research is definitely needed.

The stopper originally sold with the cruet is the same one used for Bonair and originated with that pattern. Cruets were consistently offered by Butler Brothers on what appears to be an Anona tray with salt and pepper shakers and toothpick holder in the *Swirl and Panel* design. The base motif of the latter pattern is identical to the snowflake motif found on *Feathered Medallion*. The only items found in *Swirl and Panel* are toothpicks, salt and pepper shakers, swung vases, and bowls measuring 4.25", 6.25", and 8.5". This is an odd assortment of items for a separate line, and they may have been meant to be part of the *Feathered Medallion* set.

Though the spoon holder has an inner ledge, it was not intended to have a lid. It is narrower and smaller than the sugar, closer to the size of the cream pitcher. Like other Bryce, Higbee patterns introduced after 1900, there appear to be no covered compotes. An array of unusual items on tall stems was made, however, such as rose bowls, tulip-shaped vases, bonbon (or sweetmeat) compotes, and compotes with both edges turned up like the cake baskets. Since no original company catalogs showing *Feathered Medallion* have been found, the company terms for these items and the OMN are not known.

A plate has been seen decorated on the reverse side with red and overall gold paint called goofus glass by collectors. It is uncertain when it was decorated. If done during the time frame the pattern was manufactured, it is extremely unlikely it was decorated by Bryce, Higbee in this manner.

Items Noted:

almond tray, one side up, 5.5"
bowl, collar base, round, square, ruffled, various depths and sizes
bowl, flat, oblong, 7.5", 8.25", 9.5" l.
butter, covered
cake basket, 9.5" l.
celery tray, 10.25" l.
celery vase, handled, 6" h.
comportier, low-foot, 3.5" w.
compote, jelly, high-foot, round, square, 5" w.
compote, high-foot, round, square, 8" w.
compote, high-foot, round, approximately 10" w.

compote, bonbon or sweetmeat, tall stem, square, flared, 8.5" h. x 6" w.
cream
cruet, stopper #3
goblet
nick nack, high-foot, 5" h. x 7" l. x 4" w.
nick nack, tall stem, 8.5" h. x 8" l. x 5.5" w.
nick nack tray, collar base, 11"
pickle or olive dish, "leaf" shape, tab handle, 7.25"
pitcher, quart, half-gallon
plate, collar base, round, 5.5", 10", 11.5"
plate, square, 7"
rose bowl, stemmed, 8" h.
rose bowl, tall stem, scalloped edge, small egg-shaped bowl, 7.25" h. x 2.5" w.
rose bowl, tall stem, scalloped edge, large egg-shaped bowl, 9.5" h. x 3.5" w.
salver, 6", 9.5"
spoon, handled, scalloped edge, inner ledge, 4.25" w. (not made to accept lid)
sugar, covered, handled, scalloped edge, inner ledge, 4.75" w.
tumbler
vase, tulip shape, tall stem, small belled bowl, 7" h. x 3.75" w.
vase, tulip shape, tall stem, small straight bowl, 7.5" h. x 3.25" w.
vase, tulip shape, tall stem, large belled bowl, 9.25" h. x 4.25" w.
wine, straight, belled

Reproductions and Look-alikes: No reproductions confirmed, but see text regarding an 11" salver.

Feathered Medallion 9.5" cake basket, $35–$40; 7" square plate, $25–$30; 9.5" oblong bowl, $25–$30; cruet, $30–$35.

The "Havana" assortment was made up of twenty items of *Feathered Medallion*. Baltimore Bargain House, June 1906.

5th Avenue,
year unknown

References: BH, undated
Colors: clear

5th Avenue goblet from an undated Bryce, Higbee & Company catalog, circa 1888.

A rather plain goblet is labeled "5th Avenue Goblet" on an undated Bryce, Higbee & Co. catalog page that dates circa 1888. The caption mentions that a champagne, claret, and wine were also made. These were undoubtedly the only items in the line, for the 5th Avenue name refers to a standard shape of stemware popular in that era. The bowls taper quite a bit and stems are rather thin and plain. Though the introduction date of this line is unknown, production likely lasted many years as plain patterns like this were always in demand at hotels, taverns, and other public places. 5th Avenue appears to be nearly identical to the company's No. 33, but the former has two molded bands just above the stem.

Reproductions and Look-alikes: Unknown if reproductions exist, but many companies made stemware of this shape with the same name.

Plain "Fifth Avenue" Shape.

Cup-foot line, clear crystal, fire polished, finished edges.

A709. A710. A711. A712. A713.

A709—Cordial glass, capacity 1 ounce...per doz., .38

A710—Wine glass, capacity 1 ounce......per doz., .42

A711—Claret glass, capacity 3½ ounces.....doz., .55

A712—Champagne tumbler, capacity 5½ ounces, per doz., .57

A713—Goblet, light weight, capacity 9 ounces..........per doz., .62

Fifth Avenue stemware by an unknown maker offered by Baltimore Bargain House in June 1906. Many companies made this style of stemware and gave it the same name.

Fine Cut and Fan, c. 1901

References: BB, 1901
Colors: clear

Fine Cut and Fan is called *Fine Cut Star and Fan* by Lola and Wayne Higby, but the name coined nearly thirty years earlier by authors Marion Hartung and Ione Hinshaw and used by William Heacock is endorsed here. The pattern is composed of diamond-point-filled triangles separated by deeply impressed rays in a fan-like arrangement. A star can be discerned when the multiple triangles in the design are viewed as a unit, but the earlier name *Fine Cut and Fan* is more accurate because not all items contain enough triangles to form a star. Vertical items such as the cream, sugar, spoon, pitchers, celery and flower vases, cruet, and wine display only four triangular panels that, when viewed as a unit, bear little resemblance to a star.

Fine Cut and Fan has been dated to 1903 by other authors, but it was introduced a bit earlier than that. Though the exact year has not been confirmed, a plate is first noted in "Our 'Choice Piece' Asst." in Butler Brothers catalog No. 354, dated 1901. The pattern appears into 1907, though from spring 1906 to spring 1907 only an oval bowl was offered in the "'Top Notch' Assortment of Leaders."

There is no solid evidence the pattern was continued by J. B. Higbee. A cruet is shown in an assortment called "Unmatchable" by Butler Brothers in their October 1908 and mid-winter 1909 catalogs, but this is the only assortment offered that is composed entirely of patterns made by the defunct Bryce, Higbee factory. The *Fine Cut and Fan* cruet was part of the "Delmonico" assortment from 1902 to 1904 and does not reappear until over four years later in the "Unmatchable" assortment in the aforementioned catalogs. After that, the cruet never appears again, nor do any other items in the pattern. This is no doubt because the cruet and other items in that assortment were previously manufactured stock acquired from the liquidation of Bryce, Higbee & Company in May 1908.

The *Fine Cut and Fan* cruet is shown by Butler Brothers with two different stoppers. It was first offered with the same zipper-patterned stopper used with the Paris 1900 cruet.

Fine Cut and Fan 9.5" cake basket, $45–$50; 6.5" wafer stand, $30–$35; 8" round compote, $25–$30.

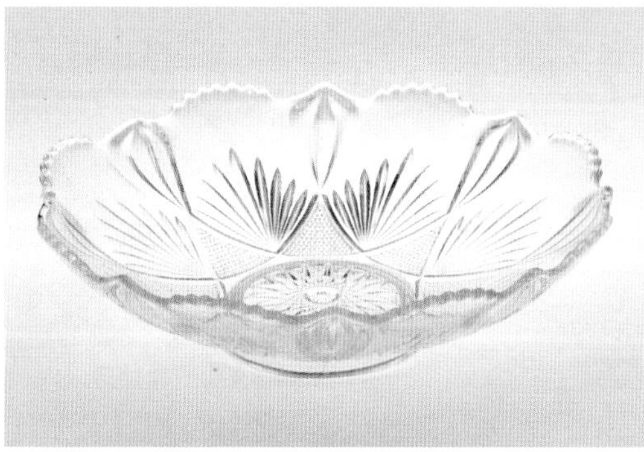

Fine Cut and Fan 10" shallow bowl, $25–$30.

Fine Cut and Fan 7.5" plates; 5.5" nick nack trays; 6.5" vase. $15–$20 each.

Fine Cut and Fan 8.5" cupped vase, $20–$25; 5.5" almond tray, $15–$20; celery vase, $30–$35; 4.5" square comportier, $10–$12; 6.5" nick nack, $30–$35; cruet with original stopper, $40–$45.

After the introduction of Bonair in 1903, it appears with the stopper designed for that cruet. Even the Paris 1900 cruet is shown with the Bonair stopper after 1904 and no longer with the stopper that was designed for it. It is notable that the *Fine Cut and Fan* cruet offered in the "Unmatchable" assortment after Bryce, Higbee closed is shown with the earlier zipper-patterned stopper, further indication the items were old stock.

Fine Cut and Fan may be either the Estoria or Tiffany pattern mentioned by *China, Glass & Lamps* in January 1901. The latter pattern seems rather fitting, as the journal notes a "nice assortment of vases" included in that line. Indeed, vases are impressive, rather prevalent, and are found in a wide variety of sizes and edge treatments in *Fine Cut and Fan.* Until documentation is found, however, it is all guesswork.

Items Noted:

almond tray, collar base, one side up, 5.5"
bowl, collar base, various depths and shapes including flared, square, cupped, from approximately 4.5"–10"
bowl, flat, oval, 8"
butter, covered
cake basket, 9.5"–10" l.
celery vase, collar base, 6.75" h.
compote, jelly, high-foot, 5" w.
compote, high-foot, round, square, 8"–9.5" w.
cream, footed
cruet, stopper #2 or #3
nick nack tray, collar base, 5.5", 8", 11.5"
nick nack, high-foot, 6.5" w.
pitcher, quart (though classified this way, it holds only twenty-four ounces)
pitcher, half-gallon
plate, collar base, round, various sizes from approximately 5.5"–11.5"
salver, 6", 9"
shaker, salt and pepper, bulbous bottom, long neck (shaped as Paris 1900)
spoon, footed, scalloped edge
sugar, covered, footed, scalloped edge, inner ledge
tumbler
vase, trumpet-shaped, various sizes and edge treatments
wafer stand, 6.5" w.
wine

Reproductions and Look-alikes: No reproductions known. A pattern known as *Coral Gables* (circa 1900) is similar to *Fine Cut and Fan* and could be confused. The most notable difference is that *Coral Gables* does not have fans between the diamond cut-filled triangles. Instead, there is a single vertical slash in this area.

Coral Gables, maker unknown (right), is similar to Bryce, Higbee's *Fine Cut and Fan* (left).

Fleur-de-lis, 1898

References: *CG&L*, 1/5/1898; MW, spring & summer 1898; BB, fall-winter 1898
Colors: clear, clear with gold trim, clear with ruby stain, clear with ruby stain and gold

Fleur-de-lis was profusely mentioned in the pages of *China, Glass & Lamps* throughout the first half of 1898. Four different full-page advertisements were shown in the first month of that year, proving the importance given the pattern by the company. These are among the very few illustrated ads from Bryce, Higbee shown in the trade journals. The company's other spring patterns, New Crescent and Simoom (or Simoon), were briefly mentioned, but the focus was clearly on Fleur-de-lis. The French-inspired pattern was offered by Montgomery Ward in their catalog for spring and summer 1898.

The fleur-de-lis represents a stylized lily and is a well-known emblem of France. The three petals are said to symbolize the medieval social classes of the people who fought, worked, and prayed. The obvious French allusion of this Bryce, Higbee pattern is carried over to the two very interesting vases termed "Flam-Beaux No. 1" and "Flam-Beaux No. 2" in the *China, Glass & Lamps* advertisement. The word is actually grammatically incorrect in reference to a single vase, for *flambeaux* is the plural of *flambeau*. A *flambeau* is a lighted torch, quite fitting for the shape of these unusual vases. The Flam-Beaux vases are much more difficult to find than the standard trumpet-shaped vase. The trumpet vase was pulled slightly after coming from the mould, so height varies.

Salvers are found in two styles. Most have wide scallops on the rim, whereas others have sixteen points containing tiny scallops. The latter salvers have the fleur-de-lis motif repeated eight times around the plate with a central design; the former have no central design and the motif is repeated six times. Cake baskets and compotes have only been seen with the wide scallops. Since salvers and cake baskets were

Fleur-de-lis celery vase, \$25–\$30; 10" round plate, \$35–\$40; 9" square bowl, \$30–\$35; 8" round compote, \$25–\$30.

Fleur-de-lis 10.25" cake basket, \$40–\$45; 9.75" salver, \$40–\$45.

Fleur-de-lis half-gallon pitcher with gold, $55–$60; tumblers, $25–$30 each.

Fleur-de-lis cruet with original stopper, $45–$50; 7" square plate, $30–$35, spooner, $25–$30; 10" trumpet vase, $25–$30.

Advertisement illustrating Bryce, Higbee's Fleur-de-lis table set appeared in *China, Glass & Lamps* on January 5, 1898.

tooled from compotes, there very well could be cake baskets and compotes in the less common variation with sixteen points.

The water set, table set, mug, trumpet vase, shakers, and toothpick are occasionally found with ruby stain and ruby stain with lush gold decoration. Some items are found with only gilding on the lilies. It is not known when items were stained with ruby, but there is no indication Bryce, Higbee decorated them.

Fleur-de-lis was a large line, but it is not certain exactly how many items were made. In December 1897, a *China, Glass & Lamps* reporter stated that Fleur-de-lis was a "very full line" of about 90 pieces, though in July 1898 the same journal mentions the line "comprises about 75 pieces." Notable mention is made of the "tall, graceful bouquet holder" producing a "splendid effect."

Other references also give credit to J. B. Higbee for producing Fleur-de-lis, but firm evidence of this has not been found. The pattern has been seen in only one jobber catalog after 1907. In 1909, G. Sommers offered an assortment of celery vases including three patterns: Alpha, *Feathered Medallion*, and Fleur-de-lis. A single, post–1907 appearance of this pattern that was such a popular seller for Bryce, Higbee & Company implies previously manufactured stock.

Fleur-de-lis Flambeaux vases illustrated in *China, Glass & Lamps* in early 1898.

Items Noted:

bowl, berry, round, 8"
bowl, dessert, round, 4.5"
bowl, dessert, square, 5"
butter, covered
cake basket, 10.25" 1.
celery tray, 11.25"
celery vase, handled, 6.25" h.
compote, round, 8.25" w.
cordial
cream
cruet, stopper #1
dish, preserve, oval, 7"
dish, square berry, 9"
jelly, handled, 5"
mug
nappy, round, 9"
olive tray, oval, 8"
pitcher, half-gallon
plate, oval, upturned edge, 10.5" x 9.75"
plate, round, 10", 12"
plate, square, 7"
salver, scalloped edge, 9.25"- 9.75"
salver, pointed scalloped edge, 10.5"–11"

shaker, salt and pepper
spoon, pointed scallop edge, handled, 3.5" w.
sugar, covered, pointed scallop edge, handled, inner ledge
toothpick
tumbler
tumbler, lemonade, applied handle
vase, Flam-Beaux No. 1, pedestal, wide flared rim
vase, Flam-Beaux No. 2, pedestal, belled rim
vase, trumpet shape, 10"–10.5" (height varies)
wine

Reproductions and Look-alikes: The square plate has been recently copied by Shannon Crystal. Sometimes they are attached to a ribbed, square-shaped pedestal. The author has seen these offered as "rare" Fleur-de-lis cake stands and selling for outrageous sums. Be aware that no such item was ever made by Bryce, Higbee. The rim is lightly scalloped, unlike original plates, which have sharply contoured edges. Also, there is a plain circle in the center of the copy, but originals have a small star in this area.

Flora, 1890

References: BH, undated; *P&GR*, 7/3/1890 and 7/10/1890; *CG&L*, 12/31/1890; BB, March 1891
Colors: clear, clear with engraving

Flora is first mentioned in the July 3, 1890, issue of *Pottery & Glassware Reporter* as a new pattern in imitation of cut glass made in over sixty-four pieces.

Patterns were generally introduced for the spring trade, less often for the fall. Most of the glass companies had a shut-down period for a few months during the summer when business was slow. Flora is later mentioned in *China, Glass & Lamps* on December 31, 1890, as being a new pattern for the coming spring. Perhaps Bryce, Higbee wanted to be a step ahead of their competition and decided to get an early start on producing and exhibiting the pattern.

Kamm misidentified some Bryce, Higbee catalog pages, which caused

Flora 5.25" covered compote, $40–$45; wine, $20–$25; 7" engraved high-foot open compote, $40–$45.

Flora cream, $40–$45; 6" low-foot open compote, $25–$30; 6.25" high-foot covered compote, $45–$50.

No. 18. Diamond Table Salts.
Heavy crystal table salts, fine imitation of cut, in boxes of 1 doz. **Price, 40c doz.**

Flora table salt sold by Spelman Brothers, February 1891..

Westmoreland's No. 501 goblet (left) is a close copy of Bryce, Higbee's Flora (right). Note the barrel shape not found on items of Flora.

her to erroneously attribute Flora to Greensburg Glass Company. There is no doubt the pattern was made only by Bryce, Higbee. Not only do trade journals confirm this, but the pattern is consistently shown in assortments from Bryce, Higbee & Company offered in different jobber catalogs.

Like other Bryce, Higbee patterns from the early to mid–1890s, Flora is made from good quality, heavy glass and there is a marked similarity to some of the company's other patterns introduced in the same time frame. Flora is sometimes found with attractive engravings including a trailing fern/leaf design that greatly complements and contrasts nicely with the heavily pressed motif. The pattern does not seem to be very plentiful.

Flora is the goddess of flowers and the springtime in Roman mythology. The name is derived from the Latin *flos*, meaning "flower."

Items Noted:

bowl, flat, scalloped edge (some originally termed "nappy"), 4.5"–9"
butter, covered
celery vase, 6.5" h.
compote, high-foot, covered, plain edge, 5.25", 6.5", 7", 8" w.
compote, high-foot, open, scalloped edge, 5", 6", 7", 8", 10.5" w.
compote, low-foot, covered, plain edge, 5", 6", 7", 8" w.
compote, low-foot, open, scalloped edge, 5", 6", 7", 8" w.
cream, applied handle
dish, rectangular, 7.5"
goblet
pickle dish, oblong
pitcher, tankard, applied handle, quart, half-gallon
salt, table
salver, 9", 10"–10.5"
shaker, salt and pepper
spoon, scalloped edge
sugar, covered, plain edge
tumbler
wine

There are undoubtedly more items, as trade journals note there were over sixty-four pieces in the line.

Reproductions and Look-alikes: No reproductions known. It seems that Westmoreland liked to copy Bryce Higbee's patterns! Mention is made in the trade journals that their designs were being imitated, but the reporter did not reveal who was imitating them. Westmoreland's No. 501 goblet is a copy very similar to Flora. Though it is not known when No. 501 was introduced, it was presumably within a few years of Flora. A goblet and wine are shown in the company's 1902 catalog, and the 1905 catalog shows only the goblet. Westmoreland's No. 76 is also a copy. At least the table set and tumbler were made, but it may have been a full line. The table set was shown in Butler Brothers October 1894 catalog and the tumbler was shown in the Westmoreland catalogs noted above. See illustrations for comparison.

Catalog images of Westmoreland's No. 501 (left) and Westmoreland's No. 76 (right), another pattern easily confused for Bryce, Higbee's Flora. This table set appeared in the October 1894 Butler Brothers catalog.

Gem, c. early 1890s

References: BH, undated; BB, April 1892; W&M, c. 1892/93
Colors: clear

Though Kamm dates Gem to the mid–1880s, it has not been observed in any catalogs from that decade. The earliest dated source is an April 1892 Butler Brothers catalog. An assortment of Gem is included in an undated Wallace & McAfee catalog. Shown throughout it are many patterns by other companies introduced for the 1892 spring market. Mention is made more than a few times that the patterns are new, and Wallace & McAfee emphatically states "All of our assortments are made up from new goods. NO OLD patterns that you will have

Gem celery vase, $35–$40; 9" salver, $40–$45; 8" high-foot covered compote, $50–$55.

Gem half-gallon pitcher, $50–$55; goblet, $25–$30; sugar, $35–$40.

to keep on your shelves." Granted, any claim could have been made regarding the newness and salability of the goods offered, but one must question whether a company would harm its integrity and risk its reputation by so boldly claiming only new patterns were offered if they really were not. If we are to believe most of the patterns were new, this catalog would date to approximately 1892/93, which coincides with Gem's appearance in Butler Brothers. There is a paucity of description of any Bryce, Higbee patterns in trade journals from 1892 to late 1894. Gem seems to date from this period. Another clue to the introduction period for Gem is the fact that a square plate is found in the pattern. Square plates began to appear in Bryce, Higbee's lines made during the 1890s.

Many years ago, Gem was attributed to the Boston and Sandwich Glass Company of Sandwich, Massachusetts. In 1954, Kamm stated that fragments of the pattern were at MIT(Massachusetts Institute of Technology) and concluded the pattern was either made by Sandwich or the fragments were samples used for study. Attempts to locate said fragments in spring 2014 proved futile. MIT told the author that it does not have the shards and that they are at the Sandwich Glass Museum. The Sandwich Glass Museum does not have the shards. They said the MIT should have them and that, if they were disposed of in any way, MIT was required to have record of that happening, which apparently they do not.

It is this author's belief that the shards thought to be Gem were actually a different pattern. There is little doubt that Gem was never made at Sandwich. The shards thought to be Gem likely shared similar pattern characteristics. Shards can be quite difficult to identify, especially if they are not compared side-by-side to actual, intact examples. It must be kept in mind that in the early years of collecting EAPG, many patterns were claimed to be of Sandwich origin with no proof whatsoever or through connections that were tenuous at best. Kamm and others once reported many dubious shards of patterns found at Sandwich that we now know never saw the factory site. A Sandwich birth certificate was once considered a mark of distinction and other pressed glass was deemed much less worthy. Kamm mentions that Gem was a highly prized pattern and this may have been due to its misguided association with Sandwich. Wishful thinking can easily obscure reality. The fact that Gem shares mould shapes with other known Bryce, Higbee patterns indicates it originated at Homestead, Pennsylvania, rather than Sandwich, Massachusetts.

Gem half-gallon pitchers are found in four variations:

Version 1: Base is ribbed; pattern on body is large. Center row of diamonds is horizontally divided. The vertical rows alternate between one and two nail heads in each row. Top edge is plain.

Version 2: Base is ribbed; pattern on body is large. Center row of diamonds is not divided. The vertical rows alternate between one and two nail heads in each row. Top edge is plain.

Version 3: Base is plain; pattern on body is large. Center row of diamonds is horizontally divided. The vertical rows alternate between one and two nail heads in each row. Top edge is plain.

Version 4: Base is ribbed; pattern on body is small. The vertical rows alternate between four and five nail heads in each row. No diamonds are divided. Top edge is scalloped.

Version 1 is pictured in this book and was shown in a September 1895 Butler Brothers catalog. Lola and Wayne Higbee picture version 2 in their book, *Bryce, Higbee and J. B. Higbee Glass*. The pitcher illustrated on the Bryce, Higbee catalog page reprinted by Kamm is the variation numbered 3 above, and version 4 is clearly shown in a Butler Brothers assortment of Bryce, Higbee items in the 1896 Santa Claus issue. The reason so many variations of the water pitcher were made is anybody's guess, but there is no doubt all were produced by Bryce, Higbee.

Kamm mentions Gem decorated with orange in the grooves as well as "clear aquamarine" (she must mean transparent blue), but no colored or decorated items have been seen. Gem would have been an outstanding pattern to decorate with ruby stain. Not only would it enhance the design, but the various elements of the pattern could be brought out by staining different areas. Unfortunately, ruby stained items are not known to exist.

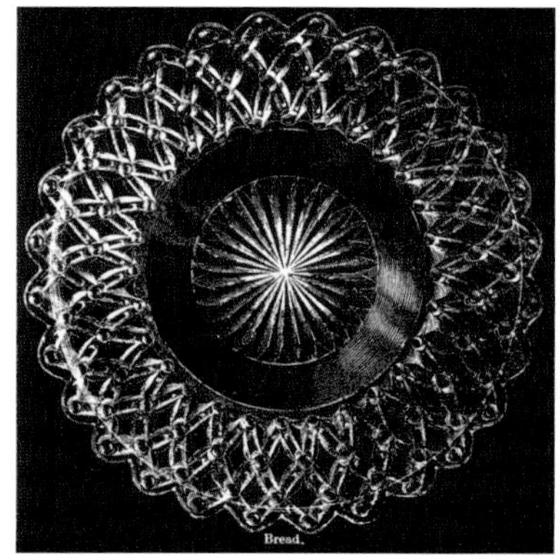

Gem 9" bread plate from a Bryce, Higbee catalog.

Items Noted:

bowl, nappy, 4"–4.5"
bowl, berry, 7"
butter, covered
celery, stemmed
compote, high-foot, covered, 6.25", 7.25", 8" w.
compote, high-foot, open, scalloped rim, 6.25", 7.25", 8", 9" w.
cream
goblet
pitcher, half-gallon, four variations (see text)
pickle dish
plate, square, 7"
plate, bread, round, 9"
salver, 9"
spoon, scalloped edge
sugar, covered, plain edge
tumbler
wine

Reproductions and Look-alikes: In approximately 1973, L. E. Smith produced a two-tiered tidbit tray with a central metal handle. Offered as part of the Regency line and cataloged as No. 9720, the pattern appears identical to Gem; however, the large plate measures 12" and the small plate measures 8.5". Original round Gem plates measure 9" and are much thicker than those made by Smith. Tom Felt reports that, in addition to clear, the tidbit tray was made in amber, antique green, and colonial blue. The clear example examined by the author at Island Mould was frosted in the crevices of the design. The plates were drilled through to accommodate the metal handle, but it is possible plates were made that were not drilled. Beware of clear, clear frosted, and colored Gem plates measuring 8.5" and 12".

Tarentum Glass Company's Albany (right) could be confused for Bryce, Higbee's Gem (left). Note the absence of the round "nail heads" in the Albany pattern.

Tarentum's Albany (1894) is very clearly based on Gem. The most obvious difference is the lack of "nail heads" in the design.

Grand, c. mid–1880s

References: BH, undated; GS, c. 1888; HB&F, spring and summer 1888
Colors: clear

Grand celery vase, $30–$35; goblet, $25–$30; 10" bread plate, $25–$30; 4.5" footed fruit dessert, $12–$15; 3.5" comportier, $18–$20; sugar, $40–$45 (with lid). Goblet with knop stem is most likely New Grand.

Grand 10" salver, $40–$45; 8.5" open high-foot compote, $35–$40.

Comparison of goblets to show the evolution of shape and stem design (l. to r.), Persian, Grand, New Grand, and Melrose.

Grand has been dated to 1885 by previous authors, but the exact year of introduction has not been documented. Trade journal reports mentioning the pattern have not been found; however, an invoice from Bryce, Higbee & Company dated June 30, 1886, has been discovered. Gowans, Kent & Company, a glassware and crockery retailer, purchased ten tierces (packages) of the Grand pattern totaling 1,360 items for $68. Not only does this give a time frame for the pattern, but it also proves that American glass was sent to Canada and sold by their retail establishments.

Some reference books claim Grand was produced in Canada. This is due to an undated advertisement from Gowans, Kent & Co. of Toronto and Winnipeg, Canada, offering items in the New Grand pattern (plain edged version). There is absolutely no evidence to indicate the pattern was made there, but there is proof that Gowans, Kent & Co. purchased items from Bryce, Higbee & Company.

It is this author's belief the Grand pattern consisted of the items with fan-and-scallop edges. Around 1888, the shapes were completely changed, but the design remained essentially the same with minor alterations. This version, done on plain, more modern shapes, was called New Grand by the company. The bread plate and celery vase were carried over to New Grand and were not redesigned.

Fan-and-scallop edges are like those found on Yale, but Grand predates Yale. Finials are an interesting geometric shape and are the same as those on Mirror (1890), New Grand (c. 1888), and Melrose (1894). Salvers and open compotes have an inner ridge and were tooled from the high-foot compotes that were made to accept lids. Salvers and compotes in the Capitola and *Chain* patterns were made the same way. Grand high-foot compotes and salvers were attached to pedestals with a glass wafer, whereas New Grand items were molded in one piece.

Though other authors list Grand items with ruby stain, none have been confirmed. Also, the syrup and decanter have not been documented, either. The listing only includes items with fan-and-scallop edges. For plain-edged items, see New Grand on page 198.

Items Noted:

bowl, flat, oval, 7", 9"
bowl, flat, round, 4.25"–4.5", 6"
compote, low-foot, fruit dessert, 3.5" w.
butter, covered, flat
celery vase, stemmed, 7.75" h.
compote, high-foot, covered, 6", 7", 8", 9" w.
compote, high-foot, open, shallow, 7", 8", 9", 10" w.
compote, low-foot, open, 4"
compote, low-foot, open, covered, 6", 7", 8" w.
cream, stemmed
goblet, plain stem
pickle dish, oval
pitcher, half-gallon, plain foot, notched pattern on foot (latter may be New Grand)
plate, bread, 10"
salver, 9", 9.5", 10"
shaker, salt and pepper , tall, cylindrical (possibly introduced with New Grand)
spoon, stemmed, 3.75" w.
sugar, stemmed, covered, inner ledge, 5.5" w.
wine, plain stem, ring stem

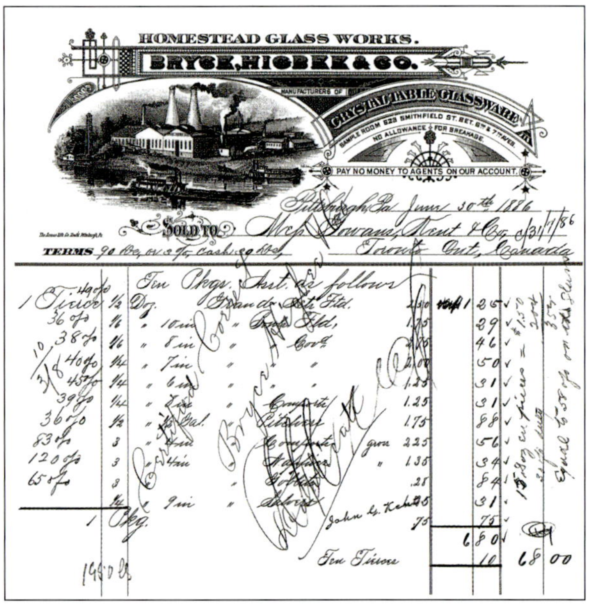

Bryce, Higbee & Company invoice enumerating items of Grand sold to Gowans, Kent & Company in 1886.

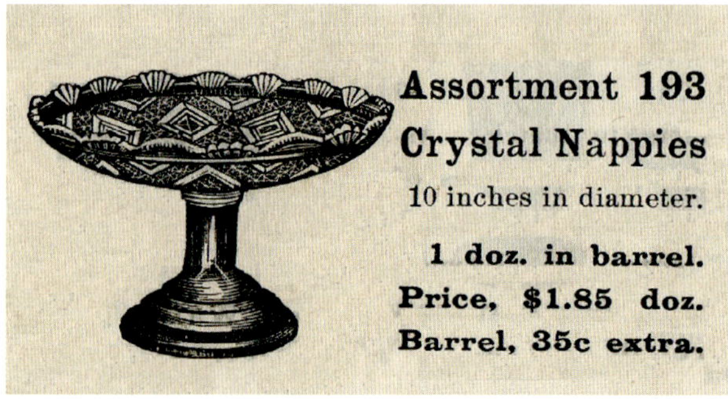

Grand 10" high-foot comport referred to as a nappy in a circa 1888 Spelman Brothers catalog.

Grand Assortment.

Grand Assortment, consisting of the following desirable patterns.

2	9-inch Salvers,	Our retail price, $0.25	.50
2	8 " High Foot Bowls	" " " .35	.70
2	7 " " " "	" " " .25	.50
4	½-gallon Jugs	" " " .25	1.00
4	8-inch Comports	" " " .20	.80
36	4 " "	" " " .05	1.80
3	4 pieced Glass Sets	" " " .40	1.20
24	Wines	" " " .05	1.20
12	10-inch Bread Plates	" " " .10	1.20
36	Goblets	" " " .05	1.80
	Total retail price		10.70
	Price for the assortment		7.50
	Net profit		3.20

Hollander, Bradshaw & Folsom offered this assortment of Grand in 1888. Notice the fan-and-scallop edges and the plain stems on the goblet and wine. *Courtesy of the Rakow Research Library, Corning Museum of Glass.*

Proof was not found that the water set was sold with a waste bowl on a Yale tray as in New Grand, so these items are not included in the listing.

Reproductions and Look-alikes: No reproductions known. Bryce, Higbee's Melrose is often confused for Grand. The arrangement of the main diamond motif is similar, but Grand consists of plain-centered diamonds against a background of tiny eight-pointed stars that appears as a fine cut design when viewed as a whole. Bryce, Higbee's Melrose has the star or fine cut design in the center of the diamonds with fans between each diamond, all set against a plain background.

Highland, 1902

References: *CG&L*, 1/11/1902; BB, spring 1902; JBH, c. 1917 and NM, undated (celery vase only); NMPL, 1921 (celery vase and covered butter only)
Colors: clear, clear with gold trim

Highland 8" square compote, $25–$30; cream, $20–$25; 7.75" plate, $20–$25; 7" bowl, $18–$20; 5" jelly compote, $18–$20.

Highland celery vase, $30–$35, and illustration from the circa 1917 J. B. Higbee *General Catalogue*. This is the only source for the pattern's OMN. *Catalog image courtesy of the Rakow Research Library, Corning Museum of Glass.*

Highland was first mentioned in the January 11, 1902, issue of *Crockery & Glass Journal*:

> The other line is called the "Highland" and comprises also about 75 pieces. It is a figured pattern, too, and equally as attractive as the other.

Like many trade journal reviews of the time, description of the pattern is sorely lacking. It was deemed sufficient to briefly describe new lines to entice the buyers to view them in person. Fortunately, the circa 1917 J. B. Higbee *General Catalogue* shows a celery vase labeled Highland, so there is no doubt which pattern it is.

According to *China, Glass & Lamps*, Highland was a rather large line. Presumably many of the items were bowls of various sizes and depths that were hand-tooled in different ways. Most of Bryce, Higbee's post–1900 lines are found in an amazing variety of bowls, yet by this time it seems that the company produced no covered compotes in their new lines as they had in previous decades. The edges of bowls were crimped, flared, squared, and curved inward to create different forms, each given its own designation. Plates were flattened from bowls, and cake baskets and salvers were tooled from compotes. This was an economical method to add to the number of items in the set because the same mould was used to create many different articles.

The only item shown in the J. B. Higbee *General Catalogue* and an undated New Martinsville Glass Manufacturing Company catalog is the celery vase. J. B. Higbee acquired the mould in the liquidation of the Bryce, Higbee factory in May 1908, and, in turn, that mould was purchased by New Martinsville from J. B. Higbee. No examples of the celery vase have been reported marked with J. B. Higbee's trademark bee. Interestingly, the images in both company's catalogs appear to be identical. A 1921 New Martinsville

Glass Manufacturing Company price list records a celery vase and butter dish to be sold per dozen at $1.40 and $1.25 respectively. It may seem odd that the covered butter dish would sell for less than the celery vase, but this was likely due to the celery vase requiring some hand-tooling. Their rims are often flared, some more than others.

The Highland name may be a reference to the beautiful and picturesque Highland Park. Dating back to the 1890s and located in Pittsburgh, it was not far from the Bryce, Higbee factory. The area also boasted a street named Highland as well as a telephone exchange by the same name. Another possibility, though perhaps less plausible, is that it relates to the fact that the Bryce family was of Scottish descent. Though they were not from the highlands, the name could have been a tribute to their native country.

Items Noted:

bowl, collar base, round, square, various depths and sizes
bowl, flat, oval, 7"
butter, covered
cake basket, 9.5" l.
celery vase, collar base, 6" h.
compote, jelly, high-foot, round, square, 5" w
compote, high-foot, round, square, 8" w.
cream, footed
nick nack, high-foot, 6" l.
pitcher, half-gallon
plate, collar base, round, 7.75", 9.5"
rose bowl, stemmed, 7.5" h.
salver, 6", 9.5"
shaker, salt and pepper
spoon, footed, scalloped edge
sugar, footed, covered, scalloped edge, inner ledge
tumbler
wine

Our "MISCELLANEOUS" Asst. of FULL FINISHED WARE.

An Assortment of Staple Sellers, Every One of Which Can Be Retailed at a "Leader" Price.

C779—All of the same beautiful pattern, which is an entirely new beautiful cut diamond design, every piece full finished and fire polished and all except three being footed. Will sell off evenly and pay you a handsome profit. Assortment comprises the following:

⅓ doz.	four piece table sets (Butter Dish, Sugar Bowl, Spoon Holder and Cream Pitcher)	$1 85	$0 62
⅙ doz.	2-qt. Water Pitchers—Fancy Shape	1 25	21
⅙ "	8-inch High Footed Fancy Bowls	1 20	20
⅙ "	9½-inch High Footed Cake Salvers	1 20	20
⅙ "	Extra Large High Celery Holder	96	16
⅙ "	9-inch Footed Flaring Salad Bowl	96	16
¼ "	9½-inch Footed Cake Plates	80	20
¼ "	7¼-inch Extra Deep Footed Round Bowl	80	20
¼ "	6-inch High Footed Salver	60	15
¼ "	5¼x5¼ High Footed Fancy Shape Deep Jelly Dish	60	15
1 "	Heavy Rich Table Tumblers	33	33
1 "	4½-inch Footed Comport	36	36
½ "	Heavy Cut Pattern Salt Shakers	29	15
½ "	Heavy Cut Pattern Pepper Shakers	29	14
⅓ "	8x4½-inch Oval Utility Dish	39	13

(Total 5½ doz. in bbl. Wt. 100 lbs. Bbl. 35c.) Total for assortment, **$3.36**

Large assortment of Highland, Butler Brothers spring 1903 catalog. Note the single *Fine Cut and Fan* oval bowl. This same assortment appeared in the spring 1902 catalog for 19¢ less.

Other items typical of Bryce, Higbee's production during this time frame, such as almond trays, 5.5" plates, 7" square plates, and nick nack trays, have not been found but could exist. Obviously many other forms are to be had, since *Crockery & Glass Journal* mentions Highland was made in about seventy-five items.

Reproductions and Look-alikes: None known.

Homestead, c. 1880s

References: BH, undated; BB, 1885; P&B, c. 1887; W&M, c. 1891; BB, May 1905; JBH, c. 1917 & NMPL, 1921 (rectangular salt dishes only)
Colors: clear, clear with frosted handles, clear with engraving; amber and blue (individual salts)

Homestead spooner, $20–$25; rectangular individual salt, $15–$20; salt and pepper shakers, $50–$55; amber oval salt, $30–$35; engraved 6" high-foot covered compote, $40–$45.

Engraving commonly found on items of Homestead. So far, it has not been found on any other pattern.

The year of introduction for Homestead is not known, but a single cream pitcher is first spotted in a Butler Brothers assortment in 1885. The pattern appears sparingly in available jobber catalogs that were observed by the author. Homestead is illustrated in an undated Bryce, Higbee catalog dating to circa 1888. Oddly enough, some Homestead and Mirror items are included together in assortments in a May 1905 Butler Brothers catalog. This may indicate items from the earlier Homestead line were added to the Mirror line, or it may suggest that old stock was being purged from Bryce, Higbee's warehouses and offered with another plain pattern. An 1898 Peaslee-Gaulbert catalog also shows a Homestead pitcher with an assortment of Mirror. A circa 1891 Wallace and McAfee catalog includes a Homestead water pitcher with an Alfonzo celery vase and items in the Mirror pattern, so it seems that plain patterns were offered together by the factory.

A salver shown in a circa 1887 Pitkin and Brooks catalog is labeled Homestead, but it is very similar to plain patterns made by other companies. The butter dishes (mammoth and standard), celery vase, cream, spoon, sugar, and pickle jar are much more distinctive with their open-ringed handles with scrolls on both sides, much like the handles found on the Capitola and *Chain* patterns as well as the New Grand pickle dish. The Homestead pickle jar and covered sugar are easily mistaken for one another, but the pickle jar is slightly narrower than the sugar. Lids are high and angular; finials are tall tapered cylinders. Stems have a raised ring at the midsection. Footed items are found with a plain base or with a distinctive twelve-pointed star design underneath the foot, which is actually a small six-pointed star placed over a large six-pointed star.

Homestead is often found engraved with a wide leaf motif, which led to the name *Cordate Leaf* given by Kamm. The OMN Homestead is preferable, however, because not all items are engraved, nor do they all have that distinctive engraving. Other engravings have been seen, which include a typical leaf and berry design as well as a variety of Victorian moss rose. Since Bryce, Higbee had its own engraving shop, additional engravings are possible.

The only items thus far found in color are an amber individual oval salt and a blue individual rectangular salt. Salts were made in oval and rectangular shapes in table (master) and individual sizes. Bryce, Higbee termed the rectangular Homestead salt "Sqr." (square) in their catalog. Homestead rectangular salts are distinguished from other similar plain salts by their concave angled edges, four tiny, rounded feet under each corner, and wide-rayed star in the base. The oval salts have the same feet and star in the base, which is a smaller version of the star found on items of Capitola, *Chain,* Alfonzo, and Butterfly. Only the rectangular salt dishes are shown in J. B. Higbee's circa 1917 *General Catalogue* as "No. 512—Star Table Salt" and "No. 513—Star Individual Salt." Clear, rectangular individual salts are found marked with J. B. Higbee's trademark bee. These salts have not been seen in any New Martinsville Glass Manufacturing Company catalogs, but they do appear in a company price list from 1921. Their descriptions are the same, but for some reason they are given different numbers.

The Homestead name is yet another one of significance, for this was the city where Bryce, Higbee & Company was located.

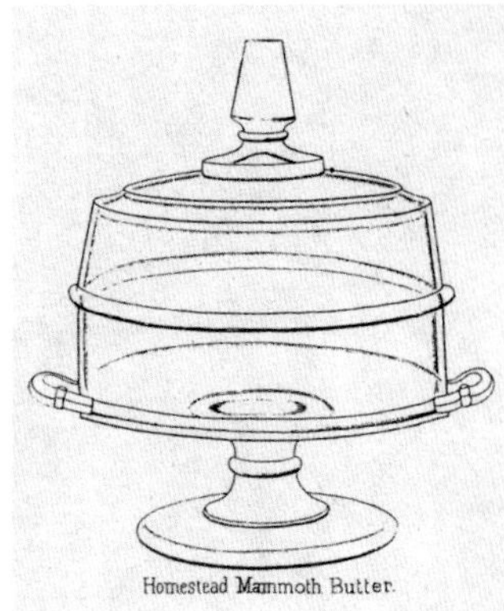

Homestead goblet and mammoth butter illustrations from Bryce, Higbee catalogs.

No. 0, Homestead,
8 inch, per doz . . $2.50.
9 " " " . . 3.00.
10 " " " . . 3.50.
11 " " " . . 5.50.
12 " " " . . 7.50.
Extra good, fine polish, more durable than common goods.

Homestead salver from a circa 1887 Pitkin & Brooks catalog. Notice its similarity to the plain wares made by many other glass companies.

Items Noted:

butter, footed, covered, shallow handled bowl
butter, "mammoth," footed, covered, deep handled bowl
celery vase, stemmed, handled, 8" h.
compote, high-foot, covered, 6", 7", 8", 8.5" w.
compote, low-foot, open, 4" w.
cream, stemmed
goblet
pickle jar, stemmed, handled, plain edge, glass lid, 3.5" w.
pitcher, half-gallon
salt, four small feet, oval, individual (2" x 1.5") and table
salt, four small feet, rectangular, individual (2" x 1.5") and table
salver, 8", 9", 10", 11", 12"
shaker, salt and pepper, stemmed, handled
spoon, stemmed, handled, scalloped edge, 6" h. by 3.5" w.
sugar, stemmed, covered, handled, plain edge, 4.25" w.
wine

Kamm mentions a footed tumbler and "many compotes, covered and open" without elaborating. It is not known if the open compotes have scalloped edges or are the same plain-rimmed bases used for the covered compotes.

Reproductions and Look-alikes: No reproductions known. Handles and finials are quite distinctive, but Homestead is difficult to distinguish from plain patterns made by other companies if the item does not have handles or a lid. The typical "cordate leaf" engraving found on the pattern could distinguish items if present. See other features mentioned above.

Ida, 1885

References: BH, undated; *P&GR*, 1/1/1885; BB 83rd Trip, 1885; GS, 1885 & 1886
Colors: clear, amber, blue, some canary

Ida 22 oz. pitcher, \$35–\$40; sugar lid (complete sugar, \$30–\$35) cream, \$20–\$25; wine, \$15–\$20; celery vase, \$30–\$35.

Ida 7.5" high-foot clear compote, \$20–\$25; amber pickle, \$20–\$25; blue goblet, \$35–\$40.

The January 1, 1885, issue of *Pottery & Glassware Reporter* was the first to mention Bryce, Higbee's Ida:

> A new pattern of tableware named the "Ida," which is made in close imitation of cut glass, and is very bright and handsome. The set is a novelty, there being several different shapes in the line, which is now complete.

The modern collector may find it interesting that the pattern was described as a close imitation of cut glass by the reporter. In the same year, B. Sommers offered an Ida bread plate in an assortment and described it as "Grecian." Our perception is often very different from that of 130 years and more ago.

An Ida pitcher is shown on an undated Bryce, Higbee catalog page that dates to 1887 or after, and a table set is shown and correctly called Ida in an 1886 B. Sommers catalog.

Some contend that Ida was originally made by the Eagle Glass Works of Keota, Iowa, and/or the Iowa City Flint Glass Manufacturing Company of Iowa City, Iowa. These companies existed for a brief time between September 1879 and the first half of 1882. There are many flaws with attributing Ida to Keota and/or Iowa City. First, if Ida originated in Iowa before Bryce, Higbee made it, where were the moulds for nearly three years? Like Earl, Ida is the Bryce, Higbee pattern found most often in color, which is very typical of the mid–1880s. The colors of amber, blue, and canary were not used in the time frame that glassware was being made in Iowa. Even if we surmise that Ida was made only in clear at Keota and/or Iowa City, the glass made there contained a lot of impurities and was not high quality ware, yet pieces of Ida are well made and of a quality consistent with other Bryce, Higbee products. There is nothing to substantiate the Iowa attribution.

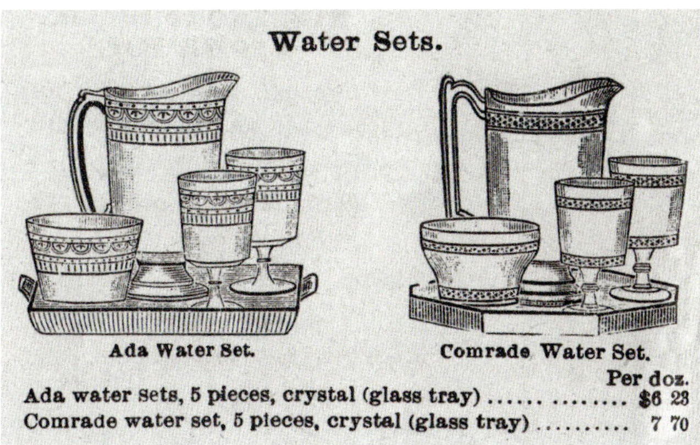

Water Sets.

Ada Water Set. — Comrade Water Set.

	Per doz.
Ada water sets, 5 pieces, crystal (glass tray)	\$6 23
Comrade water set, 5 pieces, crystal (glass tray)	7 70

Ida and Earl water sets illustrated in French, Potter & Wilson's April 1886 price list. Earl appears here as "Comrade," while Ida is more closely called "Ada." Note the waste bowls and glass trays that came with the sets.

Ida is a feminine name derived from the Germanic word *id* meaning "labor." John Bryce's youngest daughter (born 1864) was named Ida, suggesting the pattern was named after her.

Ida table set, B. Sommers' spring 1886 catalog. The pieces are not drawn proportionately to each other, a common occurrence in many jobber catalogs.

Items Noted:
bowl, round, 4", 6"
bowl, octagonal, 6", 7.5"
butter, covered
celery vase, stemmed, scalloped edge
compote, high-foot, covered, 7", 8.5" w.
compote, high-foot, open, flared, plain edge, 7.5", 8.5" w.
compote, low-foot, open, 4", 5" w.
cream, two styles: "ear"-shaped handle, flat handle with thumb rest
goblet
pickle dish, octagonal, handled
pitcher, quart, two styles, 20 oz. and 22 oz.
pitcher, half-gallon
plate, bread, octagonal, 9.75"
salver, 10"
spoon, plain edge, 3.5" w.
sugar, covered, plain edge, inner ledge, 4.25" w.
tray for water set, rectangular, handled
waste bowl, approximately 5" w.
wine

Reproductions and Look-alikes: None known.

Madora, c. 1906, possibly 1907

References: BB, spring 1907; *CG&L*, 11/8/1910; JBH, undated; JG, c. 1920–25; NM, undated & NMPL, 1921 (high-foot open compote only—see notes below)
Colors: clear, clear with ruby stain (mug and tumbler; also lemonade cup engraved "Toronto 1921" known)

There has been confusion whether Madora was introduced by Bryce, Higbee or J. B. Higbee. The pattern incorporates hexagons with daisies impressed in them just like those found on the *Ten-Pointed Star* pattern, and the design in the base of Madora items is identical to the base design of *Ten-Pointed Star*. Though no Bryce, Higbee company catalogs showing Madora are known, it confidently can be attributed to them. A rather large assortment called the "Crown Jewel" stock pattern containing fifty-seven different items of Madora appears in the spring 1907 Butler Brothers catalog. We are led to believe the glassware was manufactured before the end of 1906, for according to the December 22, 1906, issue of *China, Glass & Lamps*:

> It is announced that Bryce, Higbee & Co., Homestead,

Madora 8" bowl, \$18–\$20; 9.25" plate, \$30–\$35; lily or rose bowl, \$30–\$35.

Madora 10" shallow bowl, \$25–\$30; 7" plate, \$20–\$25; 6.5" wafer stand, \$30–\$35.

Madora wines (two styles), \$12–\$15 each; toothpick, \$25–\$30; 3.5" comportier, \$10–\$12; cruet with original Bryce, Higbee stopper, \$35–\$40. Note the hand-twisted stem on the wine second from the left. This wine is not marked, but the other two have the J. B. Higbee trademark bee.

> Pa., have shut down their tableware plant and that they will not operate pending the settlement of matters due to the death of John B. Higbee, one of the members of the firm.

The factory remained closed, and, in March 1907, the factory was damaged by flood, never to reopen. An important clue is found in the October 1908 Butler Brothers catalog. Part of the description of the "Crown Jewel" assortment reads:

> On account of the destruction of factory by flood we were compelled to omit from our catalog and disappointed many customers during past season. From now on we shall carry all items in stock and be in position to make immediate shipments.

This is obviously a reference to the loss of the Bryce, Higbee & Company factory in the 1907 flood. How is it, then, that Madora is shown in the spring 1907, issue when the factory reportedly shut down in December 1906? Butler Brothers catalogs proudly mention the vast amount of warehouse space they had, so it is possible that the glassware was manufactured prior to December 1906 and stored in their own warehouses. There is some indication the factory did not completely shut down as *China, Glass & Lamps* reported. See page 96 for more discussion. By October 1908, J. B. Higbee was producing the Madora pattern for Butler Brothers. It is interesting to note that only the earliest offerings of the assortment includes a cupped compote referred to as "C746, High Footed Lily or Fruit Bowl," which appears to be tooled from the regular 8" compote. Subsequent offerings after the formation of J. B Higbee Glass Company skip from C745 to C747 and do not picture or list the C746 compote. This can only mean that J. B. Higbee did not make this particular item for whatever reason.

Even more confusing is the fact that J. B. Higbee introduced Madora as a new pattern for the 1910 market, as evidenced by this quote from the January 8, 1910, issue of *China, Glass & Lamps:*

> The J. B. Higbee Glass Co., Room 228, Fort Pitt Hotel, have two new lines for 1910 to be known respectively as Colonial and Madora, each consisting of approximately

one hundred pieces.

Butler Brothers mentions that the "Crown Jewel" stock pattern was made especially for them, but Madora pitchers and cruets were offered in small assortments with the same items in the Alpha pattern throughout 1909. J. B. Higbee continued to produce the pattern for Butler Brothers' "Crown Jewel" assortment after Bryce, Higbee ceased to exist, but, by mid-summer 1911, it was no longer offered. The bulk of the moulds purchased from the defunct Bryce, Higbee factory in May 1908 may have been the Madora pattern. J. B. Higbee undoubtedly added items to the line, however.

The Madora name is documented through an undated, circa 1910 J. B. Higbee catalog, which comprises ninety items of the pattern under this title (incidentally, the "High Footed Lily or Fruit Bowl" from the "Crown Jewel" assortment mentioned above is not included). There is no extant proof that Bryce, Higbee called the pattern Madora, but if they did introduce it to the trade, there is no reason to think they did not use that name.

Ollie Higbee clearly followed in the footsteps of his father's company. The terms for forms found in catalogs issued by J. B. Higbee directly coincide with the same terms for Bryce, Higbee forms mentioned in trade journals and shown in Bryce, Higbee catalogs as well as catalogs of Pitkin and Brooks, Wallace & McAfee, and other jobbers issued before Bryce, Higbee closed. Terms such as berry dessert, casserole, nick nack, and comportier are very unusual and would be much too coincidental to be random, arbitrary uses for these specific forms. In fact, the word comportier is either a misspelling or a corruption of the French *compotier* and was widely used by Bryce, Higbee and J. B. Higbee.

The Madora cruet is shown in Butler Brothers' "Delmonico" and "Crown Jewel" assortments as well as the J. B. Higbee Madora catalog with the diamond and zipper patterned stopper, which originated with Bryce, Higbee's Bonair. The cruet has also been seen with the stopper found on J. B. Higbee's Alpha and Laurel patterns, and it was likely sold this way as well. This latter stopper appears in no Bryce, Higbee assortments, only those of J. B. Higbee. See pages 62–65 for photos of stoppers used by both companies.

Madora 11.25" celery tray with Old Rose Distilling Co. advertising, $50–$55.

Items Noted: *Items shown in Butler Brothers as "Crown Jewel" before flood destroyed the Bryce, Higbee factory.*

basket, applied ribbed handle, 6.5", 8.75" l.
bowl, collar base, round, "berry bowl," 5.25", 7", 8", 8.5"
bowl, collar base, "star shape berry bowl," (ruffled), 6.5", 8.5", 9.5", 10.25"
bowl, collar base, deep, "nappy or sauce dish," 4.5"; flared, 5"
bowl, collar base, shallow, flared, "fancy fruit bowl," 6", 8", 9.75", 11"
bowl, collar base, shallow, cupped, "fancy footed salad bowl," 6", 8", 9", 10"
bowl, flat, shallow, "ice cream dish," 4.25"
bowl, flat, deep, "nappy or sauce dish," 4.5"
bowl, flat, oval, "table dish," 10.25" x 7.5"
butter, covered
celery tray, "rolled up sides," 11" l.
celery vase, handled, 6" h.
comport, footed (comportier), 3.5" w. (found with twelve-pointed star or figured pattern in base)
compote, jelly, high-foot, 5" w.
compote, high-foot, shallow, cupped, 5.75", 8.5" w.
compote, high-foot, deep, 8" w.
compote, high-foot, deep, cupped, "lily or fruit bowl"
cream, table, scalloped top
cream, cafe, (mug with small tooled spout), 3.5" h.
cruet, stopper #3
cup, sherbet, deep, 2.75" w.
jelly dish, handled, round, 5"
mug, 3.5" h.
olive dish, handled, triangle-shaped, 5.5"

The "CROWN JEWEL" STOCK PATTERN

Beautiful heavy cut pattern, made especially for us. Fine quality ware. Note specially that practically all the pieces can be retailed at the popular prices of 5, 10, 15 and 25 cents. Purest heavy crystal, new deep diamond jewel and fan cut design, artistic shapes, all full finished fire polished. Every piece a sparkling gem. On account of the destruction of factory by flood we were compelled to omit from our catalogue and disappointed many customers during past season. From now on we shall carry all items in stock and be in position to make immediate shipments.

Note—Don't confuse the Crown Jewel line with the cheap unfinished glassware usually sold at similar prices, but order a sample lot and compare. **Sold in open stock.**

C697, Footed Comport—Diam. 3½ in., deep shape, footed, ht. 2⅝ in....Doz. 27c
C698, Ice Cream Dish—Diam. 4¼ in., round shape....Doz. 29c
Nappies or Sauce Dishes.
C699—4⅜ in., round deep shape....Doz. 33c
C700—4½ " round deep footed shape. " 39c
C701—5 in. footed flaring shape...Doz. 41c
Extra Deep Round Berry Bowls, Footed.
C702—5¼ in....Doz. 45c
C703—7 "...." 87c
C704—8 "...." $1.20
C705—8½ " extra deep...." $1.95
Star Shape Berry Bowls, Footed.
C706— 6½ in....Doz. 45c
C707— 8½ "...." 87c
C708— 9½ "...." $1.20
C709—10¼ "...." 1.95
Fancy Fruit Bowls—Footed flaring shapes.
C710— 6 in....Doz. 45c
C711— 8 "...." 87c
C712— 9¾ "...." $1.20
C713—11 "...." 1.95
Fancy Footed Salad Bowls—Rolled up sides.
C714— 6 in....Doz. 45c
C715— 8 "...." 87c
C716— 9 "...." $1.20
C717—10 "...." 1.95
C721, Pickle Dish—8¼ in., deep oval shape. Doz. 43c
C722, Table Dish—10¼x7½, deep oval shape. Doz. 92c
C723, Celery Tray—11 in., oval shape, rolled up sides....Doz. 96c
C724, Cake Plate—7¼ in. square....Doz. 45c
C725, Cake or Fruit Plate—9¾ in., round footed shape....Doz. 89c
C727, Handled Olive or Jelly Dish—5 in., round and deep....Doz. 45c
C728, Salts and Peppers—Asstd., ht. 3½ in. heavy cast plated tops....Doz. 48c
C729, Handled Sherbet Cup—Deep, diam. 2¾ in....Doz. 42c
C730, Handled Mug—Large size, diam. 3 in., ht. 3½....Doz. 43c
C733, Table Tumbler—New shape, thin bell edge....Doz. 45c
C734, Oil or Vinegar Bottle—Large size, full ht. 6½ in....Doz. 84c
C735, Celery Holder—Extra large size, ht. 6 in., fancy doubled handles....Doz. $1.20
C736, 4 Piece Table Set....Set, 37½c
C751—Covered butters only. Diam. 7¾ in. Doz. $1.39
C752—Covered sugars only. Extra large size double handled, ht. 6½ in....Doz. $1.30
C753—Cream pitchers only. Ht. 4⅜ in., wide top....Doz. 92c
C754—Spoon holders only. Double handles, ht. 4½ in....Doz. 89c
Jugs or Pitchers—New rich shape, wide flaring tops.
C737—Quart size, ht. 7½ in....Doz. $1.20
C738—3 pt. size, ht. 8¼ in...." $1.95
C739—Mammoth half gal. size...." 2.95
C732, Fancy Wine Glass...." 39c
High Footed Cake Salvers—Round shape.
C740—Diam. 6½ in....Doz. 48c
C741— " 9½ "...." $1.50
C744, High Footed Jelly Dish—Deep round shape, diam. 5 in....Doz. 48c
C745, High Footed Fruit Bowl—Deep round shape, diam. 8 in....Doz. $1.50
C747, Tall Flower Vase—Ht. 12 in. fancy floral shape top....Doz. 96c
Fancy Baskets—Extra deep footed shape, serpentine stuck handles.
C749—6½ in....Doz. 96c
C750—8¾ "...." $2.10
C705-699, 7 Piece Berry Set—Comprising 8 in. deep bowl, six 4¼ in. nappies....Set, 33c
C739-733, Water Set—Comprises mammoth half gallon jug, 6 tumblers....Set, 48c

A large grouping of Madora was offered as "Crown Jewel" by Butler Brothers beginning in spring 1907. This cut is from the October 1908 issue. Note the reference to the destruction of the factory by flood.

pickle dish, flat, oval, 8.25"
pitcher, quart, 7.5" h.
pitcher, 3 pint, 8.25" h.
pitcher, half-gallon, 8.5" h.
plate, collar base, round, "cake or fruit plate," 9.75"
plate, square, "cake plate," 7"
rose bowl, collar base, deep, cupped, 3.75", 4.5", 6.25" w.
salver, high-foot, 6.5", 9.5" w.
shaker, salt and pepper
spoon, handled, scalloped edge
sugar, covered, handled, scalloped edge, inner ledge, 4.5" w.
tumbler
vase, swung, four rows of hexagonal stars at base, ribbed top section, 12", 16"
wine

Additional items shown in J. B. Higbee catalog devoted to Madora:
basket, oblong, no handle, 8", 10", 11" l.
bowl, collar base, cupped, 4" (termed "individual salad")
bowl, fruit, collar base, straight sides, deep, 5", 6"
bowl, fruit, collar base, flared, 7"
bowl, collar base, round, deep, 9", 10" (termed "comportier")
bowl, collar base, crimped and square, 6", 8", 9" (termed "comportier")
bowl, collar base, flared edge, 6", 8", 9" (termed "casserole")
cake basket
compote, jelly, high-foot, belled, square, 5"
compote, high-foot, shallow, 5" (termed "sweetmeat")
compote, high-foot, scalloped base, straight, flared, square, belled, crimped
compote, high-foot, shallow, 8" (termed "sweetmeat")
compote, high-foot, square, 8"
cup, ice cream, flared
lily bowl, collar base, cupped, 5", 6", 8" w.
nick nack, high-foot, 6" l.
nut bowl, collar base, deep, flared, approximately 8" w.
plate, 5", 8", 10", 11"
rose bowl, stemmed, cupped, flared, (respectively termed "No. 1 and 2 lily vase")
salt, table, cupped
sherbet, footed, straight, belled
toothpick
wafer stand, 6.5" w.
wine, belled

Though not shown in any known J. B. Higbee company catalogs,

6" collar-based ruffled bowls, footed sherbets, straight-sided goblets and wines, as well as individual "crown"-shaped salts and toy table sets were made. Some of these items and ones listed above from the Madora catalog may have been introduced by J. B. Higbee and not made by Bryce, Higbee. The "crown" individual salts are not shown in the Madora catalog, but are first observed in a mid-summer 1911 Butler Brothers catalog. The straight-sided goblets and wines are commonly found marked and are shaped like stemware in J. B. Higbee's Colonial and Delta patterns. Obviously, if an item has the bee trademark, it was not made by Bryce, Higbee, but, since it is not known if J. B. Higbee marked every single piece of glassware they made, there is no guarantee that unmarked items were made by Bryce, Higbee. Indeed, a great amount of Madora is not marked. It must be considered that the items offered as the "Crown Jewel" stock pattern may not have been marked—even when produced by J. B. Higbee after May 1908—since Butler Brothers states the pattern was made especially for them. Presumably, moulds acquired from Bryce, Higbee were being used, which obviously were not trademarked. Since J. B. Higbee introduced Madora as their own pattern in 1910, it is reasonable to think this is when they began marking the pattern and added new items to the line. The bee trademark was most likely taken off the plungers by New Martinsville and Jefferson Glass Company, Limited, but there is no way to know for certain.

It is not known how many Madora moulds New Martinsville might have acquired from J. B. Higbee. A celery tray advertising Old Rose Distilling Company's twentieth anniversary in 1922 is known, but there is no proof it was made by New Martinsville. The only item that can be documented through company catalogs is the high-foot compote (straight bowl) with scalloped base. Oddly enough, this compote is given the same number as a similar covered compote in J. B. Higbee's Alpha pattern shown next to it. There is little doubt J. B. Higbee was responsible for this name change, for the 1921 New Martinsville price list headed "Higbee Glass Company's Moulds" includes a "21 Alpha Hi Ft Comport" as well as a "21 Alpha High Ftd Comport & Cov." These are the same captions, minus the Alpha name, shown under the compotes illustrated in New Martinsville's catalog.

There are only twenty Madora items shown as "No. 230 set" in Catalog No. 21 of Jefferson Glass Company, Limited, Toronto, Canada. Of those twenty items, thirteen appear to be identical to those shown in the J. B. Higbee Madora catalog:

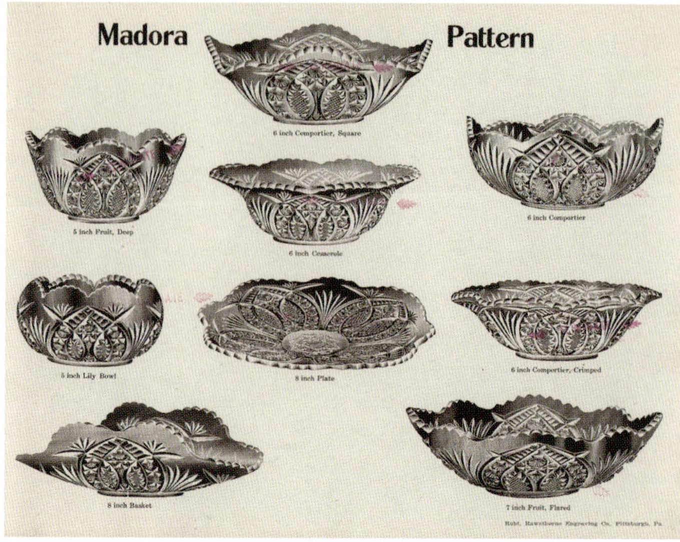

Circa 1910 Madora catalog page issued by J. B. Higbee. Note the terms used for the various bowls, especially the use of the designation "comportier" and the typographical error of "cesserole." *Courtesy of the Rakow Research Library, Corning Museum of Glass.*

- butter, covered
- bowl, footed, 6" (footed jelly, belled)
- bowl, oval, 8" (olive tray)
- cafe cream
- comport, 3.5" (comportier)
- cream
- jelly, handled, 5"
- jug, quart (quart pitcher)
- jug, half-gallon (half-gallon pitcher)
- mug
- toothpick
- spoon
- sugar and cover

The seven items that appear to be different than those shown in J. B. Higbee's Madora catalog are:

- cracker bowl, 9" (may be shown in "Crown Jewel" assortment as "8½" extra deep berry bowl.")
- nappy, 4", 5", 5.5" (two different shapes), 9"
- tumbler (looks to be narrower and slightly cupped)

New Martinsville cataloged both of these compotes as No. 21 (Alpha), but the pattern on the open compote was originally called Madora.

At this point, the only pieces of Madora that can be firmly attributed to Bryce, Higbee are those shown in the spring 1907 "Crown Jewel" assortment enumerated above. Forms typical of Bryce, Higbee (such as cake baskets) could very well have been made by them, but at this point there is no way of knowing for certain. The "high-footed lily or fruit bowl" mentioned earlier may be the only Madora item made exclusively by Bryce, Higbee.

Madora is a feminine Greek name that translates to "ruler." This would not have been the first time Bryce, Higbee used a person's name with this meaning. It may be a metaphor that the pattern would rule over others in the market.

Reproductions and Look-alikes: Amber 3.5" comportiers have been seen and other items are possible. These may have been made by New Martinsville or after they became the Viking Glass Company. Cambridge's No. 2694 (c. 1908) could be confused for Madora upon casual inspection, but comparison reveals many differences within the pattern.

Cambridge No. 2694 (right) is similar to Madora (left).

Melrose, 1894

References: *CG&L*, 10/17/1894; OM&G, 1895; P&B, 1897 & 1899; JBH, c. 1917 & NM, undated & NMPL, 1921 (water tray only)
Colors: clear

Bryce, Higbee introduced their Melrose pattern in fall 1894, as evidenced by this brief quote from the October 17, 1894, issue of *China, Glass & Lamps*:

> They [Bryce, Higbee & Co.] make a high grade of ware...Their new "Melrose" pattern is a beautiful one and sells well.

Though not described in any trade journal quotes, Melrose is shown in jobber catalogs that consistently used OMNs. A salver is shown in Ogden, Merrill & Greer's 1895 catalog as well as Pitkin & Brooks's 1897 and 1899 catalogs; in fact, the images in those catalogs appear to be identical. Bryce, Higbee's Melrose is the pattern collectors have called *Sheaf and Diamond*.

A Melrose water tray is illustrated in the circa 1917 J. B. Higbee *General Catalogue*. The same image appears in an undated New Martinsville Glass Manufacturing Company catalog, and is recorded in the company's 1921 price list at $2.50 per dozen. All three documents include the same number, 523, and caption, "Melrose Water Tray." The Higbys report this item with the bee trademark. John and Elizabeth Welker confused the Melrose water tray for Yale, leading them to believe New Martinsville reproduced the Yale pattern and called it Melrose. From this error was born the misconception that Yale was also made by J. B. Higbee, which it most certainly was not. The Melrose water tray merely utilizes the Yale blank, which includes the distinctive central medallion and fan-and-scallop design molded onto the rim. They are two completely different patterns. The Welkers also incorrectly identify J. B. Higbee's Melrose as the pattern of the same name made by Brilliant/Greensburg and later acquired by National, which it decidedly is not. Lola and Wayne Higby repeat this misinformation in their book, *Bryce, Higbee and J. B. Higbee Glass*. None of these authors mention Bryce, Higbee when discussing Melrose, nor do they make any correct connection with the *Sheaf and Diamond* pattern.

The Greensburg Glass Company of Brilliant, Ohio, introduced their Melrose design about 1888. This pattern has nothing to do with Bryce, Higbee or J. B. Higbee. The basic motif of diamonds with fans between them was used with slight variations by many other companies during the early to mid–1890s. Each company called their version something different except for Bryce, Higbee, who not only used the motif, but strangely christened the pattern with the same name Brilliant/Greensburg did.

Melrose is very similar to Bryce, Higbee's earlier New Grand pattern, and at least some items, if not most of them, were made from retooled moulds of the New Grand pattern. Once Melrose appeared in the pages of Butler Brothers, New Grand completely disappeared. Finials of the two patterns are the same, and they are also the finials used for the Mirror pattern. Oddly enough, the Melrose spoon holder is not shown in jobber catalogs, though the butter, cream, and covered sugar were offered together in assortments.

Three Melrose items have fan-and-scallop edges: the bread plate, celery vase, and water tray. Examination shows that this is due to retooling and reuse of moulds. For more detailed discussion, see Retooled Moulds on page 85.

Melrose celery vases, $25–$30 each; sugar, $40–$45; water tray, $45–$50; goblet, $20–$25.

Melrose 8" plain-edge compote, $35–$40; 8" scalloped-edge compotes, $20–$25 each.

Melrose 10.5" cake basket and 9.5" salver, $35–$40 each.

Melrose half-gallon pitcher, $50–$55; 8.25" scalloped-edge bowl, $20–$25

Melrose 5.5" jelly compote, $18–$20; 10" bread plate, $25–$30; 7.5" oval bowl, $15–$20; 6.25" high-foot covered compote, $45–$50.

Melrose salver from an 1897 Pitkin & Brooks catalog. *Courtesy of the Rakow Research Library, Corning Museum of Glass.*

To avoid confusion, the name of the company should precede the pattern name: Brilliant's/Greenburg's Melrose; Bryce, Higbee's Melrose.

Items Noted:

bowl, round, plain edge, 6"
bowl, round, scalloped edge, 6", 8.25"
bowl, oval, plain edge, 7.5"
butter, covered, flat, footed
cake basket, 9.5", 10.5" l.
celery vase, stemmed, fan-and-scallop edge, 7.75" h.
compote, jelly, high-foot, open, scalloped edge, 5.5" w.
compote high-foot, covered, open, plain edge, deep, 6.25", 7", 8" w.
compote, high-foot, open, scalloped edge, 8", 10" w.
compote, low-foot, open, flat bottom, 4.5", 7" w.
cream
goblet, ring stem
mug
pickle dish, oval, handled
pitcher, half-gallon
plate, bread, fan-and-scallop edge, 10"
salver, 9.5", 10.5"
spoon, plain rim, 3" w.
sugar, covered, plain rim, 4" w.
tumbler
wine, ring stem
vase, swirled stem, 6.75" h.
water tray, 12"

Reproductions and Look-alikes: No reproductions known. Bryce, Higbee's Melrose is often confused for the same company's Grand and New Grand patterns, which

Melrose look-alikes (l. to r.) McKee's Majestic, Co-Operative Flint Glass No. 200 AKA *Sheaf and Block*, and Indiana Tumbler and Goblet Company's No. 11 AKA *Diamond and Double Fans*. Covered sugar at far right is Bryce, Higbee's Melrose.

have a very similar layout. Grand and New Grand consist of plain-centered diamonds against a background of small eight-pointed stars, whereas Bryce, Higbee's Melrose has the star design in the center of the diamonds, with fans between the diamonds set against a plain background. There are many patterns clearly based on this popular motif that resemble Bryce, Higbee's Melrose. These include Brilliant's/ Greensburg's Melrose (c. 1888), Co-Operative Flint Glass Company's No. 200 AKA *Sheaf and Block* (1893), McKee's Majestic (1894), and Indiana Tumbler and Goblet Company's No. 11 AKA *Diamond and Double Fans* (c. 1895). See photos for visual comparison.

Brilliant/Greensburg Glass Company's Melrose was introduced in the late 1880s. Because of the same name and similar pattern, it has wrongly been associated with the Higbee companies.

Mirror, 1890 & 1901

References: BH, undated; *P&GR*, 12/26/1889; *CG&L*, 1/10/1901; JBH, c. 1917 & NM, undated & NMPL, 1921 (wine, cocktail, and egg cup only)
Colors: clear, clear with engraving

> Their other new set, the "Mirror" is perfectly plain, with beautiful and artistic outlines.
>
> —*P&GR* 12/26/1889

It was a standard practice for glass companies to offer completely plain lines in addition to those that were more ornate. Though the trade journals praised the plain designs, they also made sure to mention the plainness could be relieved by engraving, etching, or other decoration. This was an era in which color and pattern boldly reigned, and it seems that people were almost apprehensive to allow surfaces to remain uncluttered and undecorated.

Though completely plain, there are features to distinguish items of Bryce, Higbee's Mirror pattern from similar products of other companies. The finials are an interesting geometric

Mirror cream, $20–$25; 8" bowl with star bottom, $20–$25; sugar lid, note geometric finial (complete sugar, $30–$35), 7.25" compote (with lid, $40–$45).

Mirror high-foot covered compote and butter from an undated Bryce, Higbee company catalog.

shape, the same found on Grand, New Grand, and Melrose. Flat bowls have a fine cut pattern in the base, but when examined closely it becomes apparent the design is composed of tiny stars very much like those found on other Bryce, Higbee patterns. Pedestals are the same as those found on Charm salvers and are applied to the bowls of compotes and plates of salvers with a glass wafer.

Confusion arises in trying to separate and distinguish the various plain lines made by Bryce, Higbee. A circa 1891 Wallace & McAfee catalog shows an Alfonzo celery vase among items of Mirror and Homestead. At some point these plain lines were seemingly offered together by the company.

China, Glass & Lamps mentions Mirror among Bryce, Higbee's new patterns for 1901. One report reads:

> The Mirror pattern, of which there is also a full line, is imitation blown and may be set down as the prettiest plain line in the market.

This second issue of the pattern may have added more items that were originally part of other plain lines. Jobber catalogs issued after 1901 show Mirror offered with Homestead and Vici (introduced 1896). The spring 1905 Butler Brothers issue shows a grouping of Mirror, but the pitcher and celery are the Homestead pattern and two bowls are Vici. Another shows a Mirror covered compote paired with a Homestead compote that has a Mirror lid. The "Mirror 'Plain Glass' Assortment" in the June 1906 Baltimore Bargain House catalog shows a large assortment of plain items consisting mainly of Mirror and Vici. Since these assortments were put together at the factory, it could be that Bryce, Higbee mixed the plain patterns to purge older stock, or it could be that they changed the makeup of the plain lines to keep things fresh. This would make sense, especially since Mirror was eleven years old by the time the company reintroduced it as "new" in 1901.

Due to the lack of company catalogs, it becomes difficult to know exactly which items were originally included in each of the plain lines (Alfonzo, Homestead, Mirror, Vici)

KENTUCKY PATTERN.

The Best Fire Finished Plain Line on the Market. Heavy, Brilliant and Well Made.

TABLE SET

Sugar. Cream. Spoonholder. Butter.

High Covered Bowl. Salvers. Pitcher.

4 inch Nappy. Pickles. 8 inch Nappy.

Low Covered Bowl. Celery. Open Bowl.

Prices of Kentucky Pattern.

	Per Doz. Bbl. Lots.	Per Doz. Open Stock.		Per Doz. Bbl. Lots.	Per Doz. Open Stock.
Sets	$2 60	$2 85	Open Bowl 7 in	$1 05	$1 20
Sugars	85	95	" 8 in	1 40	1 60
Creams	50	60	" 9 in	1 70	1 90
Butters	90	95	Salvers, 8 in	1 05	1 25
Pitchers	1 45	1 60	" 9 in	1 25	1 50
Covered Bowl, 6 in. high	1 55	1 75	" 10 in	1 60	1 80
" " 7 in. "	2 15	2 45	" 11 in	2 25	2 75
" " 8 in. "	3 00	3 50	Pickles	30	35
" " 9 in. "	3 45	3 95	Celeries	1 05	1 20
" " 6 in. low	1 40	1 60	Nappies, 4 in	17	18
" " 7 in. "	1 96	2 35	" 5 in	22	23
" " 8 iu. "	2 75	3 25	" 8 in	65	70

Peaslee-Gaulbert offered an interesting assortment of Bryce, Higbee's Mirror as "Kentucky Pattern" in 1898. Note the items with star-patterned bases as well as the inclusion of the Homestead pitcher.

by Bryce, Higbee. The circa 1917 J. B. Higbee *General Catalogue* shows two compotes and a salver called "Plain." It is not known if this was a separate line originated by Bryce, Higbee, or if these were items originally included in one of the company's other plain lines. Lola and Wayne Higby list Plain as a pattern by Bryce, Higbee and date it to 1899. They arrive at this date due to the appearance of a low-foot compote with scalloped edge that is completely void of design in a Butler Brothers catalog from that year, but that compote appears to be from the Vici line. No documentation has been found to confirm Bryce, Higbee made a full line called Plain, but a goblet and wine labeled "Plain No. I" are shown on a circa 1888 company catalog page. As with the Homestead pattern salts, the Plain compotes shown in the *General Catalogue* may be another example of J. B. Higbee renaming items that were part of earlier Bryce, Higbee patterns. The compotes certainly have more in common with the Mirror wine shown in the J. B. Higbee catalog than with the Plain No. I stems shown in the Bryce, Higbee catalog.

The J. B. Higbee *General Catalogue* illustrates a wine labeled "No. 511—Mirror" (with notation that it was also available belled as No. 511½) and a cocktail labeled "No. 520—Mirror." The 1921 New Martinsville price list includes a "511 Mirror Wine—Optic or Plain" and a "600 Mirror Short Stem Wine (Egg Cup 600)." These items are illustrated in an undated New Martinsville company catalog. The egg cup is also shown in the J. B. Higbee *General Catalogue* simply captioned "No. 600—Single Egg Cup" and the cocktail is mentioned in the New Martinsville price list as "520 Cocktail 2 oz."

Mirror seems rather challenging to find, but this could be due to the fact that items are difficult to recognize. Glassware void of pattern is also easily overlooked and not in high demand.

The name Mirror is an obvious reference to the brilliant, reflective quality of the glass.

Items Noted: *This list does not knowingly include items from other plain lines originally issued by other names:*

bowl, preserve, flat, oval, fine cut (star) pattern in base, 7", 8", 9"
bowl, nappy, flat, round, fine cut (star) pattern in base, 4", 5", 6", 7", 8"

This 1905 Butler Brothers illustration also shows that items from the plain Homestead and Mirror lines were combined. The compote on the right is composed of a Mirror lid atop a Homestead base.

butter, low wide foot, covered
celery vase, low-foot, cylindrical, scalloped edge
compote, high-foot, covered, deep bowl, 5", 6", 7", 8", 9" w.
compote, high-foot, open, plain edge, shallow bowl, 7", 8", 9" w.
compote, low-foot, covered, deep bowl, 6", 7", 8" w.
compote, low-foot, open, plain edge, shallow bowl, rounded bottom, 7", 8", 9", 10" w.
compote, low-foot, open, plain edge, flat bottom, 4", 7", 8" w.
cream
pickle dish, oval, handled, fine cut (star) pattern in base
pitcher, wide foot, half-gallon, plain edge, scalloped edge
pitcher, pedestal foot, tapered body, half-gallon
salver, 8", 9", 10", 11", 12"
spoon, scalloped edge
sugar, covered, plain edge, inner ledge

Reproductions and Look-alikes: No reproductions known. Note features mentioned above to assist in distinguishing items in this line from other plain patterns made by Bryce, Higbee and other manufacturers. Just about all the glass companies offered severely plain glassware for more utilitarian home use and for use in hotels, restaurants, and other public establishments.

Monarch, 1902 (pattern unknown)

References: *CG&L*, 1/11/1902; NMPL, 1921
Colors: unknown, but undoubtedly clear

> Bryce, Higbee & Co, whose sample room is located at 623 Smithfield street, second floor, has two complete new lines ready to show visitors. One has been dubbed the "Monarch." It is an artistically figured pattern that has a sparkle like cut glass. The shapes are unique and handsome and there are about 75 different pieces, a few of which are fruit bowls, knick-knacks, nappies of all sizes, styles and shapes, cracker jars, oils, tall celerys and trays, sugars, creams, butters, spoons, square plates and everything else, in fact, usually made in table glassware... The "Monarch" has 10 different styles of vases and six styles of footed jellies.

The reference to cracker jars in this review is interesting and a bit perplexing, for this form is not known in any Bryce, Higbee pattern and is not typical of the company. If the report is accurate, perhaps this could be the link to match up this OMN with the pattern. It is possible that the reporter was calling a lidless vessel, perhaps a deep bowl, a cracker jar. By definition, a jar is simply a wide-mouthed container.

New Martinsville's list of "Higbee Glass Company's Moulds" includes a Monarch butter along with the annotation "No. 615," so at least one mould of this pattern was acquired by J. B. Higbee and later by New Martinsville. Unfortunately, this butter dish is not shown in any of the company's known catalogs.

Monarch refers to a person who reigns over an empire or kingdom and may be a metaphor that the pattern would rule over the market. This was not the first time Bryce, Higbee used a pattern name with the allusion of leadership.

Reproductions and Look-alikes: Unknown.

New Crescent, 1898

References: *CG&L*, 1/5/1898; BB, spring/summer 1898; NM, undated (cream only)
Colors: clear, clear with gold trim, clear with ruby stain (tumbler known)

New Crescent was mentioned without description in the January 5, 1898, issue of *China, Glass & Lamps*:

> Bryce, Higbee & Co. have their sample room at 623 Smithfield street in great shape for the reception of visiting buyers. On some of the mirror covered tables are displayed their three new spring patterns; the elegant and unique Fleur de lis, the New Crescent, and the Simoom. These are all in the purest of crystal glass and three [there] are very full lines of them.

Note the mention of "new spring patterns" for 1898 and that they are all "very full lines." *China, Glass & Lamps* describes Bryce, Higbee's Fleur-de-lis pattern the very same way, along with the notation that it would encompass ninety pieces when complete. The Butler Brothers spring/summer 1898 catalog shows the pattern collectors call *Diamond Point Discs* for the very first time. This pattern is found in a full line of tableware, and close examination reveals that it is a more ornate version of the earlier Crescent pattern made from retooled moulds. It is worthy to note that many examples of retooled patterns exist among Bryce Higbee's output. See page 85 for further discussion.

New Crescent 9.25" vases, $30–$35 each; butter, $50–$55; 7" high-foot covered compote, $45–$50; cream, $20–$25.

No. 601 cream shown in an undated New Martinsville Glass Manufacturing Company catalog. Note the crescents are not illustrated with ribs.

New Crescent; 8" high-foot open compote, $25–$30; 9" low-foot compote, $30–$35.

A New Crescent cream pitcher is shown in an undated New Martinsville Glass Manufacturing Company catalog labeled No. 601. It is not mentioned in the company's list of moulds acquired from J. B. Higbee. Interestingly, the catalog illustration lacks the vertical ribbing on the crescents that is a characteristic of the design. It was thought to be possibly another variation on the pattern, but a cream has been found that is very faintly patterned on the crescents, so it could very well be that, by the time New Martinsville made this pattern, the moulds were rather well-used and that part of the design became obliterated. It seems a bit odd that this item is not shown in any J. B. assortments in Butler Brothers catalogs, in the J. B. Higbee circa 1917 *General Catalogue*, nor in the New Martinsville list of Higbee moulds, but perhaps it appeared in catalogs unknown to us. There is always the possibility that items offered in company catalogs were no longer in production, or might have been old stock.

New Crescent 6.25" plate, $18–$20; boat-shaped pickle dish, $15–$20; 11.75" celery tray, $20–$25; ruby-stained tumbler, value undetermined; wine, $15–$20; mug with gold trim, $20–$25.

New Crescent quart pitcher, $40–$45; half-gallon pitcher, $50–$55.

This may not be the case with this cream pitcher, however. By the time it appears in the New Martinsville catalog, the mould was already approximately two decades old, which could explain why the design appears worn.

Compotes and salvers are found with different patterned stems. Some match the Worlds pattern and others match the Crescent pattern. Round bread plates measuring just about 10" were made in two styles. Some have twenty-four scallops, small starred centers, and the motif is repeated eight times around the plate. These were flattened from bowls. Others have twenty-four scallops, large starred centers, and the motif is repeated twelve times around the plate. These were formed in their own mould.

New Crescent is seen in many wholesale assortments from 1898 to 1907, and is not too difficult to acquire. A 7.25" covered compote was offered by Butler Brothers in late 1911 and was undoubtedly previously manufactured stock.

The pattern Lola and Wayne Higby identify as New Crescent is not correct, for it was not made in a full line. Only bowls and compotes tooled various ways, cake baskets, plates, and salvers have been found. See *Diamond Point Swag and Fan* on page 151.

SIX RICH "BARGAIN DAY LEADERS."—(Shipped from Pittsburgh)

Any of these goods would be cheap at a quarter, but we offer them here as **possible 10-cent articles.**

Special Requirement.—To get this price customers must order no less than 3 packages of these goods. Either 3 packages of one lot or 3 packages of different lots.

LOT NO. 1.

9½-inch Plain Salver. Best crystal glass. Scalloped edge. 2½ doz. in bbl. (Bbl. 35c.) **Price—82c Doz.**

LOT NO. 2.

9-inch Footed Dish. Best goods. Newest pattern. 3½ doz. in bbl. (Bbl. 35c.) **Price—82c Doz.**

LOT NO. 4.

High Footed Bowl. 8¼-inch large table dish. 2¾ doz. in bbl. (Bbl. 35c.) **Price—82c Doz.**

LOT NO. 3.

9¼-inch Fancy High Finished Salver. 2½ doz. in bbl. (Bbl. 35c.) **Price—82c Doz.**

LOT NO. 5.

10-inch Fancy High Finished Dish. 4 doz. in bbl. (Bbl. 35c.) **Price—82c Doz.**

LOT NO. 6.

Large 8-inch Flanged Butter Dish with High Cover. 4 doz. in bbl. (Bbl. 35c.) **Price—82c Doz**

An early offering of New Crescent with Bryce, Higbee's Vici from Butler Brothers in May 1898.

Items Noted:

bowl, flat, oval, scalloped edge, 7", 8"
bowl, flat, round, scalloped edge, 9", 10"
bowl, berry dessert, collar base, 4.5"
butter, covered
celery tray, oblong, 11.75"
celery vase
compote, high-foot, covered, 6.5", 7"
compote, high-foot, open, scalloped edge, 8"
compote low-foot, open, scalloped edge, 9"
cordial
cream
jelly, handled, 5"
mug
olive tray, oblong, scalloped edge, 8"
pickle dish, boat-shaped, four points on edge, 7.75"
pitcher, 32 ounce, rayed foot
pitcher, half-gallon, patterned foot
plate, round, scalloped edge, 6.5"
plate, round, bread, two styles, approximately 10"
salver, 9.5"

shaker, salt and pepper
spoon, scalloped edge
sugar, covered, plain edge
tumbler
vase, trumpet-shaped, swirled stem, squared top, 9.25"
wine

Cake baskets and square plates likely exist, since these forms are typical of Bryce, Higbee's production from this time frame and are found in the Crescent pattern. Theoretically, any item found in Crescent could be found in New Crescent. Barret and Heacock both show a New Crescent ruby stained tumbler (the author has the Heacock example in his collection). The three-toed individual salt identified as *Diamond Point Discs* in Heacock's *5,000 Open Salts* book (figure 2930) is actually J. B. Higbee's Banner pattern introduced in 1909.

Reproductions and Look-alikes: No reproductions known. On casual inspection, New Crescent could be confused for Ohio Flint Glass Company's Mignon (1895) and United States Glass Company's No. 15038, Electric (1896). The most obvious difference is the lack of diamond point in Mignon and Electric. New Crescent is quite similar to some early flint designs known to collectors as *Roman Rosette*. Early glass gives off a bell-tone ring, unlike the later soda-lime glass. Also see Crescent on page 146 for the earlier version of this pattern.

Ohio Flint Glass Company's Mignon (right) is similar to New Crescent (left). New Crescent 9.5" salver, $40–$45.

New Crescent (right) was clearly inspired by the early *Roman Rosette* pattern (left).

New Grand, c. 1888

References: BH, undated; BB, 1888 Santa Claus; GS, February 1891
Colors: clear

New Grand appears to have been the designation for items in the earlier Grand pattern with plain rims. The change in shapes occurred around 1888. Plain-edged items are first noted in jobber catalogs toward the end of 1888. After that, only random fan-edged items appear very sporadically. None have been spotted after 1891. *Pottery and Glassware*

New Grand 8" and 6.5" high-foot covered compotes. $50–$55; $40–$45.

New Grand 8.25" open compote, $25–$30; butter, $40–$45.

New Grand goblet, $25–$30; shaker, $30–$35; spoon, $20–$25; cream, $20–$25.

Reporter mentions a low-priced figured line on July 12, 1888, "the covered bowls being particularly noticeable." Although not named, this may be a reference to New Grand. The covered compotes (originally called covered bowls) are definitely noteworthy, mainly due to their massive appearance and unusual prismatic finials. Comparison of pitchers in this pattern to others by Bryce, Higbee reveals that they were much lower in price. The pattern does not have the weight and brilliancy of most other wares made by the company and, though of decent quality, it does seem to be a slightly lower grade of glass. The spring and summer 1890 and fall and winter 1890–1891 Montgomery Ward catalogs offer an old-style cream pitcher as well as a 4.5" low-foot compote and pickle dish with fan edges, but these odd items were in all likelihood old stock.

It was common practice, though about a decade earlier, for glass companies to offer the table set of older patterns in a new, updated shape; one was termed "old set," the other, "new set." The designation "New Grand Pattern" by Bryce, Higbee in their company catalog indicates this was the actual name. Company catalogs were rather expensive to print and were meant to last the life of the patterns, hopefully many years. They were very straightforward and relied on illustrations to depict the wares. Descriptions with the intention to entice buyers is a marketing technique not found in company catalogs; instead, is seen in retail catalogs, jobber catalogs, and trade journals, such as ads for the Era pattern that refer to it as "new" in *China, Glass & Lamps* in early 1891. All the catalog pages done in negative print shown in Kamm 8 appear to be from the same catalog, but she is not clear on this matter. If the pages are from the same catalog, they cannot date before the early 1890s, despite some being labeled "mid-Eighties" and earlier by Kamm, because Ethol and Flora were introduced for the 1891 market. The Worlds pattern is shown, and it dates to circa 1892/93. By this time, the original Grand pattern (with fan edges) certainly was not new.

The earlier Grand cream, sugar, and spoon holder underwent a complete change in design, making them more cylindrical, shorter, and smaller. Pedestals on New Grand compotes and salvers are thinner and are not applied to the vessels as they were with their earlier fan-edged Grand counterparts. New Grand items have an overall more modern appearance than items with the fan edge. Finials remained the same and are an interesting geometric design also found on Mirror and Melrose. The New Grand celery vase and 10" bread plate retained the fan edge found on Grand. The water tray is the same one used for the Yale set and does not have the Grand motif. The rim of this tray is smooth, but the fan and scallop design is molded into the glass. The mould shapes of New Grand (even the three items with the fan edges just noted) were also carried over to the later and very similar Melrose pattern introduced in 1894. Comparative study shows that at least some of the New Grand moulds were retooled to become the Melrose pattern. An interesting oddity exists on the New Grand pickle dishes. They have distinctive scrolled handles like those found on the Capitola and *Chain* patterns.

Though the goblet visible on the Bryce, Higbee catalog page has a plain stem, it appears that the goblet with ring stem was introduced while New Grand was being made. The author comes to this conclusion for a few reasons. The plain-stemmed goblet is shown on a circa 1888 Bryce, Higbee stemware page simply labeled "Grand." It is also shown in a spring/summer 1888 Hollander, Bradshaw and Folsom assortment with items of the fan-edged Grand, presumably before New Grand was introduced. The shape of the goblet, stem and all, is that of the Princeton/Persian pattern introduced in 1887. The goblet with ring stem is a slightly different shape and is that found on Tidal, introduced 1889 and the later Melrose pattern introduced in 1894.

New Grand celery vase, $30–$35; 10" bread plate, $25–$30; 8.75" salver, $35–$40. The bread plate and celery vase are the same as Grand.

Each Butler Brothers assortment of Bryce, Higbee glassware was named and they often remained the same for many seasons. When new items replaced older ones, the title of the assortment was typically altered by adding the word "new," "improved," or other similar term to reflect the change. Comparing "Our 'Bargain' 5-cent Assortment" and "Our 'Magnet' 3-cent Assortment" shown in October 1894 with the same assortments in September 1895 reveals differences: the word "improved" is added to the title of each assortment, and all the New Grand items are replaced with items in the Melrose pattern. After September 1895, New Grand completely disappears from Butler Brothers and jobber catalogs seen by the author.

Comparison of Grand and New Grand goblets (left photo) and New Grand and Melrose goblets (right photo). Note the differences in stems and bowl shapes.

All items in the listing have plain edges, except where indicated. Also see Grand on page 177.

Items Noted:
bowl, flat, oval, 7", 9"
bowl, flat, round, 4.25", 6"
butter, covered, flat, footed
celery vase, stemmed, fan and scallop edge, 7.75" h.
compote, high-foot, covered, open, 6.25", 7", 8", 9" w.
compote, low-foot, open, 4" w.
compote, low-foot, covered, open, 6", 7", 8" w.
cream
goblet, ring stem
pickle dish, oval, handled
pitcher, half-gallon, plain foot, notched pattern on foot (plain foot may be Grand)
plate, bread, fan and scallop edge, 10"
salver, 8", 9", 10", 12"
shaker, salt and pepper, tall, cylindrical
spoon, 3" w.
sugar, covered, 4", 4.5" w.
tray for water set, 12" (same as Yale; does not have the Grand motif)
waste bowl, low-foot, cupped, approximately 4" w.
wine, ring stem

There are two sizes of what look like covered sugar bowls, but one was perhaps meant to be a pickle jar.

Reproductions and Look-alikes: No reproductions known. Bryce, Higbee's Melrose is often confused for New Grand. The arrangement of the main diamond motif is the same, but New Grand consists of plain-centered diamonds against a background of small eight-pointed stars, whereas Bryce, Higbee's Melrose has the star design in the center of the diamonds, with fans between the diamonds set against a plain background.

New York, year unknown

References: BB, c. 1886
Colors: amber, blue; most likely clear

A New York goblet was offered in Butler Brothers circa 1886 "Our New '5 cent' Colored Ware Assortment" with other known Bryce, Higbee products. The goblet has three rows of honeycomb and appears to have a thin, rounded, plain stem. It is unknown whether this was a full line for Bryce, Higbee or if the goblet was the only item they made. Most know this pattern by the common collector's name, *Honeycomb*.

New York goblets by unknown makers. This pattern was made by many manufacturers during the nineteenth and early twentieth century.

Reproductions and Look-alikes: Numerous companies made New York patterned stemware and tableware during the 1800s and early 1900s, but far fewer offered it in colors. This, along with the thin stem, could be a way to distinguish Bryce Higbee's from others. A multitude of variations on the honeycomb theme applied to modern shapes became very popular during the 1930s, called Georgian by most manufacturers.

Our New "5 CENT" Colored Ware Assortment.

Last spring we first succeeded in securing an assortment of articles in this beautiful and popular colored ware to be sold at 5 cents each. It at once became a great favorite with our customers, and the sale was so great that we determined to secure a still better assortment for the fall trade, with the following result: (We predict that this new assortment will have a larger sale than any we have ever introduced.)

Our 5 CENT COLORED GLASS ASSORTMENT Comprises the Following Articles:

Butter Dish and Cover—Handsome Pattern
Tooth Pick Holders—3½ inches high. Fish pattern
6 inch Round Dishes—Vine pattern
Footed Comports—5 inch. Very handsome
Milk Pitchers—Diamond and plain pattern
Goblets, Polished—New York pattern
Fancy Tumblers—Latest shape. Diamond pattern
Octagon Dishes, 6 inch—Vine pattern
A B C Plates, 6½ inch—The Emma style
7 inch Handled Pickle Dishes—Elegant plain and Diamond pattern

Each barrel containing 1 dozen each of these items, or a total of **10 Doz. to the Barrel.**

(Assorted colors, blue and amber.)

Price, 42 Cts. Per Doz.

..............Order here.

New York goblet (lower left) in an assortment of colored ware made by Bryce, Higbee & Company and sold by Butler Brothers in 1886. Note the thin stem and honeycomb pattern low on the bowl.

No. I Plain, year unknown

References: BH, undated

A goblet and wine called No. I Plain are shown on a circa 1888 Bryce, Higbee catalog page with other stemware. Note that the Roman numeral one is used here because this is how it appears in the original company catalog. Though the introduction year is unknown, it is most likely an early product of the company. In late 1880, *American Pottery and Glassware Reporter* remarked on the large variety of stemware being produced by the company. This and the following, No. 2 Fluted, were likely part of that production. No. I Plain looks the same as the Alfonzo goblet illustrated on the same page, but appears to have a thin band molded slightly above the middle of the bowl that is not present on Alfonzo.

There are three items labeled "Plain" in the circa 1917 J. B. Higbee *General Catalogue*: an 8" flared bowl, 8" sweetmeat, and 9" salver. The first two items would be called compotes by the modern collector. It is not known if these items were originally part of Bryce, Higbee's No. I Plain line. There is no band like on the No. I Plain goblet and wine. The stems and bases are slightly different and have more in common with the Mirror wine also shown in the *General Catalogue*. No mention of Plain or No. I Plain was found in any trade journal. Unless there is some notable, distinguishing feature, plain items are among the most difficult products of the glass manufacturers to correctly identify. Each manufacturer offered plain patterns for public establishments and private use for those who wanted something more utilitarian. See Mirror on page 192 for more discussion on plain patterns.

No. I Plain goblet and wine illustrations from a circa 1888 Bryce, Higbee catalog.

Reproductions and Look-alikes: Unknown. As noted above, plain pieces can be extremely difficult to identify.

No. 2 Fluted, year unknown

References: BH, undated

Bryce, Higbee's No. 2 Fluted goblet from a company catalog, circa 1888.

A goblet labeled No. 2 Fluted Goblet is shown on a circa 1888 catalog page with various stemware in other patterns. Like No. I Plain, simple, durable stemware was a staple item of the glass companies and was much in demand by hotels, restaurants, taverns, and other public establishments. Other companies made paneled goblets nearly identical to this, so it may be difficult to distinguish Bryce, Higbee's No. 2 Fluted.

Reproductions and Look-alikes: Unknown. This is a rather common design, and goblets of this style are still being produced today. Bryce, Higbee's product might be able to be distinguished by comparing examples to the catalog illustration. The stem seems to be the most distinctive feature.

No. 33, c. early 1880s

References: *AP&GR*, 1/27/1881; P&B, 1897

American Pottery and Glassware Reporter mentions Bryce, Higbee's No. 33 in late January 1881. A detailed description is not given, but "engraved and engraved F. band styles" are noted in conjunction with No. 33. The journal then mentions the company's new banding machine, a reference to John B. Higbee's "Mechanism for Grinding Bands upon the Surfaces of Wine Glasses" which was patented just two weeks prior. It is not known what the "F. band" engraving looks like, but

Engraved goblets and plain cordial which may be Bryce, Higbee's No. 33. Goblets, $15–$20 each; cordial, $10–$12. The band engraving is like that shown in the 1881 patent illustration for John Higbee's grinding mechanism.

obviously the newly patented machine was used to engrave the ware. It could be the banded design illustrated in the patent drawing or one similar to it.

If it were not for the goblet shown in Pitkin and Brooks' 1897 catalog, we would not know what No. 33 looked like. Its shape is nearly identical to the 5th Avenue goblet shown on a circa 1888 Bryce, Higbee catalog page of stemware. The stem of No. 33 is thinner and tapered, however, and the base is wider and thinner as well. Absent are two molded rings near the base of the bowl found on 5th Avenue. The Pitkin and Brooks catalog notes the goblet is seamless and of "5th Avenue shape." This was a popular stemware shape of the time, and many other companies produced it as well. No. 33 was most likely only made in stemware. Pitkin and Brooks offered No. 33 at least sixteen years after it was first introduced, a good indication that plain, utilitarian stemware was in good demand and had a long production life.

No. 33 goblet from an 1897 Pitkin & Brooks catalog. *Courtesy of the Rakow Research Library, Corning Museum of Glass.*

Reproductions and Look-alikes: Unknown. Note differences mentioned above between Bryce, Higbee's No. 33 and 5th Avenue lines. Other companies made similar lines, so unless there is engraving or etching that can be tied to a particular company, it would be nearly impossible to confidently attribute items to a specific manufacturer.

Ola, 1889

References: *P&GR*, 12/27/1888
Colors: unknown, but undoubtedly clear

The December 27, 1888, issue of *Pottery and Glassware Reporter* relates:

> Bryce, Higbee & Co. have out some elegant new patterns for the spring trade. One of them is the "Ola," a distinctively original design, handsomely finished and clear and bright in effect. It is beyond doubt the best cut pattern in the market...

The lack of detailed pattern description is frustrating to the researcher, but, nevertheless, quite typical of the period. Nobody at the factory could have imagined that well over 100 years later historians would be trying to document their products.

The only thing conclusive about Ola is that it was an imitation cut pattern, but most pressed glass in this time frame was based on cut glass. Ola may be the pattern known as *Prism Bars*. The first observance of *Prism Bars* in a jobber catalog is May 1889, which does coincide with Ola's introduction. Also, *Prism Bars* is quite different from most patterns by other companies introduced in the late 1880s; it is nicely finished, and certainly has a bright appearance. This is purely speculation and only presented as a possibility.

As a male name, Ola is the Norwegian and Swedish variant of Olaf, meaning "ancestor" or "descendant." As a female name, Ola is the Polish short form of Aleksandra, meaning "defender of mankind." The reason Bryce, Higbee chose to use this unusual name is not known.

Reproductions and Look-alikes: Unknown.

Optic, *c.* 1906

References: BB, spring 1906; GS, 1906; JBH, undated (wines and cocktail only, see below)
Colors: clear

Although no mention of Optic was found in trade journal reports, the pattern is shown in many wholesale assortments with other Bryce, Higbee patterns beginning in spring 1906. The pattern is consistently called Optic by Butler Brothers and G. Sommers. Butler Brothers is not known for their use of OMNs, but did include them on occasion, as did Sommers.

Optic 9.5" square bowl, $25–$30.

"OPTIC" GLASSWARE ASSORTMENT.
Up-to-date goods at a popular price.

K 271—"Optic" Assortment of brilliant fire polished glassware, full finished edges, clearest crystal, pot glass, suitable for your good trade. Assortment consists of ½ doz. each of the following pieces:

Large cream pitcher.
Optic spooner.
Covered sugar bowl.
Extra size butter dish.
Full size ½ gallon jug.
Large 10-oz Optic tumbler.
8¼-inch low footed berry bowl.
4¾-inch belled fruit pappy to match.
8½-inch oval or handled pickle dish.
7-inch low footed fruit or bon bon.
Large 10-inch star bottom cake plate.
5-inch bell shape footed jelly.

Total, 6 doz. in package (no pkg. chg.). Per doz.................... .86

Optic assortment from a G. Sommers catalog, 1906.

Three Optic items are shown in the circa 1917 J. B. Higbee *General Catalogue*: two wines (one is belled) and a cocktail. They are the same shape as corresponding items labeled Mirror in the same catalog. In addition to the Optic designation, each is given a number. It is impossible to tell if the optic is on the inside or outside. These items may not have been part of Bryce, Higbee's Optic line.

The shape of Bryce, Higbee's Optic half-gallon pitcher is the same as a completely plain half-gallon pitcher offered in an assortment of Mirror by Butler Brothers in spring 1905. The small berry nappy and handled pickle have a star design in the base.

Interestingly, a Butler Brothers assortment of Optic titled "6 Big Staples" does not appear until after Bryce, Higbee closed. It is last shown in mid-winter 1909. This could have been previously manufactured stock from Bryce, Higbee or it could have been made by J. B. Higbee. The former seems more plausible because the assortment was not offered for very long. It was an up-to-date pattern that surely would have had a longer run if J. B. Higbee possessed the moulds.

The Optic pattern consists of rounded, convex ribs on the exterior. It appears to be very difficult to find. If Optic truly was made only by Bryce, Higbee, it would have had a short production of a year or less. Its absence on today's market could be due to obscurity rather than scarcity, however. Perhaps items will show up now that it has been illustrated and identified.

Items Noted: *Items shown in Butler Brothers and G. Sommers assortments.*

bowl, berry nappy, flat, fine cut star pattern in base, 4"
bowl, fruit nappy, collar base, belled, 4.75"
bowl, collar base, round, 7", 8.25"
bowl, collar base, round, square, 9.5"–10"
butter, covered

compote, jelly, high-foot, open, 5"–5.5" w.
compote, high-foot, round, square, 8.5"–9" w.
cream, footed
pickle dish, handled, oval, fine cut star pattern in base, 8.5"
pitcher, half-gallon, low dome foot
plate, collar base, 10"
salver, 10"
spoon, footed, plain edge
sugar, covered, footed, plain edge
tumbler

Certainly cake baskets must exist, for they are found in all other post–1900 Bryce, Higbee patterns and were tooled from the 8" high-foot compotes. An Optic 8" compote is shown in assortments along with the salver, which was also tooled from the compote.

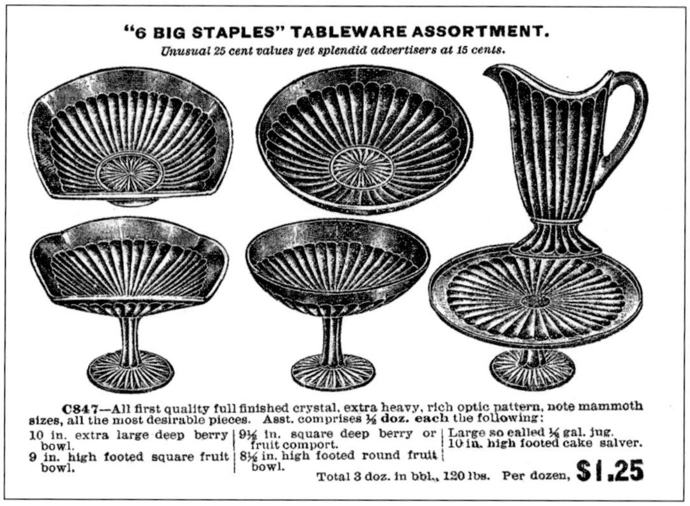

Butler Brothers "6 Big Staples" assortment of Bryce, Higbee's Optic pattern, October 1908.

Reproductions and Look-alikes: No reproductions known. Many companies made glassware with an interior optic imparted by the plunger, but Bryce, Higbee's Optic is an exterior pattern. Shapes of some items may be helpful to determine Bryce, Higbee's product.

Oregon, 1899

References: *CG&L*, 12/22/1898; P&B, 1899; BB, 1901
Colors: clear

Some may surmise the name Oregon is a reference to the thirty-third state of the Union, but because the pattern was introduced as a companion to Admiral at the same time, it is without doubt in reference to the USS *Oregon*, a battleship of the United States Navy. The contract to build her was awarded to Union Iron Works of San Francisco, California, in November 1890, and she was launched on October 26, 1893. As with Admiral George Dewey, the *Oregon*'s great fame is also related to the Spanish American War. In preparation for war with Spain, she departed San Francisco on March 19, 1898, on a 16,000 mile voyage that took a staggering sixty-six days. This was considered a remarkable achievement at the time. The USS *Oregon* took part in the battle of Santiago de Cuba, forcing surrender, and was given the nickname "Bulldog of the Navy." She was sold for scrap in 1956.

The United States Glass Company also made an Oregon pattern (introduced 1901), but theirs was part of a series

Oregon sugar, $50–$55; butter, $65–$70.

Oregon 10" cake basket, $45–$50; 8.5" bowl with collar base, $35–$40.

Oregon 10" salver, $45–$50; 8" compote, $35–$40.

named after the states. Collectors have known Bryce, Higbee made an Oregon pattern, but its appearance was not known. This has caused some to mistakenly think that United States Glass Company's Oregon was also made by Bryce, Higbee. Bryce, Higbee's Oregon is the pattern that collectors have called *Heavy Heart*, but the OMN should be used, now that it is known. As with the name of any pattern used by more than one manufacturer, the company name must precede the pattern name when speaking of EAPG in general to avoid confusion.

Oregon was one of three new patterns for the 1899 market as reported by *China, Glass & Lamps* on December 22, 1898:

> Bryce Higbee & Co. are out with three entirely new patterns in brilliant crystal glass which they will offer the trade the beginning of the new year...They have named them the Admiral, Oregon and the Bow-knot... The figured pattern of each is of the beaded cut style and they are very neat.

The only piece of Bryce, Higbee's Oregon previously reported in reference books is a tumbler. The pattern was, however, made in a full line, though it is not known how extensive the line was. Butler Brothers offered the Oregon tumbler from 1901 to 1907 as part of their New Leader Assortment, which became their Bargain Day Assortment beginning in 1902. These two assortments consisted of small items and appear to have been a way for the company to move odds-and-ends and old stock. The only other piece of Oregon seen in a jobber catalog is a covered butter dish shown in an assortment offered in Baltimore Bargain House's Unabridged Catalog No. 522 dated February & March 1907. Once again, this illustrates that stock must have been in warehouses of the jobbers, for the Bryce, Higbee factory was reported as completely shut down in December 1906 and never reopened.

It would not be farfetched to say that Bryce, Higbee's Oregon was not a success with the buying public. From the start it appears to have taken a back seat to the very similar Admiral pattern. An 1899 Pitkin and Brooks catalog offered both patterns. Oregon was not sold in open stock, yet the Admiral pattern was. The notation "Owing to lack of space, we illustrate only the [table] set in the Oregon Pattern, shapes are much like the Admiral" implies that it was not as worthy of the space given to Admiral. There are a total of sixteen pieces of Admiral shown throughout the catalog (the salver and large square bowl, called a "comportier," are even shown twice), yet only an Oregon table set (consisting of covered butter, spoon, cream, and covered sugar) is shown. When the two patterns are compared many similarities are seen and it becomes apparent that Oregon is basically a more ornate version of Admiral. Perhaps the patterns were too similar for Bryce, Higbee's Oregon to stand on its own and it was soon discontinued.

Oregon water bottle, $75–$100; 9.25" bowl with collar base, $40–$45.

Items Noted: *The list of items is compiled from the 1899 Pitkin & Brooks catalog and actual items seen and owned:*
bowl, berry nappy, collar base, round, deep, 4.5", 8.5"–9"
bowl, collar base, round, 9.5"
bowl, flat, round, 9.75"
bowl, fruit dish, round, 10"
bowl, berry, square, 8"
bowl, comportier, collar base, square, 5", 9"
bowl, flat, square, 9.5"
butter, covered
cake basket, 10", 11.5" l.
compote, high-foot, round, square, 8" w.
cream, applied handle
plate, collar base, 11"–12"
salver, 10"
spoon, scalloped edge
sugar, covered, plain edge
tumbler
water bottle

Oregon 12" plate, $45–$50; 8" square compote, $40-$45.

Oregon flat bowls, 9.5" square and 9.75" round. $40–$45 each.

Pitkin & Brooks' 1899 catalogs reveals the true identity of Bryce, Higbee's Oregon pattern. Note its similarity to Admiral. *Courtesy of the Rakow Research Library, Corning Museum of Glass.*

Reproductions and Look-alikes: No reproductions known. As noted, very similar to Bryce, Higbee's Admiral. Oregon is also quite reminiscent of a pattern known as *Crossed Ovals* (c. 1900), maker unknown. The most noticeable difference is the lack of any heart design in *Crossed Ovals*.

Crossed Ovals, maker unknown (right), is quite similar to Bryce, Higbee's Oregon (left). Note the lack of hearts in *Crossed Ovals*.

Oxford, 1901 (pattern uncertain)

References: *CG&L*, 1/10/1901
Colors: undoubtedly clear

The January 10, 1901, issue of *China, Glass & Lamps* mentioned five new lines made by Bryce, Higbee & Company, one of them the Oxford:

> The Waldorf and Oxford are short lines, comprising bowls, compotiers, berries, salvers and a few other articles.

Oxford may be the pattern called *Curlicue* or *Diamond Point Swag and Fan* in this book. See those entries in this chapter for more discussion.

The name Oxford refers to the city in southeast England, best known as the site of Oxford University. Its significance regarding Bryce, Higbee and Company is not known.

Reproductions and Look-alikes: Uncertain.

Paneled Flower and Thumbprint, c. 1901

References: BB No. 354, 1901
Colors: clear

Authors Lola and Wayne Higby call this pattern "Simoon," but give no proof or logical explanation for matching up this pattern with that factory name. In January 1898, *China, Glass & Lamps* reported that Bryce, Higbee's Simoom (or Simoon) was a "very full line" of tableware introduced for the spring trade. The pattern in question was not made in a full line and has only been found in bowls with various edge treatments. It first appears in Butler Brothers "Beauty Bright" assortment in catalog No. 354 from 1901 and was offered through summer 1904. Only bowls tooled different ways are shown.

The temporary descriptive name *Paneled Flower and Thumbprint* has been given until the correct OMN is found.

Paneled Flower and Thumbprint 10.5" nick nack tray, $35–$40; 9" square bowl, $30–$35.

Items Noted:

bowl, round, flared, square, various depths, 7.5" to 9"
nick nack tray, 10.5"

Plates measuring approximately 10.5" may exist as well.

Reproductions and Look-alikes: No reproductions known. Designs consisting of panels of punties (thumbprints) alternating with other motifs were popular at the turn of the twentieth century, but this pattern is quite distinctive because of the flowers with Star of David centers.

Our "BEAUTY BRIGHT" Assortment.
Six Fine "Leaders." Every Piece Full Finished and Fire Polished.

C311—This good assortment includes six large heavy pieces that are *supposed* to be retailed at 25 cents. Of course you will do as you choose, but we would suggest that you make a profit and an advertisement by selling them for less.

The "Beauty Bright" Assortment Comprises 1-2 Doz. Each of the Following:

6½-Inch Flared Fruit Bowl—Unites bigness with beauty.
8½-Inch High Footed Fancy Dish—Easy to get 25 cents for this.
8½-Inch Deep Round Utility Dish—A dish of a sort that always sells.
8-Inch High Footed Round Bowl—Good seller, better ware, best bargain.
9-Inch Fancy Square Corner Table Dish—Showy Dish for a "leader."
9¼-Inch High Footed Cake Salver—Usually retails for a quarter.
(Total 3 doz. to bbl. Sold only by bbl., wt. 105 lbs. Bbl. 35c.)
Per dozen, **$1.15**

The "Beauty Bright" assortment included bowls in the *Paneled Flower and Thumbprint* pattern. Butler Brothers catalog illustration, spring 1903.

Paris 1900, 1900

References: *CG&L*, 12/28/1899; P&B, c. 1900; BB No. 354, 1901; JBH, c. 1917 & NM, undated & NMPL, 1921 (celery vase, ice tub, mug, family shaker, and sugar duster—see below)
Colors: clear, clear with gold trim

Paris 1900 cream, \$40–\$45; butter, \$55–\$60; square plate, \$45–\$50; salt and pepper shakers, \$40–\$45 pair; large cruet with original stopper, \$40–\$45.

Paris 1900 6.5" nick nack, \$30–\$35; 6.5" wafer stand, \$35–\$40; 5.25" square jelly compote, \$18–\$20.

Paris 1900 10.5" cake basket, \$45–\$50; 9.5" salver with foot pattern variation, \$40–\$45.

Paris 1900 was Bryce, Higbee's leading pattern for the new century. It is strikingly modern and a bit stark in appearance when compared to the company's complex, frilly Admiral, Oregon, and Beaunot patterns introduced just one year prior. In December 1899, *China, Glass & Lamps* reported that "they [Bryce, Higbee & Company] have several new things in preparation for the coming season," but did not elaborate. Only Paris 1900 was specifically mentioned. The December 28, 1899, issue announced the special new pattern:

> Bryce, Higbee & Co., will take a rest between Christmas and New Year's days...Meantime they have got out a brand new pattern which, out of compliment to the great French exposition of the coming year, they have named "Paris, 1900." This is an imitation cut, elegant in design and finish, and will contain in all probably about 125 pieces. The shapes are new and unlike any hitherto made and the line includes every necessary for table use, such as set, bowls, nappies, celeries, oil cruet, pitchers, etc., as well as several sizes of vases. This will be put on the market for the first time in January and the firm think they are justified in predicting that it will be a trade winner of the first magnitude.

Even though the pattern is not described in detail, we know what it looks like because items are shown in the circa 1917 J. B. Higbee *General Catalogue* labeled Paris. Pitkin & Brooks featured the pattern as "No. 1900" on the first few pages of their circa 1900 catalog. Montgomery Ward offered the pattern as Paris in their spring and summer 1900 and fall and winter 1900–1901 catalogs, further proof this mail order retailer did not exclusively offer old glassware.

The trade journal quote gives some valuable information. First, it tells us that the pattern was named in honor of the 1900 Paris Exposition and was brand new and "unlike any hitherto made." For too long, Paris 1900 has been irrationally claimed to be a product of the Portland Glass Company of Portland, Maine. There is absolutely no basis for the Portland attribution other than fanciful thinking. This eastern glass company operated from 1863 to 1873. Most of the forms and shapes in which Paris 1900 is found did not even exist in the 1860s and 1870s; furthermore, if the pattern truly did originate at Portland, where were the dormant moulds for over a quarter century? Gerald Stevens includes Paris 1900 in his 1982 book, *Glass in Canada—The First One Hundred Years,* as "Nova Scotia Ribbon and Star." There is nothing whatsoever to prove Paris 1900 was produced in Canada.

Another point the quote establishes is that Paris 1900 was not available until January 1900. Lola and Wayne Higby and others incorrectly date the pattern to 1899, but it clearly was a new pattern for the 1900 market. Its name alone tells us that. The trade journals announced the new spring patterns near the end of each year, but at that point they were only samples. These samples were presented to the trade for the first time at the annual glass and crockery show in Pittsburgh and orders were then taken. This marks the introduction of the patterns, not when they were first mentioned or even first illustrated in the trade journals.

Large compotes, cake baskets, and salvers were all made from the same mould. These forms are found with a slight variation in the design on the underside base. The base design most often found has three short, horizontal bars between each vertical ray, which perfectly matches the patterned stem. A second base design appears less often and does not have the horizontal bars. There are other minor differences, but the horizontal bars are the most obvious. Though the drawings are a tad crude, the Montgomery Ward catalogs cited above clearly illustrate both base styles. It is not known if the smaller jelly compote and other items tooled from the same mould (nick nack, small salver, and wafer stand) were made with this base variation, but the potential certainly exists.

J. B. Higbee had at least some hand in producing the pattern, for some items are found marked with their trademark bee. The "Great 'Victory' Assortment" consisting of a dozen Paris 1900 items was offered by Butler Brothers from 1908 to 1910, but only four pieces labeled "Paris" appear in the circa 1917 J. B. Higbee *General Catalogue*: ice tub, celery vase,

Paris 1900 6.5" vases (note different shapes), $15–$20 each; 12" swung vase, $35–$40.

Paris 1900 7.5" high-foot compote with paneled stem and rayed base, $25–$30.

large family shaker, and sugar duster. An undated New Martinsville catalog shows a mug, ice tub, and sugar duster, and the company's 1921 price list records a mug, ice tub, sugar duster, and celery vase. High foot 7.5" compotes and 9" salvers are known with plain, paneled stems and rayed bases that greatly differ from other Paris 1900 footed items, but are very much like those found on J. B. Higbee's Colonial, Delta, and Iris patterns. This variation was most likely made by J. B. Higbee. The toothpick holder called "Paris" by J. B. Higbee and listed as "Paris Beauty" by New Martinsville was not part of the original Paris 1900 line. It was called Our

Paris 1900 was featured by Pitkin & Brooks at the front of their circa 1900 catalog. *Courtesy of the Rakow Research Library, Corning Museum of Glass.*

Toothpick by Bryce, Higbee. For discussion, see Our Toothpick in the Novelties section on page 262.

Paris 1900 cruets were made in two sizes and offered with three (possibly four) different stoppers. Pitkin & Brooks, Montgomery Ward, and Butler Brothers illustrate the large size cruet with the stopper used for the Banquet pattern. Beginning in spring 1904, Butler Brothers show it with the large Bonair-patterned stopper. The large cruet is also illustrated with a similar diamond-patterned stopper, but no actual examples have been seen. The small Paris cruet is shown by Butler Brothers in the "Delmonico" assortment through January 1904 with the matching zipper-patterned stopper designed for it. Beginning in spring 1904, the assortment changed to offer cruets in the Bonair and *Fine Cut and Fan* patterns.

As noted, the name Paris 1900 is a direct reference to the Paris Exposition of 1900. The *Exposition Universelle* celebrated the achievements of the nineteenth century and presented visitors to new ideas aimed to encourage progress in the new century. The exposition ran from April 15 to November 12 and attracted over forty-eight million attendants. One trade journal noted how brilliantly this World's Fair was illuminated at night by 12,554 incandescent lamps (light bulbs) on the exposition buildings and 174 arc lights on the Champs Elysees. It is difficult for twenty-first century minds to fathom how breathtaking such a sight must have been to those millions of spectators in 1900. They must have truly felt they entered into an exciting new modern age with the arrival of the twentieth century.

Items Noted:

bowl oval 8.25"
bowl, "berry casserole," collar base, round, 4.5", 8", 9", 10"
bowl, "comportier," collar base, square, 5", 9"
bowl, collar base, cupped, 7.5"
bowl, flat, round, 9"

butter, covered
cake basket, two base styles, 10.5" l.
celery vase, collar base. 7.25" h.
compote, jelly, round, square, 5.25"
compote, round, square, standard stem, two base styles, 8"–8.5" w.
compote, round, paneled stem with rayed base, 7.5" w.
cream, footed, applied handle
cruet, small, rounded base, stopper #2
cruet, large, wide base, stopper #1 or #4
ice tub, handled, 6.25" w.
mug
nick nack, high-foot, 6.5" w.
pitcher, half-gallon
plate, round, 8", 10"
plate, square, 7"
salver, 6"
salver, standard stem, two base styles, 9.5"–10"
salver, paneled stem with rayed base, 9"
shaker, salt and pepper, bulbous bottom, long neck
shaker, salt and pepper, cylindrical, large
shaker, sugar, cylindrical
spoon, footed, scalloped edge
sugar, covered, footed, scalloped edge, inner ledge
syrup, metal lid
tumbler
vase, footed, various edge treatments and sizes
vase, footed, swung, 12" (height varies)
wafer stand, 6.5" w.
wine

Reproductions and Look-alikes: None known.

Persian, 1889 (first introduced as **Princeton**, 1887)

References: BH, undated; *PGR*, 7/28/1887 & 12/27/1888; BB 89th Trip, 1888; HB&F, spring and summer 1888
Colors: clear; amber and blue (mug and tumbler known)

Minnie Watson Kamm includes some undated catalog pages of Bryce, Higbee's Persian in *An Eighth Pattern Glass Book.* Also shown is a circa 1888 catalog page of stemware that includes a goblet in the same pattern, but it is labeled "Princeton." This discrepancy has been long thought to be an error, however, evidence has been found that shows this was the original name Bryce, Higbee gave the pattern. The journal *Pottery and Glassware Reporter* first mentions Bryce, Higbee's Princeton pattern on July 28, 1887:

> Bryce, Higbee & Co... have a new pattern in tableware just completed and it comprises quite an extensive line. It is of round shape and bears a very pretty figured design. The pieces are without any obstrusive [*sic*] feet or other parts likely to be knocked off, and are made with a view to practical utility as well as ornament. These points are exemplified in the pitchers, set, comports and other articles. They have called this the "Princeton" pattern, and it is the third new one they have produced this year.

This report dates no less than a year prior to the catalog page of goblets shown by Kamm with the Princeton designation because a Royal goblet is also shown, and that pattern was first mentioned in July 1888. Hollander, Bradshaw & Folsom illustrates and lists items in the pattern we know

Persian cream, $35–$40; spoon, $35–$40; sugar, $50–$55.

Persian goblets, $25–$30 each; 9.75" and 8.75" oval bowls, $20–$25 each, 4.5" covered jelly compote, $30–$35.

Persian 4.5" and 9" open compotes with smooth edge, $15–$20; $30–$35.

as Persian in their spring and summer 1888 catalog, and they are also labeled Princeton. The pattern was offered in the "Torrence" assortment by Butler Brothers in 1888, but no name is given to the pattern itself. Three different original sources, two showing illustrations, and, very importantly, one of which is a company catalog, can hardly all be in error in calling the pattern Princeton. The December 27, 1888, issue *Pottery and Glassware Reporter* states:

> Bryce, Higbee & Co. have out some elegant new patterns for the spring trade...The "Persian" is a pretty figured pattern, of which they also have a full line.

The Bryce, Higbee catalog pages shown by Kamm in negative print include three pages labeled "Persian Pattern" and obviously date after the December 1888 report in *Pottery and Glassware Reporter*. From May 1889 to at least 1892 individual items are described as "Persian pattern" in some Butler Brothers assortments. It is not common for Butler Brothers to use OMNs, but there are other confirmed instances where they did. Spelman Brothers also refers to the pattern as Persian in the same time frame.

The overwhelming evidence shows that Bryce, Higbee introduced the pattern as Princeton in July 1887 for the fall trade and either changed the name to Persian or reintroduced the pattern as Persian for the spring 1889 market. Is it mere coincidence that earlier in 1887 the company introduced their Yale pattern, also named after an Ivy League school?

Persian refers to someone or something from Persia, now known as Iran.

Persian blue mug, $50–$55.

Items Noted:

bowl, "nappy fruit dessert," round, 5"
bowl, "footed fruit dessert," 4"
bowl, "nappy fruit," round, deep, 6", 7", 8", 9"
bowl, oval, 8", 9", 10"
butter, low-foot, covered
butter pat
celery tray, shallow, approximately 11"
celery vase
compote, jelly, high-foot, plain rim, open or covered, 4.5" w.
compote, high-foot, covered, 6.5", 7.5", 8", 8.5" w.
compote, high-foot, open, shallow bowl, smooth edge or bullet edge, 7", 8", 9", 10.5" w.
cream
goblet
mug
pickle, oval, handled
pitcher, half-gallon
plate, bread, oval, 11"
spoon, 3.75" w.
sugar, covered, inner ledge, 5" w.
salver, plain edge, scalloped edge, 9"–12"
tumbler
wine

The only items known in color are the mug and tumbler. They have been found in ambler and blue.

Reproductions and Look-alikes: None known.

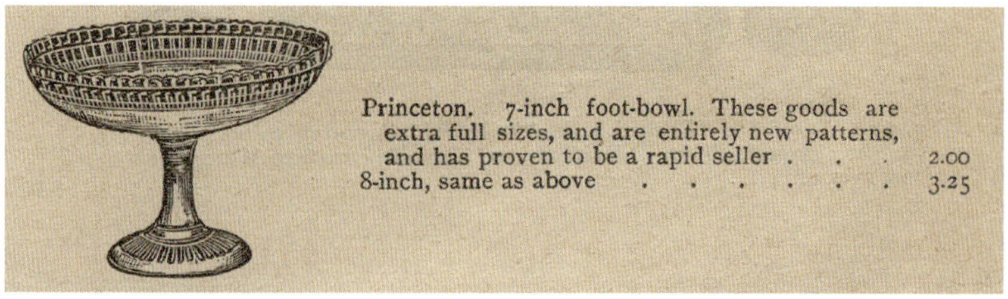

Goblet and compote labeled "Princeton" from circa 1888 Bryce, Higbee company catalog (right) and 1888 Hollander, Bradshaw and Folsom catalog (above).

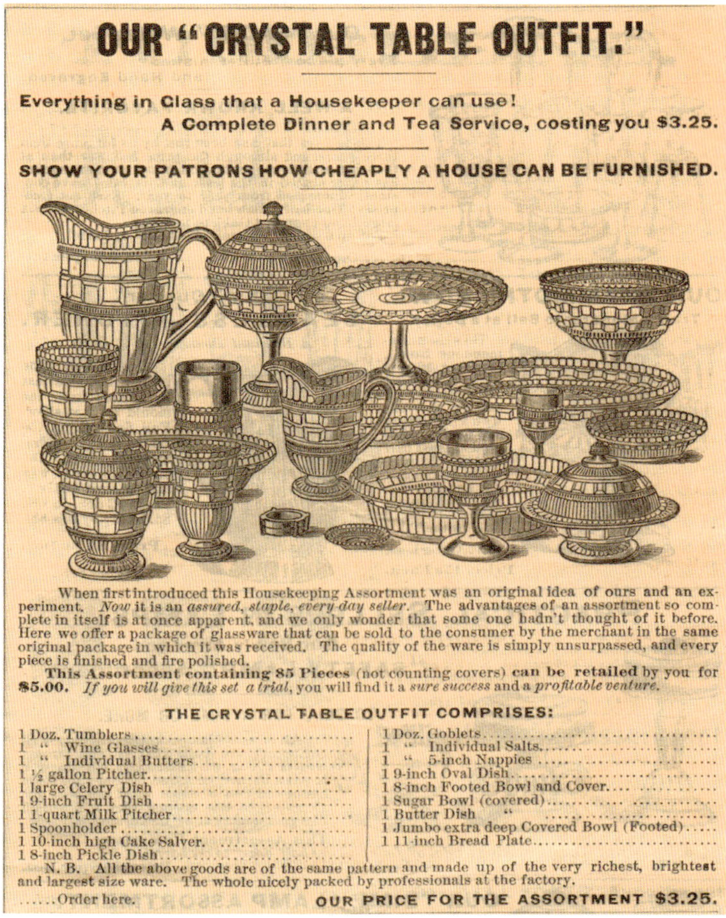

Persian was sold by Butler Brothers as a "Crystal Table Outfit" in September 1889.

Prism Bars,
c. late 1880s

References: BB, May 1889
Colors: clear

Prism Bars 6.25" high-foot covered compote, \$50–\$55; celery vase, \$35–\$40.

Prism Bars 8" oval bowl, \$18–\$20; 7.5" handled pickle, \$20–\$25.

Prism Bars 8" high-foot covered compote, \$60–\$65.

Prism Bars was first noted in a May 1889 Butler Brothers catalog in the "Our 'Wonder' 5 Cent Assortment," and may have been a new pattern for spring 1889. It disappears from Butler Brothers by April 1892.

In *Bryce, Higbee and J. B. Higbee Glass*, authors Lola and Wayne Higby state that *Prism Bars* "appeared in an 1886 Bryce, Higbee catalog along with items in the Persian and Acme patterns" and enumerate each piece they saw on that page. This is impossible because the Persian pattern did not exist in 1886. All the items they mention are shown in the May 1889 Butler Brothers assortment noted above. If the Higbys truly found the pattern in an 1886 Bryce, Higbee catalog, surely they would have listed it by its OMN. The only Bryce, Higbee catalog pages known are those in Kamm 8, and there is nothing that shows *Prism Bars*. Somehow the Higbys mistook a Butler Brothers catalog for a Bryce, Higbee catalog and incorrectly dated it as well. There is little doubt they were looking at the Butler Brothers "Wonder" assortment because all the items they mention are in it. In addition, the cream pitcher is drawn disproportionately larger than the sugar bowl and they mistakenly refer to it as a water pitcher. Unlike the creamer, the *Prism Bars* water pitcher has a plain, wide band at the top. The "fan-shaped olive dish" the Higbys mention is listed as a "7-Inch Fan-Shaped Plate" in the assortment and is actually part of the Bijou pattern. Due to the inclusion of this dish in a 1905 Butler Brothers assortment, they wrongly assign a 1905 date to *Prism Bars*.

The "beehive"-shaped finials are the same as those found on Gem and many items are shaped like Gem as well. *Prism Bars* is distinguished from other ribbed patterns by two notable features: each convex rib has a flat surface and is beveled at the top. The pattern seems a bit challenging to find.

It is possible that the OMN is Ola, but this has not been confirmed.

Items Noted:

bowl, flat, wide base, 4.5", 8"
bowl, oval, 8"
butter, covered
compote, high-foot, covered, 6.25", 8"
celery vase, stemmed, scalloped edge, 7.5" h
cream, footed
goblet
pickle dish, oval, plume handles (shaped as Earl), 7.5"
pitcher, half-gallon, footed
plate, bread, 9"
salver, 10"
spoon, plain edge, footed
sugar, covered, footed, plain edge
tumbler
wine

Items common to lines of glassware of this period undoubtedly exist, such as bowls and compotes in additional sizes and heights.

Reproductions and Look-alikes: No reproductions known. *Prism Bars* is very similar to Columbia Glass Company's No. 73, AKA *Vertical Bar*. The convex ribs are flat on Bryce, Higbee's *Prism Bars*, but are pointed on No. 73. The stemmed celery vase shown in the book *Findlay Glass: The Glass Tableware Manufacturers, 1886–1902* as *Vertical Bar* is actually Bryce, Higbee's *Prism Bars*.

Columbia Glass Company's No. 73 pattern is very similar to Bryce, Higbee's *Prism Bars*, but the convex ribs are pointed on No. 73.

Butler Brothers May 1889 "Wonder Assortment" that the Higbys mistakenly refer to as an 1886 Bryce, Higbee catalog. Note the items of *Prism Bars*, Acme, Persian, and the Bijou *Shell* plate.

Prism Bars half-gallon pitcher and sauce set. Butler Brothers, 1889.

Rival, 1883

References: *C&GJ*, 1/11/1883; SB, April 1884; BB 83rd Trip, 1885; BS, fall and winter 1885-86, spring 1886; GS, spring and summer 1888

Colors: clear; amber and blue (pickle jars with silver-plated lids known)

Rival celery vase, $35–$40; sugar, $45–$50; spoon, $30–$35; cream, $30–$35.

For over half a century it has been accepted that the OMN of the pattern collectors commonly call *Sprig* is Royal. Minnie Watson Kamm based this on catalog pages showing Bryce, Higbee's Royal pattern. In *An Eighth Pattern Glass Book,* she states, "Apparently it was thought the pattern would sell better with a bit of decoration, added later to the mold for each item in the set. Hence collectors may find the pattern with or without the added delicate spray." Kamm assumed they were the same pattern, but they are not. One telltale difference (which, surprisingly, nobody has noticed or noted until now) is the fact that the Royal sugar, spoon holder, and celery do not have handles, but these forms with the added sprig do. Trade journal reports confirm Royal was introduced in 1888, yet this pattern with the sprig decoration was offered as early as April 1884 by Spelman Brothers. Obviously the leafy sprig design was taken off the moulds rather than added. The OMN for *Sprig* is not Royal, but Rival.

> Among the patterns lately produced by this house [Bryce, Higbee & Co.] are the "Acme" and "Rival" sets, the latter just out. Both are very pretty, and will, no doubt have a large sale. A butter and honey dish of the last named pattern are especially noticeable, the design and execution of the work being equally effective.

Note the mention of the "especially noticeable" honey dish in the above quote from the January 11, 1883, issue of *China, Glass & Lamps*. The pattern commonly called *Sprig* by collectors does, indeed, contain an unusual diamond-shaped honey dish that is very worthy of note. Honey dishes are not standard forms made by Bryce, Higbee. The only other honey dish known in any of their lines is Ethol, though one could potentially exist in Royal.

Rival covered honey dish, $200–$225.

Further clue of the OMN is the fact that two different jobbers used the Rival name for this pattern. A Spelman Brothers April 1884 catalog clearly illustrates a table set labeled Rival. This jobber is known to have used OMNs. Among others, in the same catalog are items in Bryce Brothers Derby pattern (AKA *Pleat and Panel*) correctly named. Catalogs of B. Sommers (spring and summer 1886) and G. Sommers (spring and summer 1888) include a goblet in "Our 'Rival' Assortment" with the caption "Rival Goblet—Heavy fine polish goblet." Sommers is known to have used OMNs on occasion as well.

By July 1888, the moulds were retooled to become the Royal pattern. Rival must have been quite popular, for it is not too difficult to acquire. The handles on the celery vase, spoon holder, and covered sugar are very vulnerable and often found damaged.

The name Rival is an obvious reference to it being a preferred opponent to other patterns in the glass market. The reader will note how often the theme of competition and preeminence appear in the names Bryce, Higbee chose for their patterns.

Rival 8.25" salver, $50–$55; wine, $20–$25; 4" flat bowl, $8–$10; handled pickle dish, $15–$20; oval bowl, $15–$20.

Rival 7" high-foot covered compote, $45–$50; 7" low-foot covered compote, $40–$45; 8" high-foot covered compote, $50–$55.

Spelman Brothers April 1884 catalog offered a Rival table set by name. Note the incorrect mention of "engraved panels." Misleading descriptions in jobber catalogs are common and were used to boost the sales appeal of the goods.

Items Noted:

bowl, nappy, flat, covered, open, 6", 7", 8" w.
bowl, nappy, flat, open, 4"
bowl, flat, oval, 7", 8", 9"
butter, footed, handled
celery vase, stemmed, handled, 8.25" h.
compote, high-foot, covered, deep, 6", 7", 8" w.
compote, high-foot, open, flared, 6", 7", 8" w.
compote, low-foot, covered, 6", 7", 8" w.
compote, low-foot, open, 4", 6", 7", 8" w.
compote, low-foot, open, scalloped edge , 7.5", 8.5"
cream
goblet
honey dish, diamond-shaped, flat, footed
mustard, covered, base approximately 2.5" x 2.5"
pickle dish, oval, handled
pickle jar, glass lid
pitcher, half-gallon
salt, oval, 3"
salver, 8", 9", 10"
spoon, footed, handled, plain edge, 3" w.
sugar, footed, covered, handled, plain edge, 4.25" w.
wine

Pickle jars with silver-plated lids and frames are known in amber and blue. The base to the mustard is often sold as a "master salt."

Reproductions and Look-alikes: Newly made 7" high-foot open compotes have been seen with transparent labels reading © Two's Company Made in Taiwan. At first glance they are quite convincing, though close inspection reveals that the sprig design is poorly molded and lacks the fine detail of the old.

Royal, 1888

References: BH undated; *P&GR*, 7/12/1888; BB, May 1889
Colors: clear

Collectors have accepted that the patterns known as *Sprig* and Royal are one and the same, an incorrect assumption that has persisted for over six decades. Kamm makes this connection in *An Eighth Pattern Glass Book* stating: "Apparently it was thought the pattern [Royal] would sell better with a bit of decoration, added later to the mold for each item in the set. Hence collectors may find the pattern with or without the added delicate spray." The July 12, 1888, issue of *Pottery & Glassware Reporter* states:

Royal sugar, $45–$50 (lid is Rival); oval salt, $15–$20; half-gallon pitcher, $55–$60.

> The "Royal" is another new line just out. It is of plain glass, without figuring, and is in imitation of cut glass. The shapes are beautiful and it will prove a ready seller, the demand for glassware without much ornamentation being on the increase in many places. The glass in this line shows with great brilliancy and clearness, the more so from its being free from any intricacy of design.

Note how the trade journal quote draws great attention to the plainness of Royal by pointing out this quality three times in the course of four sentences. Nowhere is there mentioned any variation including a leaf design. Bryce, Higbee catalog pages illustrate Royal completely plain. This is because Rival and Royal are two separate patterns. It was logical of Kamm to guess that the sprig decoration was later added rather than taken away, but evidence confirms the latter is the case. Items with the sprig design are Rival, introduced in 1883 and first noted in a Spelman Brothers catalog dated 1884, four years before Royal was introduced. The sprig-patterned pieces also appear regularly in Butler Brothers assortments during the mid–1880s. All items are shown with the sprig design on every other panel. The completely plain version, Royal, is first spotted in the May 1889 Butler Brothers catalog. It should come as no great surprise that items with the sprig design no longer appear after 1888. The moulds were retooled, eliminating the leafy design as well as the handles on the sugar, spoon, and celery.

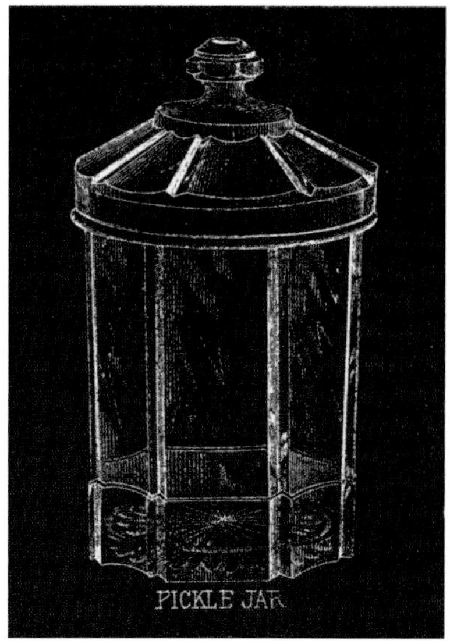

Royal items from original Bryce, Higbee catalogs.

Hands-on examination of Rival and Royal sugar bases shows that they were not made from the same mould, however.

Some sources give an AKA of *Sprig Without Sprig* to the plain Royal pattern, but this name should be abandoned. It implies one is a variant of the other rather than acknowledging they are two separate lines. The appellation is also very confusing and nonsensical, for why should we identify a pattern by a motif that is not present? An AKA for Bryce, Higbee's Homestead is *Cordate Leaf* due to an engraving commonly found on items in that line. Many were not engraved and are found completely plain. Using the same logic, why then should we not refer to the plain Homestead items as *Cordate Leaf Without Cordate Leaf*? This is just as ridiculous as using the name *Sprig Without Sprig* for Royal. Using OMNs is preferable and eliminates such confusion.

Royal appears to be more difficult to find than its sister pattern, Rival.

Items Noted:

bowl, nappy, flat, covered, open, 6", 7", 8" w.
bowl, nappy, flat, open, 4"
bowl, flat, oval, 7", 8", 9"
butter, footed, handled
celery vase, stemmed, 8.25" h.
compote, high-foot covered, open, deep, flared, 6", 7", 8" w.
compote, low-foot, covered and open, 6", 7", 8" w.
compote, low-foot, open, 4" w.
cream
goblet
pickle dish, oval, handled
pickle jar, glass lid
pitcher, half-gallon
salt, table, oval, 3.25"
salver, 8", 9", 10"
spoon, footed, plain edge, 3" w.
sugar, footed, covered, plain edge, 4.25" w.
wine

The same items found in Rival should potentially exist in Royal, such as the covered mustard and diamond-shaped covered honey dish.

Reproductions and Look-alikes: None known.

Scroll, c. late 1890s

References: BB, spring/summer 1898
Colors: clear

Scroll 7" oval bowls, $20–$25 each. Note the two varieties, with and without diamond point in the design.

An oval "7-inch Scroll Dish" appeared in the "Leader" assortment offered by Butler Brothers from 1898 to 1900. There are two versions of the dish. On one, the scrolls and ovals contain a diamond point motif found within many other Bryce, Higbee patterns from this time frame, including Surprise, Fleur-de-lis, and New Crescent. Some *Scroll* dishes are found without this diamond point design, which is the version illustrated by Butler Brothers. On both varieties there is a star with twenty-four points in the base surrounded by a zigzag pattern. The design with diamond point is very reminiscent of New Crescent, introduced in 1898; in fact, the *Scroll* oval bowl appears to be the same mould shape as found in New Crescent. These two patterns were clearly influenced by much earlier designs and are quite suggestive of patterns dating fifty years prior. It is not known if other items were made in *Scroll*. The author has wondered if this could possibly be Simoom, but no documentation has been found. Until future research yields evidence, the name *Scroll* will prove most satisfactory.

Reproductions and Look-alikes: A similar pattern was made by Indiana Glass Company, circa 1905, called *Shooting Star* by collectors. *Shooting Star* has a pinwheel design in the center of each of the "eyes." This area on Bryce, Higbee's *Scroll* contains diamond point or is plain.

Butler Brothers' Leader assortment included this *Scroll* pattern bowl with items of Melrose, Charm, Banquet, and New Crescent in May 1898.

Catalog image of Indiana Glass Company's *Shooting Star*, which could be confused for Bryce, Higbee's *Scroll*.

Simoom or **Simoon,** 1898 (pattern unknown)

References: *CG&L*, 12/22/1897,1/5/1898, and 2/16/1898
Colors: unknown, but undoubtedly clear

Simoom is first mentioned in *China, Glass & Lamps* on January 5, 1898:

> Bryce, Higbee & Co. have their sample room at 623 Smithfield street in great shape for the reception of visiting buyers. On some of the mirror covered tables are displayed their three new spring patterns; the elegant and unique Fleur de lis, the New Crescent, and the Simoom. These are all in the purest of crystal glass and three [there] are very full lines of them.

Regarding the name Simoom, the December 22, 1897, issue of *China, Glass & Lamps* informs the reader:

> This is the name applied by geographers to a powerful wind that sweeps over Southern Europe and Northern Africa at certain seasons and the firm believe it especially applicable to this pattern inasmuch as they claim that it will sweep the board when the dealers come to see it.

The pattern is mentioned in three different issues of *China, Glass & Lamps*. It is spelled Simoom twice and Simoon once. According to *Webster's Dictionary* both are correct, so the spelling Bryce, Higbee intended is not clear. Despite the company's claim for Simoom's imminent success, this does not appear to have been the case, and the identity of pattern remains undocumented.

The pattern that Lola and Wayne Higby label "Simoon" in their book, *Bryce, Higbee and J. B. Higbee Glass,* cannot be correct. See discussion under *Paneled Flower and Thumbprint* on page 210.

Reproductions and Look-alikes: Unknown.

Surprise, late 1896/early 1897

References: *CG&L*, 1/6/1897; BB, 1896 Santa Claus; P&B, 1897
Colors: clear

The January 6, 1897, issue of *China, Glass & Lamps* gave a lengthy report about Bryce, Higbee & Company and described their new Surprise pattern:

> The company [Bryce, Higbee] has this year taken a somewhat higher position than at any former time, and have placed two strong tableware patterns, the Banquet and Surprise, on the market...The Surprise is a combination of plain and figured pattern, less ornate, but a strong set, abounding in a great variety of shapes...

The August 4, 1897, issue of the same journal reported:

> Their [Bryce, Higbee & Company's] Banquet and Surprise table patterns, of which they have very extensive and complete lines, have been much favored by buyers...

Surprise sugar, $45–$50; 8" oblong bowl, $25–$30; 10" oval bread plate, $25–$30; butter, $55–$60.

Surprise wine, $18–$20; footed salt, $20–$25; 8.75" high-foot open compote, $25–$30. Note the Crescent-patterned stem.

Surprise oval (bread plate) from an 1897 Pitkin & Brooks catalog.

Though a detailed description of the pattern is not given, there are some particularly important features noted about Surprise. First, it is stated to be a very extensive and complete line. Second, it is described as a combination of plain and figured pattern. This terminology is repeatedly used by reporters in the trade journals of this era and refers to a specific type of pattern; namely, one that has a patterned lower section and plain top, or one that contains alternating plain and patterned sections. Patterns described this way in period journals include Heisey's No. 1220 AKA *Punty Band* and Riverside's No. 420 AKA *Box in Box*, which both have plain top sections and patterned bases, and Fostoria's Carmen and Indiana Tumbler and Goblet Company's No. 140, Columbia AKA *Herringbone Buttress*, which both have alternating plain and patterned panels.

The pattern that Lola and Wayne Higby call "Surprise" is not correct. That pattern is not a full line and is only found in bowls, plates, compotes, and cake baskets. Also, it is not a combination of plain and figured pattern by any stretch of the imagination. For this pattern, see *Curlicue* on page 148.

The pattern Bryce, Higbee called Surprise has been known to collectors as *Paneled Diamond Point*. Not only does the trade journal description truly fit the design, but an oval bread plate is shown in Pitkin & Brooks's 1897 catalog labeled Surprise. As noted throughout this book, Pitkin & Brooks is known for their use of OMNs. *Paneled Diamond Point* has been dated by previous authors to 1890, but this is clearly incorrect since trade journals confirm Surprise was new in early 1897.

Very interestingly, Surprise is a grandchild of the Worlds pattern. The Worlds moulds were retooled to create a design known as *Bowline*, which in turn was tooled yet again to become Surprise. It may not be pure happenstance that Bryce, Higbee decided to call this pattern Surprise, for its origin certainly is a surprise!

Surprise first appears in Butler Brothers 1896 Santa Claus issue in the "X Rays" assortment. This is a very early offering of the pattern that was not on the market for very long. The early appearance of Surprise in the pages of Butler Brothers is further evidence that this wholesaler did not offer only old, outdated merchandise.

Our "X RAYS" 10-Cent Assortment.

All Large--All of the Purest of Rich Glass, and All Prompt Sellers.

It is not enough to say these goods are "fire polished," "full finished," etc. We beg you to order a package and see if they are not superior to anything you've seen.

The "X Rays" Assortment Comprises 1 Doz. Each of the Following:

8-Inch Round Dishes—Large, deep and beautiful.
7-Inch Footed Dishes—Usually sold from 15 to 25 cents.
Stuck Handled Milk Pitchers—A large and elegant table necessity.
7½-Inch Flared Butter Dishes and Covers—An every day necessity.
5-Inch High Footed Bowls with Covers—For sauces or preserves.
8x10-Inch Oval Bread Plates—An attractive, self-selling item.

(Total of 6 doz. to pkg. Sold only by pkg. Bbl. 35c.) **Price, 74c Doz.**

☞ Shipped only from our Pittsburgh warehouse.

Surprise was first offered by Butler Brothers as "Our 'X RAYS' 10-Cent Assortment" in their 1896 Santa Claus issue.

Items Noted:

bowl, flat, point and scallop edge, 8"
bowl, oblong, bubbles on scalloped edge, 8"
bowl, oval, deep, 8"
butter, covered, scalloped edge with stars (as Vici)
compote, high-foot, covered, 5", 7", 8"
compote, high-foot, open, scalloped and point and scallop edge, 7", 8", 9"
cream, applied handle
pitcher, half-gallon, footed, point and scallop edge
plate, bread, oval, 10"
salt, flat, 1.5"
salt, footed, 2.5"
salver, 9"
shaker, salt and pepper, barrel-shaped
spoon
sugar, covered, plain edge, 4" w.
tumbler
wine

Cake baskets should exist, but none have been found. Since *China, Glass & Lamps* described Surprise as a very extensive line, there are undoubtedly more items than listed here.

Reproductions and Look-alikes: No reproductions known. Other companies made similar patterns with panels of diamond point. Richards & Hartley's Diamond AKA *Flat Diamond* could be easily confused, but as the AKA implies, the diamonds are flat. The diamonds on Surprise are small and pointed; the plain panels are convex and the diamond point panels are slightly concave. Also, look for Bryce, Higbee stems and finials, which are the same as Worlds. Open compotes are also found with the same stem used for Crescent, however.

Swirl and Panel, c. 1905

References: BB, spring 1905
Colors: clear

There are only four different shapes known in *Swirl and Panel.* The design in the base is identical to the flower motif of *Feathered Medallion*, and the first appearance of both patterns is in the spring 1905 Butler Brothers catalog. It seems a bit unusual that Bryce, Higbee would make so few miscellaneous articles in this pattern, and it is quite likely these items were intended to be part of the *Feathered Medallion* line. The *Swirl and Panel* toothpick and salt and pepper shakers are consistently shown by Butler Brothers as part of a caster set including a *Feathered Medallion* cruet

Swirl and Panel toothpick, $20–$25.

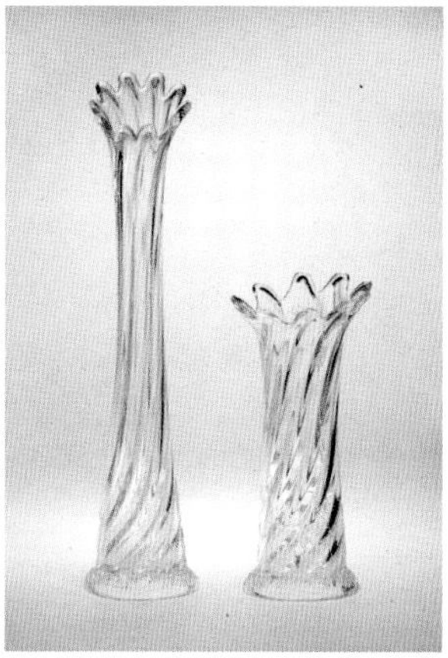

Swirl and Panel 10.25" and 17" swung vases, $35–$40 each.

and what appears to be an Anona tray. Though the motifs differ quite a bit from those found in the *Feathered Medallion* design (except for the aforementioned base pattern), it was a common practice in this time period to include items in a line of glassware that did not match exactly. This concept baffles collectors today, but it was considered a desirable quality meant to give the set variety and, ultimately, attract the attention of the buyers. The toothpick is the item most often seen in this design.

Items Noted:
bowl, round, 4.25", 6.25", 8.5"
shaker, salt and pepper
toothpick
vase, swung, 10.25", 17" (height varies)

Reproductions and Look-alikes: None known.

Teardrop Row, c. early to mid–1890s

References: OM&G, 1895; BB, September 1895; BB, 1896 Santa Claus
Colors: clear, clear with engraving

Teardrop Row engraved sugar, $45–$50; spoon, $30–$35; butter, $60–$65.

Bryce, Higbee's *Teardrop Row* is another pattern for which original company material is lacking. No trade journal reports have been found that describe the pattern and the OMN is unknown.

The earliest jobber catalogs in which *Teardrop Row* has been found are dated 1895. Ogden, Merrill and Greer offered a pickle and celery tray in their "Victor Package." Butler Brothers offered a 9" scalloped-edge bread plate in two different assortments in September 1895. A 6.25" handled bowl with inner ledge was sold in Butler Brothers "Chieftain" assortment in the 1896 Santa Claus issue. This is actually the butter dish base, though it was sold without a lid in this assortment. This odd mélange of individual items offered with other patterns suggests leftovers of a slightly earlier line.

There is an uncomfortable gap in what is known of Bryce, Higbee's production between 1892 and 1894, and no doubt *Teardrop Row* falls within this time frame. An important clue is the use of the Worlds pattern stems applied with a glass wafer to compotes, cake baskets, and salvers. This particular stem/pedestal originated with Worlds, circa 1892/93, so it can be deduced that *Teardrop Row* does not date before that. During the early 1890s, Bryce, Higbee introduced patterns that included a very heavy salver utilizing a separate mould rather than being flattened from high-foot compotes. The plate part is completely flat with a molded gallery rim, and the pedestals are applied. These include Era, Flora, Ethol, Worlds, and *Bowline. Teardrop Row* salvers are also of this type and must fall within this same production period.

Teardrop Row plates were flattened from bowls, and both are found with a raised, ground, and polished circle on the outside center. This is because bowls were also used to make the compotes. The pedestals were attached to the small raised circle, but in the case of bowls and plates, the circle was finished when the pedestal was not added. 9" plates were flattened from the 7" bowls. Since other sizes of bowls are known, the potential exists that plates were made by flattening them as well. Cake baskets were hand-tooled from 8.5" bowls attached to pedestals. Lids are very highly domed; finials are pointed and composed of stacked teardrops. Bases have teardrops molded in high relief. The convex design protrudes quite a bit from the body, and items often have scuffs, wear, and flakes. An engraved trailing leaf design is sometimes found on the wide plain border.

Teardrop Row has been called *Job's Tears* by some, but this is a long-established AKA for Adams & Company's Art pattern and should not be used. The two patterns are similar, and using this common name only causes confusion.

Items Noted:

bowl, scalloped edge, rayed base, 4.25"
bowl, round, scalloped edge, ground and polished circle in base, 7", 8.5"
bowl, rectangular, approximately 8"
butter, handled, inner ledge, 6.25"

Teardrop Row 10.75" cake basket, $45–$50; 6.25" covered compote, $45–$50.

Teardrop Row 10.5" salver, $125–$150.

Teardrop Row 7" and 8.25" engraved open compotes. $30–$35; $45–$50.

Teardrop Row custard cups, $18–$20 each; 9" plate, $25–$30; shaker, $20–$25; 8.5" bowl, $20–$25.

Adams & Company's Art pattern (left) is often confused for *Teardrop Row* (right). The most noticeable difference is that Art has diamonds in the pattern.

cake basket, 10.5"–10.75" l.
celery tray, 12"
compote, jelly, high-foot, open, scalloped edge, 5"
compote, high-foot, covered, scalloped edge, inner ledge, 6.25", 8.25"
compote, high-foot, open, scalloped edge, 7", 8.25", 9.25" w.
cream
custard cup, small looped handle (appears applied, but is molded)
mug
pickle dish, 8"
plate, scalloped edge, ground and polished circle in base, 9"
salver, scalloped gallery, 10.5"
shaker, salt and pepper
spoon, scalloped edge, 3.5" w.
sugar, covered, scalloped edge, inner ledge, 4.25 w.
tumbler

No doubt more items exist, such as a celery vase, water pitcher, and compotes in other sizes.

Reproductions and Look-alikes: No reproductions known. Adams & Company's Art AKA *Job's Tears* (1889) is often confused for *Teardrop Row*. The heaviness and brilliance of the glass is similar, but the Art pattern contains flat, beveled diamonds not present in *Teardrop Row*.

Ten-Pointed Star, 1906

References: BB, spring 1906
Colors: clear

The discovery of a photo dated January 1906, taken in the Bryce, Higbee office, has helped confirm a date of introduction for *Ten-Pointed Star*. In the foreground of the photo is a table with many items of this pattern. These were no doubt samples of a new line of tableware in preparation for the annual January glass show. Toward the back of the photo are a half dozen more articles in the same design stacked on a desk.

The pattern is first noted in Butler Brothers spring 1906 catalog in a rather large grouping. The assortment was offered continuously for about a year, but the mid-spring 1907 issue notes the assortment was temporarily out. The June 1907 issue makes the same statement, and the mid-winter 1908 issue (issued in December 1907) does not offer it at all. When one studies the timeline of the company during this corresponding period, a clearer picture is formed. John B. Higbee died in December 1906 and, according to trade journal quotes, the factory shut down. Butler Brothers still offered the pattern either because they had stock remaining in their warehouses or because the Bryce, Higbee factory did not completely shut down as *China, Glass & Lamps* reported. The spring 1907 Butler Brothers catalog was issued in late February and still offered *Ten-Pointed Star*. Flood destroyed the Bryce, Higbee factory in March 1907. By the publication of the mid-spring 1907 catalog (effective in May), Butler Brothers was out of the pattern and could no longer be supplied with it.

The OMN is unknown, but hopefully will soon be discovered. Kamm first mentioned the pattern in 1940 and named it *Ten-Pointed Star*. It is quite amazing that, at the time, the pattern was only thirty-four years old, yet the OMN had already been lost. Kamm's name does not adequately describe the motif because only a few of the items display stars with ten points. The stars are overlaid with a band composed of hexagons with rayed centers and only six points are exhibited on most items. The rectangular bowls show only three points. It is a very elaborate, exotic-looking design meant to imitate rich cut glass.

In *Glass Salt Shakers*, Peterson shows a shaker that appears to be *Ten-Pointed Star*, but calls it *Hawaiian Lei*. It definitely is not J. B. Higbee's Gala AKA *Hawaiian Lei*. Gala contains star-centered octagons separated by diamond point in an X configuration. The shaker in question has none of these motifs and displays only the band of star-centered hexagons found in *Ten-Pointed Star* pattern. The shape appears to be the same

Ten-Pointed Star celery vase, $25–$30; 10.5" plate, $30–$35; butter, $45–$50; half-gallon pitcher, $45–$50.

Ten-Pointed Star 7" nick nack, $30–$35; 7.5" plate, $15–$20; 6.75" wafer stand, $30–$35.

as Bryce, Higbee's *Swirl and Panel* shaker and it may be shown in a spring 1907 Butler Brothers catalog as part of a *Ten-Pointed Star* cruet set, but the illustration is not clear enough to be certain. It is worthy of note that the stopper shown in the cruet is not drawn true to reality, either.

The handled olive and handled jelly are from the same mould, but the jelly is round whereas the olive has a hand-tooled lip. The cafe cream and handled baskets are unusual items for Bryce, Higbee and are not as easily found as other articles in the pattern. Tooled from the mug, the cafe cream is a late form and more commonly appears in patterns made by J. B. Higbee. An abundance of *Ten-Pointed Star* bowls were made in various sizes and depths. Edges were hand-tooled in numerous ways, including cupped, flared, square, and ruffled. As was typical for Bryce, Higbee, round plates were flattened from bowls. For some reason the cake basket is not as commonly found as those of other Bryce, Higbee patterns.

Ten-Pointed Star does appear in a few random items in Butler Brothers catalogs issued as late as 1910. The large open compote and salver were offered with J. B. Higbee's Alpha from August 1909 to the end of 1910. The tumbler and 4.5" berry bowl show up in the "Bargain Day" assortment from spring 1909 to late 1910. All other items in that grouping are J. B. Higbee's Alpha, and, prior to spring 1909, the tumbler and small berry bowl were also. By mid-summer 1911, all items are J. B. Higbee's Banner with a single *Swirl and Panel* toothpick holder. Why were those two items of the Alpha pattern replaced with the same items in *Ten-Pointed Star*? The "Bargain Day" assortment seems to have been an outlet for Bryce, Higbee, and later J. B. Higbee, to sell odd, small items as well as stock of older patterns. This would explain why over the years individual items randomly appear in the assortment for short amounts of time.

Ten-Pointed Star has not been seen or reported with the J. B. Higbee trademark bee. The pattern must have been produced in huge quantities, for most items are not too difficult to find. The liberal availability of *Ten Pointed-Star* belies the fact that, according to the timeline presented above, Bryce, Higbee produced it for only a year, so a suggestion that J. B. Higbee also made it cannot be discounted.

Ten-Pointed Star cruets, \$30–\$35 each; square plate, \$25–\$30; mug, \$15–\$20; cafe cream, \$35–\$40; stemmed lily or rose bowl, \$40–\$45.

Ten-Pointed Star 8.25" basket with applied handle, \$55–\$60; 9" cake basket, \$45–\$50.

Ten-Pointed Star 8" square compote, \$20–\$25; flat rose bowl, \$25–\$30; 9.5" salver, \$40–\$45.

"CRIMPED" BERRY SET ASSORTMENT.

A806—Pure crystal fire polished brilliant glass, new 1906 pattern, 3 different shapes; one 9-inch flared square, one 9-inch flared, and one 8-inch crimped. Set consists of 1 large bowl and six 4½-inch nappies to match. Six sets of each pattern in barrel, total 18 sets............per set, **21c**

Ten-Pointed Star bowls were made with many different edge treatments as this June 1906 Baltimore Bargain House assortment illustrates.

Items Noted:

basket, applied ribbed handle, oval, 6", 8" l.
bowl, collar base, round, oval, square, flared, ruffled, cupped, various depths and sizes
butter, covered
cake basket, 9.25" l.
celery tray, 11.25"
celery vase, handled, 6" h.
comportier, low-foot, 3.5" w.
compote, jelly, high-foot, round, square, 5.5" w.
compote, high-foot, open, round, square, deep, shallow, 7.5"–8.5" w.
cream, cafe, 3.5" h. (mug with hand-tooled lip)
cream, table
cruet, stopper #3
cup, custard
jelly, handled, 5.5"
mug
nick nack, high-foot, 7" l.
nick nack tray, collar base, 7", 10.25" l.
olive, handled, pointed lip, 5.5"
pitcher, quart
pitcher, half-gallon
plate, round, collar base, various sizes
plate, square, 7"
rose bowl, collar base, scalloped edge, square opening, 6" w.
rose bowl, stemmed, scalloped edge, 7.5" h.
salver, 6.25", 9.5"
sauce dish, rectangular, 7", 8" l.
spoon, scalloped edge
sugar, covered scalloped edge, inner ledge
tumbler
vase, swung, approximately 12"–14" (height varies)
wafer stand, 6.75" w.
wine

Reproductions and Look-alikes: None known.

Photo taken January 1906 in the Bryce, Higbee & Company office. Displayed on the table in the foreground, as well as on a desk at back, are items of *Ten-Pointed-Star,* a new pattern for the 1906 spring trade.

A rather large grouping of *Ten-Pointed Star* was offered as the "Brilliant" assortment by Baltimore Bargain House in June 1907. Butler Brothers offered a similar assortment by the same title in spring 1906.

Ten-Pointed Star Variant, year uncertain

References: BB, mid-winter 1907
Colors: clear

Ten-Pointed Star Variant 9" flared bowl, $25–$30; 10" ruffled bowl, $25–$30; 11" plate, $30–$35; 7.5" oval bowl, $15–$20.

Ten-Pointed Star Variant 3.75" toy butter base (sold as an individual butter or almond dish), $15–$20; 11" plate, $30–$35. Note the star motif on the individual butter is the same as on the plate.

Like *Ten-Pointed Star*, the pattern called *Ten-Pointed Star Variant* by Lola and Wayne Higby is also a misnomer because not all pieces contain stars with ten points. The Higbys acknowledge this fact and mention a possible third variation in reference to a bowl with only eight points to each star, but they use the name *Ten-Pointed Star Variant* regardless. When coining descriptive titles for patterns, it is best to use a name that applies to all pieces in the set, even ones with a slight variation (in this case, stars with differing numbers of points). Patterns were often altered to fit the allotted space by taking away some elements or adding to them; despite this, they were intended by the manufacturer to be part of the same line. The use of the term "variant" in a pattern's name is weak and confusing. It implies slight changes in the design of the same line of glassware rather than a different design of a completely separate line of glassware. If the slightly different items were meant to be part of the same line of glassware, there is no need to call them something other than the name the manufacturer gave, or a good, inclusive AKA if the OMN is not known. Though the author considers the name *Ten-Pointed Star Variant* extremely inadequate, no attempt has been made to change it, lest greater confusion will ensue. The OMN shall be endorsed, however, if and when it is found.

The author strongly feels the toy table set illustrated here was actually intended to be a part of this pattern. There has been much confusion as to which pattern line the toy set rightfully belongs. In *Bryce, Higbee and J. B. Higbee Glass*, the Higbys note that Bill Heacock states the toy set has been known as "10-Pointed Star." They do not agree with Heacock and refer to the set as "Fine Cut Star and Fan." Even though they admit they are not convinced it is part of that pattern, they date it to 1903 as they erroneously date the rest of that line that is presented in this book by the first AKA given to it, *Fine Cut and Fan*. This toy set is most definitely not a part of that pattern.

The ornate star in the base of the toy butter dish has ten points and is the same motif found on items of the pattern called *Ten-Pointed Star Variant*. The butter lid has eight points to the star, and the tiny sugar lid has only six. The bodies of the cream, sugar, and spoon holder also display six-pointed stars. The rays of the star on the butter dish and sugar lid are filled with a file design, but the same areas on the six-pointed stars each contain three tiny slashes. The variations here noted within the same set are due to the amount of available space and are no indication the items are part of a different pattern. There is a common characteristic between the toy cream, sugar, spoon and the full-sized items of the set, albeit slight. The tops of the medallions that contain the stars clearly come to a point as they do on other pieces of *Ten-Pointed Star Variant*.

The author debated whether to present this toy set as part of the *Ten-Pointed Star Variant* pattern because the name does not correctly describe it, but the name does not describe every item in the set, either. The author cannot feel responsible for such a poorly conceived name and must be true to himself and report his findings. The toy items are illustrated on the last page of an undated J. B. Higbee catalog devoted to the Madora pattern and labeled "Special toy set." The pattern bears no resemblance to Madora, however. It appears that J. B. Higbee used the "special" designation to denote items that varied (sometimes ever-so-slightly) from others in the same line. It is interesting to note that the Madora toy table set is not shown in this catalog, so it must have been added to the line after the catalog was issued. The *Ten-Pointed Star Variant* toy set may have been manufactured only by Bryce, Higbee & Company. The set in the J. B. Higbee catalog may have been previously manufactured stock and sold with the Madora pattern before the matching toy table set was designed.

Both *Ten-Pointed Star* and full-sized items of *Ten-Pointed Star Variant* share common elements, but the placement of the motifs results in two completely different patterns. There is little doubt they were meant to be two separate lines, for the

Ten-Pointed Star Variant toy sugar, $35–$40.

Ten-Pointed Star Variant toy spooner, $30–$35.

Ten-Pointed Star Variant toy cream, $25–$30.

Ten-Pointed Star Variant toy butter, $40–$45.

The last page of a circa 1910 catalog of the Madora pattern issued by J. B. Higbee shows the *Ten-Pointed Star Variant* child's items as Special toy set.

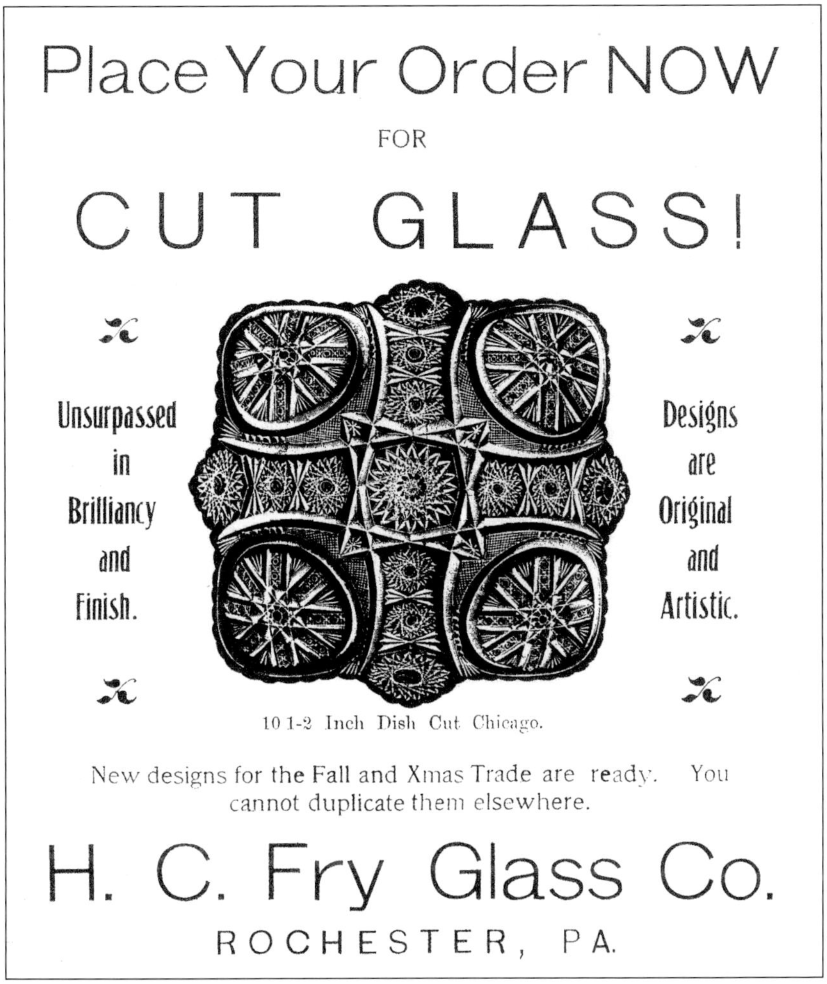

Ten-Pointed Star Variant shows obvious similarity to H. C. Fry Glass Company's Chicago pattern, confirming that pressed glass often closely imitated rich cut glass. This ad appeared in the July 16, 1904, issue of *China, Glass & Lamps.*

same forms exist in each pattern. Evidence shows *Ten-Pointed Star* was introduced in 1906. *Ten-Pointed Star Variant* is first noted in Butler Brothers mid-winter 1907 catalog (issued in December 1906). Here the toy set was offered for 96¢ per dozen sets. The base to the butter dish was also offered in this same issue as an "individual butter or almond dish" for 18¢ per dozen. The mid-spring and mid-summer 1907 catalogs note the items "Temp-Out," and they do not appear again after that.

Two *Ten-Pointed Star Variant* bowls are shown in an assortment composed entirely of Bryce, Higbee patterns in an October 1908 Butler Brothers catalog. The pieces and patterns offered are odds-and-ends, some being approximately five to seven years old by 1908. Most items in this assortment do not appear again in the pages of Butler Brothers (a few appear very sparingly), so it may be that this grouping was compiled from previously manufactured stock made by Bryce, Higbee before the factory reportedly shut down in December 1906. Butler Brothers offered a ruffled 9.5" *Ten-Pointed Star Variant* bowl and 8" vase for about a year beginning in April 1909.

No pieces of *Ten-Pointed Star Variant* have been reported marked with J. B. Higbee's trademark bee. The pattern is quite similar to H. C. Fry Glass Co.'s Chicago and appears to be based on it. A dish in Fry's Chicago is shown on the cover of the July 16, 1904, issue of *China, Glass & Lamps*, but the author feels *Ten-Pointed Star Variant* was made even later. *Ten-Pointed Star* and *Ten-Pointed Star Variant* (other than the toy set) both share marked similarities to Madora, using the same starred hexagonal motif as well as containing the very same design in the base. The three patterns are clearly related and are quite characteristic of the patterns made very late in Bryce, Higbee's history.

Items Noted:

bowl, flat, lobed, 6.5"
bowl, flat, oval, shallow, 7.5"
bowl, collar base, deep, 8"
bowl, collar base, flared, ruffled, 9"–11"
pitcher, quart
plate, collar base, 10", 11"
rose bowl, collar base
toy table set (covered butter, covered sugar, cream, spoon holder)
vase, cylindrical, 8"

Presumably, many other forms exist such as a half-gallon pitcher, tumbler, table set, etc.

Reproductions and Look-alikes: None known.

Tidal, 1889

References: BH, undated; *P&GR*, 7/11/1889; BB, September 1889
Colors: clear

Some modern references incorrectly date Tidal to 1900, but the pattern was first mentioned in the July 11, 1889, issue of *Pottery & Glassware Reporter*:

> The firm have now ready for the market a new line, the "Tidal," which possesses highly attractive and meritorious features, which cannot fail of being appreciated by the trade...

New patterns were usually introduced at the beginning of the year for the spring trade. A pattern introduced in mid-July was less common. Most of the glass companies had a shut-down period in the summer, but the trade journals indicate that Bryce, Higbee was often operating when most other glass companies took their annual break.

Tidal was earmarked for the fall trade. A water pitcher is first noted in the Butler Brothers September 1889 catalog. It was offered for $1.80 per dozen and described as "a very handsome pattern, so made that the seams from the mould do not show." A few years later an assortment of eighty-five pieces (not counting lids) was offered for $3.25 with the notation "everything a housekeeper can possibly require...you can sell them off quickly enough at $5.00 per package."

By misidentifying some Bryce, Higbee catalog pages, Kamm incorrectly attributes Tidal to Greensburg Glass Company. Lola and Wayne Higby mistake Kamm's drawing of a cream pitcher for a water pitcher despite Kamm stating the illustrations in the section in which Tidal appears are creamers. The Tidal water pitcher does not have four feet like the cream. The bowls shown on plate 54 of Kamm's *An Eighth Pattern Glass Book* are not Tidal. Though they resemble the pattern, they are actually part of Bryce, Higbee's Bijou line. See page 48 for more detailed discussion.

In her eighth pattern glass book, Kamm mentions that Tidal appeared in a 1904 Montgomery Ward catalog under the name "Perfection," adding another unneeded AKA to the list and instigating the Higby's claim that Tidal was in continuous production until at least 1904. I had always been quite skeptical

Tidal 8" high-foot covered compote, $60- 65; 8.25" high-foot open compote, $40–$45.

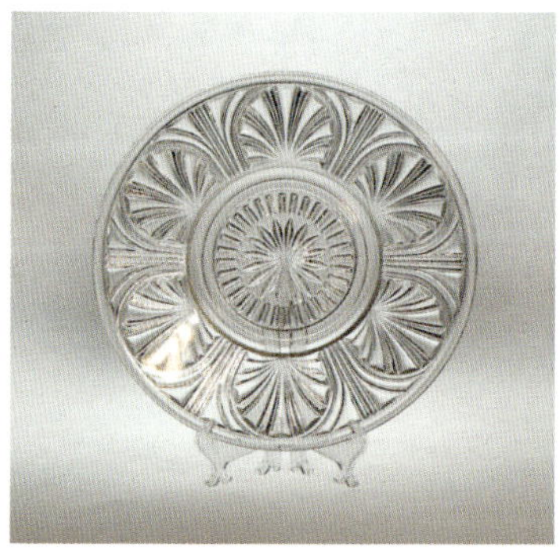

Tidal 9.25" bread plate, $25–$30.

Tidal cream, $30–$35; sugar, $45–$50; spoon, $30–$35; celery vase, $40–$45.

of this, for it is highly unusual for a full line of glassware of this era to have been produced by the same company continuously for a solid fifteen years. Exceptions are found with items in extremely popular lines like Adams & Company's Excelsior AKA *King's Crown* or Palace AKA *Moon and Star*, but they were actually continued production by the regime of the United States Glass Company. Most patterns introduced during this time frame did not have very long lives. With the plethora of new lines introduced every year, it did not take long for patterns to become "old" as these trade journal quotes illustrate:

> ...the popular Fleur de-lis, which held the boards for so long, is still called for largely.
>
> —*China, Glass & Lamps*, 3/1/1900

This entry is notable because Fleur-de-lis made its debut as a spring pattern for 1898, yet it is described has having held the boards for "so long" in the duration of about two years.

> ...they [Bryce, Higbee & Co.] still have their old lines on deck of which their Tiffany pattern continues to be a strong favorite.
>
> —*China, Glass & Lamps*, 1/11/1902

In this January 1902 quote, Tiffany is described as an "old line," yet it had been introduced to the trade just one year prior to this report.

It has taken over sixty years to be researched and exposed, but Tidal's 1904 date and the AKA *Perfection* can finally be discarded. Mrs. Kamm refers to a Tidal carafe shown in a 1904 Ward catalog as "Perfection" in her third book on pattern glass pitchers. When one carefully studies Montgomery Ward's catalog No. 72 for fall and winter 1903–1904, it becomes apparent that she made an error. Toward the end of the glassware section is a Bonair water bottle (called a carafe by some) near a plain water bottle. Bonair is similar to Bryce, Higbee's earlier Tidal pattern. Kamm mistook the Bonair water bottle for Tidal and thought the caption with the Perfection title was meant to go with it. The description that includes the Perfection name goes with the bottle shown to the right and clearly

Tidal butter, goblet, and oval bowl from an undated Bryce, Higbee catalog.

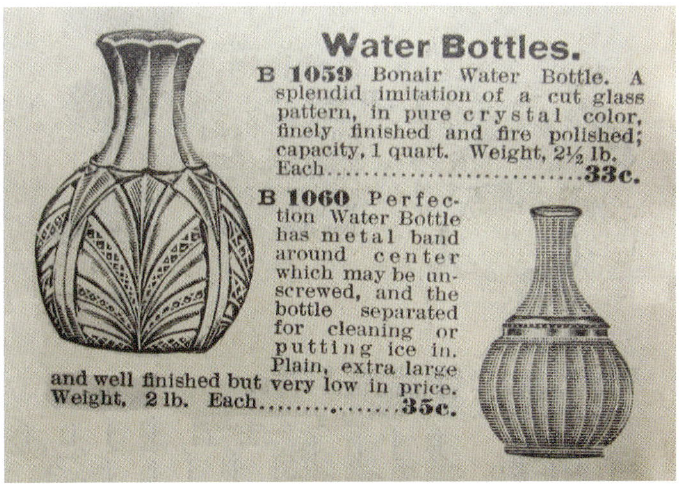

Water Bottles.

B 1059 Bonair Water Bottle. A splendid imitation of a cut glass pattern, in pure crystal color, finely finished and fire polished; capacity, 1 quart. Weight, 2½ lb. Each.......................**33c.**

B 1060 Perfection Water Bottle has metal band around center which may be unscrewed, and the bottle separated for cleaning or putting ice in. Plain, extra large and well finished but very low in price. Weight, 2 lb. Each..................**35c.**

1903 Montgomery Ward catalog illustration showing Bryce, Higbee's Bonair water bottle next to a Perfection separating bottle. Kamm created a lot of confusion by misinterpreting this catalog entry.

Ad for Perfection separating glassware, the type of water bottle shown in the Montgomery Ward catalog.

mentions it having a metal band, which may be unscrewed and "separated for cleaning and putting ice in." These were features of the separating glassware made by the Perfection Manufacturing Company of Washington, Pennsylvania, and this is what is shown in the accompanying illustration. Presented earlier in the same Ward's catalog are a separating cruet and syrup made by the same company, both given the Perfection title as well. We know the Bonair caption goes with the patterned water bottle because other items in this design are labeled Bonair elsewhere in the catalog. Bonair is the OMN for the pattern Kamm named *Palm Leaf Fan*. See page 132 for more information.

Further proof that Kamm mistook the Bonair water bottle for Tidal is the fact that in *A Second Two Hundred Pattern Glass Pitchers* she mentions that a water bottle, berry set, and footed jelly in the *Palm Leaf Fan* pattern were offered in 1904 by Montgomery Ward. These are the exact items shown as Bonair by Montgomery Ward in catalogs No. 72 (fall and winter 1903–1904) and No. 73 (spring and summer 1904). There is no Tidal water bottle at all.

The name Tidal obviously refers to the ebb and flow of tides. The shell motif found in this pattern makes the name particularly fitting.

Items Noted:

bowl, dessert, flat, 4.5"
bowl, berry dish, flat, 6", 7", 8"
bowl, flat, oval, 7", 8", 9"
butter, four-footed, covered
celery, four-footed, 6.5" h.
compote, high-foot, covered, open, 6"–10" w.
compote, high-foot, open, flared bowl, approximately 9" w.
compote, low-foot, covered, open, 6"–10" w.
cream, four-footed
goblet
jelly dish, four-footed, covered, open (may be same as butter)
pickle, oval, tab handles
pitcher, half-gallon, solid foot
plate, bread, 9.25"
salver, 9", 10", 11", 12"
spoon, four-footed, scalloped edge, 4.5" h.
sugar, covered, four-footed, plain edge
tumbler
wine

Reproductions and Look-alikes: No reproductions known. The author has encountered stemware that could be confused for Tidal, though the design actually looks more like *Bijou Shell*. The most distinguishing feature of the look-alike items is the rayed, octagonal base not present on Tidal. Their origin is not known, but they were not made by Bryce, Higbee.

Tiffany, 1901 (pattern unknown)

References: *CG&L*, 1/10/1901
Colors: unknown, but undoubtedly clear

> Bryce, Higbee & Co. are showing five new patterns at their sample room, 623 Smithfield street, and they are eminently worthy of the attention of buyers. The first is the Tiffany, an imitation cut pattern, comprising over 80 pieces. It has all the usual articles for table use and a nice assortment of vases.

Some past authors have surmised that Bryce, Higbee's Tiffany is really the Banquet pattern. This false assumption is based on the fact that Butler Brothers called the Banquet individual cream, toothpick, and mug "Tiffany" in their catalogs. This appellation appears four years before Bryce, Higbee introduced their Tiffany pattern in 1901, so it is obviously not a reference to this pattern. Incidentally, an assortment of Banquet offered in 1898 is titled "Waldorf," but this is not a reference to Bryce, Higbee's Waldorf pattern, as it appears three years before that pattern was introduced. The names Tiffany and Waldorf were often used by jobbers and retailers to denote a distinctive, rich quality.

As of this writing, the Tiffany pattern remains unidentified. It surely must be known to collectors by its alias, but its identity is uncertain.

Reproductions and Look-alikes: Unknown.

Triad, c. 1880s

References: patent illustration, 1884
Colors: clear, clear with engraving

Triad cream (value unavailable). *Courtesy of Jim Chafin.*

Triad is a pattern that would hardly be linked to Bryce, Higbee & Company, for the design is not typical of their output. A table set (cream, spoon, covered sugar, and covered butter) are shown in an illustration of a patent granted to John B. Higbee on June 17, 1884. Though the patent is for the tray that holds the set, it is hardly likely that a prolific, respected glass manufacturer like Bryce, Higbee would illustrate items made by a competing glass company or show items they blatantly copied from another firm.

The design on the flat corners of items found is different than that shown on the patent illustration, but patent illustrations often vary from the actual items. Besides, the design of the table set is not what the patent covered. The tray that holds the items was obviously designed specifically to hold them, although the specification mentions that any configuration and shape could be employed. There is also citation that the tray could be made of glass "or any other suitable material," but any such trays by Bryce, Higbee would have been made of glass. The patent covered the invention of an open-topped, center-handled tray having compartments to hold items.

Triad sugar and spooner (value unavailable). *Courtesy of Jim Chafin.*

In her fourth pattern glass book, Kamm calls the pattern *Triad* and notes a cream, sugar, and spoon holder. She makes an interesting observation that the items fit together to form a semi-circle and would sit nicely on a cupboard shelf. This is similar to the configuration shown on the patent illustration and *Triad* appears to have been made to sit on a polygonal tray.

Interestingly, the leafy design shown on the patent illustration is very similar to that of Rival. It is assumed the illustration indicates engraving rather than molding, however it is not certain. The *Triad* cream drawn in Kamm 4 is engraved, but the design is different than shown on the patent.

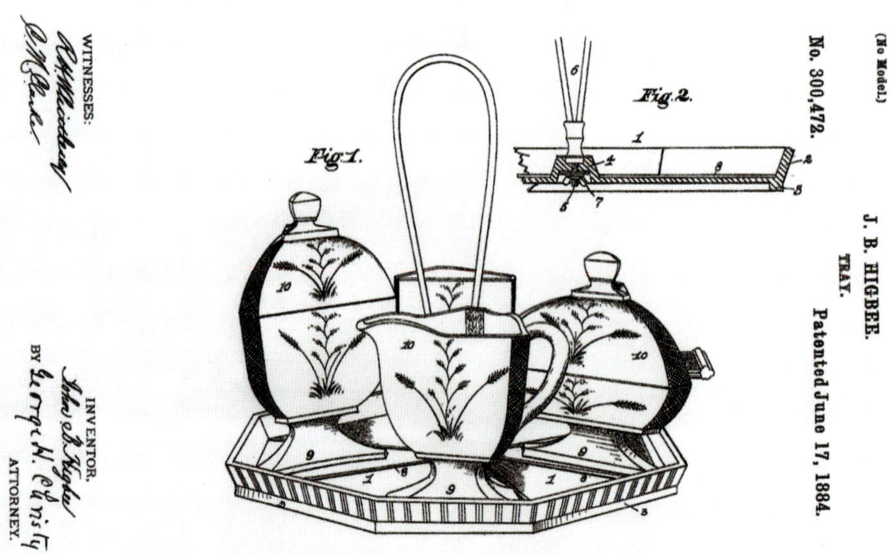

Patent illustration showing *Triad* table set on a glass tray with metal handle. The tray was patented by John Higbee on June 17, 1884.

The *Triad* spoon holder has a plain rim and could be easily confused for a sugar missing its lid. As with other EAPG, the sugar is larger than the spoon holder. Each side of the sugar measures 5", whereas the sides of the spoon measure 4". *Triad* certainly appears quite difficult to find. Only the cream, covered sugar, and spoon holder have been reported, but there is little doubt the butter exists as well. Perhaps only the table set was made with the intention to sit on the tray. The author has not encountered a glass tray like the one shown in the patent illustration.

Reproductions and Look-alikes: None known.

Vesta, late 1879 or early 1880 (pattern unconfirmed)

References: *C&GJ*, 2/19/1880 and 3/4/1880
Colors: undoubtedly clear

Vesta was mentioned in the February 19, 1880, issue of *American Pottery and Glassware Reporter*, but unfortunately without illustration or description:

> Their [Bryce, Higbee & Company's] styles have the advantage of being all new, and comprise full lines of table ware in different designs. Among their patterns, "Capitola" and "Vesta" are worthy of mention for neatness of decoration, while their designs in plain crystal ware are as handsome in shape and proportion as any yet shown.

Vesta was mentioned again in the March 4, 1880, issue of *Crockery & Glass Journal* without a specific description of the pattern. It appears to have been one of Bryce, Higbee's earliest patterns and may have been an imitation cut design introduced for the spring 1880 market. It could be the pattern known as *Chain*, but the author was not able to find documentation.

The Welkers date Bryce, Higbee's Vesta to 1888, noting a December 1888 trade journal, but they do not identify the day or the journal. The trade journals generally reported on new or recent patterns, so it seems rather unlikely that the same pattern would be mentioned eight years later. The Higbys repeat the undisclosed 1888 trade journal reference gleaned from Welker. The association of Vesta with Bryce, Higbee in 1888 is an error, for the December 21, 1888, issue of *Pottery & Glassware Reporter* mentions the Adonis and Vesta patterns made by the Ætna Glass & Mfg. Company. The glass companies often used the same names as their competitors for their own patterns, and such is the case with Vesta.

Vesta is the virgin Roman goddess of the hearth, home, and family.

Reproductions and Look-alikes: Uncertain.

Vici, 1896

References: *CG&L*, 1/9/1896; BB, 1896 Santa Claus; P&B, 1899 and c. 1900
Colors: clear; undoubtedly clear with engraving

In early 1896, *China, Glass & Lamps* briefly described Bryce, Higbee's Vici as "elegant in shape, quite plain" and implied it was a large line. An 1897 Pitkin and Brooks catalog illustrates a completely plain salver labeled Vici as part of an assortment with Bryce, Higbee's Melrose and Gem salvers. All three are the same shape overall. Presumably, other items in the Vici set have scalloped edges, too, as another review in *China, Glass & Lamps* mentions this feature.

A Vici butter dish, 9" salver, and 7" oval bowl are first noted in Butler Brothers 1896 Santa Claus issue. A fall 1897 Butler Brothers catalog shows a large Melrose compote in an assortment with a completely plain, low-foot, scalloped-edge 9" compote (or bowl), which is undoubtedly Vici. Low and high-foot 7" compotes were offered in the "Top Notch" assortment from circa 1901 to 1905. Lola and Wayne Higby refer to these items as "Plain" and cite the items in J. B. Higbee's circa 1917 *General Catalogue*, but they are decidedly not the same. Not only are the stems quite different, but unlike the stems of Vici, those found on the Plain compotes smoothly emanate from the bowl into the base with no ledge or plinth whatsoever. The "Mirror 'Plain Glass' Assortment" in the June 1906 Baltimore Bargain House catalog shows a large assortment of plain items including seven Vici compotes. Vici items were offered in jobber assortments along with Mirror after the reintroduction of the latter pattern in 1901. A 1909 G. Sommers catalog offered an assortment of high-foot 8" compotes from J. B. Higbee, including one which appears the same as the Vici compote shown in earlier Butler Brothers catalogs. The possibility that it was previously manufactured stock by Bryce, Higbee cannot be ruled out.

Flat items of Vici include a star in each scallop as well as a leafy central design identical to that found on the Yale pattern. Unfortunately, the Higbys mislabel these items as "Charm" because they say it is a "delicate and charming pattern." The pattern Bryce, Higbee called Charm is commonly known to collectors as *Rosette and Palms*.

Comparison of Yale and Vici bread plates reveals that the same valve with the leafy central design was used. Vici finials are the same shape as those found on Yale with the addition of a star on the crown. Mould shapes of compotes and other items in the set indicate that Vici was made from reworked moulds of the old Yale pattern. This should hardly come as any surprise, seeing how often Bryce, Higbee ingeniously reused moulds to create different, interesting patterns.

By the time Vici was introduced in 1896, the company had already issued at least three plain tableware lines: Alfonzo, Homestead, and Mirror. These plain items were offered together in jobber assortments, and it seems that Bryce, Higbee included some items from the earlier plain lines with the more recent ones. Because of this mixing of items and their lack of pattern, it is very difficult to know exactly which articles originally belonged to each line. Known forms of Vici consistently match up with those of Yale, so the collector should observe this guideline to identify items.

Vici 9" bread plate, \$25–\$30; 9" low-foot compote, \$20–\$25.

Vici salvers were sold by Pitkin & Brooks in their circa 1900 catalog. *Courtesy of the Rakow Research Library, Corning Museum of Glass.*

Vici salver and footed dish (low-foot compote) from a May 1898 Butler Brothers catalog.

Eight items of Vici were included in the Baltimore Bargain House "Mirror 'Plain Glass' Assortment" in June 1906. The open compotes and half-gallon jug are Vici, the "finger fluted" tumbler is Optic, and the celery vase originated with the earlier Alfonzo line. The remaining seven items are from the original Mirror line of 1890, reintroduced in 1901.

Vici half-gallon jugs were offered with Homestead jugs by Butler Brothers in spring 1906. Vici is on the left.

The plain cream pitcher Kamm shows in *An Eighth Pattern Glass Book* as "Utility" appears to be Bryce, Higbee's Vici. Since most items of Vici are difficult to distinguish from other plain patterns (which generally have low demand), its availability is uncertain. Perhaps now that the author has endeavored to separate and identify the plain lines made by Bryce, Higbee & Company collectors will appreciate their timeless simplicity and seek them out.

Vici is Latin for "I conquered" and is obviously a metaphor that the pattern would capture the market, though stated affirmatively in the past tense.

Items Noted:

With star border and Yale leaf design in base:
bowl, oval, 7"
bowl, round, 4.5"
butter, covered
pickle, oval, handled (fan handles like Yale)
plate, bread, round, 9"

Plain items, shaped as Yale:
compote, high-foot, scalloped edge, 7", 8", 9 w."
compote, low-foot, scalloped edge, 4.5", 5", 7", 8", 9" w.
cream, footed, scalloped edge
pitcher, half-gallon, low-foot, scalloped edge
salver, scalloped edge, 9.5" w.

Many other items were obviously made, including the covered sugar, spoon holder, and celery vase, but their exact appearance is not known. The author has seen plain, high-domed lids measuring approximately 5.5" and 7" with finials identical to the Vici butter dish. These lids had widely flanged, scalloped edges and were undoubtedly lids for compotes. Presumably, the Vici sugar bowl employs such a lid. To assist in identifying items of Vici, look for scalloped edges and mould shapes like Yale.

Reproductions and Look-alikes: McKee's Ionic is very similar to Vici, especially the low-foot compotes; however, there are some easy ways to distinguish the two patterns. Ionic high-foot compotes have paneled stems and low-foot compotes have paneled bases with a star in the center. Vici high-foot compotes have plain stems and low-foot compotes have no star in the base. Patterns void of design are some of the most difficult to positively identify. Nearly all the glass factories made them. These lines often had longer lives than others due to continual demand for basic, utilitarian ware. See discussions in this chapter of other plain patterns, including Alfonzo, Homestead, and Mirror.

FOOTED BOWL ASSORTMENTS.

K 1520—Duplex Footed Bowl Assortment. A small lot of good selling footed bowls; made of very best brilliant crystal glass; all new designs; full 8 in. size; ½ doz. each of four patterns; total 2 doz. in bbl.; no less sold; no pkg. chg., (wt. 75 lbs.). Per doz. 1.75

G. Sommers sold this J. B. Higbee assortment of footed bowls in 1909. Clockwise from left: Alpha, Banner, Madora, and Vici. This grouping is interesting because J. B. Higbee did not introduce Madora to the trade until January 1910. The Madora and the Vici compotes may have been old stock acquired from Bryce, Higbee.

Waffle and Rib, year uncertain

References: BB, March 1891 to September 1895
Color: clear

Waffle and Rib tumbler from an October 1894 Butler Brothers assortment comprised of Bryce, Higbee's wares.

From 1891 to 1895, in their Magnet and Bargain assortments, Butler Brothers consistently offered a tumbler in a pattern composed of two rows of beveled cubes over vertical ribs. The Magnet and Bargain assortments comprised patterns made by Bryce, Higbee including New Grand, Tidal, Bijou, and in later assortments, Melrose and Charm. The *Waffle and Rib* tumbler was more often than not described as "beautiful Persian pattern" by Butler Brothers, though it is most decidedly not Bryce, Higbee's Persian. It is not a quirk of the catalog illustration, as this tumbler was offered for at least four years and they did illustrate the true Persian patterned tumbler accurately.

It is unlikely the *Waffle and Rib* tumbler is part of a full line of exact matching pieces, and it actually may be part of the Bijou line, which consisted of several different patterns. With no real evidence, however, the author decided to give it a descriptive name until proof is found. The tumbler could have been left out of this book, but that would be a disservice to the intent of cataloging and attempting to document as many of Bryce, Higbee's products as possible.

Reproductions and Look-alikes: None known. The elements of the design are found in the products of other companies from the same time frame, but not in the same combination and configuration.

Waldorf, 1901
(pattern uncertain)

References: *CG&L*, 1/10/1901
Color: undoubtedly clear

The January 10, 1901, issue of *China, Glass & Lamps* announced Bryce, Higbee's five new patterns, one of them the Waldorf:

> The Waldorf and Oxford are short lines, comprising bowls, compotiers, berries, salvers and a few other articles.

Unfortunately, no description of Waldorf or Oxford was given, so we can only surmise which patterns they might be. The patterns presented in this book as *Curlicue* and *Diamond Point Swag and Fan* are logical choices. Both are short lines found in the very items mentioned in the report and first appear in the pages of Butler Brothers during 1901.

It is interesting that one of the other patterns introduced at the same glass show was referred to in the journal as Estoria, possibly a misspelling for the phonetically same or similar "Astoria." One cannot help but to think of the Waldorf-Astoria Hotel in New York City and wonder if there was some sort of allusion in the names chosen. The Waldorf-Astoria was born from two separate hotels: the Waldorf Hotel built by William Waldorf Astor in 1893 and the Astoria Hotel built next to it three years later by his cousin, John Jacob Astor VI. The latter hotel was designed to connect to the older Waldorf Hotel by Peacock Alley. The combined hotel then became known as the Waldorf-Astoria, at the time the largest hotel in the world. It was quite known for its grandeur and well-appointed rooms. At the annual glass show in January 1901, Bryce, Higbee was to unveil their newly renovated showroom:

> Bryce, Higbee & Co. have made a large increase to the extent of their already commodious sample room, 623 Smithfield street, second floor. They have secured the apartment adjacent to the original room, torn out the separating partition, repainted and renovated the whole, and the result has been a big accretion of floor space and a much ampler opportunity for the display of wares. They have put in several new tables, all of them topped with mirror glass, laid new carpets and the whole place has undergone a complete transformation. The full extent of the improvement will not be realized, however, until the new patterns are put on exhibition...
>
> –*China, Glass & Lamps*, 12/6/1900

If Bryce, Higbee truly named the pattern Astoria, by introducing it alongside another named Waldorf were they making a subtle reference to their elegant, newly enlarged showroom by comparing it to the famous hotel? Certainly, the names Bryce, Higbee chose for their patterns are colorful and significant. The association of grandeur, elegance, and richness with the Waldorf-Astoria Hotel would have been more than understood by the general public.

Reproductions and Look-alikes: Uncertain.

Worlds, c. 1892

References: BH, undated; W&M, c. 1892/93; MW, spring & summer 1894; BB, September 1895
Colors: clear

Though Kamm assigns a date of the mid–1880s to Worlds, no evidence has been found to verify this; however, evidence has been found to support a date of 1892 or 1893. Worlds was offered in a circa 1892/93 catalog of Wallace & McAfee, a wholesaler based in Pittsburgh, Pennsylvania. The assortment contains the caption "Another new pattern and is already a favorite." For more information about this catalog, see discussion under Gem on page 174.

Many have wondered about the significance of the name Worlds. It is difficult to think of it as a plural noun as written because there is only one world as we know it. Worlds is quite possibly a reference to "World's Fair" which would coincide with an introduction date of 1892/93. The Columbian Exposition World's Fair was slated for 1892 to mark the 400th anniversary of Columbus's arrival in the New World, but due to delays the fair actually opened in May 1893. Perhaps Bryce, Higbee gave this pattern the name Worlds with no apostrophe as a dedication in the form of a triple reference to the World's Fair, the New World of the Americas, and the Old World of Columbus's time. Names which have some sort of significance or specific meaning are encountered often with Bryce, Higbee patterns, so this reference certainly is within reason.

Virtually nothing is known about the patterns Bryce, Higbee introduced in 1892 and 1893. The only insight is a report published in the January 19, 1907, issue of *China, Glass & Lamps* as part of a recollection of fifteen years back regarding the Pittsburgh glass show. The reporter mentions that in January 1892 "Bryce, Higbee & Co., of Homestead were showing full line at their regular office, 623 Smithfield street. They showed three new sets which were very pretty, besides a complete line of staple goods." We can only wonder what the patterns were, but it is tempting to think one may have been Worlds.

Worlds is quite difficult to locate; in fact, neither Kamm nor the Higbys had an actual piece for study. Kamm erroneously

Worlds 8.25" and 7.25" covered compotes. $100–$125; $75–$100.

Worlds 10" salver, $125–$150.

Worlds celery vase, $50–$55, 4.5" dessert, $18–$20; sugar, $55–$60 (with lid).

describes the pattern as having "plain convexed columns" when in reality the plain panels are concave. Lola and Wayne Higby repeat Kamm's misinformation and illustrate a fuzzy sketch of a spoon holder that does no justice to the pattern. In actuality, the design has a prismatic quality that creates some interesting optical illusions depending on the light and angle the pattern is viewed. A 10" salver is shown in *Early American Pattern Glass Cake Stands & Serving Pieces* by James and O'Brien, but it is misidentified as Jenkins's *Stars and Stripes* pattern.

Worlds items are very thick and heavy. The celery vase weighs a hefty 2.5 pounds. Worlds must have had a limited production due to low sales because the pattern was retooled to another design, which did not seem to sell much better. The name *Bowline* is endorsed for the retooled pattern until the OMN is discovered.

Items Noted: *The list of items is compiled from the Wallace & McAfee catalog referenced above, Kamm's Bryce, Higbee company catalog listing, as well as actual items found.*

bowl, oblong, scalloped edge, 8"
bowl, scalloped edge, 7" and 9"
butter, covered
celery vase, 6.75" h.
compote, open, scalloped edge, 5", 6", 7", 8", 9"
compote, covered, scalloped edge, 5", 6", 7.25", 8.25"
cream
dessert, 4.5" (per catalog description)
pickle dish
pitcher, half-gallon
salver, scalloped gallery, 10"
shaker, salt and pepper
spoon, scalloped edge
sugar, covered, scalloped edge, inner ledge, 4.5" w.
tumbler

No doubt 10" oval bread plates and other items exist as well. See *Bowline* and Surprise patterns in this chapter and the discussion of the interesting relationship between Worlds, *Bowline*, and Surprise on pages 85–87.

Reproductions and Look-alikes: None known. See *Bowline* for similar retooled pattern.

605 ASSORTMENT.

¼ dozen	½ gallan	Pitchers	$1 00
2 "		Tumblers	1 00
½ "		Pickle Dishes	38
½ "	8 inch	Oblong Dishes	62
¼ "	10 "	Cake Stands	75
½ "	7 "	Nappies	70
½ "	9 "	"	1 13
2 "	4½ "	Desserts	90
½ "	6 "	Open Bowls.	87
½ "	7 "	" "	1 25
½ "	5 "	Covered Bowls	88
¼ "	7 "	" "	87
½ "		Shaker Salts	23
½ "		Shaker Peppers	22
Package			70
		PRICE OF ASSORTMENT	$11 50

Another new pattern and is already a favorite.

Selection of Worlds included in a circa 1892/93 Wallace & McAfee catalog. Note the caption "Another new pattern and is already a favorite."

Yale, 1887

References: BH, undated; *P&GR*, 1/13/1887; HB&F, spring and summer 1888; HLS, c. summer 1888; MW, spring and summer 1895 and P&B, 1897 (pickle dish only)
Colors: clear, clear with engraving; fruit and dessert dishes in colors (according to *P&GR*)

Yale, a new pattern for 1887, was well-described in a review in the January 13, 1887, issue of *Pottery and Glassware Reporter*. Mention was made that Yale was available engraved in "several handsome designs," and that the fruit and dessert dishes were made in colors. Though none have been found, the colors made are without doubt amber and blue.

Oddly enough, Yale has not been seen in any Butler Brothers catalogs, but it was sold by other firms. Hollander, Bradshaw and Folsom sold Yale salvers in 1888. As late as 1897, Pitkin and Brooks offered Yale pickle dishes competitively priced at 42¢ per dozen. The same pickle dish was sold by Montgomery Ward in their spring and summer 1895 catalog for 5¢ each, an average retail price at the time for this type of item.

Lola and Wayne Higby incorrectly state Yale was made by J. B. Higbee and the New Martinsville Glass Company. This is based on their and the Welkers' error of confusing the Melrose water tray (shown in J. B. Higbee and New Martinsville catalogs) for Yale. Though the trays utilize the same mould, they are decidedly not the same. Yale was made only by Bryce, Higbee & Company.

The fan-and-scallop edge motif is also found on the Grand pattern. Yale items encountered today are often worn and scratched from years of use. Any wear is quite visible because the pattern is so plain. The handles of the cream and water pitcher look applied, but seams running down their length reveal they are molded. Bryce, Higbee appears to have reworked the Yale moulds for their later Vici line introduced in 1896. The handsome central design in the base of flat items is found on flat items of Vici as well. This motif is also displayed on the lid of the Utility Boot ink, introduced the same year as Yale.

Yale is a private Ivy League university at New Haven, Connecticut, founded in 1701.

Yale cream, \$25–\$30; 10.75" bread plate, \$25–\$30; butter, \$50–\$55; sugar, \$40–\$45.

Yale 7.5" bowl, \$20–\$25; 10.75" bread plate, \$25–\$30; 4" bowl (possibly a fruit dessert), \$12–\$15. Note inner rims on this pattern are not necessarily an indication that the items originally had lids.

Yale open compotes were offered in three sizes in a circa 1888 Bryce, Higbee catalog.

Items Noted:

butter, covered
celery vase, footed
compote, jelly, high-foot, open, 5.25" w.
compote, high-foot, covered, 6", 7", 8" w.
compote, high-foot, open, deep, shallow, 7", 8", 10" w.
compote, low-foot, covered, 6", 7", 8" w.
compote, low-foot, open, deep, shallow, 7.5", 8.5" w.
compote, low-foot, fruit dessert, 4" w.
cream, footed
goblet
olive dish, oval, flanged edge
pickle dish, oval, fan handles
pitcher, half-gallon, footed
plate, bread, 10.75"
salver, 9"
spoon, footed
sugar, covered, inner ledge, 5.25" w.
tray, water, 12"
waste bowl, low-foot, cupped, approximately 4"–5" w.
wine

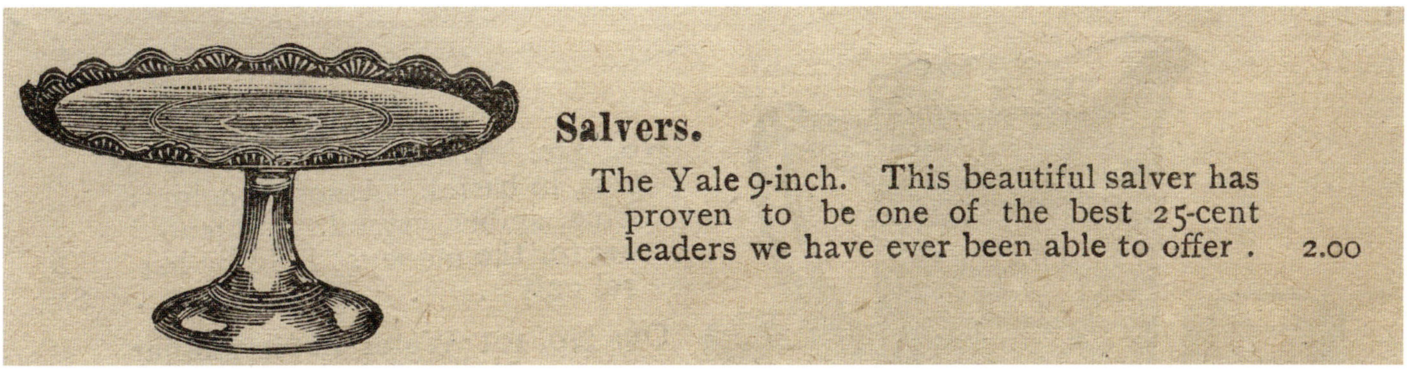

Hollander, Bradshaw & Folsom sold 9" Yale salvers for $2 per dozen wholesale in their catalog for spring and summer 1888. They suggested the retailer offer them to their customers as a leader for 25¢ to stimulate business.

Reproductions and Look-alikes:

None known.

NOVELTIES

ABC Plate,
year unknown

References: BH, undated; BB, March 1891; JBH, c. 1917; NM, undated
Colors: clear

Shown on an undated, circa 1888 Bryce, Higbee catalog page labeled simply "ABC Plate," this is one of three alphabet plates made by the company. There have been no trade journal quotes found to precisely date any of these plates. The scalloped, beaded edge is also found on the Capitola pattern, but there is no documentation to show it was included as a part of that line. The attractive central star is the same as that found on other Bryce, Higbee patterns including Capitola, *Chain*, Alfonzo, Butterfly, and Acme.

The plate appears in the c. 1917 J. B. Higbee *General Catalogue* with the caption "No. 530—Plain ABC Plate." Here it is shown without the beads on the edge. The mould was apparently reworked to remove the beads and sharpen the letters. The curves of the letters are more pronounced and the period was eliminated between the letters A and Z. The plate has been reported with the J. B. Higbee trademark bee. It is also shown in an undated New Martinsville Glass Manufacturing catalog, but with the caption "No. 530 Star A-B-C Plate."

Bryce, Higbee's A B C Plate, $45–$50. Note the beaded scallops and period between the letters A and Z. These features distinguish examples made by Bryce, Higbee.

Star A-B-C Plate made by New Martinsville from the mould acquired from J. B. Higbee. J. B. Higbee called it "Plain A B C Plate." Note the lack of beads on the edge and no period between the letters A and Z.

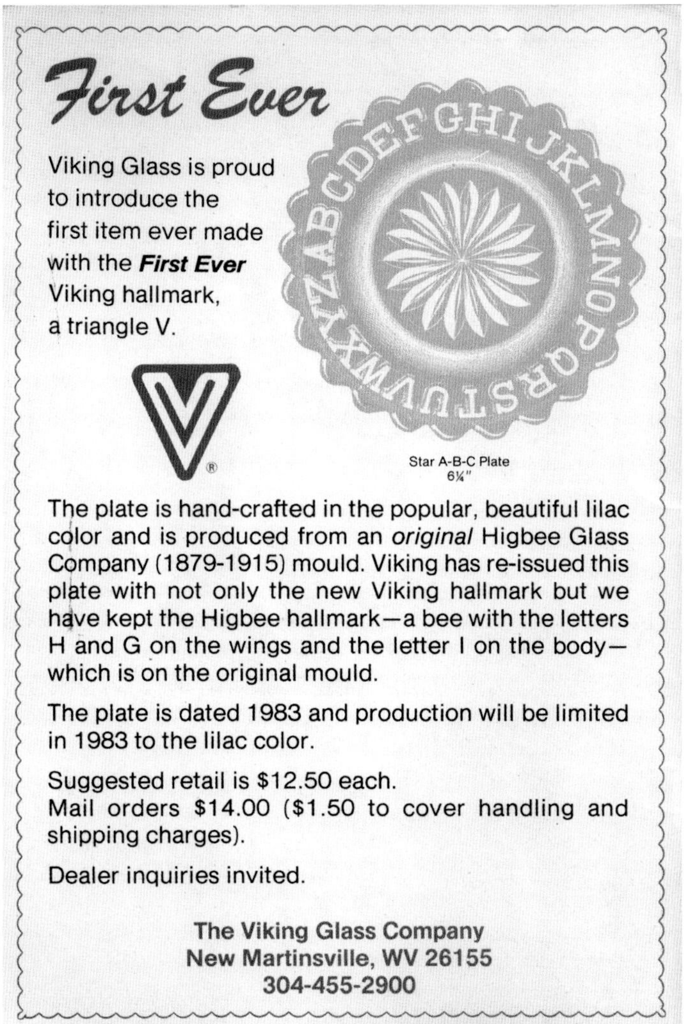

1983 ad for Viking's Star A-B-C Plate. Note the ambiguous mention of "Higbee Glass Company (1879–1915)." At the time of this advertisement, precise and in-depth study of Bryce, Higbee & Company and J. B. Higbee Glass Company had not yet been undertaken.

Bryce, Higbee originals are distinguished from all of the later issues by the presence of beads on the scalloped edge and a period between the letters A and Z. Original plates measure 6.25" wide.

Lola and Wayne Higby list the ABC plate in amber and blue, but no old colored examples have been seen.

Reproductions and Look-alikes: This plate has been recently reproduced by Mosser Glass of Cambridge, Ohio, in clear and various colors including cobalt blue, light blue, vaseline, and pink. Reproductions are J. B. Higbee's/New Martinsville's version and do not have the beaded border. Beginning in 1983, Viking Glass Company made the plate, calling it "Star A-B-C Plate" from original J. B. Higbee moulds. The company themselves stated the original moulds were used, which retained the Higbee trademark bee. In addition, each plate was dated with the year of issue along with a large "V" in an upside down triangle. This was touted in an ad as the "***First Ever*** Viking hallmark" and its use began on July 18, 1983. Each year a different color was issued, and the date changed on the mould. Island Mould & Machine Company has a clear example in their collection dated 1984, which includes both trademarks mentioned above. This information is quite important because it shows New Martinsville did not take the bee trademark off all the moulds acquired from J. B. Higbee. The New Martinsville Glass Company changed its name to the Viking Glass Company in 1944. This is how Viking became connected with the Star A-B-C Plate. When Viking closed, Mosser acquired this and other moulds from them. Some Star A-B-C plates have been seen marked with a capital "M" inside the silhouette of the state of Ohio, one of Mosser's trademarks, along with the bee trademark. Mosser called it "Child's ABC Plate," still offering it in cobalt, rose (pink), and vaseline in their 2012 catalog. In *Antique Fakes and Reproductions* (1950), Lee reported that 6.5" "star center" alphabet plates were reproduced in "clear and colors." If this is so, they may have been reissues by New Martinsville/Viking. No further information is available at this time.

Boat Covered Dish, year unknown, but undoubtedly 1880s

References: pattern characteristics
Colors: clear known

The *Boat Covered Dish* is ingeniously molded to represent a boat floating upon waves of water. It was more than likely intended to serve as a novelty butter or pickle dish. This item is presented here as a possible Bryce, Higbee product. It is risky to attribute a pattern to a specific glass company based on design elements alone, but it cannot be ignored that the design in the bottom of the boat appears on other Bryce, Higbee products in identical and near-identical forms. These include the ellipses in the *Chain* pattern, the base of the Alaric bread tray, and bases of full-sized Drum cream, sugar, and spoon. The small star motif was used extensively by Bryce, Higbee. There is a striking overall continuity between the *Boat Covered Dish* and the 7" oval bowl in the Earl pattern. The quality, color, and feel of the glass are consistent with glassware made by this firm during the 1880s.

The January 22, 1885, issue of *Pottery & Glassware Reporter* mentions a line that could possibly describe this item:

> Dalzell Bros. & Gilmore, Wellsburg W. Va...have some very beautiful salvers, handled tumblers, berry dishes, bread plates, and a line of "Boat" ware, including toilet set, caster set, individual salt and pepper, table salt, celery and cigar stand. These pieces are made with a boat for the base and it is an exact representation.

Boat Covered Dish, value undetermined.

Comparison of the motif in the base of the *Boat* dish with the central design of the Alaric bread tray and the ellipses of the *Chain* pattern.

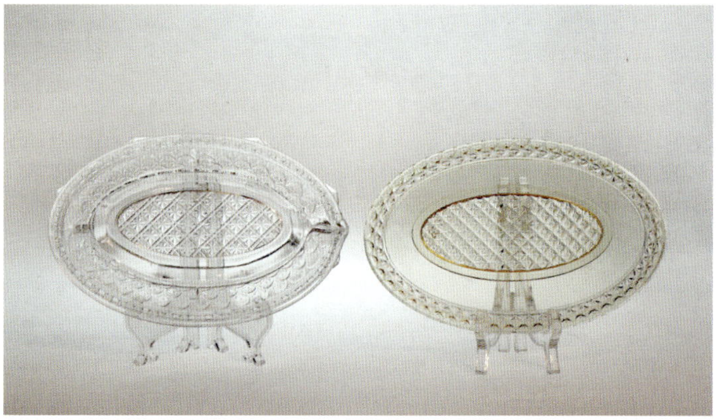

Comparison of the *Boat* dish with Bryce, Higbee's Earl reveals many similarities. Note the diamond and star motif in the boat base is identical to the ellipses of the *Chain* pattern.

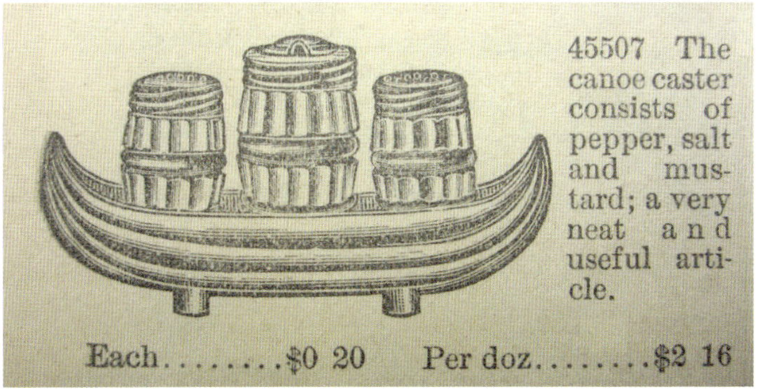
45507 The canoe caster consists of pepper, salt and mustard; a very neat and useful article.
Each........$0 20 Per doz........$2 16

The canoe caster sold by Montgomery Ward in the early 1890s may be a line of "Boat" ware mentioned in *American Pottery & Glassware Reporter* in January 1885.

Note, however, that there is no mention of any covered dishes. Dalzell's boat items are described as only having a boat for the base. The *Boat Covered Dish* is a full figure of a boat with masts, not just a base. There is also no mention of the unique representation of the boat floating upon water. Montgomery Ward catalogs from the early 1890s illustrate two items with boat bases mentioned above: a caster set and individual salt and pepper set. These very well may be the items described in the trade journal report.

The author feels quite comfortable attributing the *Boat Covered Dish* to Bryce, Higbee and Company, but hopefully a catalog will someday be found to confirm the maker of this unusual novelty. The base measures 7" long by 4.75" wide.

Reproductions and Look-alikes: None known.

Busy Bee Hive Ink, 1887

References: BH, undated; *P&GR*, 2/10/1887
Colors: unknown, but presumably clear

Busy Bee Hive Ink from a circa 1888 Bryce, Higbee & Company catalog.

The Busy Bee Hive Ink is briefly mentioned in the February 10, 1887, issue of *Pottery and Glassware Reporter*. The journal states that the novelty was introduced that week. It is shown on an undated Bryce, Higbee catalog page with an Ida pitcher and other novelties. Lola and Wayne Higby say the inkwell was made in amber and blue, yet they disclose that they have never seen an actual example. No mention of color is made in the Bryce, Higbee catalog or the trade journal. The Busy Bee Hive Ink could very well exist in amber and blue, but none have been spotted.

Reproductions and Look-alikes: Unknown.

Cucumber Dish, 1887

References: BH, undated; *P&GR*, 1/13/1887
Colors: clear, blue, undoubtedly amber; possibly others

The January 13, 1887, issue of *Pottery and Glassware Reporter* states:

> They [Bryce, Higbee & Company] have also out several novelties, conspicuous among which are a cucumber dish made in the exact shape of a cucumber though somewhat larger than the general run of these vegetables. It is in several colors as well as crystal and is got up very attractively.

The Cucumber Dish is known only in clear and blue. It was most likely made in amber as well, which would be typical of Bryce, Higbee's color production for the late 1880s. Since the report mentions "several colors" it is tempting to wonder if the Cucumber Dish was also made in canary and/or apple green. Bryce, Higbee is known to have made these colors, but slightly earlier and on a much more limited basis. None of the company's novelties are known in those colors, though green would certainly be most appropriate for this item. The Cucumber Dish measures 8" long by about 3.75" wide and is not very common.

Reproductions and Look-alikes:

None known.

Blue Cucumber Dish, $200–$250.

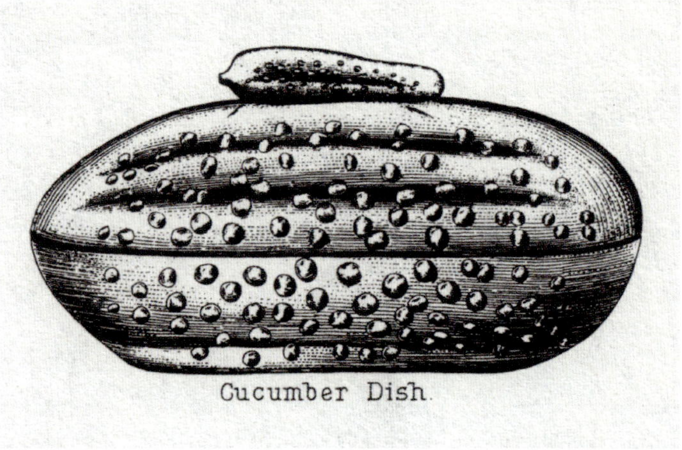

Illustration of the Cucumber Dish from an undated Bryce, Higbee company catalog.

Dog Match Box, c. mid- to late 1880s

References: BB, 1888
Colors: clear, amber, blue

Blue *Dog Match Box* lid, $150–$175 (complete).

BELOW
Butler Brothers offered the *Dog Match Box* with the Tub Soap Dish in their 1888 Santa Claus catalog.

Our 10-cent "HOUSEHOLD ASSORTMENT,"

A little 2 dozen lot "of Dime Bargains."

This little assortment consists of 1 dozen Novel-shaped Soap Dishes, and 1 dozen large Dog Match Boxes, with covers. They will sell as soon as shown.

A total of 2 dozen to the case (1 dozen each). Sold only by the case. (No charge for case.)
......Order here. **Price 83c. Doz.**

The *Dog Match Box* depicts a reclining Scotty or Terrier on a ribbed base. Butler Brothers offered the box during 1888 with the Tub Soap Dish in "Our 10-cent 'Household Assortment.'" Color is not mentioned, but amber and blue are known as well as clear. The *Dog Match Box* measures 3" wide by 5" long. Since the OMN is unknown, the Butler Brothers appellation is endorsed here.

Reproductions and Look-alikes: None known.

Emmas, c. mid–1880s

References: BH, undated; BB, c. 1886; P&B, c. 1887; HB&F, spring and summer 1888; JBH, c. 1917; NM, undated
Colors: clear, amber, blue

Emmas is one of three alphabet plates made by Bryce, Higbee & Company. Lola and Wayne Higby wrongly date this ABC plate to 1893, saying it first appeared in an 1893 Butler Brothers catalog. No trade journal has been found that mentions the plate, but the earliest date it has been seen by this author in a jobber catalog is Butler Brothers 86th Trip which dates circa 1886. Here it is shown in an assortment of colored ware with the notation "ABC Plates—The Emma style." It was also offered in a circa 1887 Pitkin & Brooks catalog as well as the spring and summer 1888 catalog of Hollander, Bradshaw & Folsom. These two catalogs call the plate "Emma." It is also shown on an undated, circa 1888 Bryce, Higbee catalog page.

The plate is labeled "Emmas" with no apostrophe in the Bryce, Higbee catalog, signifying a plural proper noun rather than a singular possessive. Indeed, Charles K. Bryce, foreman of Bryce, Higbee's mould shop, had more than one Emma in his life, his wife and daughter.

J. B. Higbee acquired the mould for Emmas, but it is shown in the undated, circa 1917 *General Catalogue* as "No. 531—Boy ABC Plate." Plates are found in clear glass with J. B. Higbee's trademark. The same illustration of the plate appears in an undated New Martinsville Glass Manufacturing Company catalog with the caption "No. 531—Boy A-B-C Plate." One would assume New Martinsville took the bee off the plunger, but there is no way to confirm this. Bryce, Higbee made Emmas in clear, amber, and blue. Apparently J. B. Higbee made the plate in clear glass only.

Reproductions and Look-alikes: Reproduced in clear and many colors with the portrait frosted. These plates were marketed by A. A. Importing as early as 1969 and likely made in Taiwan. Reproductions are very easy to distinguish because they are marked "Clays Crystal Works" under the bust and measure 8". Originals measure 6.5" and are not frosted. In *Antique Fakes and Reproductions* (1950), Lee reported that 6.5" alphabet plates with "Boy's head in center" were reproduced in "clear and colors" in 1937. If this is so, they may have been reissues by New Martinsville. No further information is available at this time.

Amber Emmas plate, $50–$55.

Emmas plate from an undated Bryce, Higbee catalog.

Frog Butter (Duke), 1886

References: BH, undated; *P&GR*, 3/11/1886
Colors: clear, amber, blue; possibly others

The March 11, 1886, issue of *Pottery and Glassware Reporter* gives a rather charming description of the Frog Butter:

> Bryce, Higbee & Co. have plenty of orders on hand and are running their two furnaces full. They have a new butter dish which they have named the "Duke," in complement to the creature it represents, namely a frog. For the frog is a cool complacent animal, self-contained, pompous and given to including himself, all of which qualities are eminently character of the duke. Seriously, this is a very neat article and ought to have a good sale. It is ready in crystal and several colors.

Frog Butter shown in an undated Bryce, Higbee company catalog.

Though called Duke in the trade journal, the item appears on an undated Bryce, Higbee catalog page as "Frog Butter." Like the Cucumber Dish, the reporter notes "several colors" and it is possible canary and/or apple green was made. The latter color would be most appropriate for a dish in the shape of a frog, but none of the company's novelties are known in green or canary. There is a marked similarity to Bryce Brothers Fly covered dish, proving that the glass companies were well aware of the products of their competitors. The Frog Butter measures 8.25" long by 6.25" wide.

Reproductions and Look-alikes: L. G. Wright had the Frog Butter reproduced as their 77–127 Frog Candy. It also appears in Wright catalogs as 70–6, depending on whether it was classified as a candy box or miscellaneous item. Reproductions are shown in Wright catalogs in blue marble and vaseline opalescent, though other colors were made. The reproduction Frog Butter is readily found in plain vaseline with a muddy appearance darker than canary glass made in the 1800s. A medium green, also with a murky look, has been seen as well. At the 1999 L. G. Wright liquidation auction, the mould was sold to the National Milk Glass Collector's Society. They commissioned Mosser to produce it in green opaque in 2003 and in white milk glass in 2008. Each is marked with the NMGCS rabbit logo and the last two digits of the year preceded by "OH-."

Gatling Gun, 1887

References: BH, undated; *P&GR*, 2/10/1887; P&B, c. 1887
Colors: clear, amber, blue

Clear Gatling Gun, $25–$30. Note the ribbed base.

The Gatling Gun is shown on an undated Bryce, Higbee catalog page and was mentioned in the February 10, 1887, issue of *Pottery and Glassware Reporter* as being a brand new novelty introduced that week. It is also shown in a circa 1887 Pitkin and Brooks catalog. Company catalogs must have been available to the artists who sketched the items, for the Gatling Gun is illustrated by Pitkin and Brooks and in a Butler Brothers assortment at a very odd angle, just as it is shown in Bryce, Higbee's company catalog. The item's purpose is not given by the trade journal, Pitkin and Brooks, or even the Bryce, Higbee catalog page, but Butler Brothers notes them as "Gatling Gun Toothpick Holders" in their "Magnet" assortment. Some of them have fine vertical ribs on the base to strike matches, but only clear examples have been seen with this addition. The Bredehofts and Sanfords show two with lids (in amber and blue) in their book *Glass Toothpick Holders,* which, like the Utility Boot, indicates some were sold as inkwells. The Gatling Gun is shown with a plain base and no lid on the Bryce, Higbee catalog page shown in Kamm 8.

Reproductions and Look-alikes: None known.

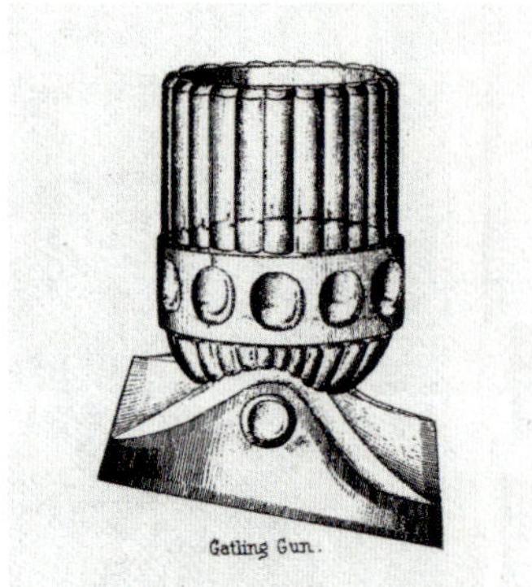

Gatling Gun illustrated in an undated Bryce, Higbee & Company catalog. Note the plain base.

Grant Plate, 1885

References: BH, undated; *AG*, 5/15/1885 & 7/31/1885
Colors: clear, amber, blue

Ulysses S. Grant was born on April 27, 1822, in Point Pleasant, Ohio, and was a successful military commander in the Civil War. Under his leadership, the Union Army defeated the Confederates, which led to the surrender of Robert E. Lee. Grant later served as the eighteenth president of the United States from 1869 to 1877.

Despite assumptions by other authors, the Grant Plate was most definitely not intended to be a death memorial. The novelty is mentioned in the trade journal *American Glassworker* on May 15, 1885:

> The new Grant bread plate, made by Bryce, Higbee & Co., is such a beautiful work of art, that a Diamond alley Italian artist has taken plaster paris casts from the reverse side, and is retailing the diamond surrounded bust of the "patriot and soldier," at 25 cents a piece. Quite a compliment, eh?

Since Grant passed away over two months later on July 23, 1885, it was obviously not made as a death memorial.

Though the trade journal calls it a bread plate, which it undoubtedly was intended to be, the Bryce, Higbee catalog

Grant Plate, $40–$45.

page labels it simply "Grant Plate." It measures 9.25" square. The fine cut design in the background was used quite a bit by Bryce, Higbee as filler. It is also found in the bottom of the flat Mirror and Optic bowls, in the base of the oblong (rectangular) Bijou dish, on the back of the Tramp match safe, and underside the base of the Utility Boot. The same eight-pointed star motif, which makes up the fine cut design, is found in the background of the Grand pattern, in the center of the diamonds in the Melrose pattern, in the ellipses of the *Chain* pattern, and others.

Reproductions and Look-alikes: A shallow bowl with the image of Grant surrounded by the words "THE PATRIOT AND SOLDIER GEN. ULYSSES. S. GRANT." in beaded letters has been recently made and distributed by A. A. Importing. It is more appropriately referred to as a fantasy piece since it is not a direct copy of Bryce, Higbee's Grant bread plate. Nonetheless, it still causes confusion. The new bowls measure about 9.5" wide and vary from about 1.5" to 1.75" deep. Some sellers list them as plates. They are found in clear, amber, blue, vaseline, and possibly other colors. Grant's portrait is frosted. For a newer item it is rather well done, and many are fooled into thinking they have found an old and rare commemorative item.

Kaiser Wilhelm Plate, c. 1888

References: BH, undated
Colors: clear

Kaiser Wilhelm Plate illustrated in a circa 1888 Bryce, Higbee catalog.

In their book *Bryce, Higbee and J .B Higbee Glass*, authors Lola and Wayne Higby say this plate was made in 1888 as a souvenir to commemorate the crowning of Kaiser Wilhelm II as King of Prussia. This plate clearly portrays the older, mutton-chopped Kaiser Wilhelm I rather than the much younger, oddly mustached Kaiser Wilhelm II and was without doubt a death memorial. The very fact that the portrait is identified as Kaiser Wilhelm I rather than simply Kaiser Wilhelm implies the second Kaiser Wilhelm had already ascended to the throne. Wilhelm I was born March 22, 1797, became King of Prussia June 2, 1861, and died March 9, 1888. Wilhelm II was twenty-nine years old when crowned on June 15, 1888. This plate most certainly does not depict a man in his twenties!

The Kaiser Wilhelm Plate is labeled as such on an undated Bryce, Higbee catalog page from circa 1888 (see

Kaiser Wilhelm I and Kaiser Wilhelm II. The bread plate made by Bryce, Higbee clearly portrays the former.

page 44 for more discussion about this particular catalog page). The plate is bordered by a finely detailed wreath of oak and either laurel or bay leaves. This decoration was not arbitrarily chosen, for one must remember the "language of flowers" was extremely popular and highly regarded in Victorian times. Many manuals were written to decipher the hidden meanings behind trees and flowers, oftentimes the symbolism going back to ancient times. Sometimes the meanings varied, depending on the author and source, but in this case two original guides from the 1880s were consulted and both are in complete agreement. The oak symbolizes bravery, and the laurel or bay wreath signifies ambition, glory and reward of merit, a most appropriate tribute to honor the life of Kaiser Wilhelm I.

Reproductions and Look-alikes: None known.

Menagerie Toy Set and Bear Mustard or Horse Radish, 1886

References: BH, undated; *P&GR*, 2/11/1886; BB, c. 1886
Colors: clear, amber, blue

The clever and whimsical Menagerie Toy Set was introduced in 1886 and consists of a bear covered sugar, fish spoon holder, owl cream, and turtle covered butter. The bear covered sugar was also sold with a notched lid for use as a mustard or "Horse Radish" according to an undated Bryce, Higbee catalog page. The fish spoon holder was offered by Butler Brothers in "Our New '5 Cent' Colored Ware Assortment" as a toothpick in amber and blue. See page 43 for a catalog illustration of the toy table set.

Bear Covered Mustard, $100–$125. This is the same as the covered sugar to the toy table set, but with the addition of a slot at the back of the lid.

The small owl cream has caused much confusion because Challinor, Taylor & Company and Bryce, Higbee both made a version of it and they are very similar. Other authors have said they are from the same mould, but they are not. Challinor's owls are known to this author in opaque white, opaque blue (both with smooth base), and clear (with stippled base). It is not known if Challinor made them in transparent colors. Their opaque owls came with separate glass eyes affixed with adhesive. If glass eyes are not present, the molded sockets will be concave. Bryce, Higbee's Owl cream was made in clear, amber, and blue and has convex molded eyes. They were not made with separate glass eyes. There are other slight differences (especially in the feathers), but the eyes are the most obvious and easiest characteristic to discern.

Bryce, Higbee's Owl cream from the Menagerie Toy Set. Note the molded convex eyes.

Reproductions and Look-alikes: The Higbys mention Doris Lechler's conclusion that the Menagerie Toy Set was copied, due to her observation of two different shades of amber. Shades of color could and did vary quite a bit from batch to batch, and any variation in color is not necessarily an indication of a copy or reproduction. The Imperial Glass Corporation of Bellaire, Ohio, reproduced the owl cream with separate eyes, but there is no confusing this for Bryce, Higbee's version since it is a copy of the Challinor owl. They should be marked with the I G trademark on the underside of the base. Imperial also made a small companion sugar, also with separate eyes, and has the owl figure on opposing sides. This does not replicate any original form. The Boston and Sandwich Glass Company of Sandwich, Massachusetts, made a bear pomade jar that could be mistaken for Bryce, Higbee's bear sugar. There are many differences, but the most noticeable are that Sandwich's bear wears a muzzle and is not seated on a base.

Challinor, Taylor & Company's very similar Owl cream. Note the addition of glass eyes that are not found on the owls made by Bryce, Higbee.

Owl cream in clear glass from a circa 1891 United States Glass Company catalog. Note the concave eye sockets and stippled base, features not found on Bryce, Higbee's Owl cream.

Mortar Mustard or Horse Radish,
c. mid–1880s

References: BH, undated; FP&W, April 1886; P&B, c. 1887
Colors: clear, amber, blue

Though it is not known when Bryce, Higbee's Mortar was introduced, it was most likely in the mid- to late 1880s when the company was producing other novelties in color. It is shown on an undated Bryce, Higbee catalog page from circa 1888 and is labeled "Mortar Mustard or Horse Radish." The earliest dated reference for this novelty is an April 1886 illustrated price list from the Chicago jobber French, Potter & Wilson. Correctly called Mortar, they were offered only in clear glass for 72¢ per dozen. A circa 1887 Pitkin and Brooks catalog offered them in clear glass for 60¢ per dozen. The 12¢ variance in price may seem minor today, but in the mid–1880s this was a significant difference. The Mortar Mustard or Horse Radish measures 4.25" high with lid, which is notched to accommodate a spoon.

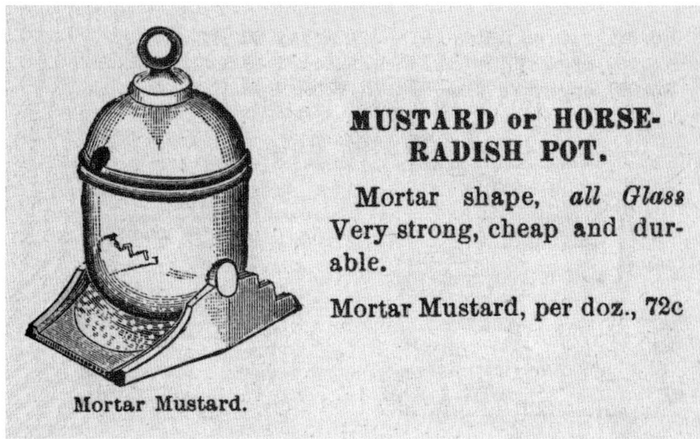

Mortar Mustard illustrated in French, Potter & Wilson's price list, April 1886.

Reproductions and Look-alikes: None known.

Our Toothpick,
c. mid- to late 1880s

References: BH, undated; P&B, c. 1887; BB, 1888; HB&F, spring-summer 1888; SB, c. 1888; JBH, c. 1917 (labeled No. 503—Paris Toothpick); NM, undated; NMPL, 1921 (labeled 503 Paris Beauty Toothpick)
Colors: clear, amber, blue

The Our Toothpick certainly had a long life. It was made by three different companies and appeared in jobber catalogs with variations for approximately forty years. It is shown with the caption "Our Toothpick" on an undated, circa 1888 Bryce, Higbee catalog page. The exact year of introduction is not known, but it was likely in the mid- to late 1880s, when the colors of amber and blue were being made. The toothpick is first sighted in a Pitkin and Brooks catalog that can be dated to circa 1887 due to the known introduction years of the various patterns offered. Our Toothpick is shown in the circa 1917 J. B. Higbee *General Catalogue*, but with the caption "No. 503—Paris Toothpick." Although J. B. Higbee called it Paris it was not originally part of the Paris 1900 line introduced by Bryce, Higbee in 1900. Lola and Wayne Higby are clearly confused about this and make much ado about the different names. Many items shown in the *General Catalogue* that originated with Bryce, Higbee were given different names by J. B. Higbee. The toothpick holder also appears in an undated New Martinsville Glass Manufacturing Company catalog with no name, only the notation "42 Doz. To ½ Bbl." This indicates a quantity of 504 toothpick holders were packed in a half barrel. A 1921 price list of the same company includes it on the roster of Higbee moulds as "503 Paris Beauty Toothpick." At that time the company's list price was 50¢ per dozen, showing obvious inflation since the time Butler Brothers was selling those made by Bryce, Higbee for 28¢ per dozen wholesale about twenty years earlier.

There are four distinct versions of the Our Toothpick. The first version matches the image shown on the circa 1888 Bryce, Higbee catalog page. This toothpick has twenty-four ribs, which are sharply pointed at the top. The center band is composed of three rows of beveled cubes with flat top surfaces. In the base is a design of a circle surrounded by twenty-four rays.

The second version has only twenty-one ribs, which are a bit wider and slightly rounded at the top. The center band is composed of three rows of beveled squares, each one coming to a sharp point. In the base is a design of a circle surrounded by twenty-one rays. Though it is not known when this version was first made, it is shown in Montgomery Ward's catalog No. 53 for spring and summer 1893.

The third version contains twenty ribs that are quite rounded at the top. Like the second version, the center band is composed of three rows of pointed beveled squares, but they are much smaller. In the base is an ornate, faceted, eight-pointed star. The overall barrel shape tapers less toward the rim than the previous toothpicks. This version is clearly shown in an 1897 Pitkin and Brooks catalog. Butler Brothers does not illustrate this version until spring 1904, indicating they still sold stock of the older models or they continued to use previous illustrations of the old-

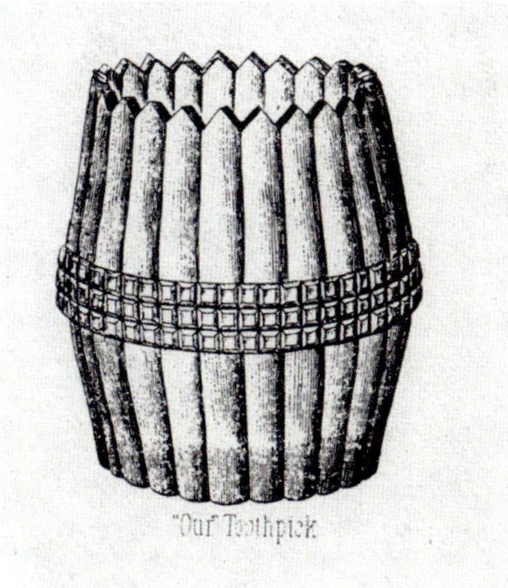

The first and original version of Our Toothpick from an undated Bryce, Higbee catalog. Note the flat cubes.

Group of Our Toothpick holders showing a variety of styles and colors.

Our Toothpick, version #1. Note the band of flat cubes and twenty-four ribs in base. $25–$30 each.

Our Toothpick, version #2. Note the band of pointed cubes and twenty-one ribs in base. $20- $25 each.

style toothpicks. This third version is shown in the J. B. Higbee *General Catalogue*, and appears to be the same shown in the New Martinsville catalog as well.

The fourth version contains twenty ribs that are even more rounded at the top. The center band appears to be composed of sparse dots, but close examination reveals they are actually tiny, uneven squares. These squares are most prominent between each rib. They are also on the convex ribs, but are so faint that they are hardly noticed and appear to be reflections of the other squares. In the base is the same eight-pointed star seen on the third version, but the star much less defined and is smaller on some. Some fourth version toothpicks in clear are found marked as illustrated nearby, a trademark of the New Martinsville Glass Manufacturing Company. It is not known exactly when the company used this mark, but it appears infrequently on wares produced during the 1920s. The trademark obviously dates prior to 1944, the year the company became the Viking Glass Company. This toothpick seems to be a reworked, or more likely, a very well-used mould of version three. The differences are probably due to years of cleaning with abrasive tools, which obscures fine details.

By the mid–1890s, the Our Toothpick was offered by jobbers only in clear. The first two versions were made in clear, amber, and blue by Bryce, Higbee only. The third version was being produced by 1897 and is only found in clear. This would logically be the mould acquired by J. B. Higbee when Bryce, Higbee closed. J. B. Higbee did not make this toothpick in colors, and none have been seen with their bee trademark. The fourth version appears to be quite late and made from a well-used mould by New Martinsville, though judging from catalog illustrations, they likely made the third version as well. Fourth version toothpicks are found in clear, deep blue (quite different than cobalt blue), light "apple" green, and canary/vaseline. These are colors New Martinsville produced during the Depression era and may date from those years. Marigold iridescent is also found, but New Martinsville is not known to have used this treatment on its glassware. The scalloped edges of each successive version of toothpicks one through three are more rounded than the last, implying that the moulds were altered because the edges were easily chipped. A great number of the earliest models found today have damage on the vulnerable top points.

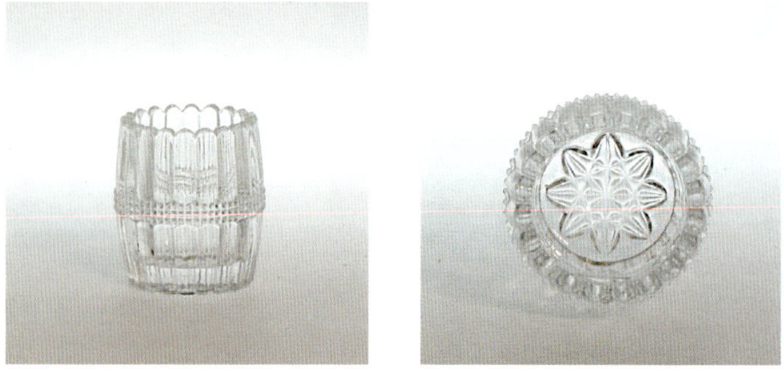

Our Toothpick, version #3. Note the band of small pointed cubes and star in base. $15–$20.

Two Our Toothpicks have been found with ground and polished flat tops. One is a blue first version and the other is an amber second version. At first the author thought they were done by glass repair persons, but close examination indicates they may have come from the Bryce, Higbee factory like this. The top edges are rounded, smooth, mellow,

Our Toothpick, version #4. Note the sparse band of cubes and less distinct star in base. Clear, $15–$20; deep blue, $25–$30.

Flat-topped Our Toothpick, version #1. The precisely beveled edge is ground and polished, possibly done at the factory.

and extremely well done with a tiny, rounded bevel at the top of each rib. Each bevel is perfectly even and centered on each rib. The amber toothpick had beveling done on each rib at the base as well. This hand work was obviously done by someone very skilled, and it is hard to fathom a repair person taking such extreme care to put this meticulous detail into an item where the amount of time and labor incurred would far exceed its market value. Besides, two were encountered with the same detailed ground and polished rim. If these toothpicks truly left the factory this way, then there are six distinct versions. A flat top amber first version is shown in *A Collector's Book on Toothpick Holders* by Florence Mighall (1973), but the edge detail is not discernable. The author would like to hear from anybody who has a flat-topped Our Toothpick.

Reproductions and Look-alikes: See text above for variations.

Owl Pitcher, 1886

References: BH, undated; *P&GR*, 2/11/1886; FP&W, April 1886
Colors: clear, amber, blue

Bryce, Higbee and Challinor, Taylor & Company both made a half-gallon pitcher in the form of an owl. Kamm notes the two pitchers are identical, and the Higbys take this a step further and imply that the same mould was used to make them. Those authors could not have closely compared the pitchers, because they are not identical. In his book *Tarentum Pattern Glass*, Robert Irwin Lucas suggests that the same mould maker from an independent firm made the Owl pitcher for Bryce, Higbee & Company and Challinor, Taylor & Company. Bryce, Higbee had its own mould shop, so there would have been no need for them to hire an outside establishment to make the mould. One is obviously a copy of the other, but it is not known who did the copying. Challinor's version certainly has finer overall detail than Bryce, Higbee's, especially in the feathers, but this does not prove the finer came first. *Pottery and Glassware Reporter* confirms that Bryce, Higbee's Owl Pitcher was introduced in early 1886, but it is unknown when Challinor, Taylor & Company first made theirs. Lucas gives the introduction date of 1885 for Challinor Taylor's Owl pitcher. This could

Amber Bryce, Higbee Owl Pitcher, $200–$225.

be correct, but the accuracy and preciseness of his dating must be questioned. Of the forty-six Challinor tableware lines and novelties Lucas assigns introduction years to, four are dated 1888, one is given a less definite "circa 1885," and a staggering forty-one are strictly dated 1885. It is completely

Owl Pitcher illustrated in a Bryce, Higbee company catalog. Note the image is reversed from the actual item, a common occurrence with old catalog cuts.

Owl Jug

Challinor's Owl Jug illustrated in an early United States Glass Company composite catalog offered after the merger. This image is also reversed, but note there is a flower at the point where the spout meets the rim.

unrealistic to think a single company could produce that many different patterns and novelties in a single year, and an abbreviated year at that, for Mr. Lucas states that Challinor, Taylor & Company did not become a reality until March 10, 1885.

At first glance the Owl pitchers of both companies do appear the same, but close inspection reveals many differences between the two. Below are some of the most prominent and easiest to distinguish.

Bryce, Higbee:

- **Spout** meets the rim above a leaf.
- **Eyes** are convex with a slash molded into the eyeballs to simulate pupils.
- **Feet** come to a triangular point where they meet the owl's body.

Challinor, Taylor:

- **Spout** meets the rim above a flower.
- **Eye sockets** are concave to accept separate glass eyes which were affixed with adhesive. The author has seen photos of clear Challinor pitchers that appear to have convex molded eyes, but it was very difficult to tell for certain. If the eyes were indeed convex, there was no slash to simulate the pupil.
- **Feet** meet the owl's body in a straight line.

Challinor Owl pitchers are known to the author in opaque white and clear. They may also exist in other opaque colors, as well as transparent amber and blue. Bryce, Higbee is not known to have made any opaque glass. Their Owl pitchers are found in clear, amber, and blue. The images are reversed on the original catalog pages of both companies, like many catalog illustrations of the time. When the actual pitchers face the viewer, there are two bunches of cherries on the left side, and one bunch of cherries with a bunch of flowers on the right side.

Reproductions and Look-alikes: No reproductions known. See information above concerning look-alikes.

Pope Leo XIII Bread Plate, c. 1887

References: BH, undated; HLS, summer 1888
Colors: clear, clear with frosted portrait

Pope Leo XIII was born Vincenzo Pecci on March 2, 1810. He studied diplomacy and law at the Academia dei Nobili, and in his youth received awards for academic excellence. He soon caught the attention of Vatican officials. Pope Gregory XVI appointed Pecci as his personal prelate in February 1837, and he was ordained a priest on December 31, 1837. Pecci was elected pope on February 20, 1878, and died on July 20, 1903.

Others have assumed that this plate was made in 1903 to commemorate the Pope's death, but this is not correct. The summer 1888 catalog of H. Leonard's Sons & Co. lists a bread plate described as "Pope Leo, with his picture in the glass" at 18¢ each. The undated Bryce, Higbee catalog page showing this plate definitely does not date as late as 1903; it more than likely dates to 1888 (see discussion in chapter 4). Since the plate was not a death memorial, it would be very likely that some other momentous event inspired its creation. When the life of Pope Leo XIII is examined, it becomes quite apparent what that event was. The Pope celebrated the golden jubilee of his ordination as a priest on December 31, 1887, quite an accomplishment and one to be commemorated. The plate was no doubt made to recognize this grand occasion, hence the dating noted above.

Reproductions and Look-alikes: None known.

Pope Leo XIII Bread Plate, \$25–\$30. Some are also found with a frosted portrait.

Portrait of Pope Leo XIII from a packet of souvenir pictures printed in Munich, Germany. This image is one of six issued by Obpacher Brothers in 1887 for the Pope's jubilee to celebrate fifty years in the priesthood.

Rovers,
c. mid- to late 1880s

References: BH, undated; P&B, c. 1887; HB&F, spring and summer 1888; JBH, c. 1917; NM, undated
Colors: clear, amber, blue

One of three ABC plates made by Bryce, Higbee, this example depicts a dog and is given the caption "Rovers" on an original company catalog page. Lola and Wayne Higby wrongly date this ABC plate to 1893 saying it first appeared in a Butler Brothers catalog that year. Though an exact introduction date is not known, it was undoubtedly in the mid- to late 1880s. Rovers is first noted in a circa 1887 Pitkin and Brooks catalog where it is called "Rover." The plate was also offered in the spring and summer 1888 Hollander, Bradshaw & Folsom catalog under the listing "Rover and Emma, 6-inch fancy alphabet, assorted colors." The other plate is Bryce, Higbee's Emmas ABC plate. Both actually measure closer to 6.5".

J. B. Higbee acquired the mould and offered the plate in their circa 1917 *General Catalogue* as "No. 532—Dog ABC Plate." Clear plates are sometimes found with the J. B. Higbee trademark bee. Like the other ABC plates that originated with Bryce, Higbee, Rovers is also found in the undated catalog of the New Martinsville Glass Manufacturing Company and is given the same caption used by J. B. Higbee. Presumably, New Martinsville removed J. B. Higbee's trademark bee, but there is no way to know for certain. Since Plain ABC plates were made much later with the original bee mark along with a Viking trademark, it cannot be assumed that the bee mark was taken off all the plungers.

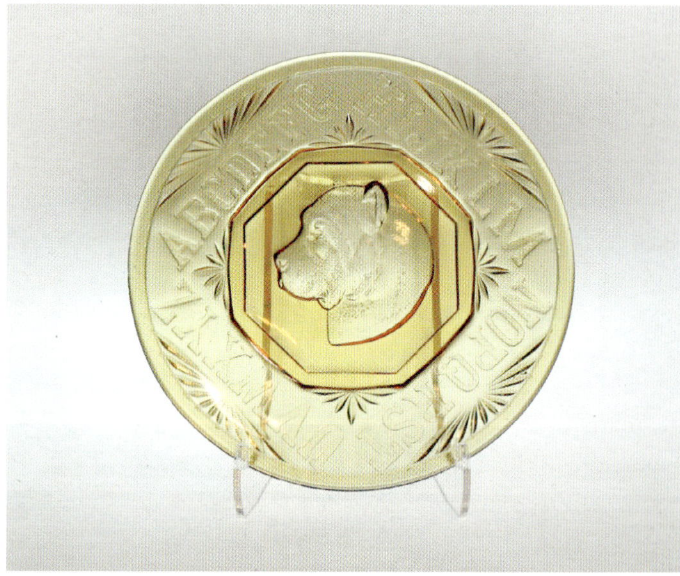

Amber Rovers plate, $55–$60.

Rovers plate illustrated in an undated Bryce, Higbee catalog.

Reproductions and Look-alikes: Rovers was reproduced for the Smithsonian Institution by the Imperial Glass Corporation of Bellaire, Ohio, beginning in 1977. Reproductions are marked "S I" at the bottom of the plate between the letters "T" and "U" in the alphabet. Some have been seen by the author with original Imperial labels. In *Antique Fakes and Reproductions* (1950), Lee reported that 6.5" alphabet plates with "dog's head in center" were reproduced in "clear and colors." If this is so, they may have been reissues by New Martinsville/Viking. No further information is available at this time.

Royal Special Covered Jelly, year uncertain

References: JBH, c. 1917; NM, undated; NMPL, 1921

The Royal Special Covered Jelly is included as a possible Bryce, Higbee item. It certainly was made by J. B. Higbee and later New Martinsville, but there are indications the mould may have originated with Bryce, Higbee & Company. Gail Bardhan, head librarian at the Rakow Research Library at the Corning Museum of Glass, kindly sent the author copies of a price list of the New Martinsville Glass Manufacturing Company dated 1921. The roster is headed with the notation "Higbee Glass Company's Moulds." Among the items enumerated are patterns known to have originated at Bryce, Higbee & Company, including Anona, Bijou, Bonair, Highland, Melrose, Monarch, and Paris. Note the original Bryce, Higbee names were retained (though the 1900 designation was omitted from Paris). Included on the list is a "524 Royal Spl Cov'd Jelly." This provides a pattern name for the piece illustrated in the J. B. Higbee *General Catalogue* as "No. 524—Special Covered Jelly" and in an undated New Martinsville catalog as "No. 524—Covered Jelly." The New Martinsville catalog that illustrates items made from Higbee moulds retains the numbers and descriptions, but generally leaves out the pattern names.

Everett and Addie Miller call the No. 524 covered jelly "Landberg" and indicate this was the original name given by J. B. Higbee, but it is not shown in any known company catalog as Landberg. Since the New Martinsville price list utilizes OMNs from Bryce, Higbee and J. B. Higbee, certainly Royal is the correct OMN. The name Landberg is used on the price list in conjunction with the number 125 shaker in the Colonial pattern. This 125 shaker is shown in J. B. Higbee's *General Catalogue* without the Landberg designation and bears no resemblance whatsoever to the jelly dish. J. B. Higbee's catalogs indicate the "special" designation was given to items which varied (some more than others) from the rest of the set, but J. B. Higbee had no Royal pattern as far as the author knows. J. B. Higbee used much of the same terminologies as Bryce, Higbee. It would make sense for Bryce, Higbee to use the "special" designation for this item because they did have a pattern completely different from this jelly dish called Royal.

Royal Special Covered Jelly lid, $35–$40 complete.

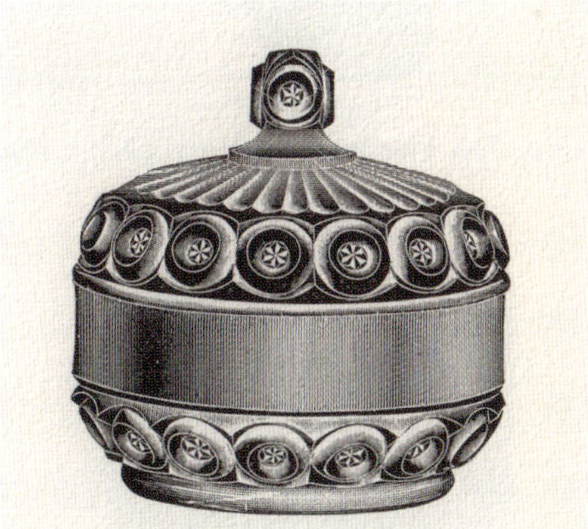

No. 524—Covered Jelly

Royal Special Covered Jelly illustrated in an undated New Martinsville Glass Manufacturing Company catalog. Note the catalog only refers to it as "No. 524—Covered Jelly," but the full designation "Royal Spl Cov'd Jelly" is given in a company price list.

The name Royal attached to this covered jelly is quite notable because the pattern is nearly identical to Co-Operative Flint Glass Company's Royal pattern introduced in 1894. The only noticeable difference is the addition of stars inside the circles in the design. This dating and name both imply that the Royal Special Covered Jelly was originally produced by Bryce, Higbee & Company in the 1890s. Patterns were generally copied when they were new or, at the very least, were still popular and had the attention of the buyers. It does not seem very likely that J. B. Higbee would be the first to copy Co-Op's Royal pattern and use the same name approximately two decades after its introduction. Bryce, Higbee copied Brilliant's/Greensburg's Melrose pattern in 1894 and even gave it the very same name; however, there is a huge gap in what is known of Bryce, Higbee's production between mid–1891 and late 1894, so, regarding this covered jelly, we cannot be certain who copied whom.

The Royal Special Covered Jelly is smaller than one might expect, measuring approximately 4" wide. None have been seen or reported with the J. B. Higbee trademark.

Illustration of Co-Operative Flint Glass Company's Royal pattern from a T. M. Roberts wholesale catalog from 1898. The similarity of the Royal Special Covered Jelly is very obvious. *Courtesy of the Rakow Research Library, Corning Museum of Glass.*

Reproductions and Look-alikes: No reproductions known, but as stated above, Co-Op's Royal is nearly the same.

Tramp Match Safe, 1887

References: BH, undated; *P&GR*, 1/13/1887; P&B, c. 1887
Colors: clear, amber, blue

The Tramp Match Safe depicts an old boot coming apart at the sole, hence the colorful name given by the company. There is a hole at the back for hanging, and the rectangular area containing raised dots on the front of the boot serves as a match striker. The back is impressed with a fine cut design found on many other Bryce, Higbee products. It is shown on an undated company catalog page, which Kamm dates to the mid–1880s, but fortunately the novelty is clearly mentioned in the January 13, 1887, issue of *Pottery and Glassware Reporter*, establishing the exact year of introduction for this item.

Tramp Match Safe in amber, blue, and clear. $20–$30 each.

Tramp Match Safe illustration from an undated Bryce, Higbee catalog.

Reproductions and Look-alikes: The Tramp Match Safe has been reproduced in clear as well as original and new colors, including amethyst, cobalt blue, light green, dark green, and peach. It is not known who remade the boot match holders, but reproductions were reported as early as 1977 and at least some were marketed by L. G. Wright. The new is a close copy of the old. Any color other than clear, amber, or blue is obviously new. It is difficult to distinguish reproductions done in clear and the original colors. Many, but not all, new boots have a thin web of glass in the hole at the top and, thus, cannot be hung. New boots have been observed that have very clean, smooth holes. Old ones usually have some roughness or sharpness around the hole. The fine cut pattern on the back of the boot is often not as clean or crisply molded on reproductions and much new glass feels slick or oily to the touch.

Tub Soap Dish (Chinese Laundry), 1887

References: BH, undated; *P&GR*, 1/13/1887; P&B, c. 1887; BB, 1888
Colors: clear, amber, blue

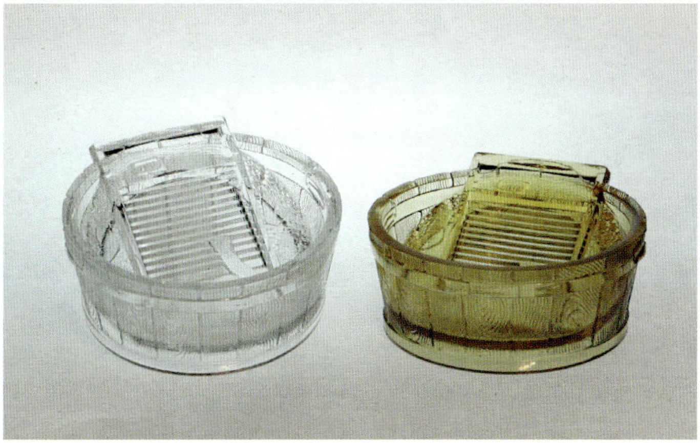

Tub Soap Dish in clear and amber, $100–$125 each.

This novelty is listed here as Tub Soap Dish because that is how it appears in original company material. It is shown among other novelties and an Ida pitcher on a circa 1888 Bryce, Higbee catalog page. Pitkin & Brooks calls it Chinese Laundry as does this January 1887 review from *Pottery & Glassware Reporter*:

> The most original article of all is the Chinese laundry, rendered more conspicuous by the prominence given to the Chinaman, and it must be regarded as the prime novelty of the season.

Tub Soap Dish shown in an undated Bryce, Higbee & Company catalog believed to date to circa 1888.

Since the trade journal and jobber catalog both refer to the soap dish as Chinese Laundry, that name must have originated from the factory. Perhaps Bryce, Higbee felt the function of the item would not be understood solely from a catalog illustration marked Chinese Laundry, so the more descriptive Tub Soap Dish was used. The design at the top of the washboard is reversed in the illustrations shown in the Bryce, Higbee and Pitkin & Brooks catalogs.

Items of this nature obviously received daily use and are difficult to find in top condition. The Tub Soap Dish measures 4.75" wide.

Reproductions and Look-alikes: No reproductions known. Novelties in the shape of wooden tubs were made by other glass companies. One even included a tiny, separate glass washboard, but Bryce, Higbee's Tub Soap Dish is quite different with its molded washboard surrounded by articles of clothing and soap bubbles.

Twin Cornucopia, 1887

References: BH, undated; *P&GR*, 1/13/1887
Colors: clear, clear engraved, bi-colored clear and amber, bi-colored clear and blue

The Twin Cornucopia is mentioned in a pleasantly lengthy review of many new Bryce, Higbee items in the January 13, 1887, issue of *Pottery and Glassware Reporter*. Concerning this novelty, the reporter states:

> The twin cornucopia in crystal glass, engraved, is a very tasteful ornament for the mantel piece, where it can be used for a flower holder or similar purpose.

It is shown with a design of lilies-of-the-valley on an undated Bryce, Higbee catalog page. This is most likely an engraving as noted in the trade journal report, though the catalog caption makes no mention of this and merely reads "Twin Cornucopia."

In addition to all clear, some are found in bi-color combinations of clear and amber and clear and blue. It is possible the Twin Cornucopia may have been made in solid amber and solid blue as well, though none have been seen.

This item measures 5.75" tall and is not plentiful.

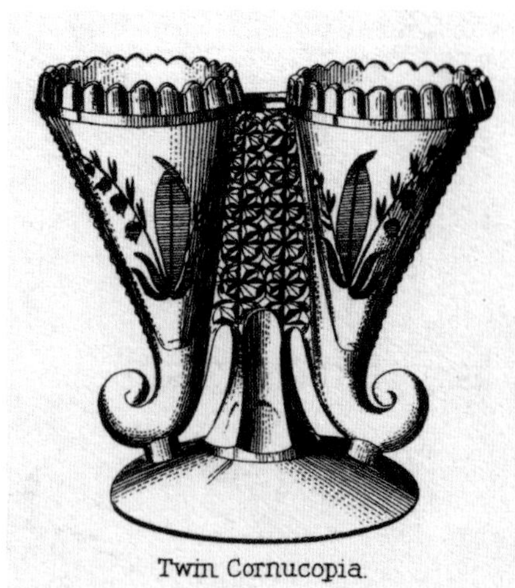

Original catalog illustration of the Twin Cornucopia. Note the floral design which is most likely engraved.

Reproductions and Look-alikes: None known.

Twine Holder, 1891

References: *CG&L*, 4/25/1891
Colors: unknown, presumably clear

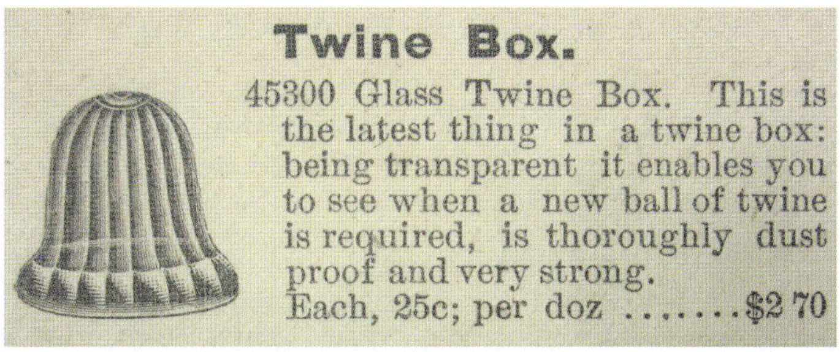

A twine holder (here called a "twine box") illustrated in an 1891 Montgomery Ward catalog. Though the appearance of Bryce, Higbee's *Twine Holder* is unknown, it may show some resemblance to the common design of glass twine holders such as this.

Twine holders were useful items in businesses and homes of the nineteenth century into the first decades of the twentieth century. This was before tape was used for home and commercial use. Figural chalk ware twine holders were made in quantity during the 1920s and 1930s. Many of them were wall-hung whimsical faces of people and animals with a hole in the mouth to dispense the string. Those made of glass are dome-shaped with a dispensing hole at the top.

The April 25, 1891, issue of *China, Glass & Lamps* mentions a new twine holder brought out by Bryce, Higbee & Company that could be hung or used on the counter. No description was given, and its appearance is not known. Glass twine holders were mainly designed to sit on a table or counter, so the fact that Bryce, Higbee's was able to be mounted on the wall is unusual and could possibly distinguish it from those made by other companies.

Reproductions and Look-alikes: Unknown.

Utility Boot, 1887

References: BH, undated; *P&GR*, 1/13/1887; P&B, c. 1887; BB, 1888 Santa Claus; SB, September 1889
Colors: clear, amber, blue

The January 13, 1887, issue of *Pottery and Glassware Reporter* mentions many new Bryce, Higbee products, among them the Utility Boot. The writer for the journal refers to it as "Rip Van Winkle's utility boot," but an undated, circa 1888 Bryce, Higbee catalog page simply refers to it as "Utility Boot." With lid it is labeled "Ink;" without lid, "Toothpick or Match Safe," proving it was sold both ways by the company.

A September 1889 Spelman Brothers catalog offered the Utility Boot under the description "Colored Glass Boot Inkwell" with a small bottle of Stephanotis perfume for $1.88 per dozen. Interestingly, the lid was included even

Clear Utility Boot, \$30–\$35. These were originally sold with and without lids.

Utility Boot ink shown in an original Bryce, Higbee company catalog.

though the bottle of perfume set inside the boot prevented the lid from being in place. The same catalog offered the Utility Boot inkwell on its own for 45¢ per dozen in clear, amber, and blue. One can see the perfume added greatly to the cost. Butler Brothers 1888 Santa Claus catalog sold the covered Utility Boot for 78¢ per dozen as "Our 'Funny' Ink Stand" in assorted colors, noting it was "the best of new dime favorites."

The Utility Boot lid is small and fragile, and no doubt many were lost or broken over the course of time. The lid displays an ornate six-pointed leafy star that is the same design found on the bases of flat items of the Yale and Vici patterns. This is not too surprising since Yale was introduced in the same year as the Utility Boot. Montgomery Ward offered a brass match safe in the shape of a boot from spring 1886 to 1887. Bryce, Higbee's Utility Boot bears such a resemblance to it that one cannot help but wonder if the metal version may have inspired the glass version.

Reproductions and Look-alikes: No reproductions known. There is a glass look-alike boot with lid that could be confused for Bryce, Higbee's Utility Boot, but it is crude by comparison, smaller, has an oval-shaped opening, and does not sit on a base. The design on the lid is similar, but fuller with fern-like leaves with five berries in the center. It has been seen in amber. By whom and when it was made is not known.

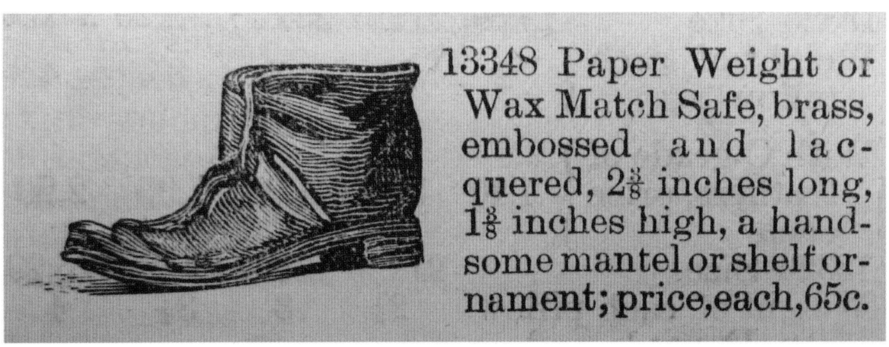

This brass boot match safe bears a striking resemblance to Bryce, Higbee's Utility Boot. It was first offered by Montgomery Ward in their spring and summer 1886 catalog.

10 COLLECTING TIPS

- Building a Collection
- Condition
- Flaws and Marks Inherent in the Manufacturing Process
- Make-Dos
- Sun-Colored Glass
- Value and Price
- Care and Maintenance
- Re-purposing

Unity Boot-Ink

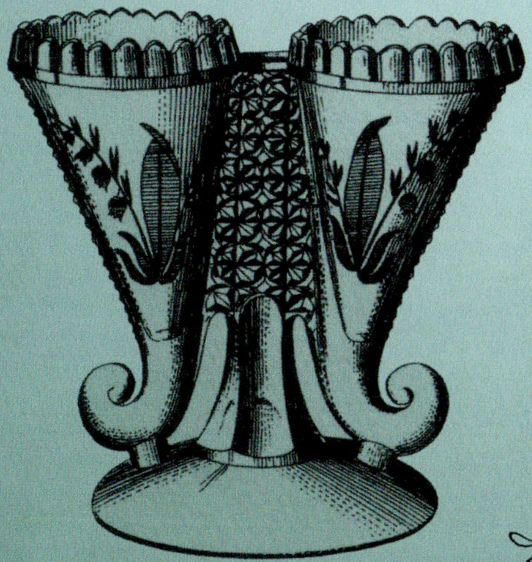

Twin Cornucopia

Building a Collection

Each person's collection is unique in the items represented. Some collect glassware made in a certain city or by a particular company. The Pittsburgh and Ohio Valley areas were large, prolific glass making centers for decades. Some collect by focusing on a particular color. There are many collectors for vaseline glass, originally called canary by its makers, but blue and amber are just as attractive. Amber generally has a low demand, so bargains can be found. Glass made by Bryce, Higbee in canary is challenging to find and is a welcome addition to a collection. There are collectors who focus on a certain form, whether it be cake stands, cruets, toothpicks, salt and pepper shakers, or goblets. A collection of cake baskets or square plates would be very interesting and would feature many of Bryce, Higbee's popular patterns.

Some collectors love the thrill of the hunt and seek antique glassware at thrift stores, resale stores, flea markets and similar places. Others prefer to buy only from auctions and dealers specializing in antiques. This may seem more expensive in some ways, but often the choice items are only obtainable through these outlets. Reputable dealers and auction houses should have no problem guaranteeing the authenticity or condition of an item. This is not the case with flea markets, thrift stores, and similar venues where the term *caveat emptor* must be at the forefront of the shopper's mind.

Internet shopping sources often have return policies, but some sellers can be difficult to work with when there is a problem. Also, there can sometimes be an added expense involved with shipping the item back to the seller. It is always best to work with Internet marketplaces that have clear return policies. Many shy away from buying glassware through the Internet because of the fear of breakage in shipping. This can really be a problem if the seller is not experienced in packing antique glassware for a safe trip. Horror stories abound about buyers having glass items shipped to them with inadequate packaging, sometimes in nothing more than a padded envelope. Buyers should review a seller's feedback and note comments about how items were packed for other buyers. It is paramount for buyers to mention in feedback how well items were packed by the seller. This is the only way others will know. Sellers are responsible for adequately packing their items. A little care and respect goes a long way. Apply the Golden Rule to shipping and pack your items as you would like someone to pack yours.

Cake baskets are an unusual form and are readily available in most Bryce, Higbee patterns. Left to right: *Beautiful Lady*, Oregon, and *Fine Cut and Fan*. $45–$50 each.

Square plates were made in many of Bryce, Higbee's patterns and make an interesting collection. Patterns from l. to r. are Crescent, Admiral, and Paris 1900, $45–$50 each.

CONDITION

Most collectors strive to acquire the best possible examples for their collection. Others tolerate minor damage, especially for hard-to-find or very desirable items. There are some collectors who buy damaged glass to save it from the shelves of thrift stores where it is not appreciated. Some purchase it for everyday use so they can regularly enjoy it without the worry of damaging a valuable piece. The amount of damage a collector accepts is a personal decision, but some guidelines will be given.

If one chooses to sell their collection, the best price will be realized from glassware in the best condition possible. Remember, EAPG was mass produced, so if one searches diligently another example will likely be found. There are many items and patterns that can be truly classified as hard to find and even rare, and for those pieces the collector might be more willing to accept a certain amount of damage without ever expecting to find a better example to upgrade their collection. Production was extremely limited for certain items in particular colors.

Some items and patterns are very difficult, if not impossible, to find completely undamaged due to the nature of the forms or design. One must pose the question to oneself: "How likely am I to find another in better condition, and how long might it take me?" Though there are many dealers who specialize in EAPG and a whole slew of online sources, some items are just not found often. One cannot simply go to the corner store and pick items from the shelf as needed! This must be considered when seeking items for one's collection. For obscure patterns, especially many of those presented in this book for the first time as products of Bryce, Higbee & Company, it may just be a matter of time before more examples show up. A pattern must be recognized and properly identified by its seller in order for the collector to easily find it. This is especially true for Internet auctions and virtual stores where literally thousands of items are offered. It is possible to find a prize that has been misidentified or placed in the wrong category, but sifting through the chaff can be a tedious process with no guarantee of reward.

It is a great conundrum how some sellers can claim an item for sale is in "mint condition, except for a chip or two" (perhaps three). There is no allowance for the word "except" when using the term mint. Mint refers to something in perfect, completely unblemished condition. It is better to not use the term at all than to misuse it. Mint condition was once referred to as "proof" some seventy years ago or more, even in reference to glassware. These are terms the numismatist uses, and there are strict criteria established by the American Numismatic Association (ANA) which coins must meet in order to warrant a certain grade. Since glassware does not have established, specific grading standards such as poor, good, very good, fine, and so on set by an accepted authority, why use the term mint at all? It is better and more than adequate to clearly and concisely state the presence or lack of damage rather than include a much overused term in hopes of attracting a potential buyer's interest. In truth, very few EAPG items should truly be called mint. Even those in the best condition possible will typically show normal wear commensurate with their age.

There are sellers who say damage is to be expected on glassware of a certain age and should be overlooked. This conviction usually arises when the buyer points out damage the seller has missed and is particularly problematic buying online from sellers who lack experience with glassware. Damage is damage whether an item is one year old or one hundred years old. It is for the buyer to decide what amount of damage, if any, is acceptable to them. It is imperative for sellers to accurately state the condition of items, especially with Internet sales, since the buyer does not have the luxury of examining them in person. Buyers should be wary of the terms "as found" and "vintage condition" when purchasing online. These expressions are vague and can be misleading. Some sellers state that photos of the item are part of the description. This is a red flag that the seller will not take responsibility for missing any damage and often indicates the seller is putting the burden on the buyer to notice any damage from a photo. Photos can be deceiving and cannot reveal exactly what one can observe in person.

Damage includes chips, flakes, bruises, cracks, scratches, heavy wear, cloudiness, and, to some, sun-coloring (see separate section on sun-colored glass on page 281). Chips, flakes, and scratches can be repaired to some extent, at no small cost, however. A bruise is a type of fracture in the glass caused by trauma to the item. The area in question looks chipped, but the glass is still intact and has a slight whitish reflection when held at just the right angle. Thick areas in the glass, especially bases and sometimes rims, are prone to this type of damage. There is no way to repair a bruise. Cloudiness, also called sickness, is actually a change in the chemical composition of the surface of the glass brought on from oxidation. It is a hazy, whitish residue often found on the inside of vases, cruets, and other items where liquid remains for an extended time. It will not come out with any sort of cleaning. Acids from fruit can cause the same reaction on plates and bowls if left too long. Just as metal rusts and pits from oxidation, glass can become sick. Like metal, the affected surface can be polished out, but this is expensive. It would cost approximately $75.00 to $100 to restore a sick bowl. Cloudiness can be masked with liquid floor wax and other commercial products, but should be done only on display pieces. To avoid sickness, be sure to change the water in any item used to hold fresh flowers every few days and clean the vessel immediately after discarding the contents. Sickness can also occur from the use of a dishwasher. Scalding hot water and chemicals are harsh on glass. Storing glassware wrapped in newspaper in damp areas may cause oxidation as well. Most sickness is found on the inner surface of items, but it can also occur on the outside within intricate patterns. It seems that this is just old soap residue and will come clean, but many times it does not. Be aware of this before buying an item with hazy white areas. If white scum is present and does not budge when scratched with a fingernail, it probably will not come out with any amount of scrubbing.

Serious collectors want their items as original as possible. The term marriage refers to two parts put together that did not originate together, such as a butter lid of one pattern paired with a base of another. Most collectors stay away from married items or purchase them with the goal to find the correct component parts. Original stoppers in cruets are preferred and avidly sought by purist collectors. Many cruets were sold with different stoppers, so it is sometimes difficult to know what is truly original. See pages 62-64 for examples of stoppers used by Bryce, Higbee & Company. If the stopper in a cruet is not original, many collectors prefer having one proportionate and appropriate to the style of the cruet rather than no stopper at all. The value of a cruet can be diminished by half or more if the stopper is missing or not original. Metal salt and pepper shaker lids were discarded when they became corroded or excessively worn. Sometimes it is difficult to tell if a lid is original or an old replacement. The author has observed many Bryce, Higbee shakers from the 1880s with lids that have stars and crescents for the holes. These are most likely original. It is preferable to have original lids, but better to have replacement lids for shakers than no lids at all. If using the shakers, new, clean lids ought to be used instead of original, oxidized lids. The original lids should be kept, however.

Original lids found on early shakers made by Bryce, Higbee & Company. The same lids are found on shakers from other companies suggesting the glass companies purchased the lids from a common source.

FLAWS AND MARKS INHERENT IN THE MANUFACTURING PROCESS

Some flaws are inherent in antique pressed glass. Bryce, Higbee's glassware was lauded in the trade journals as being of a uniform and high quality, yet many items are found containing flaws. This was a product marketed to the masses, and quality control was not quite the same back then as is expected now. Colors (and also clear glass) often varied from batch to batch. Particles, small stones, and streaks may be found in the glass. These flaws are often the result of improper mixing or an unintentional addition of foreign elements in a batch of glass. A rough, grainy surface has been observed on the top or inner surface of many items. Sometimes it is not easily seen, but can be felt. Items are found with dents and scars that occurred at the time of manufacture. Tools used to manipulate the glass into different forms may have come into contact with the item before the glass was completely firm. Though some of these marks are smooth, some are rough and can be easily confused for chips. One often hears the term mould roughness used to describe small chips that occurred in the glass making process. Some items truly left the factory in this state. EAPG items have been observed where the original gilding was applied over small chips. Sometimes small chips were obscured and smoothed out when the glass was fire polished. During the cooling stage when the glass was still in a somewhat plastic state, items sometimes sagged. Compotes and other stemmed items are found that lean, and items may not sit flush on a level, horizontal surface. This could have been caused from less than careful removal from the mould, but often this occurred when the glass was being tooled by hand. More perfect examples can be sought if the collector deems manufacturing flaws unsightly or disfiguring, but the historian accepts these imperfections as a true testimony the glassware was handcrafted in factories lacking modern conveniences to which we are now so accustomed.

A shear mark, incorrectly called a straw mark, is a line, usually on the inner surface of an item, resembling a stitch. They are inherent to the manufacturing process. Shears were used to snip off a quantity of molten glass (called a "gather") into the mould. The glass cooled a bit faster at the point where the shears came in contact with the glob of molten glass. Some collectors still believe a shear mark in the glass resulted from being set or even thrown upon a bed of straw to cool after removal from the mould. This is a myth, and quite possibly the most insidious one regarding glass making techniques. If hot glass taken from a mould came into contact with straw a fire would ensue. If wet straw was used, as some contend, the hot glass would shatter. Furthermore, if any of this were true, items would literally be covered with scars on the entire surface from coming in contact with a bed of straw. Has anybody who believes this figment stopped to think how it would be

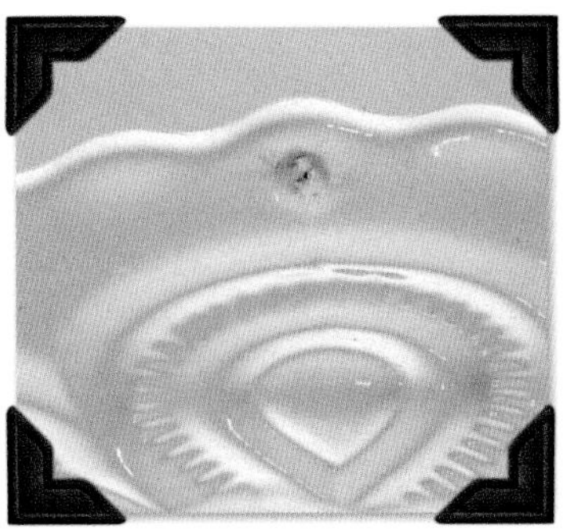

Curlicue cake basket has a particle imbedded in the glass. Such flaws are common in pressed glass from the EAPG era.

This *Curlicue* cake basket is called a "leaner" by collectors. Some view items like this as inferior while others cherish them for their whimsical quality that shows items were handmade.

The center of this Oregon bowl has a dark swirl imbedded in the glass possibly from improper mixing.

This Worlds compote has areas that might be confused for chips, but the scuffs were fire polished over and were done at the time of manufacture.

possible for only one prominent mark to remain on the *inner* surface of the glass? When one employs simple logic, this misguided notion is seen as so utterly ridiculous that it is amazing it has managed to persist to this day. In order to relieve the stress and strengthen glass taken from moulds, it must be gradually cooled under controlled conditions in annealing ovens or lehrs. The process is not as simple as one might think.

Sometimes a small crack is present at the point where an applied handle is attached to the body of a pitcher. This can also appear on the top of a salver or inside a compote that has a pedestal attached to the body with a glass wafer. These types of cracks were caused by incompatible temperatures of the body and applied glass. They can also occur by mis-handling glass, i.e.: putting a hot item on a cold piece of glass and vice versa. Though some of these fissures truly happened at the time of manufacture, it is often difficult, if not impossible, to tell for certain and should be noted as damage or, at the very least, a flaw.

Annealing marks are light cracks or crazing in the glass, often difficult to see unless the item is held at a certain angle when the light hits the area just right. These marks are sometimes found on edges and bases that are thicker than the body of the item. After glassware was taken from the moulds it went through a series of steps to gradually cool at certain temperatures. Different areas may have cooled slower or faster depending on the thickness of the glass. Annealing marks can also be in the form of straight or squiggly lines that look like little cuts in the glass. They can resemble shear marks, but are usually not as prominent. Shear marks are most often found on the inside, near the center. Some collectors avoid items showing annealing marks, whereas others accept them as a part of the manufacturing process.

As an educational aside, EAPG cruets, water bottles, and other narrow-necked vessels that have a dimple on the base were not mould blown as many insist. The rough mark found on the underside of the base is not a "pontil" but is a cut-and-shut (sometimes simply called "cut shut") mark. These items were pressed upside down and had an extra flap of plain glass in the area that would become the base. Once the item was removed from the mould, the area of excess glass was warmed in, closed, and cut shut.

This rough mark on the bottom of cruets and other narrow-necked EAPG items is not a pontil mark; it is a cut-and-shut mark.

MAKE-DOS

We live in a rather disposable society, but our ancestors lived in a time when things were not thrown out unless they were completely useless. When a mishap occurred, such as breaking the handle off a jelly dish or smashing the base of a cream pitcher, the prudent and resourceful repaired or re-purposed the item themselves with anything

Make-dos are damaged items given industrious repairs much more creative than glue and staples. The broken handle of this jelly dish in J. B. Higbee's Alpha pattern was replaced with an ornate, monogrammed sterling silver hollow handle.

handy and that which would allow the item continued use. A lamp or compote that had its font or bowl broken from the pedestal could be transformed into a footed pincushion with a bit of ingenuity. The broken base of a spoon holder could be replaced with a block of wood. These items are called make-dos and have a following of collectors who avidly seek them. Because the materials utilized for the repairs were usually very different from the composition of the items themselves and mismatched proportions often resulted, make-dos display a juxtaposed, homely charm that speaks of an earlier time very different from our own.

SUN-COLORED GLASS

Sun-colored glass, also called sun-tinted glass, is clear glassware that has taken on a color ranging from light grayish-lavender to a deep purple. Glassware made prior to approximately World War I will turn due to the presence of manganese dioxide, a compound once used as a stabilizer in the batch for colorless soda-lime glass. When too much manganese was inadvertently added, the glass took on a grayish-lavender color without exposure to the sun. Sometimes the tinting is a natural occurrence from sitting near a sunny window; other times it is done deliberately by allowing the glass to sit in the sun for prolonged periods of time or by subjecting it to intense ultraviolet rays. The latter is a quicker, mechanical method called irradiation. Glass can obtain quite a dark purple hue. Some people do this because they feel clear glass has no market and color enhances its value. Unscrupulous sellers pass the altered glass off as a "rare" color to the unsuspecting. Sun-coloring glassware is not a new concept; in fact, Lee and Kamm mention it seventy years ago and refer to the color as amethystine. Kamm speaks favorably of it. The Early American Pattern Glass Society and serious collectors adamantly

Examples of sun-purpled EAPG. Note the grayish lavender tint.

frown upon sun-colored glass. They consider the glass historically altered and damaged because the process is (for all intents and purposes) irreversible. There are people who simply like the color and admire sun-colored glass as a decorative object. Some collectors feel that items with a very light tinting are acceptable because they likely became that way naturally, though there really is no way of knowing for certain. Sun-colored glass is quite a controversial topic, and many have taken a stand by reporting dealers who sell the glass and by educating collectors on the undesirable qualities of the altered glassware. How can one ascertain whether an item has been irradiated, sun-colored, or is true amethyst colored glass? Here are some hints to assist the collector:

- Light lavender was not a glass color made during the EAPG era.
- An overly dark purple with no life or body to it that is muddy in appearance has most likely been achieved through artificial methods.
- Dark sun-colored or irradiated purples often look unnaturally glossy.

Beware of patterns not normally found in amethyst color. Original amethyst from the 1880s was predominately produced by Bryce Brothers and exhibits an underlying subtle pinkish or cranberry tint. Amethyst was made again in the late 1890s by Riverside, then in the early 1900s by Northwood, Jefferson, Dugan, and others. The shades from these companies can vary and are darker than the amethyst of the 1880s, but there is warmth to the original tint generally not found in glassware artificially turned purple. Bryce, Higbee is not known to have produced true amethyst colored glass.

Value and Price

Establishing value and/or price is quite possibly the most difficult part of buying and selling antiques and collectibles, especially in this day and age. It is quite ironic because the Internet brings so many resources to us which were not thought possible even a decade ago. This plethora of resources is the very reason pricing has become so difficult because it encompasses such a broad, seemingly boundless marketplace that is constantly changing.

Through the Internet, information is presented and exchanged at a lightning-fast pace. It is the ultimate twenty-first century paradox, a blessing and a curse at the same time. The Internet has proven to be a useful tool in the fruitful acquisition of antiques and collectibles from the comfort of our own homes. Here one is able to find items previously unattainable by other means. All this convenient ease has its repercussions, however, and with such an abundance of items on the marketplace the rules of supply and demand have more poignantly made themselves known to collectors. In general, prices have dropped from what they were before the Internet auction became the king of consumer cyberspace, but the market has been slowly picking up. Antique glassware is being discovered by a whole new generation of collectors, an essential element needed to sustain a strong market. The many forums and groups on the Internet devoted to the discussion of EAPG have greatly assisted in recruiting new collectors. Staying abreast of the prices supported in different marketplaces, virtual and actual, is important to both buyer and seller in order to ensure items continue to be bought and sold. Items sitting in dealers' inventories and packed away in boxes do not contribute to a thriving market or healthy economy.

The laws of supply and demand must be considered in order to price items to sell. A strong price is often obtained when the supply is low and the demand high. The opposite scenario, a high supply and low demand causes a weak or low price and sometimes no sale at all. Attachment to an object can cause an inflated asking price on the part of the seller or an inflated price paid by a buyer. Attachment on the buyer's part can also be viewed as desire for an object and often explains why some items sell for a much higher price than what the market generally supports. This often happens with Internet and live auctions when at least two bidders have a great desire for a particular object. For this reason auction prices are sometimes not consistent and may not be an accurate representation of the market.

Many sellers check Internet auctions as a method of pricing their own items. To do this wisely, one must make sure the same or similar items are being compared. This includes an object's form, color, pattern, and, very importantly, the item's condition. Postage costs must be considered as part of the final selling price as well. Also keep in mind that opening bids of current auctions and "Buy It Now" (also referred to as BIN) auctions are nothing more than asking prices. Anybody can ask anything they want for their item. The asking price might be highly inflated and unrealistic, so it is best to check listings of items that have actually sold. The savvy seller—and buyer—also checks completed auctions for items that have not sold. Chances are if the same item has been re-listed time and time again and has not sold, the BIN or opening bid is too high or the item has very little demand—or both.

CARE AND MAINTENANCE

Many collectors like to use their antique glassware rather than just let it sit untouched. Glassware is a bit of a paradox because it is quite durable, yet fragile at the same time. Proper care will allow you to enjoy your treasures for many years to come and to pass them on to the next generation in a good state of preservation.

Refrain from overcrowding china cabinets and display shelves. Edges and handles are particularly prone to damage, so allow adequate space between items. Place paper plates, napkins, or paper doilies between plates and bowls if being stacked. Make sure shelves are secure and able to bear the weight. Multiple items may be heavier than first thought.

Wash only when needed, otherwise dust or wipe between washings. Save old toothbrushes for cleaning your glassware. A toothbrush is ideal for scrubbing grime and residue out of intricate patterns. Mix a paste of baking soda with a dab of dish soap and a bit of water for a mild, safe abrasive. This concoction is particularly effective for removing years of built up dirt and grease. It is adequate to wash antique glassware with warm water. Use antibacterial soap if food will come in contact with the item during use, and be sure to rinse thoroughly. The water temperature should not be too hot. Never subject cold glassware to hot water or warm glassware to cold liquids or food such as ice cream. Use a dishpan lined with a towel to wash your glass and exercise caution. Glass is slippery when wet and easily dropped. Dry with a soft, lint-free cotton towel to avoid water spots and soap residue collecting in the crevices of the design. Sudden temperature changes can crack and even shatter glassware, particularly when antique. If glassware is acquired during cold weather, especially in the mail, resist the temptation to open the package upon receiving. Let it slowly come to room temperature away from a heat source. Glass can crack and even break from abrupt temperature changes. Merely handling cold glassware can cause it to crack.

Do not put antique glassware in the microwave. Some people clean their antique glassware in the dishwasher. This is not recommended, even if there is a special china and crystal setting. EAPG was not made to withstand the modern dishwasher or other modern conveniences we commonly use today. If the item in question was made before the advent of a certain technology, do not use it for that item.

RE-PURPOSING

Giving new purpose to items once intended for something else is quite popular at present. Most people do not decorate or entertain on the grand scale, which was common when EAPG was made. Garden art is the term for taking "found objects" (i.e.: garage sale, auction, or thrift store finds) and attaching them together by means of glue or screws. The end result resembles a haphazard stack of dishes, bowls, trays, and similar items, sometimes in mixed materials. Glassware is often incorporated into these creations (some may be less kind than the author and refer to them as monstrosities). Another popular "art form" is putting together cake stands by gluing a plate to something resembling a pedestal. Again, glassware is frequently utilized. These are things people either love or hate, but I have never met a collector of EAPG who had any fondness for them. Sometimes a good piece of glassware is ruined from being drilled through. When using glass for decorative/artistic purposes, take the preservationist's point of view and refrain from doing anything that cannot be easily reversed. You may have little regard for the item in question, but that does not mean it should be treated as a worthless object.

Items can be used as they were originally intended, but there are many fun and creative ways to decorate and use antique glassware that cause no harm. For, example, many collectors do not know what to do with spoon holders, but they are among some of the most versatile

EAPG forms. Here are some ideas for using them:

- Battery-operated votive candle or tea light holder for the dining room table or anywhere in the house. Do not use real candles; the heat from the flame can crack the glass. Rose bowls and toothpick holders work well, too. Using colored and ruby stained glassware is particularly effective.

- Pen and pencil holder on the desk, kitchen or anywhere in the home. They can also hold crayons and artist's supplies.

- Utensil holder for a buffet table. Use separate holder for knives, forks, and spoons. Plastic utensils can be used for casual gatherings, and they will not scratch the spooner like metal could.

- For holiday and party displays, use to hold pretzel sticks, candy canes, and other stick candy.

- Use spooners in the bathroom for holding cotton swabs, disposable razors, toothbrushes, combs, brushes, makeup, etc.

- Keep them on the sewing table for holding small crochet and knitting needles. Celery vases are ideal for longer ones.

New collectors often gravitate toward items they remember their families having and using. This is the nostalgia factor. Many a collector was born after being gifted an item they remember from childhood. Involve your friends and family with your collection and give gifts of glass. A batch of homemade cookies received on an EAPG plate is much more memorable than the same cookies put on a paper or plastic plate. Include the plate as part of the gift and be sure to attach a small note card with information about the glassware. To encourage the future generation of collectors, expose others to EAPG in actual use, not just sitting in the china cabinet. Bring out your treasures for special occasions and holidays. Allow a child or grandchild to choose a pretty dish to serve a particular treat in. Designate a certain salver for birthday cakes. Create your own traditions and engage others in imaginative ways. These are just a few suggestions to considerately use and repurpose items in your collection. Above all, be creative and enjoy your glassware!

Acknowledgments

So many people have been very generous with their time, sharing of documents, gifts, and encouragement. I probably would not have written this book if it was not for Bob Sanford and others who kept nudging me with periodic messages asking "When are you going to write that book?" to which I would jokingly reply "What book?"

I would like to acknowledge every person and list each individual gift they gave me, whether it was a material item, a gift of love and support, or both, but space will simply not permit such a list because it would fill an entire volume. It is amazing to recall the number of times I received a surprise package in the mail containing a piece of Bryce, Higbee glassware for this book. For two-thirds of my life I have known that collecting brings people together and attracts benevolence like a magnet. Those who are well acquainted with me understand that I never forget a kindness and I will always remember exactly what you have contributed.

I wish to express my sincere thanks to the Early American Pattern Glass Society (EAPGS) for believing in me and choosing me as a grant recipient for 2014; Sarah Karr and Rob Tompkins for the use of their photographic equipment; those who loaned items, provided important research materials, lists of items made in specific patterns, and general information, including Bob Sanford, Tom Felt, Sid Lethbridge, Brad Gougeon, Tom Bredehoft, Jim Chafin, Lee Marple, Dean Six, Darryl Reilly, Robin Cisne, Richard Moon, Chris Schafer, Roger Haworth, Bob O'Grady, and Gary Fredrickson; the wonderful and dedicated librarians at the Rakow Research Library in Corning, NY, including Stephen Chervenak, Mary Chervenak, and especially head librarian, Gail Bardhan, who mailed copies of documents and used her vacation time to meet at the research library to fetch me even more catalogs to study; Amanda Stow and the helpful staff at the American Heritage Center in Laramie, WY; John J. Weishar, Thomas J. Weishar, Robert C. Roth, David J. Schmid, and Mark W. Tuttle of the Island Mould & Machine Company, Wheeling, WV, who liberally shared their amazing wealth of knowledge of mould making and glass making techniques. They truly are a link to the past who keep the memories of the old glass factories and workers alive and well. My gratitude goes to those who gave me items so important to my research including Phyllis Messerla, Dean Six, April Nyarango, Margaret Malloy, Jim Schmidt, Will Carmichael, Steven Skeim, Gene Serbus, Elaine Henderson, Fiona ni'Giollarua, Donnah Brnger, Christine Browning, Sharon Blanks, Brad Gougeon, M. Zak McCamey, Anna May Vanderbilt, Nancy Tibbits Smith, Bob Mason, Jacqueline Ann Lane, Jayne Stoll, Gail Curley, and Paula Slimak. Finally, last but not least, eternal gratitude to Patricia Kirk, Alice Jean Javorsky, Frank Edward Dvorak, John Kurt Entsminger, and Fred Boreali for all the love, guidance, and support they have given, which has made me who I am today. Though some of these people are no longer with us, I shall think of them and each and every one of you whenever I open this book.

BIBLIOGRAPHY

Barret, Richard Carter. *Popular American Ruby-Stained Pattern Glass.* Manchester, VT: Forward's Color Productions, Inc., 1968.

Bredehoft, Sanford, et al. *Glass Toothpick Holders.* Paducah, KY: Collector Books, Second Edition, 2005.

Felt, Tom. *L.E. Smith Glass Company: The First One Hundred Years.* Paducah, KY: Collector Books, 2007.

Hartung, Marion, and Ione Hinshaw. *Patterns and Pinafores Pressed Glass Toy Dishes.* Des Moines, IA: Wallace-Homestead Co., 1971

Heacock, William. *Encyclopedia of Victorian Colored Pattern Glass Book 7 Ruby-Stained Glass From A to* Z. Marietta, OH: Antique Publications, Inc., 1986.

Higby, Lola and Wayne. *Bryce, Higbee and J. B. Higbee Glass.* Marietta, OH: The Glass Press, Inc. dba Antique Publications, 1998.

James, Bettye, and Jane O'Brien. *Early American Pattern Glass Cake Stands & Serving Pieces.* Paducah, KY: Collector Books, 2009.

Kamm, Minnie Watson. *A Fourth Pitcher Book.* Detroit, MI: Motschall Company, Second Edition, 1950.

_____. *An Eighth Pattern Glass Book.* Grosse Point, MI: Kamm Publications, Fifth Printing, 1970.

Lee, Ruth Webb. *Early American Pressed Glass*, Lee Publications, Wellesley Hills, MA, thirty-sixth edition, 1960.

Lucas, Robert Irwin. *Tarentum Pattern Glass.* Tarentum, PA: Robert Irwin Lucas, 1981.

National Imperial Glass Collectors' Society edited by James Measell. *Imperial Glass Encyclopedia Volume III M-Z.* Marietta, OH: The Glass Press, Inc. dba Antique Publications, 1999.

Peterson, Arthur G.. *Glass Salt Shakers.* Radnor, PA: Wallace-Homestead Book Co., 1970.

Reilly, Darryl and Bill Jenks. *Early American Pattern Glass, Collector's Identification & Price Guide*, second edition. Iola, WI: Krause Publications, 2002.

Stephens, Clarence. *The Water Ambering of Clear Glassware.* Slaterville Springs, NY: Clarence Stephens, circa 1972.

Welker, John and Elizabeth. *Pressed Glass in America.* Ivyland, PA: Antique Acres Press, 1985.

West Virginia Museum of American Glass. *L. G. Wright Glass.* Atglen, PA: Schiffer Publishing Ltd., 2003.

Whitmyer, Margaret & Kenn. *Children's Dishes an Illustrated Value Guide.* Paducah, KY: Collector Books, 1993.

Magazines and Other Publications

Brothers, J. Stanley, personal notes. Held at the Rakow Research Library at the Corning Museum of Glass, Corning, NY.

Heacock, William. *The Glass Collector.* Premiere issue, winter 1982. Columbus, OH: Peacock Publications, 1982.

Ibid, issue number four, fall 1982.

Kirk, Paul. "Bryce, Higbee's Crescent and New Crescent." *All About Glass* (publication of the West Virginia Museum of American Glass, Ltd.), Volume X, No. 1, April 2012.

_____. "Bryce, Higbee & Company's Melrose." *All About Glass* (publication of the West Virginia Museum of American Glass, Ltd.), Volume X, No. 4, January 2013

_____. "Bryce, Higbee & Company's Admiral and Oregon." *The News Journal* (publication of the Early American Pattern Glass Society), fall 2012.

_____. "Bryce, Higbee & Company's Worlds, '*Bowline*,' and Surprise." *The News Journal* (publication of the Early American Pattern Glass Society), winter 2012.

Glass Review, Volume 13, Number 6. July/August 1983. Published by Barbara Shaeffer. Marietta, OH.

Rainbow Review Glass Journal, Volume 7, Number 6. June 1977. Publishers: Ben and Barbara Shaeffer. Costa Mesa, CA.

Trade Journals

American Glassworker

American Pottery and Glassware Reporter

China, Glass & Lamps

Crockery and Glass Journal

Glass and Pottery World

Pottery and Glass Reporter (formerly *American Pottery and Glassware Reporter*)

Company Catalogs:

Bryce, Higbee & Company, circa 1888 and circa 1892/93.

Federal Glass Company, July 1914.

J. B. Higbee Glass Company, circa 1917 *General Catalogue*; individual catalogs for Banner, Era, Fortuna, and Madora patterns (all undated).

Jefferson Glass Company, Ltd, Toronto, Canada, circa 1920/25.

New Martinsville Glass Manufacturing Company, undated.

Jobber and Retail Catalogs:

Butler Brothers, various issues, 1884–1924

French, Potter & Wilson

H. R. Eagle & Co.

T. Eaton and Co. Limited

Hollander, Bradshaw & Folsom

H. Leonard's Sons & Co.

Montgomery Ward & Co., various issues

Ogden, Merrill & Greer

Pitkin and Brooks

Sears, Roebuck and Co., various issues

B. Sommers & Co.

G. Sommers & Co.

Spelman Brothers

Wallace & McAfee

INDEX

Paul Kirk

PAUL KIRK has been collecting and researching antique glassware for over twenty-five years. His research philosophy is to go straight to the source whenever possible. Paul is a trustee for the Early American Pattern Glass Society and also does pattern identification for the organization. He is a prolific fiddler and tunesmith and has composed over 500 folk tunes.

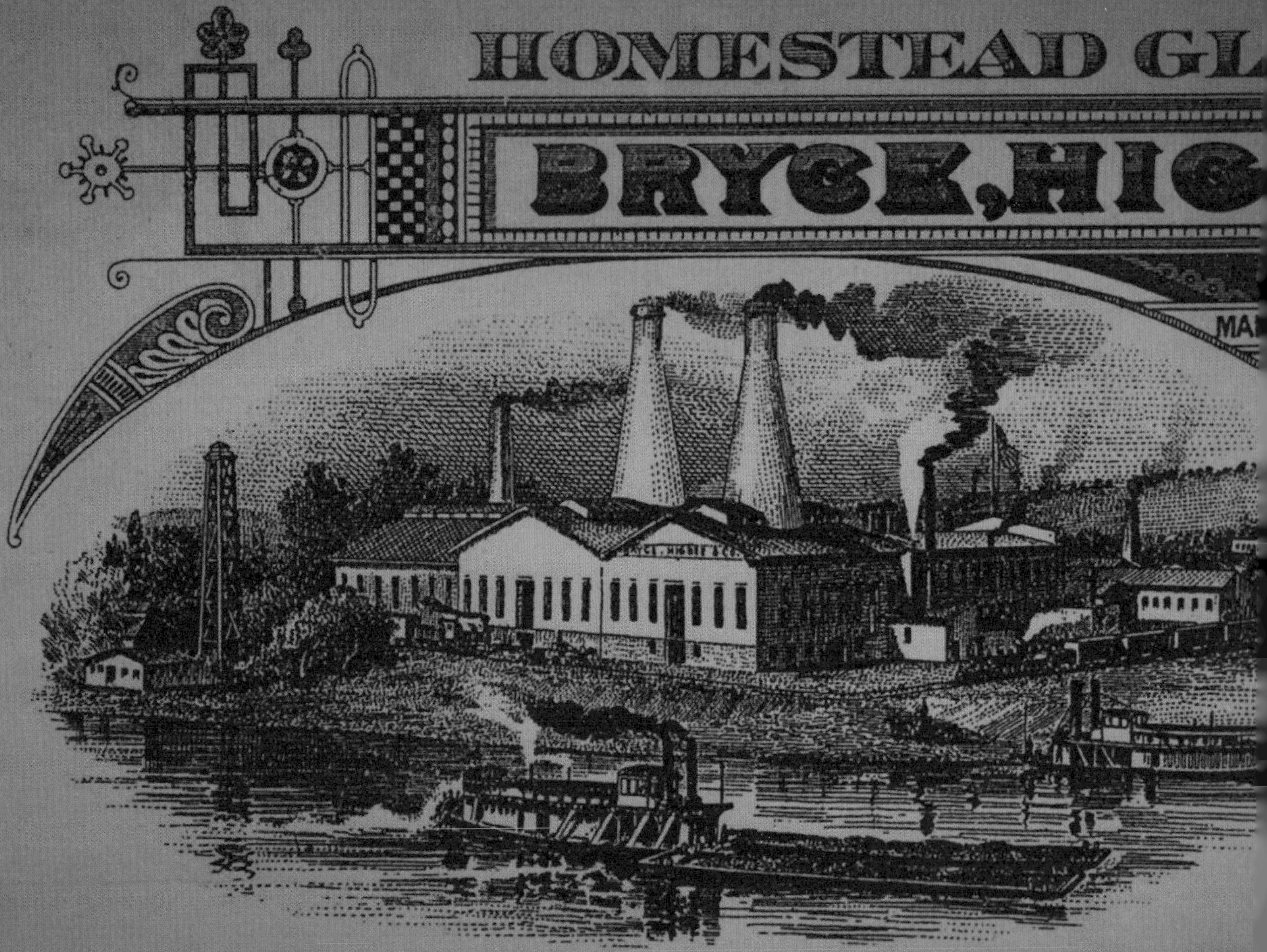
HOMESTEAD GL
BRYCE,HIG

Menagerie
THIS SET MADE IN
OLD GOLD, BLUE AND CRYSTAL
FULL SIZE